AYAHUASCA WISDOM
Achieving Personal Spiritual Healing with a Quantum Model of the Psyche

Jules Henry Rivers

Quantum Books
San Juan, Puerto Rico
2020

Published by Quantum Books (First Edition)
San Juan, Puerto Rico
ayaquantum@protonmail.com

Copyright © Jules Henry Rivers

All rights reserved. No part of this publication may be reproduced or transmitted in any form or by any means without the written permission of the author and the publisher.

The author of this book does not intend nor actually offer medical advice or prescribe the use of any technique as a form of treatment for physical, emotional, or medical conditions without the help of a certified physician. The positive intent of the author is to share with the reader some general guidelines gained from direct experience that has not been scientifically tested in any way. Such information may or may not help the reader in the quest for emotional and spiritual wellbeing. The author and the publisher assume no responsibility for the consequences of any action initiated by using information contained in this publication.

Credits: Refer to the last page

ISBN: 978-1-7357293-0-5

Printed by: CreateSpace in the USA

MY DEDICATION TO: Karen

The Divine Female Principle

Mother Ayahuasca

My Mother

My Wife

October 15, 2020

To a dear sister in the path of ayahuasca healing with love & respect,

Jules
3/21/21
EQUINOX

Acknowledgements

I start with whom I ended in the dedication, my beloved wife, Rosalia Galindo. I must continue honoring her at the top of these acknowledgments because she has been the critical factor for a quantum leap in my spiritual development. Without her, it would have never been the same. Since I met her at an ayahuasca session in 2009, our souls merged in a mission of love that has not shown signs of slowing down. Thank you, my sacred wife, for your resilient dedication to become the best ayahuasca advisor you can possibly be. Thank you for your unconditional support for this project—eternal love for you.

My infinite gratitude to my dear parents for the guidance and loving care in the myriad of ways they positively influenced my childhood development. You both live in me, literally.

My daughter Stefany was a key player during the entire process of producing the initial book manuscript. Thank you, dear Stefy, for the long hours of cut/paste dedication for several months along this journey.

There are a handful of souls that have displayed fantastic support to my efforts leading up to this book. They have been there since the first day I decided to embark on this project, and their support continues to this day. In alphabetical order, from the deepest of my heart, I gladly acknowledge Alexandra Klaric, Bruce Jacobs, Sameet Kumar, and Saswata & Anjna Roy.

TABLE OF CONTENTS

CHAPTER ONE 10
Ayahuasca, the Unknowable 10
The Safest Medicine Ever? 13
During the Session... 14
After the Session 15
Ayahuasca's Experiential Uniqueness 17
The Most Feared Emotion... 21
Ayahuasca and the Medical Establishment 23
The Need for Integration & Spiritual Advice 25

CHAPTER TWO 26
And Ayahuasca Said: "Know Thyself"................................. 26
The Empirical Process: Observation & Practice 29
Observational Basis of the Model.. 31
The Need for a Theoretical Framework 32

CHAPTER THREE 35
Mind-Body Quantum Mechanics 35
Basic Concepts Of The Quantum Model 35
About Naming Our Protagonist 36
The Challenge of Understanding Consciousness 37
The Solution to the Mind-Body Problem........................... 41
The Mind-Body Quantum Mechanics................................. 43

CHAPTER FOUR 51
The Urgent Need of a New Model 51
A Note on Semantics 55

Who Am I? 56
The Quantum Model of the Psyche in a Nutshell 59
The Self Identity Envelope ("SIE") 60

CHAPTER FIVE 63
The Torus and our Self Identity Envelope 63
The Toroidal Shapes of our Psyche 63
The Nature of Thought-Forms 68
A Pause to Review 69
What is "Mind"? 70
The Quantum Realities Within our SIE 71
Ego-Self Reality 72
Subconscious-Self Reality 74
Soul-Self Reality 76
Alignment Within Our Self Identity Envelope 78
The Collective Unconscious 78
The Divine Source 82

CHAPTER SIX 85
The Ego-self is Compelled to Believe 85
Free Will and the Bridge of Belief 85
Belief System Mechanics and You 93
Scrutinizing Your Belief System 94
Belief and the Placebo Effect 95
Some Life Influencing Beliefs 98

CHAPTER SEVEN 100
Principles of Quantum Psychology 100
The Soul's Master Program 105
Memory and Holograms 107
The Subpersonalities in Us 112
Entities: Subpersonalities Gone Rogue 115
Embrace The Paradignm Shift 120

CHAPTER EIGHT 122
Brain & Behavior Programming 122
Ayahuasca and Brain Neuroplasticity 122

This Neural Network is the Gate to the Soul 126
An Inconvenient Truth: Early Behavior Imprinting 128
Imprinted Behavior and our Unfortunate Human Condition 136
Transgenerational Transference of Trauma and Beliefs 139
The Bright Future of Psychedelic Therapies.. 142

CHAPTER NINE 146
Beyond Psychological Projection 146
Introduction to the Projection Principle... 146
Plato's Cave, The Matrix Movie and Other Reminders 150
The Matrix Movie 152
More Cultural Reminders of the Projection Principle........................ 153
The Projection Concept in Psychology... 155
Why Are We Projectors of Ourselves? 156
The Law of the Mirror: Spiritual Advisor's Most Valuable Tool 157
The Law of the Mirror Mechanics... 159
Some After Thoughts.. 161

CHAPTER TEN 163
Achieving Personal Spiritual Healing 163
The Nature of Spiritual Healing.. 163
Understanding Spiritual Awakening... 165
Understanding Ayahuasca Visions.. 167
The Pineal Gland and Third Eye Mysticism 171
Ayahuasca-Induced Near-Death Experiences 172
AINDE's and the Mind-Body Dilemma 175
Medical Healing vs. Spiritual Healing 177
The Osteopathic Medicine Healing Paradigm 179
The Psychosomatic Medicine Healing Paradigm 180

CHAPTER ELEVEN.. 183
The Power of Consecutive Ayahuasca Sessions 183
Three Times is Better than One 183
Who Benefits Most from Consecutive Sessions? 186
Those Who May Benefit More, But Don't 188
Happiness Is Not The Goal 190
Aligning and Instilling Direction to our Ego-self 191

Contemplation: Navigating Our Human Existence 191
The Paradoxical Existentialism of our Ego-Self 192
The Wisdom of Impulses vs. Compulsive Behavior........................... 194
Our Honorable Ego-self 196
Surrendering our Ego-self to our Soul-self... 198
In Summary 198

CHAPTER TWELVE..200
Ayahuasca Spiritual Advisors... 200
ASA's Principles and Assumptions 203
Screening Participants to Determine Eligibility 205
Developing a Basic Practitioner Profile 206
Advising for the Feeling of Isolation 208
Some Standard Instructions Before Ayahuasca Sessions 210
The Existential Challenge of ASAs and Psychedelic Therapists 214

CHAPTER THIRTEEN...216
During Ayahuasca Sessions.. 216
The Art of Holding Space 216
Observing Purging Reactions During Sessions 218
Preserving the Established Collective Trust 221
About Wearing White Clothing.. 222
I Quit, This is Not for Me! 222

CHAPTER FOURTEEN..224
Limiting Beliefs and Ayahuasca Myths... 224
Sexual Abstinence and Ayahuasca Work 224
Menstruation During Ayahuasca Sessions 228
Too Young or Too Old to Experience Ayahuasca?............................. 229
Ayahuasca During Pregnancy 232

CHAPTER FIFTEEN 235
Ayahuasca's Anomalous Outcomes... 235
About Fatalities Associated with Ayahuasca Sessions....................... 235
VIRS: Visionary Intense Release Syndrome 238
Benevolent Ayahuasca Lies? 240
Nudity and Eroticism 243

Failure to Feel Significant Effects 244
Negligent Psychonauts and Bad Trips 245

CHAPTER SIXTEEN 248
How to Advise for Psychological Wellbeing 248
Spiritual Guidance for Enduring the Storms 248
Setting Intentions & Asking the Right Questions 249
How to Dissolve Resistance Barriers 250
The Tricks of the Trickster 251
Is the Progress in Spiritual Healing Fast or Slow? 254
The Joy of Feeling Healed and the Agony of Relapse 257

CHAPTER SEVENTEEN 260
Integration and Closure 260
The Ideal Ayahuasca Session for Spiritual Healing 260
Watching for the Shaman's Moral Integrity 261
Integration Work 262
The Power of Journaling after Ayahuasca Sessions 265
Emotional Healing and Writing from your Heart 265

CHAPTER EIGHTEEN 267
Doing Your Part After Ayahuasca 267
Bypassing Roadblocks 267
Psychological Traps 268
Spirituality Traps 269
Harmful Legal Addictions 272
Practice the Moral Integrity Technique 278
Contain the Quantum Leakage 279
Going Entity Hunting 280
The Challenge of Entity Healing 281
Waging War with your Entity 282
You Can't Out Smart Your Entity 284

CHAPTER NINETEEN 286
Epilogue 286

BONUS SECTION 288

Tales From The Quantum Field 288
A Jungian Psychologist's Dream 288
An Unborn Girl Named Penelope 293
A Deceased Mother Helping Her Son in Depression............................ 297
Helping Elder WW2 Veterans to Die in Peace....................................... 300
The Daughter of Audrey Hepburn That Never Was 303
A Baby Soul Complains to His Future Dad.. 307
Ayahuasca Composes A Song and Becomes A Hit............................... 308
My Banking Career in Imminent Danger 311

Acronyms and Definitions... 314

Bibliography & Notes 316

Credits 328

Image References & Credits 329

Preface

During the summer of 2019, I embraced an opportunity that life presented, which allowed me to experience a few months of isolation from the civilized world. This time allowed me to undertake a project which had been in my thoughts for some time, but which I had been consistently postponing. During this period, I was finally able to develop the discipline of early morning meditation seven days a week, a task which had previously proved impossible due to the requirements of our modern lifestyle.

Feeding the fish at the pond and walking across a field of pine trees calmed my cluttered brain. Gradually, I started receiving a stream of information, feelings, and memories associated with the lessons and insights previously gained from decades of personal self-realization work with ayahuasca. Indeed, I'd already forgotten some of these lessons as the months and years passed; this meditative state reignited these memories. Writing a book about the numerous insights received throughout twenty years of continuous ayahuasca work was something I felt would be meaningful to share with others. I felt these insights would do interesting reading to the growing ayahuasca community. I realized that I had received enough pieces of wisdom to assemble a harmonious body of knowledge about the nature of the human psyche. The more I thought about writing a book about it, I consciously began to integrate a sort of model about how things work in the supersensible realm. I partially attributed the clarity of these insights to the fact that I have consciously cleared my mind from conceptual notions of how reality works.

My journey began when I was nineteen and experienced cannabis for the first time. That initial experience changed my life forever. I was an intellectually arrogant high school student with a strong Newtonian mindset programmed by the Catholic teaching methods of Jean-Baptist La Salle. During those times as a youngster, I lived exciting days in which I rejoiced myself and imbued in the scientific paradigm of Newton, Darwin, and Einstein. It only took one cannabis experience to shatter my then recalcitrant notion of reality, the idea that reality was a three-dimensional box, and that tridimensional space was all there it is. In my idealistic view, I believed it was only a matter of time before science would explain everything. Such a notion was also capitulated during this experience.

After overcoming and recovering from the initial shock, I began a twenty-year journey into non-conventional knowledge. I read dozens of books about the esoteric traditions, Ancient religions, Hermeticism, Gnosticism, Greek philosophers, and even medieval alchemy. I delved into fringe disciplines such as astrology, palm reading, pyramid mathematics, Reiki, acupuncture, popular metaphysics. I investigated Reich orgone devices, lucid dreaming machines, extraterrestrials, and followed various celebrities of channeling, including Cayce, Seth, and Ramtha. In the following years, I was hijacked by the 'conspiracy theory virus'; I became an expert in the JFK assassination, the New World Order, and 9/11, among many others.

My experience with cannabis triggered an intense curiosity for psychedelics. I intuitively felt that there was something underneath the fiber of reality that was waiting to be discovered and experienced. The notion that chemically-induced altered states of consciousness were possible was captivating and intellectually challenging. I embarked on a journey to satisfy my resilient curiosity. I pursued answers to questions which I didn't yet know how to articulate. During the late seventies, I experimented with psilocybin mushrooms, LSD, and even smoked opium. However, I left these experiences behind with a sense of emptiness, something was missing in them, but I couldn't pinpoint what.

As life progressed, I got married and joined the professional 'rat race,' pursuing the economic success symbols which many of us are programmed to chase. Then, it happened. One Friday afternoon in July 1998 remains etched in my memory as an essential milestone in my life path, my first experience with ayahuasca. I encountered ayahuasca with an overloaded mind that was ready for a major conceptual purge. Over the following ten years, I drank the sacred medicine with my teacher shaman Don Jose Campos before coming to the realization that I needed to surrender to Mother Ayahuasca and let her do what she does best in me.

In this initial experience, I had finally found the missing link which I had craved and searched for many years. I found a qualitatively different connection with my spiritual nature, which was different from the other psychedelics I had previously experienced. There is a famous saying: 'when you experience ayahuasca, your life story splits into two parts, before ayahuasca and after ayahuasca,' which I later realized how true it was. My life after ayahuasca gradually led to intriguing and fascinating uncharted territories.

After 20 years of dedicated work, I can attest to only having scratched the surface of what appears to be a portal to unmapped realms of knowledge and wisdom. "Thy Yourself" holds the same truthful sentiment today, as it did in the ancient days of the Delphi Oracle of Greece. The quest for inner growth with the assistance of this natural substance can become the path for a new era of long-lasting health and satisfaction to the currently dysfunctional human species. This may sound overly ambitious, but so were the dreams of traveling to outer space, and today we have thousands of satellites orbiting Earth.

Being a devoted ayahuasca user and facilitator for decades, I have researched the Internet for the latest ayahuasca advancements in the healing practices outside the shamanic paradigm. There is little to be found in this regard. Of course, there is a tidal wave of scientific research that has started to report favorable results. Several Ayahuasca World Conferences so far, and dozens of other related conferences and forums, are beginning to present empirical information. These presentations may lack the rigor of science, but are inspiring enough to make many speculate about a promising trend toward a brighter future in health care.

Ayahuasca began her vast expansion into mainstream western civilization in the 1990s. At present, 30 years later, this expansion has produced a generation of truth seekers. This is the first crop of individuals who recognized the existence of an ayahuasca path, embraced it with passion, and tried to assimilate her wisdom. Many practitioners experience ayahuasca at every opportunity, expanding, learning, taking notes, evolving as one of her students. I consider myself a member of such a generation.

I reflect on my journey with the utmost gratitude, fulfillment, and completeness. By no means, I have reached a pinnacle, nirvana, or anything of that sort. I am not speaking from the top of the mountain, looking down as an enlightened one. I humbly feel like the early cartographers exploring unknown territories, using their rudimentary instruments, remaining cautious of wild animals, hidden traps, and dangerous terrain that may derail or distract from the goal of mapping. With this map, future travelers will finetune our understanding and gradually will evolve from a rough sketch into an accurate and elaborate delineation of complex territorial regions. As a cartographer constructing useful tools for future explorers, I aimed to avoid as much as possible what some medieval cartographers did when they included in their maps mythical drawings about dragons and unicorns, which no one had ever seen.

I feel I have reached a plateau where I can look back and reflect on the view of the path already walked, with the knowledge that it shall continue for much longer. After twenty years of intense work with ayahuasca, I feel the call to point the way to the next generation, to make things easier for them, allow them to benefit from the pioneering work of the early adventurers. With this guidance, these new explorers may reach the plateau faster and be able to obtain a higher level of this eternal evolution. The standard will be higher than that of the original adventurers but still will remain short of those that will follow them.

This is my legacy to future ayahuasca facilitators, explorers, healers, and guides. By no means is this the truth, just a map from the early cartographers which may help future explorers navigate the previously uncharted waters of ayahuasca. I hope that this map will aid in the construction of a more granular and useful depictions or totally different versions of the ayahuasca realities.

I would like to express my gratitude to Dr. Joseph Tafur for his fantastic work in his book "The Fellowship of the River." In it, he described a series of fascinating ayahuasca experiences of patients visiting his retreat center in Iquitos. In those cases, the spiritual context of the healing experience during the ayahuasca retreats was directly associated to a physical healing process, with patients getting healed or experiencing substantial improvement in their health conditions. Those experiences deeply resonated in my psyche as I profoundly comprehended that to which he was referring. His work reminded me of a handful of similar cases, for which I had first-hand knowledge that could have been included in his book.

Moreover, his work also reminded me of a myriad of other cases that were not necessarily of the kind he was portraying in his medical-spiritual paradigm but were equally fascinating in different ways. While reflecting deeply on the diversity and number of these cases, it ignited my imagination, followed by an exciting muse of inspiration to write this book. In other words, Dr. Tafur's book [1] inspired me in a way, to write this one.

I am pleased with the advent of a new breed of scientists and authors that have severed the ties of scientific tradition and have published novel ideas exploring the mind-body connection. Observing this, I can see that such a link is broad and widely encompassing, with literature covering the metaphysical, spiritual nature of our reality. Ayahuasca experiences challenge and encourage us to consider the multidimensional nature of reality. These may initiate curiosity regarding the bubble we are all living in, the matrix, the illusion. One can convincingly realize that we, as humans, are genetically designed or hardwired to experience the reality inside this three-dimensional box, and never beyond it. However, sometimes you may stumble with a thin crack in the cosmic egg into which you can peek at other dimensions with the help of certain entheogens provided by nature. It is as though these magnificent compounds were placed there with the explicit purpose for us to find them when ready, to help us discover our divine nature.

Ayahuasca is an important key that opens the portal to the universal quantum field. Similarly, many people unexpectedly open this portal without such means during revealing dreams or other waking state epiphanies. Scientific discoveries such as the helical, spiral shape of the molecular structure of human DNA, or the hexagonal shape of the benzene molecule, were possible because their discoverers received the groundbreaking insights during their night dreams. Undoubtedly, there is a pool of knowledge or wisdom in the quantum realm, which has been accessed by many in a variety of ways throughout the ages. I believe ayahuasca acts like a sort of chemical password to access the 'cosmic Internet.' Only a handful of plants can do the trick, and despite other entheogens may claim the same, in my biased opinion, I can attest that ayahuasca is the queen of all of them discovered to date.

The knowledge or wisdom that can be experienced by consciously peeking through the crack is of such magnitude that overwhelms the rational mind. This often makes the experience somewhat incomprehensible, indescribable, or, usually, both. Considering this, I will attempt to provide insight and perspective into ayahuasca with a dual approach. One aspect will be rooted in the 'left brain,' providing some speculative hypotheses regarding the non-physical nature of those realities. At the tail end of the book, you will find the other 'right-brain' perspective with some engaging storytelling. I hope that this collection of ayahuasca tales combined with some healthy scientific speculation will create fertile ground in your psyche to foster your own personal stories.

After years of facilitating ayahuasca with hundreds of participants, I have gained a few valuable insights regarding the valuable tools of spiritual and emotional healing, as well as their appropriate use. I share them here with several intentions in mind: (i) to spark a conversation in the spiritual healing community about new approaches to stimulate and accelerate the evolution of this expanding playing field, (ii) motivate other ayahuasca enthusiasts to exercise the principles of spiritual advising hereby proposed, (iii) provide therapists, psychologists and other alternative health practitioners with a reference point which may induce them to consider implementing novel variations in their work, (iv) inspire experienced ayahuasca practitioners to develop the spiritual advisor expertise to help others to receive maximum benefit from ayahuasca experiences, and (v) equip experienced practitioners with a self-help manual to boost their healing process.

About Speaking the Same Language

Before beginning, it's essential to clarify some aspects of language and delivery contained in this book. Let's begin with semantics or operational definitions. Depending on the context of the topic at hand, I refer to ayahuasca in different ways, for instance: the brew, Mother Ayahuasca, the sacred medicine, her spirit, the substance. Despite ongoing debate regarding the gender of ayahuasca's plant spirit, I will refer to ayahuasca as a feminine aspect.

The language or perspective used here may differ from that of many readers because the understanding of ayahuasca is multifaceted. For a comprehensive explanation, I refer to the work of Dr. Jordan Sloshower from Yale University, presented at the 2nd Ayahuasca World Conference in Brazil. This work is particularly relevant at the current juncture, as it elucidates aspects of communication in the ayahuasca world. Extracting from an in-depth article [2]. Dr. Sloshower wise-

ly concluded that the ayahuasca is a complex field that has adopted, in his view, four different ontologies. When communicating, the parties must pay attention and "tune in" to the same "language" to foster effective and productive understanding. He identifies four distinct ontologies with their unique narratives.

When speaking about ayahuasca, parties should be aware in which ontology they will be connecting, or at least know that they may switch from one or the other without confusion. If done incorrectly, parties may end up being judgmental about each other and sometimes even offended by the views offered in one ontology or another. Therefore, it is critical to remember that this book gravitates between the second and third ontologies, spiritual and psychological. There is less reference to the first or fourth, indigenous, and biological. I invite the reader to review the perspectives of your ontology to ensure that any disagreement you may have with the views in this work is not the product of "ontological dissonance."

The perspectives explored within this text relate to transpersonal psychology, upon which a new model will be presented. Reference to "entities" within the book refers more to Carl Jung's shadow work or ego subpersonalities than to shamanic references to demons or evil spirits. You won't find references to demonic possessions, spirit attachments, attacks, or similar topics. While these experiences may be real, there is little practical knowledge about how these can be understood and managed.

Although this work focuses on the spiritual and psychological ontologies, there should be no detraction from the value of indigenous or biological ontologies. These perspectives should be appreciated equally. While these are not discussed at length within the present work, they are not entirely dismissed. The shamanic/ indigenous paradigm with all its icaros, rituals, remedies and beliefs, has proven to be effective in many instances, sometimes with results that can only be described as unexplainable or "magical".

Similarly, the biological/chemical ontology, which is the cornerstone of the pharmaceutical industry has contributed to a richer understanding of ayahuasca, through a variety of molecular and chemical experiments. Moreover, dozens of peer-reviewed papers have illuminated some of the unknown biological properties of the sacred medicine.

Beyond the Scope

The phenomena that surround ayahuasca are unusual and diverse. We need to acknowledge that in the ayahuasca path to spiritual healing, we often witness experiences that can only be described as uncanny, strange, or simply weird. Some of them are thematic in the stories presented in the last section of the book. Questions regarding these stories are left open to the imagination of the reader.

When journeying into the unknown, we must choose wisely which parts will be dissected first with the scalpel of reason and leave the others for subsequent revisions. To that effect, I have deliberately excluded entire areas that can be considered outside our immediate target of interest. Instead, we ought to focus our undivided attention on the fundamentals of spiritual healing.

Areas which are beyond the scope of this work are: (i) profound teachings from the indigenous shamanic ontology such as the power of chants or "icaros" to attain spiritual healing without conscious effort of the patient, (ii) occult practices such as sorcery and witchcraft, (iii) demonic possession, exorcisms, astral parasites, curses, etc., (iv) Spiritism and mediumship, (v) practices and rituals of Brazilian religions such as Uniao Do Vegetal and Santo Daime.

Finally, a note about the scope and fundamental assumption of this work. You will appreciate while browsing through these pages, that there is little basic information about ayahuasca. This work does not intend to detail what is already well-known about the brew itself, how it's prepared, its chemical properties, mechanism of action, or cultural aspects. Much of this information has already been widely documented in the ayahuasca literature. As we enter the third decade of the 21st century, we must aim to build on top of the valuable knowledge already gained. It is now time to work toward the next level of the ayahuasca paradigm. In that sense, this book may be considered to contain advanced information targeted to those who already have learned, theoretically or empirically, the basics of the ayahuasca path.

Some Definitions

Ayahuasca Session is the term used to refer to any type of ayahuasca ceremony in any of its modalities shamanic, religious, or therapeutic.

Ayahuasca Spiritual Advisor or simply **Spiritual Advisor** is used to referring to any person acting as counselor, coach, or therapist in any capacity.

Ayahuasca Facilitator is used to referring to the person that facilitates or serves the ayahuasca brew during an ayahuasca session. The medicine has been traditionally facilitated by a curandero, shaman, or facilitator. However, a more generic term is more appropriate considering its recent internationalization. Sometimes an ayahuasca advisor also acts as a facilitator in a therapeutic context, in which case we make the necessary distinction. It's important to clarify that the facilitator's job is tenfold more complicated than merely serving the brew. Hence, this simplified definition should not be interpreted as an underestimation regarding the essence of its work.

Three different terms are used to refer to the person that drinks the medicine. Most frequently used is the term "**participant**," referring to individuals participating in specific ayahuasca sessions or healing retreats that offer ayahuasca sessions. Participants may have experienced the medicine previously. When the individuals find value in the ayahuasca path and embrace a more committed healing journey, we refer to them as ayahuasca "**practitioners**". Finally, we occasionally use the term "**client**" to describe strictly to a professional relationship of an ayahuasca advisor, which person may or may not have prior experience with the medicine.

Numerous Subheadings

Note that each section contains numerous subheadings intended to facilitate reading in a modular fashion. This not only fosters enhanced cognitive absorption but also promotes a more relaxed review of the contents after the initial reading. Moreover, subheading should enable the quick location of specific passages when referencing or discussing the material with others.

Computer Analogies

Since computers are now prevalent in modern life everywhere, I found it useful to borrow a few terms for educational purposes in this book. Throughout this work, the reader will find frequent analogous references to computers associated with the inner workings of the psyche and brain. Pre-existing advanced computer knowledge of the reader has not been assumed, but much of the references surmise some grasp of the basic concepts. Having a basic understanding of terms such as memory storage, programs, processing unit, and circuit board will be enough to follow the examples and analogies presented throughout the text smoothly. I apologize in advance to those readers not familiar with those terms if they interfere with the conveyance of the intended message.

Use of "Quote Marks"

Quoted-marked words or phrases are often used to add semantic clarity and not necessarily are an indication of a unique term. When used, the reader should pause to reflect on a deeper meaning of the word or phrase; often, these will have additional intuitive content besides its literal meaning. This is a "poetic license". I am attempting to improve semantics while covering subjects of abstract complexity.

The Use of the Terms "Spirit" and "Soul"

It should be noted that the model presented frequently refers to the soul, but not so much to the spirit. The reason being more practical than philosophical, as both terms have very similar meanings depending on the context in which they are used. The word "spirit" is often used within religious scriptures of different faiths, and many times "spirit" is used interchangeably with "soul". The main difference between the meaning of both words is subtle. According to different sources, "soul" refers to the immortal but 'human' aspect of the self, while "spirit" is also immortal but is positioned more closely to the source, or God. For the purpose of this work, we are not neglecting the "spirit" part of the human being. Instead, we assume "spirit" to be synonymous with "soul." After all, the book is about spiritual healing, denoting that it comes from the higher planes of existence, the spirit, or the soul.

Book Synopsis

The book begins with some anecdotal accounts of my internal process leading to producing this work. This hopefully adds some context to the reader in terms of how and why the proposed model of the psyche came about. We start with the introduction of the basic concepts of consciousness and the old problem of understanding ourselves. The quantum nature of reality is then introduced with the fundamental quantum structures and their interactions while providing current scientific hypothesis that supports their plausibility. With the basis of the model established, we move into presenting the underlying healing principles of the model. The Projection Principle is described in detail as the working framework for the application of the model of the psyche to the spiritual advisor's clients. Finally, we introduce the logical conclusion of the proposed model, the ayahuasca spiritual advisor principles, and some suggested techniques learned along the way with the empirical process described in Chapter 1. We conclude with a Bonus Section of 26 pages, which moves away from the left-brain analysis and synthesis of concepts into the right-brain verbal domain. A collection of nine short stories is presented to leave the reader with a sense of intriguing thoughtfulness. If you ever sequentially reach the last pages of this book, you will better understand a part of yourself, which always knew all about it.

CHAPTER ONE

AYAHUASCA, THE UNKNOWABLE

As humans, we seek happiness, understanding, and illumination to bring light into our lives and our hearts. We often look to the future or to new ideas and perspectives which we have heard. We search for the keys to our wholeness and happiness as if they could be found outside of ourselves.

We reach outside, especially during moments when our personal world is filled with darkness and despair. There is no human being who holds power to avoid being touched by pain. There are no defenses strong enough to make us invulnerable to the unpredictability of life's changes. We may attempt to anesthetize ourselves in many different ways to the experiences of life, and in this numbness, we end up increasing our isolation and pain. In times of such darkness, we find ourselves longing for an ideal future or seeking miraculous formulas to protect us from pain and conflict.

Learning how to live with life's challenges and hardships, to discover light amid darkness, and to heal ourselves and the world around us, is an art. As is the case for any other art, the practice of living in peace calls for great love and discipline. We must be willing not to turn away from or shun the shadows. Instead, we must turn toward them. This is the first and most significant step, for, in our confrontation of these shadows, we begin to cast away our fears, despair, and self-doubt. It is not darkness that is our opponent but our rejection and denial of it. It is in our greatest difficulties that we can find a sense of everlasting light in the world - refulgent light indeed.

Mother Ayahuasca can assist us with an open heart and a clear, mindful focus in our confrontation with the specific shadows in our lives. Unlike other psychoactive substances, the motivations of those participating in ayahuasca sessions are typically related to physical or emotional healing, personal development, self-awareness, spirituality, religious commitment, or treatment for addictions. These are the courageous souls who wish to cease reacting and resisting. Instead, they seek to begin a journey of understanding. In order to do this, we must learn to feel deeply. This means we must listen carefully to the mystery that is right in front of us, rather than to preconceived ideas we have about things. Learning to listen with this same sensitivity inwardly allows for the discovery of new depths of calmness, new resources of energy, and effectiveness. In a state of calm, we begin to understand that peace is not really the opposite of challenge and hardship. We know that the presence of light is not the result of darkness ending. Peace is found not in the absence of a problem but in our capacity to experience hardship without judgment, prejudice, and resistance. We discover that we have the energy and faith to begin to heal ourselves and the world by meeting each moment with an open heart.

This book is a humble invitation to the world to embrace the developing methodologies of spiritual healing using ayahuasca to empower ourselves, expand our conscious presence, and take action to assist others and create a better world for everyone. Although the spiritual healing principles in this book were developed while walking the ayahuasca path, it became evident to me that most of them are also applicable to the practices of psychedelic-assisted therapies. These principles could apply to psilocybin, LSD, MDMA, and possibly others.

In the spirit of self-discovery and desire to become better human beings, we begin by describing the impressive journey of expansion and recognition of ayahuasca over the past thirty years. The history of ayahuasca begins with early references chronicled by 16th Century Christian missionaries while exploring the Ecuador-Peru region. Following this, we find anthropological descriptions documented by several 20th-century scientists. However, Western interest in ayahuasca was ignited by the experiences of American psychonauts during the 1980s and 90s. My teacher, shaman Don Jose Campos [1], shared with me many interesting stories about his encounters during those early days. He was at the Peruvian end of the bridge of connections with American individuals who later became well known. Don Jose spoke about his experiences with Dr. Rick Strassman and Terrence McKenna. With the latter, he described when he traveled and participated with him at an event in the Esalen Institute [2] during the early '90s. Don Jose also met and worked closely with a scientist Dr. Jacques Mabit who joined forces with Don Jose to create the Takiwasi Center [3], an addiction treatment center, which uses ayahuasca. The Takiwasi Center has operated successfully for more than twenty consecutive years. Retreat centers offering ayahuasca dietas started to appear during the '90s as Peruvian and Colombian curanderos began to travel the world, offering the novel experience.

Moving forward to 2020, we find an exciting ayahuasca world that has developed beyond the expectations of many. Timing is everything, and we can attribute this fast expansion to the power of the Internet. The new medium created an exponential explosion of ayahuasca information, including the promotion of a growing number of places that offer the ayahuasca experience. A quick Internet review during 2020 revealed the existence of over 140 retreat centers, mostly in South America, which offer ayahuasca sessions in a diverse array of formats. Over twenty documentary films have been produced with ayahuasca at the heart of the subject matter. There are also over 100 published books regarding ayahuasca, and several million links retrieved by Google using the "ayahuasca" search term. By taking an in-depth inventory of information available across the Internet, we find:

- Thousands of anecdotal accounts, written and video, mostly from neophytes in the ayahuasca path. These describe specific breakthroughs in their personal lives after experiencing just one or a few ayahuasca sessions.

- An astounding collection of articles, research papers, books, and documentaries relating to ayahuasca. This is indicative of the massive widespread acceptance of the sacred medicine.

- The existence of several ayahuasca-based institutional churches in Brazil and elsewhere, all of which have reported dramatic increases in their memberships during this century.

- Significant coverage of ayahuasca by the global mainstream media. This has become particularly prevalent in the Americas, Europe, and Australia due to the participation of actors, musicians, scientists, and celebrities in ayahuasca sessions.

- The celebration of several World Ayahuasca Conferences organized in several countries. These congresses bring together recognized scientists, writers, and indigenous personalities to share the latest developments and trends.

- The publication of the first medical book about ayahuasca in 2015, "*The Therapeutic Use of Ayahuasca* "[4] The work presents an impressive compilation of scientific papers synthesized by a medical book publisher.

- The establishment of The Global Ayahuasca Project, a multidisciplinary research project based in Australia. [5] The project provides centralized access to hundreds of ayahuasca related peer-reviewed, scientific papers.

- The award of religious freedom legal protections to several Brazilian ayahuasca churches such as the Santo Daime and UDV. These protections allow the use of ayahuasca as a religious sacrament in several countries, including the U.S.

It is evident that ayahuasca has found its niche as a recognized name associated with a new healing modality that is rapidly gaining worldwide acceptance. Ayahuasca will further continue to ascend this path of acceptance, aided by the fact that it is safe to consume.

The Safest Medicine Ever?

Ayahuasca sessions have gained broad recognition in mainstream Western culture. Media outlets now provide coverage of positive stories about powerful healing effects relating to depression, anxiety, PTSD, and addictions. One of the primary reasons for this wide-scale acceptance and popularity it owed to evidence which supports the safety of ayahuasca. Side-effects are generally mild, short term, and related to the specific use. These effects rarely persist for longer than a couple of days. Some official bodies concluded, based on the available evidence, that ayahuasca is not detrimental to health when used in a ceremonial setting. These conclusions have been made by the U.S. Supreme Court (concerning the UDV church), the government of the Netherlands, and a review conducted by the National Council on Drugs (CONAD) in Brazil.

Of course, to ensure a favorable experience, you must follow a previous regime. It is critical to ensure your body is relatively free from substances which may adversely react with the medicine. Guidelines for adequate preparation are available on various reputable websites and forums which provide necessary information about the medicine.

Over the past twenty years, a wealth of research has investigated the chemical mechanisms which underpin the foundations of how ayahuasca operates in humans. This research has been conducted with scientific rigor, impartiality, and remains free of misconceptions from the indigenous traditions. Based on these findings, a list of contraindicated foods and drugs has been developed to alert potential participants to the risks involved. Although the list of contraindicated items continues to grow as more doctors and nutritionists turn their attention to this matter, the fact is that the human body has demonstrated a robust capacity to process the medicine without serious complications smoothly. The most important compounds of concern are those who interfere with the monoamine oxidase enzymes since the ayahuasca brew already contains monoamine oxidase inhibitors (MAOIs). This category includes:

- Any other MAOI's
- SSRI's (any selective serotonin reuptake inhibitors)
- Amphetamines (meth-, dex-, amphetamine)
- Antihypertensives (high blood pressure medications)
- Appetite suppressants (diet pills)
- Medicines for asthma, bronchitis, or other respiratory problems

- Antihistamines, medicines for colds, sinus problems, hay fever, or allergies (Actifed D.M., Benadryl, Benylin, Chlor-Trimeton, Compoz, etc.)
- Central nervous system (CNS) depressants
- Antipsychotics
- Alcohol

There are many other lists of food items which may interact dangerously with ayahuasca. However, to be candid, the risk is not as dangerous as in pharmaceutical MAOIs. You may need to consume large amounts of these foods to really induce a reaction that could be dangerous to your health. To err of the side of caution is recommended to follow a vegetarian diet and stop taking all prescription and over-the-counter medications forty-eight hours before the scheduled ayahuasca session. It's important to note that while there are no reports of fatalities from food interactions with ayahuasca, these types of interactions could conceivably be life-threatening for a person with severe high blood pressure or severe heart disease. People with these conditions should follow the MAOI safety diet very strictly before taking ayahuasca.

We need to recognize that many participants in ayahuasca sessions come unprepared and experience unsatisfactory results. These vary from confusing and nightmarish episodes to psychotic crises, which may last many hours. There are even cases of participants who have fallen into a comatose state and have been hospitalized for weeks, a few of which have died. The problem with adverse reactions to ayahuasca has not been formally researched. None-the-less, we can make a reasonable assessment by thoroughly reviewing the anecdotal and news agency reports about these adverse cases. In Chapter 15, we include an in-depth discussion about fatal cases and the significant amount of misinformation surrounding their circumstances.

Regarding the mild discomforts that could be encountered, here is a general list of problems experienced by participants:

During the Session:

Participants may fall into an unbalanced mental state manifested by acting-out what some erroneously describe as some kind of "possession", which is truly a subpersonality of the participant that needed emotional release. The participant may start acting incoherently or intellectually disabled by engaging in babbling noises, uncoordinated arm movements, rolling around in the floor, speaking nonsense statements, speaking in "tongues" or screaming. These cases are typically handled by the facilitator or shaman with compassion while controlling the person to avoid possible interference with other participants' experiences. Participants can be interrupted momentarily from their behavior but will return to it as soon as they are allowed. Their true personality remains hidden for an hour or two until the effects of the medicine begin to fade off. Then, while still in the experience, they recover and continue their journey normally. Generally, participants do not retain the memory of what happened during these episodes. These episodes are subject to discussion by shamans and facilitators who have elaborated on various "theories" to explain them.

Some participants begin to feel an inexplicable fear regarding something which has arisen during their experience and express their desperate desire to finish the experience abruptly. Although not enjoyable for the participant, this is a good indication that a breakthrough is brewing up inside. Experiences such as these indicate that a strong psychological blockage is about to be released; the subconscious is about to give-away one of its dark secrets. Healing is about to happen. Here the facilitator must encourage the participant to find the courage to face it to generate a satisfactory resolution.

After the Session:

While sessions are expected to end after four or five hours, a particular participant may continue in their journey for an additional five to eight hours. Some participants remain lying down passively going through the process, sometimes sleeping or semi-conscious and sometimes hyper-aware of their surroundings but too weak walk unassisted.

- A participant may remain dizzy or confused with the feeling of not having come back entirely from the experience. The experience seems to fade away very slowly for some participants, and it may take several hours after the session has ended for them to feel grounded again.

- For a few hours, a participant may remain living or acting out in the illusion of a previous vision experienced during the session. They may believe they are in another location, another dimension, or even in heaven or hell.

- Some participants report having difficulty sleeping during the days following a session. A milligram or two of melatonin can alleviate this problem. Melatonin is a hormone that is primarily produced by the pineal gland. The hormone regulates the circadian rhythms and sleeps patterns of our bodies; increased production of melatonin prepares the body for sleep. It may be that there is a connection between the DMT in the brew and the pineal gland's capacity to regulate melatonin production.

It's important to note that most of the above inconveniences are an integral part of the experience. Despite the session and experience appear to have ended, there are still many active processes at work during the delayed recovery or unusual feelings experienced in the aftermath. With the right preparation and mental attitude, these situations should be considered opportunities to extend the learning and inner healing of the experience.

Another relevant angle to consider while assessing the safety of ayahuasca is the ability of the brew to induce vomiting in participants. This vomit-inducing property is a convenient feature as it constitutes a self-protective mechanism against overdosing. We have never found or even heard about a case of ayahuasca overdose; it merely does not exist. After drinking the medicine, the stomach begins the absorption process. When the medicine gets absorbed into the system, it starts preparing to expel any excess not required for your experience. After other things happen in your subjective experience, such as cleansing non-physical energies, nausea may reach a point of becoming unbearable just before the vomit reflex takes over. The feeling of relief and wellbeing, which immediately follows, makes you forget about the previous discomforts of nausea and involuntary diaphragm contractions. If you insist on taking another dose of ayahuasca after throwing up, likely, you will violently vomit soon after ingestion. The digestive system will not tolerate more medicine, and if it does, it means that you are prepared for it. The good news is that this protective mechanism means we will never hear of a participant dying from an ayahuasca overdose. We will cover the topic of vomiting in more detail in the later chapters.

Based on its historical performance, ayahuasca should never be an object of concern regarding health risks. It is one of the safest medicines ever discovered. To offer some perspective, consider the long list of warnings included in the written disclosures of any pharmaceutical prescription medication. The list often includes potential adverse effects that range from significant discomforts to fatality, a chilling warning indeed.

In an article published by the Journal of Law, Medicine, and Ethics, the authors describe the results of analyzing the large volume of Adverse Drug Reaction Reports submitted to the U.S. Food and Drug Administration. It indicates that "up to 2.7 million hospitalized Americans each year have experienced a serious adverse reaction. Of all hospitalized patients, 0.32 percent died due to adverse drug reactions, which means that an estimated 128,000 hospitalized patients died annually, matching stroke as the 4th leading cause of death. Deaths and serious reactions outside of hospitals would significantly increase the totals." [6]

It's important to note that the above statistics do not include cases of drug overdoses, which account for another large number of deaths. These refer only to the cases where the medication was being used as indicated. This is an astounding number of deaths caused by products sold at an enormous profit to the general public. No compensation can be offered to families that lose dear relatives to prescription medications as the legal liability of pharmaceutical companies is well protected by the carefully crafted legal disclosures included in those tiny printed informative leaflets inserted in each package. We all consume them at our own risk; case closed. Considering such realities of life, you may feel confident that ayahuasca is extremely safe.

Ayahuasca's Experiential Uniqueness

Another reason that explains ayahuasca's meteoric rise in popularity is the unique imprint and the sense of awe, which it elicits in the memory of those who experience it. This is the single most crucial difference between ayahuasca and all other psychedelics, which I experimented with during my exploration stage. Ayahuasca causes a somewhat indescribable sense of meaning. As previously mentioned, I found interest in my experience with many other psychedelics, having tried them several times. However, there was always a sense of emptiness and a feeling that something was missing. What my soul was looking for was nowhere to be found. It was a strange feeling as I didn't know exactly what my soul was searching for. However, once I had experienced ayahuasca, I knew that I had found it. The ayahuasca experience provided me with an extraordinary sense of spirituality, a solemn sacredness to the nature of my own existence. No other psychedelics were able to deliver an experience or feeling such as this. I felt a unique sense of respect for the work I was doing with myself. It is difficult to articulate, but those readers who have experienced ayahuasca may understand the feeling I am trying to express. An alternative way to describe it is that no matter how materialistic or reductionist we want to approach the ayahuasca experience, there it is, a sacredness factor, a divinity factor, a respect factor, a factor that humbles the ego and fosters acceptance of its inconsequential nature in relation to the vast expanses of the universe.

Another adjective applicable to the sacred medicine is "numinous," invented by the religious scholar Rudolph Otto. Carl Jung used the term with a particular frequency in his writings to describe the heightened states of consciousness in the creative breakthroughs of spiritual innovators, artists, and scientists. A numinous experience has an overwhelming feeling of fascination with the mysteriousness and tremendousness of life and the universe. In that sense, the ayahuasca experience often provokes numinous feelings.

Ayahuasca produces emotionally moving experiences. Inevitably, these experiences carve out a special place for the sacred medicine within the hearts of participants. The soul appreciates and feels the gratefulness, while the ego regrets the experience as it feels fear. The feeling which is predominant in you can indicate how influential these two parts are in your psyche. When you think about it, it is a great thing to realize that a chemically induced spiritual experience is possible for anyone. It is uplifting to know that you don't have to wait for the circumstances to favor you with the blessing of connecting directly with your divine nature. A spiritual or mystical experience maybe just one cup of ayahuasca away. That reality mesmerized me shortly after my first few sessions, and I was quickly enrolled as a devoted follower of the ayahuasca path.

With the emotional and spiritual awakening of the ayahuasca experience comes the realization of aliveness in our existence. We realize that we were previously living in a state of partial and sometimes total numbness. The ayahuasca experience is for many very refreshing and life-changing as it allows forgotten memories to reach the surface of consciousness. Often these are parts of you which, until then, were buried in a dark corner of your subconscious. Sometimes recovering lost memories, especially of the repressed type, can be shocking for the conscious self. Ultimately, in the end, reality wins, and we embrace these memories even if they include a dose of pain. You become powerfully reassured that ayahuasca is a potent medicine when a vivid memory deeply hidden in your subconscious, sometimes by decades, arises to the surface of your conscious awareness with just one single session without major technicalities.

Then we have ayahuasca's purgative effects. For many, the mere act of thinking about vomiting triggers that same queasy feeling in the belly. But ayahuasca vomiting is not akin to any type of vomiting you have experienced previously. From the outside, it looks the same, the expulsion of bodily fluids into a bucket, but the subjective experience is one of profound physical relief paired with some sort of redemption. In hindsight, you end up finding it fulfilling instead of repulsive. People generally categorize pleasurable experience as "good" experiences and any experience involving hardship or intensely challenging as "bad" experiences. In ayahuasca, these forms of categorizing do not apply for most participants. When you ask anyone who was vomiting and struggling for hours re-living past traumatic experiences, they often reply while grinning, "that was very good." This is yet another aspect where ayahuasca separates from anything conventional. However, before the vomit, there is another unique element - the awful and disgusting taste of the brew.

I have a particular theory about the natural body reaction to the notorious awful taste of the sacred medicine. As a facilitator, I have the privileged point of view of watching the participant in front of me at the moment of ingestion. Over the years, I found a pattern in the reaction of participants. I was curious about why participants that were trying ayahuasca for the first time, which I call first-timers, were consistently surprised with the taste. The way they react, and later confirmed in interviews, showed that the taste was not as bad as they initially thought. The concept they had heard from others, in testimonials, books, and videos, was that the taste is literary horrendous. After trying it for the first time, they tend to disagree with such notions. They invariably find the taste relatively strong, but nothing out of the ordinary. Some describe it like molasses, others a little bitter, and a handful even find it agreeable. But then, when the same participants return another day to drink for a second time, their reaction is dramatically different. From the moment they hold the cup in their hands, and sometimes before, the struggle begins. The act of swallowing becomes a clash of contradictory forces. When they overcome the resistance and succeed in the mission, their reaction to the taste catches up with the reputation they had heard before. I find a bit amusing to see the surprise in their faces and sudden change in body language when they reach out to grab the cup full of sacrament. At that moment, they have joined the club of haters of its taste.

The question is, why do they find the taste so unpalatable the second time they drink it, but not the first? After all, we are talking about the same person with the same taste buds and the same batch of medicine. The variables of the experiment are constant. The only changes were that the time was a different day, and the subject was no longer a first-timer. One possible explanation is related to a neurological effect found in neural pathways involved in flavor aversion learning. It has been found that a novel taste produced more brain activity than a familiar taste, suggesting the existence of a forebrain neophobia system. [7] Neophobia is the characteristic fear of novel foods and ensures that animals ingest only small quantities as if to sample the food to determine if it is safe to eat.

But a psychological explanation is that the experience that followed the ingestion the first time turned out to be traumatic for a quantum structure, which we will describe later as the ego. The mentioned neophobia system may have established a sort of "red alert" connection between the medicine and the life-threatening experience that followed. Like the child that learns the hard way when it gets burned when playing with fire, it creates a fear-based reaction to protect the organism from harm or pain in the future. The big difference here lies in the fact that the ayahuasca experience is threatening only to the ego, but not to the soul. That's why participants force themselves to drink it despite challenging resistance. Their souls want to grow despite the ego's defiance. Clearly, there are two opposing forces at play in the act of drinking the medicine.

Another unique element of ayahuasca practice is the major effect of the psychological attitude of the participant before the session. It is common knowledge to ensure having a clear intention before stepping into an ayahuasca session. Although this rule of thumb is valid, a more critical factor is to ensure having a profoundly open attitude to whatever is in store for you during the experience. Sometimes participants focus too much on the intention before the session. This can be especially counterproductive if the intention is not well crafted for easy transference to the subconscious. Since there is no guidance as to what a good intention looks like, participants often develop intentions that impair their journey and obstruct instead of assisting a productive session. For example, "I want to heal my soul" is extremely vague, while "I want to find out should I accept this job offer" is too specific or even irrelevant to a spiritual process. The truth is that there is no formula to articulate the right intention. However, in general, the most effective intentions are those who are targeted to the deepest aspects of your psyche.

The ayahuasca is exceptionally effective to anyone that comes with a strong desire to make fundamental changes in their lives. The sessions serve those who are fed up with their old ways and crave for a renewed sense of self. The experience favors participants who are prepared to view the absolute truth and the darker aspects of themselves. Intentions crafted around those feelings will bring extraordinary breakthroughs in your inner quest. If you don't come with such intentions, your experience may not impose a significant impact or elicit emotional growth. Many times, the medicine only induces the "drug experience" with little or no transformative power. This is mostly due to the inner attitude brought into the session. If you are not genuinely engaged with transforming yourself, the medicine is not going to impose a new agenda within your conscious self. The right attitude is a mandatory prerequisite to profound healing, cleansing, and learning experience. Without this, your experience shall be limited to only a deep physical cleansing with some amusing hallucinogenic geometry.

Following the cartographer metaphor, the explorer who meticulously makes observations about the terrain to sketch the best map possible is aware that the job is totally unpredictable and full of surprises. One of the most counter-intuitive features of ayahuasca is the intriguing ambiguity surrounding the required dosage to induce a worthwhile experience. Rational and analytical minds invariably fall perplexed about the unexplainable ways in which ayahuasca operates. Experienced and seasoned ayahuasca practitioners tend to admit she is highly capricious, fickle, changeable, mercurial, not to mention another appropriate adjective, unpredictable, that is. Dosage is an excellent example of this fickle nature.

You can knock out an athlete of two meters and 130 kg with one cup of ayahuasca. However, on the same night and using the same brew, you may need to serve three cups to a tiny 50kg lady for her to feel some effects. During my early days in ayahuasca work, I frequently felt intrigued by the fact that every time I had a theory about how ayahuasca works, my experience shortly after that showed me otherwise. Rationally, there are just too many variables to attempt to predict anything about ayahuasca. You must take it as it comes. I have learned more about her by going with the flow, observing non-judgmentally, non-analytically, than that trying to theorize about how she works. As I said, ayahuasca is dosage irrelevant. The intensity of the experience is materially affected by the physical, mental, and emotional condition of the user. This is perplexing, to say the least, as in the case of conventional drugs, if you ingest triple the dose, you will experience a more potent effect. In ayahuasca, you may swallow a teaspoon and go to heaven for two hours, or drink four cups and experience just a little dizziness. There appears to be no convention dose-response effect with ayahuasca.

This is because ayahuasca connects directly to your subconscious. The quality and intensity of the experience don't depend on the number of molecules of the substance in your bloodstream but on your inner state of being. You may drink her one day and have a considerable effect and drink the same brew the next day without any noticeable effect. Even within the same ceremony, the sound of a musical instrument can take all the effect away or hit you with a massive tsunami wave. Your thoughts, emotions, and your intention surrounding the ceremony definitely contribute to your subconscious reaction. If your subconscious is resistant to the potential outcome of the session, it can alter the outcome of your experience. Your subconscious may produce a crushingly strong experience, which may leave you powerless to pursue anything or leave you with a weak experience or constant physical distractions, such as back and limb pains, diarrhea, a continuous need to urinate, spasms, terror and infinite other distractions. Major breakthroughs occur when there is subconscious harmony with what you need to experience. It is stunning to the rational mind to accept that the chemical reaction of ayahuasca is subservient to your subconscious. These are some of the elements that define ayahuasca's experiential uniqueness. These must be considered by anyone undertaking ayahuasca spiritual advice or integration work with others.

But the most significant reason which explains ayahuasca's popularity in the world is the ability of the brew to work wonders in most sessions for most participants. We need to acknowledge, on the other hand, that the biggest deterrent of ayahuasca's expansive properties is the human emotion of fear.

The Most Feared Emotion

It's deeply rooted in the primal structures of our brains – fear. All of us carry fear as evolutionary heritage encoded in our DNA. It is one of the essential tools for the survival of the species. The paradox of fear is that it is both the most necessary, yet most undesirable, of the emotions. We cannot survive without it, but we hate to face it. Fear propels us to safety, but it's also the jail of our absolute freedom.

Fear is instrumental in the presence of imminent physical danger such as conflicts of war, street fights, criminal assaults, or when moving through unfamiliar environments. Interestingly, as humans developed into more organized and safer civil societies, the fears of humans began to shift from real physical threads to imaginary ones. Hypochondria and the ever-increasing list of pathological phobias are examples of fears which have become uncontrollable.

Although fear is a necessary genetic program that protects us from danger, it can easily damage and inhibit our abilities. It seems that when real threats are absent, the limbic system needs to invent them to justify its own existence. Rather than holding a mere vigilant stance, it starts to imagine dangerous situations. This is what I call *"bad fear,"* opposite to the *"good fear"* of real dangers. Good fear is healthy, while bad fear is pathological.

Fear is the most hated, undesirable, and avoided all the emotions. In order to ensure survival, we also carry another genetic program that encapsulates into a protective layer, the memory of anything that undermines the healthy pursuit of survival. This mechanism stores these memories away in an encrypted area located in the subconscious, where you will find a vast collection of fears, of all sizes and colors. In order to move forward in life, this survival program "forgets" endless instances of painful events filled with sorrow, despair, shame, and guilt. From all of these, we may not object to remember some of them when reflecting and thinking about our past. However, we certainly will avoid at all costs to re-live the memory of them ever again.

Moreover, there are very twisted dark events stored in our subconscious, of which we are often entirely unaware of its existence. These are so profoundly encrypted in your hidden data banks that there are no practical ways to retrieve them, no matter how hard you may consciously try. You cannot remember something that you ignore exists. Such is the power of your subconscious, a process designed for our protection and wellbeing.

There are instances that you may suspect lay hidden somewhere, such as certain traumatic events in your early childhood. However, you may find a lack of clarity and uncertainty regarding these because you can't find any images in your memory to support your intuitive feelings. Especially challenging to retrieve is the experience that occurred during your early toddler stage. This is because our brain had not yet developed adequate mechanisms of committing information in long-term memory. Even more complicated are other prenatal events. These can leave biological hallmarks or imprints which persist throughout development and into the adult brain, having been directly experienced as a fetus. These may include physical accidents and injuries, as well as emotional traumas experienced by the mother during pregnancy. We will see later how these are transferred to us before birth. All these factors directly determine who we are as adults, our behavior patterns, preferences, insecurities, and limiting beliefs that prevent us from having the healthy and happy inner world we all want and deserve to enjoy.

Unfortunately, modern science is poorly equipped to make significant advancements in the realm of subjective personal reality. Besides the variety of hypnotic regression techniques currently available, which are considered unreliable by many, there is not much more in the scientific toolbox that may help us open the subconscious data banks, much less to modify or reprogram the hidden traumas stored therein.

You must be aware when considering the possibility of participating in an ayahuasca session that you will deal with one or several of your fears. Some participants are exempt from this in the first or first few sessions as they instead go through enjoyable experiences with little discomfort if any. Never-the-less, those as everyone else, will experience and face their fears sooner rather than later. In light of such unavoidable effects, ayahuasca should be regarded as a powerful medicine for spiritual, emotional, and psychological health.

It is essential to understand that it is in facing your own darkness and fears that you can find long-lasting emotional and spiritual health. Doing nothing while staying in your comfort zone shall take you nowhere. To achieve true psychological balance and inner personal happiness, you must find your inner courage and be willing to "suffer" and embrace the discomfort of facing your darkness and fears. Ayahuasca is highly recommended to those that recognize its enormous potential and grab the opportunity without much hesitation. The experience favors those who are willing to trade a few hours of difficulty in exchange for a lifetime of wellbeing.

Ayahuasca and the Medical Establishment

As mentioned earlier, the expansion of ayahuasca has brought a growing body of scientific research with promising results. The list of potential benefits continues to expand over time. The first series of discovered benefits included the treatment of alcohol and drug dependence. Dr. Jacques Mabit from the Takiwasi Center in Peru, reports that using ayahuasca in combination with conventional psychotherapeutic methods yields positive treatment outcomes in around two-thirds of patients. Moreover, positive effects have been documented in the treatment of mood and anxiety disorders, including PTSD. Other psychological benefits have also been supported by scientific studies. This includes increased confidence, optimism, and independence. Ayahuasca has also be demonstrated to increase assertiveness, foster calmness, peace, compassion, and love. The sacred medicine can also result in reduced judgmental feelings and foster a kinder and more grateful attitude. Cognitive skills and improved creative capacity, along with improvements to other adaptive skills, have also been associated with ayahuasca.

Given such a wide variety of demonstrable physical and mental health benefits, one would expect the medical community to embrace the use of ayahuasca with positive reception. Recently, a favorable case has been made for MDMA and psilocybin, but not for ayahuasca. Two major factors may explain this situation.

First, we have the pharmaceutical industry, which has not only influenced but dominated and dictated, governmental medical policy-making globally. During the recent psychedelic renaissance, we have seen significant progress in the regulatory processes. These changes shall eventually bring MDMA and psilocybin into the pharmaceutical world. When these medications are finally approved for controlled medical use, it is not unreasonable to foresee the introduction of patented derivative products that would exclusively benefit the corporations that launch them. It will be of interest to see whether the less expensive generic versions of natural molecules as psilocybin are made available in the marketplace.

Another natural molecule that deserved to be available in pharmacies decades ago is one of the active ingredients of the ayahuasca vine, harmine. The current scientific literature regarding harmine indicates the incredible benefits of the molecule and a promising future. The issue is that, by being a natural molecule, harmine doesn't qualify for protective patents that warrant exclusive profits to the pharmaceutical corporations. These companies are currently pursuing the development of harmine's chemical analogs with enhanced features that allow the claim of a new patentable substance. Despite harmine, in its natural state, having the ability to provide effective healing to millions of people with neurodegenerative conditions, we most likely won't see harmine-based products until patentable analogs are developed. Such are the realities of the modern world.

The pharmaceutical industry was interested in ayahuasca decades ago, but the circumstances did not favor them at the time. Not many people know the story, and many find it unbelievable that the ayahuasca plant once was a patented item. From 1986 to 1999, Loren Miller, a pharmaceutical entrepreneur, was the exclusive owner of the trademark and rights to cultivate the ayahuasca plant. He had filed and obtained approval from the U.S. Patent and Trademark Office, which is the government agency responsible for granting U.S. patents and registered trademarks. When the news of the patent became well known in the Amazon basin in 1994, it prompted many indigenous tribes of South America to organize opposition to the patent because the vine was a sacred religious symbol and a known medicinal herb.

In 1999, the Center for International Environmental Law (CIEL) filed a legal challenge against the U.S. patent over the "ayahuasca" vine, Barnisteriopsis caapi, which is native to the Amazon rainforest. CIEL acted on behalf of the Coordinating Body of Indigenous Organizations of the Amazon Basin (COICA in Spanish) and the Coalition for Amazonian Peoples and their Environment (Amazon Alliance). After years of administrative and legal maneuverings, the patent expired, and the case was closed. One can only imagine how developed or repressed would have been the role of ayahuasca in the medical industry today absent from the brave resistance of the indigenous movement. [8]

The economic factor has historically been a significant determinant for the direction of the revolutionary discoveries within science and medicine. For this reason, ayahuasca is not in a favorable position to enter the club of pharmaceutical products. One of its chemically active components, harmine, is the only viable candidate to qualify for the honor. Yet, it seems as though ayahuasca, as a whole and natural substance, shall never be accepted for medical use. There is another non-economic reason for this.

The other obstacle of ayahuasca becoming a widely accepted medical alternative is the chemical complexity of the brew. Unlike MDMA and psilocybin, which have become increasingly accepted by the regulatory agencies in the USA, ayahuasca remains further down the list of serious consideration. The complex nature of the brew has contributed to this.

Substances such as MDMA and psilocybin are chemically well defined, clearly separable, and consist of a single molecule, which is ideal for laboratory studies. On the other hand, the effectiveness of ayahuasca use doesn't rest in a single molecule that can be isolated and studied. Instead, ayahuasca is a cocktail of substances that constitute an enormous challenge to any medical researcher. The analytical chemistry of an ayahuasca brew sample will define a long list of components. The N, N-dimethyltryptamine (DMT), and harmine families of molecules are the most well characterized. However, several more active ingredients combine with each other in a multifactorial and complex manner. The problem is further complicated by the fact that we are unable to reproduce an ayahuasca experience by merely combining harmine with DMT, plus a few other ingredients. There is no accepted chemical formula for ayahuasca. This leads us to another problem. Given these limitations, the research community has resigned to this issue by accepting the only remaining alternative, which is to study ayahuasca in its traditional form. Ayahuasca researchers resort to suppliers of the brew and do their best to work with non-standardized samples, as standardization is virtually impossible to achieve.

Based on these observations, I believe we are decades away from ayahuasca, making an honorable entrance into the hallways of modern medicine. Meanwhile, I hope the research community continues to explore its effects with unstandardized samples of ayahuasca, and it continues to be practiced as a natural plant remedy, religious sacrament, or shamanic ritual, indefinitely.

The Need for Integration & Spiritual Advice

Besides the physical safety of the sacred medicine, we must address a different aspect regarding its psychological effects. There are critics of the ayahuasca community who raise questions about the safety of ayahuasca for specific individuals who don't have the psychological strength required to withstand its powerful psychoactive effects. The ayahuasca experience, as we know, often brings up past traumas and may lead to new traumatic experiences that may be difficult for some people to assimilate.

Psychological distress following ayahuasca ceremonies has been reported, with a small number of case reports of severe depression and psychotic states. Mental health professionals have proposed that these episodes of psychological distress are triggered or stimulated by the ayahuasca experience in situations where little or no adequate assistance is provided to the participants. I believe these are valid concerns. This issue has become increasingly evident over the years as the ayahuasca practice has been disseminated around the globe. Organizers of ayahuasca sessions in modern settings frequently ignore the importance of integration after the experience and fail to provide supportive alternatives to in-situ or post-session. This is the case in South America, most retreats undervalue the importance of integration, and offer little psychological or cultural support to help participants frame their experiences in a healthy context.

At this time, we will not delve deeply into the additional problems of unethical facilitators or shamans who cross sexual privacy boundaries. However, we should acknowledge that the ayahuasca practice and integration support are two activities that must be considered inseparable. As discussed above, the practice of ayahuasca is unlikely to transition into a regulated medical practice. Hence, the ayahuasca community must assume a proactive role of self-regulation and aim to raise the integration function to the same level of importance as the medicine facilitation itself. It is just the right thing to do for the wellbeing of participants and the generalized acceptance of the ayahuasca practice in modern society.

One of the aspirations of this work is to provide tools for the enhanced development of the ayahuasca spiritual advisor as a practice that combines cultural, psychological, and emotional support to ayahuasca participants in the future.

CHAPTER TWO

AND AYAHUASCA SAID: "KNOW THYSELF"

The journey of developing my concept of ayahuasca spiritual advisor began with my fascination for the type of psychedelic connection that I found during my ayahuasca sessions. My ayahuasca experiences gave me a deep conviction that what I was sensing or perceiving contained a fundamental sense of truth. The symbolic language which I experienced had multiple layers of meaning. The information contained dual messages, somewhat analogous to the experience of stereo music. The visions conveyed a message which was not necessarily self-evident, but in a separate channel, I received non-verbal information, which allowed me to comprehend the intrinsic meaning of the visual message. The non-verbal channel was not always entirely clear, but in combination with the visual channel, I was able to interpret its meaning in the context of my life events and timeline.

This was my experience during the first few years as a practitioner. During this time, Don Jose Campos, who initiated me in the path and eventually accepted me as one of his many apprentices, came to Puerto Rico every summer and offered a season of sessions to the growing group of friends that eagerly awaited his annual pilgrimage. It took seven years for Don Jose to give me permission and means to drink the medicine regularly. He left me with enough medicine to continue my work during the rest of the year until his next visit. I was no longer limited to a dozen or so sessions each summer.

This enabled me to establish a discipline of self-exploration in solitude, drinking under the conditions I considered ideal and at a frequency which felt convenient. Craving for answers about myself, I embarked on a journey of self-discovery, intending to understand the underpinning feature of myself and what made me who I was. Journaling was a valuable tool that fostered a practice of reflection on the new snippets of wisdom gained through every session. I gradually discovered the art of asking the right questions before every session. I realized that the most valuable matters which I had to learn about did not specifically concern me. Instead, the lessons concerned human nature in general, with the bonus of realizing that I was only a specific manifestation of a generalized pattern.

This process produced gradual and fundamental changes in my perception of reality, my motivations, and my aspirations in life. I began to perceive others around me with a deeper awareness of what existed behind their persona. This was especially true in my professional environment. As a relatively well-positioned bank officer, I recognized the emptiness of my ultimate contribution to society through my job. Then, I saw the role-playing, which is prevalent in corporate life where personal relationships are as real as a comedy movie script.

Ayahuasca self-advisory was being born in my life. I gradually redesigned myself with the assistance of the medicine, which answered the most profound questions I could conceive. The reprogramming of my habits followed; toxic thought patterns were removed, while alcohol and recreational drugs were eradicated. I then became aware of my distorted and limiting beliefs about my relationship with women. I saw how these beliefs had been rooted in childhood traumatic experiences with my mother.

With such inner growth, I began to notice patterns of behavior and internal conflicts in others, especially those sincere truth-seekers who often attended the ayahuasca sessions of Don Jose. These patterns were clearly analogous to mine in many ways. From here, my first advisor sessions with others began to materialize. I realized that the spiritual healing principles which I was starting to comprehend extended far beyond myself and could be applied to others as well. I was not a psychic. Instead, I was just developing a deeper understanding of human nature with the prodigious assistance of sacred medicine. In a nutshell, the journey to discovering ayahuasca spiritual advising turned out to be a journey of self-realization. How can anyone deeply understand anybody without understanding themself?

Correlating self-observations with the life circumstances of others became a passion for on-going discovery. I began to share this with all participants who showed an interest in the subject. By this time, I was already facilitating monthly ayahuasca sessions at a Reiki Healing Center in South Florida. These sessions exposed me to many participants and practitioners from a wide diversity of cultural and socioeconomic backgrounds. I remained diligent and attentive to my learning over the sixty consecutive monthly sessions, which concluded in 2013. Throughout the years, I realized that I was developing a methodology which I named ayahuasca spiritual advisory. In essence, the methodology is composed of a process whereby the participant is orientated by the advisor before the session, is observed throughout the session, and is engaged in integration afterward.

Something of great significance occurred during my five years of ayahuasca facilitator at the Reiki Center. I fell in love with Rosalia, a beautiful ayahuasca practitioner from Colombia with whom I found a shared a vision of life and the future. Rosalia began to assist me in the monthly sessions as our relationship crystallized into plans to share our lives. Interestingly, ayahuasca spiritual advising turned into a mutually absorbing endeavor that enriched our relationship and, subsequently, our lives.

In fact, my decision to open up to a new loving relationship was a remarkable product of my self-advising with ayahuasca. A couple of years earlier, during my question and answer interactions with Mother Ayahuasca, I realized that childhood programming had led me into a persistent pattern of seeking romantic relationships with women excessively younger than me. I hold nothing against couples with wide age gaps. However, in my particular case, it stemmed from a subconsciously biased compulsion and wasn't a product of the random mechanics of destiny.

Over fifteen years earlier, I divorced a woman one year older than me, an event that unleashed a subpersonality that compulsively followed deeper instincts of attraction to younger women. During the first ten years of the new Century, before meeting Rosalia, I emerged from a series of four failed monogamous relationships, none of which exceeded two years in length. All four ladies were at least ten years my junior. In my self-advising with ayahuasca, I inquired multiple times about these situations, which I intuitively knew were not working well. There was something awry, but I couldn't pinpoint what or how. In a series of sessions intended for this purpose, Mother Ayahuasca revealed the connections with childhood issues. Ultimately, this released me from the unconscious behavioral mechanisms which were guiding my life. With the benefit of such an astounding breakthrough in self-awareness, I set a conscious intention to open up to new romantic relationships. This time the process was not driven by a conscious targeting of women who met specific criteria concerning age, beauty, or physical appearance. Instead, my focus laid on personality, spiritual values, and a shared vision of life. This time age was circumstantial, not a selection parameter. It is amazing how this works, as we will see later with the projection principle; once I had reorganized my psyche with new eyeglasses through which to view the world, Rosalia entered serendipitously to fit the missing link.

My relationship with Rosalia developed to enjoyable highs. In 2014, we decided to commit to marriage and create a life together in the path of ayahuasca, not only to heal ourselves but also with a mission to heal others. We decided to create our own space in a suitable location to express our passion as ayahuasca spiritual advisors freely. After a series of failed attempts, we found a property that had been previously described to us in incredible detail by a psychic friend two years earlier. Thus, it began the mission of love, which eventually led to most of the material in this book.

We started to facilitate ayahuasca sessions several times per month in conjunction with Rosalia's son, Inti. Incidentally, it was him, a young Colombian immigrant, student of anthropology, and sincere follower of Mother Ayahuasca, who introduced me to his mother, now my wife. In his tremendous devotion for the sacred medicine, he had legally changed his first and last names to Inti Munay, two words from the South American Quechua language that literary means "Sun Love". A family vessel was leaving the dock in a mission of healing, and who knows where it may lead us all.

Determined to create a body of work and leave a tangible record for future reference, we began meticulously documenting all sessions with legal disclosures and personal information from every participant.

The Empirical Process: Observation & Practice

After several years of observational study and learning, I began to realize that we were accumulating a body of data that could be organized in a quasi-scientific way. This data could be used to develop an educational model to share our lessons with those interested in learning from our experience. I thought this might be useful to others in numerous ways. This was the birth of the idea of articulating the healing principles of ayahuasca advising to share with the general public.

Without realizing it, our mission of healing ourselves and helping others to help themselves had become a quasi-scientific research project. It was exciting to see that we had reached a point where we were reaping the benefits of a five-year-long study. Our main contribution to this study was the careful observation of hundreds of participants. We had evaluated each of these participants with a careful assessment of their psychological profile and followed their evolution after going through one, or a whole series of ayahuasca sessions.

What is the definition of scientific observation in the social sciences? Technically, observation is defined as systematic data collection in the field of study for a research project. It should have the following characteristics: (i) examination of people in natural settings or naturally occurring situations, (ii) prolonged engagement in a setting or social situation, (iii) clearly expressed, self-conscious notations of how observing is done, (iv) methical and tactical improvisation in order to develop a full understanding of the setting of interest, (v) imparting attention in ways that are in some sense 'standardized' recording one's observations. [1]

When reviewing the work which we have undertaken for years, it is clearly not far from the textbook definition of observation in social sciences. When I investigated the recommended guidelines regarding the rationale which underpins the collection of observational data, I found some definitions which were even more relevant to our work.

There are a variety of reasons for collecting observational data. Some of these reasons include: (i) when the nature of the research question to be answered is focused on answering a how- or what-type question, (ii) when the topic is relatively unexplored and little is known to explain the behavior of people in a particular setting, (iii) when understanding the meaning of a setting in a detailed way is valuable, (iii) when it is important to study a phenomenon in its natural setting, (iv) when self-report data (asking people what they do) is likely to be different from actual behavior (what people actually do).

Based on these textbook definitions, we had been making very relevant field observations for years and extracting empirical knowledge in a very particular way. Perhaps technically unscientific, but never-the-less, incredibly well-defined, rational, and structured. After all, qualitative methods are scientific and widely accepted by much of the scientific community. These methods focus more on the meaning of different aspects of peoples' lives, and on their accounts of how they understand the behavior and beliefs of themselves and others.

Concerning the method of data collection we have been using, unstructured interviews, it transpires that these are also a widely accepted method in the social sciences: unstructured interviews are open-ended and informal. The researcher is seeking a detailed picture and tries to bring no preconceptions. This type of interview is often used in narrative research. Generally, the researcher asks one question and then allows the interviewee to talk or 'tell their story.' The infographic below briefly illustrates the empirical process which yielded the principles outlined in subsequent chapters.

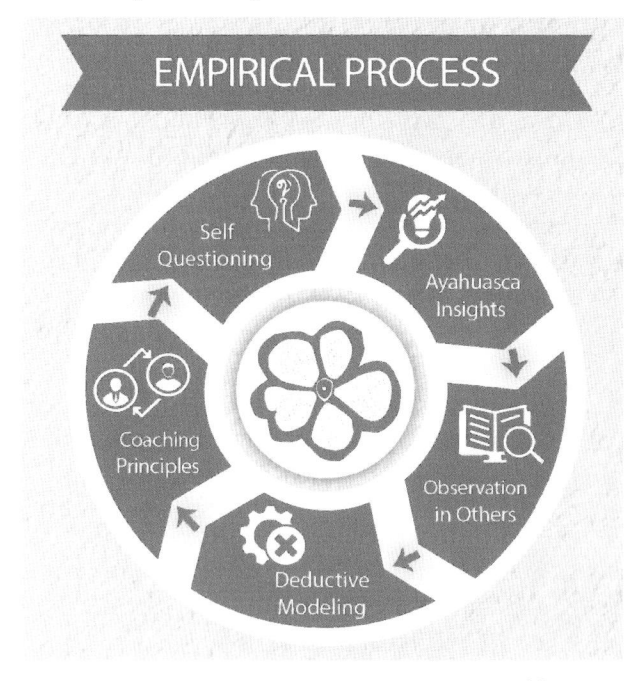

The more consciously aware we were of the connections between our own transpersonal processes with the ones of the participants, the easier it became to pinpoint their personal issues during the confidential and intimate interviews prior and after the sessions. In other words, the process of transposing our own cognitive process onto the participant's circumstances became increasingly easy. The empirical assumption for such a natural transition is that we are all fundamentally similar in our psychological composition. This further reflects the metaphysical principle that we are all one. Over the years, these connections developed into generalized patterns that we started employing as our operational guidelines to practice ayahuasca advising with others. The following chapters describe in detail the product of this process.

Observational Basis of the Model

It should be clear that the assertions regarding the quantum model of the psyche are not entirely the product of ayahuasca insights. These are also a significant amount of observational data that strengthened and confirmed our convictions of such insights. We are referring to thousands of participants of which my wife, stepson, and I have facilitated ayahuasca sessions. Sufficient first-and experience has been a fundamental factor in fine-tuning the spiritual healing principles described in the following sections of this book. It is appropriate to disclose a cross-sectional description of the sample of participants included in our observations. Here is an infographic description of the participants that have received our ayahuasca coaching sessions during the five-year period between 2015-2019.

The sample consists of 1,000 subjects, who experienced between 1 to 27 sessions during a five-year period comprising from January 2016 to December 2019.

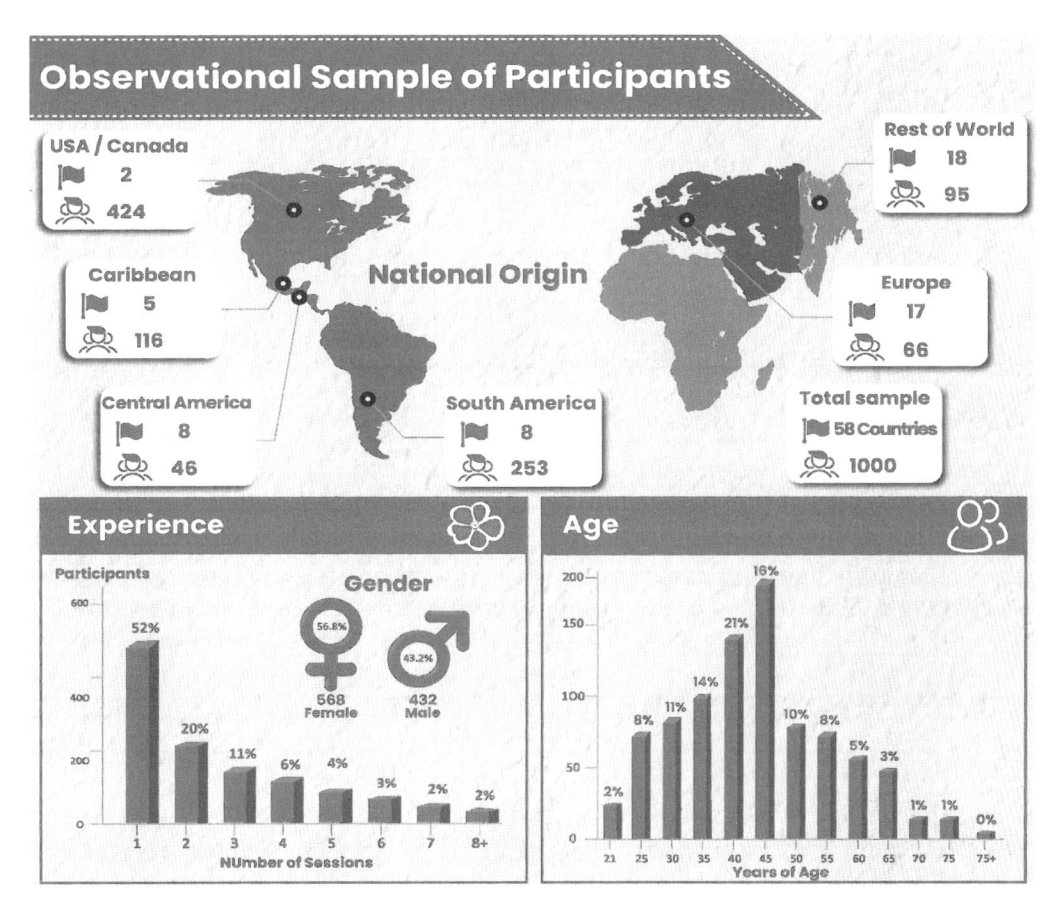

Observational Sample of Participants

National Origin

- USA / Canada: 2 flags, 424
- Caribbean: 5 flags, 116
- Central America: 8 flags, 46
- South America: 8 flags, 253
- Rest of World: 18 flags, 95
- Europe: 17 flags, 66
- Total sample: 58 Countries, 1000

Experience (Number of Sessions)

Sessions	1	2	3	4	5	6	7	8+
%	52%	20%	11%	6%	4%	3%	2%	2%

Gender

- Female: 568 (56.8%)
- Male: 432 (43.2%)

Age (Years of Age)

Age	21	25	30	35	40	45	50	55	60	65	70	75	75+
%	2%	8%	11%	14%	21%	16%	10%	8%	5%	3%	1%	1%	0%

Collectively, participants consumed 2,270 doses of ayahuasca, excluding the instances where participants consumed more than one dose during any particular session.

The observations were collected from an average of 30 sessions per year, with an average of 15.1 participants per session.

With regards to frequency of use within the participant sample, 52% participated in only one session and 22% engaged in two. The remaining 26% took part in three sessions or more, up to a maximum of twenty-seven sessions.

For obvious reasons of location, the national origin of participants was skewed, with 42% of them from the US or Canada. The other significant group was South America with 25%, and 16% from continents other than the Americas.

The gender distribution reflected a 58:42 female to male ratio, which indicates a tendency of women to be more inclined to explore disciplines leaning towards the emotional aspects of the individual.

Participant age distribution was significantly skewed toward the 31 to 45 age bracket (51%). This speaks clearly about the age at which people reach out to engage in a deeper understanding of their life process.

The Need for a Theoretical Framework

The story of the material in this book continues further. When I began to develop the outline of the healing principles and advising, I realized that the understanding of those principles was based on a model of reality that I had gradually constructed through many years of synthesizing my ayahuasca insights with the latest speculative theories about quantum physics. Unknowingly, I had constructed a conceptual model in my efforts to connect the dots of the myriad separate but meaningful insights built through numerous years of ayahuasca insights and scientific reading. I needed to find a way to communicate these concepts effectively. Otherwise, the ideas would be received as unintelligible nonsense when interpreted with the mechanistic paradigm of reality. The challenge lay in the paradox of translating my mental abstractions and nonlinear concepts into a linear, sentence-by-sentence structure. Beyond this, it was necessary to address the nature of human consciousness itself, a strange area at the perimeter of which the sciences have all drawn back. The work necessarily led to the intellectual territories of advanced theoretical quantum physics.

But there is no need to worry that some erudite intellectual capacity is required to digest this material. It is not; if you feel uneasiness with the "hard-to-understand" quantum physics, I recommend that you browse the book page by page, looking at the illustrations, and the section subtitles as in a reconnaissance mission before beginning the reading in-depth. It's like surveying new terrain from an airplane: on the first pass, it all looks unfamiliar; the second time around, it starts to make sense, and we finally gain familiarity through simple exposure. The inborn pattern-recognition mechanism of the subconscious takes care of the rest. When you "get it," you will later exclaim, "I always knew that!".

Before we explore the material in-depth, it is appropriate to address an essential aspect of the speculative nature of the quantum model. The geometric shapes of the quantum structures which are proposed in the model should be considered imaginary constructs for the simple reason that these are not detectable from the physical side of reality. Regardless of their adherence to reality, these constructed shapes are unquestionably useful for visualization exercise applications. This notion shall become increasingly understandable after review of the following chapters.

A necessary clarification should be made with regard to the generalized perception of the word "speculation." Let's start with a dictionary definition: Speculation (noun): [a] Reasoning based on inconclusive evidence; conjecture or supposition. [b] A conclusion, opinion, or theory reached by conjecture. [c] Archaic: Contemplation or consideration of a subject; meditation. [d] The act or process of reasoning a priori from premises given or assumed. A conclusion to which the mind comes by speculating; mere theory; notion; conjecture.

Anyone interested in the history of science will be well-acquainted with the centrality of speculation to the growth of scientific knowledge. Science historians have painstakingly chronicled the evolution of particular ideas, revealing a steady flow of speculative thought and hypotheses which have preceded significant advances in the natural sciences and mathematics. Interestingly, early scientists such as Galileo, Boyle, and Newton were avid critics of speculative assertions unsupported by documented observations. I believe this was their understandable reaction to centuries of Aristotelian authoritarianism. However, the historical-philosophical arguments in their published works contain a substantial amount of speculative thought at different stages of their scientific propositions.

That's not the case with contemporary scientists, who express more intellectual honesty and often recognize that speculative thinking is what drives scientific inquiry into new territory. This is evidenced by a common practice found within the majority of modern scientific writing. Scientific articles now contain speculative statements regarding experimental findings, most of them motivated by their desire to instill impetus and suggest directions for further investigation into the topic at hand.

We must bear in mind that in addition to the well-established scientific knowledge which is widely known, there is also an emerging scientific dialogue which includes new and less "solid" knowledge, often representing novel findings or new thoughts. Although we routinely rely on established scientific principles, we use emerging, novel data in the transformation of speculative ideas into testable hypotheses.

When I finished creating the illustrations of the quantum structures of the psyche, I immediately realized the value of developing visualization techniques to be used in reprogramming subconscious behavior. These could be utilized during visualization exercises and mindful meditation sessions, as well as during well-prepared ayahuasca sessions.

Because scientific measurements can't be made in the quantum field, the proposed quantum model of the psyche may barely classify as scientific speculation, despite being based on the latest emerging scientific knowledge. Although indirectly testable hypotheses may eventually be developed, the reality is that it can safely be considered scientific philosophy. If this isn't possible due to a reader's extremely rigid criteria, then we may settle to classify the model as a useful imaginary construction. Regardless of the label we ultimately apply, the model remains a powerful educational model for the psychedelic healing field of study.

Visualization techniques in psychedelic therapy are fundamental tools. The proposed quantum model provides the elements which the average psychedelic patient needs to obtain a believable self-diagnosis of their psychological state. Once the patient is able to grasp a firm understanding of their own condition, they can effectively navigate towards self-responsibility and reduce or eliminate dependency on the therapist or advisor.

While speculative and not currently testable for specific hypotheses, the model remains a valuable scientific contribution. With its foundations based solidly on existing scientific literature and data, the model cannot be dismissed with labels of unreliable, unscientific, or useless.

CHAPTER THREE

MIND-BODY QUANTUM MECHANICS

Basic Concepts of the Quantum Model

Our work aims to propose a new model of the psyche that is congruent with the realities experienced under altered states of consciousness induced by the ayahuasca brew and possibly other psychedelic substances. The model also incorporates the latest novel theories about the nature of physical reality, primarily within the field of quantum physics. Such a model may provide a substantial contribution to the understanding of the human psychological reality as experienced by the conscious awareness of the individuals. Subsequently, this may provide a robust theoretical framework that can validate new ayahuasca-based therapeutic models for spiritual and emotional healing. With reasonable widespread acceptance, a model of this type may warrant the propagation of courses, workshops, self-help books and other alternatives which could allow the general public to reach levels of psychological wellbeing which have been previously unachievable due to an insufficient understanding of the inner dynamics involved in the spiritual healing processes.

The elusive characteristics of ayahuasca, coupled with the epistemological problem of dealing with phenomena residing in other people's minds, make developing such a model a challenging task. Many complex questions have arisen during this undertaking. How are these formidable results produced as a product of drinking a chemical substance? What sequence of events occurs to manifest such life-changing visionary insights? And, how can we harness this knowledge to help suffering people in the areas of ego, mind, and spirit?

The quest for a new model is the result of an innately human wish: to comprehend the world in which we live and to construct theories to help make sense of it. In my experience, because the inner workings of ayahuasca defy easy explanation, most ayahuasca facilitators tend to cease their efforts to understand her at some point. Instead, they content themselves with whatever relatively fragmented understanding they have achieved. While attempting to broaden the horizons of our knowledge, we find ourselves grappling with the difficulty of extracting knowledge from the subjective experiences of other humans. Despite the widely held conviction that the rigor of the classical scientific method can unpick the underpinning mechanisms of any phenomena, doing it with the minds of others has consistently demonstrated otherwise. The intimate experiences, thoughts, and perceptions of others, especially those within the domain of ayahuasca, remain elusive and resist conventional scientific inquiry. Thus, in the face of such limitations, it appears unlikely that we will never attain a strictly scientific understanding of the human mind. Carefully crafted and testable hypotheses, which may remain unverifiable by science alone forever, offer the second-best tool which we can employ. We present such well-crafted and considered hypotheses in the following chapters in an effort to address the void of knowledge in this area. This knowledge gap desperately needs to be addressed. We present a model that enables humans to conceptualize their own inner psychological dynamics and strive forward with direction and hope. Despite imperfections, this awareness is tenfold better than remaining under the hopeless shadows of uncertainty and ignorance.

About Naming Our Protagonist

Upon facing the challenges of constructing an entirely novel theoretical framework for a therapeutic model, I began by borrowing from the popular vocabulary of the shamanic world; the concept of plant spirit and Mother Ayahuasca, specifically.

With permission of you, the reader, I will adopt an adaptive poetic license throughout this book, by frequently using the term "Mother Ayahausca" to describe the essence of what ayahuasca does to the structure of the human psyche. I have found this to be a useful and convenient shortcut to communicating the complex cognitive phenomena which occur during the ayahuasca experience. For lack of a better scientific term to articulate the wide variety of spiritual and emotional healing manifestations, I shall borrow this term from the popular vocabulary. Rather than elaborately describing different variations of parts of the psyche experiencing insights and epiphanies, I will simply say, "Mother Ayahuasca showed me…".

I find this preferable to simply "ayahuasca" because this term only refers to the physical substance, the liquid brew, and neglects the notion of plant intelligence or other higher quality in its functionality. How plants exhibit intelligent behavior without a 'brain' has fueled much discussion in biological science. This discourse is reasonably relevant to our work. Without digressing, my assertion here is that "Mother Ayahuasca" set us free from the limiting and somewhat intimidating name of aya-waska, which literally means "rope of death". Yes, not "vine of the soul," as it seems to be the preferred translation found in other publications geared toward ayahuasca tourism. Perhaps this translation is used as a replacement in an attempt to avoid the shocking first impression it may conjure in inquiring novices. Just in case there is doubt about its literal meaning, consider that aya p'ampay means "burial" in the Quechua language, and aya wantu means "coffin". [1] There are more than a dozen other names given to the ayahuasca brew, which are dependent on the geographical location within the Amazon basin. We know that it was associated with death because ancient curanderos were well aware of the fear of dying that often comes with the experience. However, the name doesn't do justice to the exquisite properties of the brew.

About a century ago, the brew came close to getting a better name, but history duped this move. This occurred in the early days of ayahuasca research. During that time, chemists were trying to identify the active chemical ingredient of the *Barnisteriopsis Caapi* vine, a component responsible for ayahuasca's intriguing effects. Inspired by the so-called "telepathic properties", they baptized the chemical with the name of "telepathine". Later, the chemists realized that the molecule had already been discovered in the Syrian Rue plant several decades earlier and had been called "harmine". The name telepathine quickly fell into oblivion. That said, in my attempt to better describe the essence of this brew, which is far from death as we popularly understand it, I will use the terms "Mother Ayahuasca" and "sacred medicine". I will also refer to the brew as "her" in the feminine gender, as an intelligent, loving, and compassionate plant spirit.

The Challenge of Understanding Consciousness

Initially unveiled by Sigmund Freud, the concept of ego has gone through a long parade of definitions for over a century. The concept has been fueled by dozens of prominent psychologists and scholars. Innumerable debates have ensued over its composition and inner workings, and most of these disputes remain unsettled.

Due to its metaphysical nature, it is understandable that the ego has proven elusive and difficult to define categorically. In essence, due to the uncertainty principle in the quantum arena of science, the scientific method has reached an epistemological firewall. Absent of a significant and paradigm-shifting breakthrough, science will indefinitely remain stagnant in the quest to understand human consciousness. Neuroscience is still in its infancy, and we are only just beginning to uncover the mechanics of the brain. For example, there remains much to be untangled regarding the challenging concept of "qualia".

The term "qualia" is used in philosophy [2] to refer to properties of experience. Examples of experiences with qualia are perceptual experiences (colors, taste, including subjective perceptions such as visions and hallucinations) and bodily sensations (such as pain, hunger, and itching). Emotions (like anger, envy, or fear) and moods (like euphoria, apathy, or anxiety) are also usually taken to have qualitative aspects.

The core of the philosophical debate regarding qualia resides on the notion that there are aspects of experience that science, no matter how advanced the physical explanation may be, shall never fully explain. Let's take the experience of the physical pain caused by a burning flame. In the future, we may be able to tell the specific neural location, mechanism, and neurological signature, which underpin the experience of pain. However, the qualia of the pain remain unexplained, as we are dealing with the consciousness aspect of the experience. Even a well-articulated explanation of someone's burning pain cannot adequately convey the sensation of burning skin. What is this scorching thing that hurts?

We are taught in school about the mechanics of vision with the well-known illustration of a human eye acting as the lens of a camera and the eye's retina receiving the inverted image. Upon interacting with retinal cells, light photons are digitalized and encoded by nerve impulses that are transferred to the optic nerve. These electrical signals feed-forward to deep brain regions, where they dissipate further into the neural jungle. The initially encoded neuronal signals become untraceable, entangled within brain-wide feed-forward, and feed-back neural networks. Where is the display screen of the image that we refer to as vision? How is the experience of watching a beautiful sunset scientifically understood or explained? Moreover, how is the sensation of touch that "I" feel when soft silk caresses my skin ever so slightly? How might science articulate the indefinable superior zest of a first-class wine?

A remarkable Artificial Intelligence theorist, Douglas Hofstadter, in his Pulitzer Award-winning book flirts with the notion of qualia. Notice how he tries, albeit unsuccessfully, to reconcile the consciousness paradox while acknowledging the analytical observer must exist outside the system:

"There is a famous breach between two languages of discourse: the subjective language and the objective language. For instance, the "subjective" sensation of redness and the "objective" wavelength of the red light. The former comes from the vortex of self-perception in the brain, and the latter is how you see things when you step back, outside the system." [3]

This is the challenge of the rational human mind. It is incapable of explaining its own experience of knowing. How consciousness arises from biological matter, from a network of neurons, remains one of the most significant mysteries in science. Science is helpless in even approaching a hypothetical explanation of the miracle of our own sense of self.

Where can we find the self that experiences the experience? There is a highly publicized consciousness experiment led by John-Dylan Haynes, a neuroscientist at the Max Planck Institute for Human Cognitive and Brain Sciences in Leipzig, Germany, in which neuronal activity of subjects was monitored via functional magnetic resonance imaging (fMRI). fMRI enables researchers to record regional network activation within the brain by measuring the vascular level of oxygenated activity as an indicator of 'activation'. As a result, activity in brain regions can be measured throughout experiments. It's important to note that only spatial and temporal patterns of regional activity can be measured through this method. Other aspects of neuronal network connectivity, such as signaling rate, pattern, and oscillatory activity (brain waves), cannot. While fMRI can provide a good idea of brain regions that are implicated in certain processes, it doesn't provide the entire picture.

During Haynes' study, researchers recorded fMRI during a decision-making task in which participants had to press buttons on a keyboard. Intriguingly, upon assessing EEG activity, researchers found that they could predict which keyboard keys participants would press, up to seven seconds ahead of the conscious action of tapping the key. The study showed that activity within the frontal and parietal cortical regions could predict the decision of a participant well in advance of a motor decision. This suggests that the subject's awareness of the decision had been influenced by brain activity, which occurred at least seven seconds prior to the conscious motor output. Interestingly, these predictions could actually be recording the higher-order cortical regions, which have generally been associated with conscious thought. How did the brain know the correct decision so far in advance of the participants' conscious action? This temporal dimension of decision-making remains somewhat unexplained. To a neuroscientist, this delay reflects a preparatory time in which higher-order cortical neuronal networks can begin to shape decisions prior to conscious awareness.

Many on the Internet interpret these results to refute the concept of free will. But is this really what the study indicates? Having observed me, it is true that I am normally an unconscious machine moving and making selections around my house without being consciously aware of these choices. For example, I may simply leave my computer chair and go elsewhere without consciously deciding it. I select from my breakfast cereals without consciously deciding it. I run on automatic, as though on 'auto-pilot'. These examples speak to the wonder of the brain. However, I am not a slave of the unconscious brain. Perhaps, what this study suggests is that many of our selections are made unconsciously, without the deep engagement of higher-order cortical regions. Most of our lives and decisions become automated. In a sense, there is no free will when we act robotically and follow a learned pattern of behavior. However, this is only the case for non-salient decisions such as which cereal to choose or in which room to sit. When there is a critical choice to be made, which in some way relates to survival or self-realization, the decision moves from an automated choice to a conscious one. This suggestion is in line with a wealth of psychological research, which has shown a large percentage of our decisions are based on unconscious heuristics. These heuristics allow for the conservation of vital energy within the brain by automating non-salient and frequent decisions that must be made. Ultimately, while these heuristics do not always produce the most effective decisions, they reduce the amount of energy expenditure required for everyday tasks. These unconscious decisions evolved to minimize inefficiency and reserve energy and focus on critical tasks.

Incidentally, it is worth mentioning that these claimed experiment results were based on a 66% success rate in prediction, which is only 16% above chance. The relevant point derived from this experiment is not the debate of whether or not we have free will; at some level, we inherently know that free will exists. The point is the fascinating question of who is making these constant unconscious decisions? In brief, my answer is that we are witnessing abilities that arise from the soul level, but that is a subject that will be addressed shortly.[4]

When we review the field of pure mathematics, we can appreciate that the problem of understanding consciousness comes from the world of pure ideas; a realm that transcends the world of neuroscience and physical matter. A brief explanation of Gödel's Incompleteness Theorem adds another layer of intrigue in the quest of the human mind to understand its own nature.

Kurt Gödel was a young and brilliant Austrian logician who undertook the challenge of investigating the world of the pure mathematics of the early 20th Century. After being a cornerstone of knowledge for centuries, mathematics was going through a turbulent "theoretical crisis" dealing with inconsistencies that had been found in the advanced theories of the times. He carefully examined the latest attempt to reconcile these theories, the mammoth treatise "Principia Matematica", and responded with his celebrated theorem. The publication of this theorem sent shock waves through the field of mathematics and the wider academic world.

Gödel implemented a novel approach of using mathematical reasoning to reach conclusions about mathematical reasoning. He invented the mathematical equivalent of thinking about thinking, a mathematical introspection. Gödel was able to unequivocally prove that all formal systems, not only Principia Matematica, would always find true statements unexplainable with the formal system at hand. When a system fails to fully explain reality, when the truth refuses to be "theorized", we conclude that the formal system is incomplete. Thus, we derive the name of the theorem. The implications of this are enormous and expand beyond mathematics into many other fields of knowledge. In a nutshell, the theorem bluntly says, "don't even try to explain everything, because it's impossible". It sounds so intellectually arrogant that it makes one question the possibility anyone could provide supporting evidence for this argument. But Gödel did it. This happened the day when mathematics, the purest form of thought, reflected on itself and "realized" it had an absolute limit in explaining reality. This was one of the great blows to the hope of a unified field or system of human knowledge -- and it came not from outside, not from romantic detractors who would deny the importance of scientific knowledge, but it came from inside. Logic has always been the cleanest, the most certain of all fields of human knowledge. And from logic came a decisive strike against our dream to explain the human mind scientifically.

I can even visualize a group of Buddhist masters grinning somewhere in Tibet when they learned of the discovery, as such an idea would have been very old news to them. For centuries, Buddhism has been predicated on the principle that words and truth are incompatible, or at least that words cannot capture truth.

The Solution to the Mind-Body Problem

If we can't find consciousness in the physical brain, but we are the evidence that it exists, "I think; therefore I am," then it must be somewhere, right?

Understanding our consciousness is extremely important to our psychological wellbeing, to our potential to reach self-realization, and it's a question that can't remain unaddressed. We have waited too long, and it has become evident that science will not deliver the answer during our remaining lifetimes.

These are the answers that humankind has sought for eons by embarking in a plethora of meaning-seeking endeavors that range from religion, metaphysics, philosophy, and many versions of pragmatic secularism. This is why the use of psychedelic substances has historically provided existential relief to the human soul. These entheogens, as they are now called, have opened significant windows of understanding. Unfortunately, the use of this knowledge has either been excessively controlled in the past by a priesthood minority or repressed by emotionally insecure kings or political leaders. We are now privileged to live in an era where entheogens are widely available, and those who use them wisely are not being burned like witches in a bonfire, at least in a literal sense. In my case, ayahuasca, for example, is an entheogen that has dramatically changed my perception of reality. With the resources of the Internet and self-publishing of books, we are living in information "heaven," if we could ask 17th Century's Gutenberg for his opinion. To that effect, we must not miss this historical opportunity to propose new answers to primordial questions.

Although science has been unable to provide those answers, it has provided us with an advanced understanding of the visible world. Equipped with an excellent scientific toolbox, we can now dive into the waters of the unexplained, unassisted by formal scientists. We can now embark on our mission of cartography and draw our maps. We are sufficiently equipped to dodge the dangers of superstition and successfully cross the abyss of myth. We have the tools to use scientific speculation to create a belief system that serves the purpose of our human condition and gain renewed momentum to evolve toward an improved civilization.

It's time to introduce the concept of quantum reality. This is a subject that has been widely discussed over the last few decades. By now, you may have already gained a basic understanding that allows you to follow this line of thought. Let's review some basic concepts to ensure we are all on the same page.

> **Quantum Field:** (i) A continuum of energy potential encompassing the entire Universe where every wave and every particle in existence is simply a partial excitation of such continuum. (ii) a discrete quantity of energy proportional in magnitude to the frequency of the vibration it represents

It is interesting that after the last few centuries of scientific inquiry, the journey of discovery had led us to the concept of unified field, which includes everything in existence. Although arriving at such an idea was the product of centuries of experimentation and hard work, it is perplexing to learn that it was already part of the cosmology of ancient civilizations. There is nothing new about quantum fields if you carefully examine the definition of the Hindu concept of Akasha as described by Swami Vivekananda:

"The Akasha is the omnipresent, all-penetrating existence. Everything that has form, everything that is the result of combination, evolved out of the Akasha. It is the Akasha that becomes the air, that becomes liquids, that becomes solids; it is the Akasha that becomes the sun, the earth, the moon, the stars, the comets; it is the Akasha that becomes the human body, the animal body, the plants, every form that we see, everything that can be sensed, everything that exists. At the beginning of creation, there is only the Akasha. At the end of the cycle, the solids, liquids, and gases all melt into the Akasha again, and the next creation similarly proceeds again out of the Akasha." [5]

Akasha is the universal quantum field, which is the basis of our proposed model of the psyche. The quantum field is universal; it covers everything that you may conceive in size or physical extension. It is the blanket that covers everything below the smallest atom of our organic tissues. It is consistent with the metaphysical notion that we are all one, the unity principle, that there is no separation, and that individuality is an illusion. We will see later how "chunks" of this quantum continuum are manifested as contained envelopes that constitute our individual identity. In other words, the quantum realm is a subtle world that includes our physical reality but reaches far beyond it.

The problem of understanding consciousness is the problem of understanding our spiritual nature. We will start with the assumption that consciousness permeates everything. In a sense, when we interpret consciousness in this fashion, we are equating it with the physical notion of the quantum field.

Much has been written about the mind-body problem. This relates to the old debate concerning the relationship between consciousness in the human mind on one hand, and the brain as part of the physical body in the other. The "problem" or paradox has to do with the presumed distinction of mind and body based on their completely different natures. How can two substances with completely different natures causally interact to give rise to a human being capable of having voluntary bodily motions and sensations? Said differently, if the mind consists of an unknown substance which is different from the brain's physical nature, how can such unknown substance influence the physical brain?

Within the proposed model, we can understand the mind-body relationship with the analogy of the modern personal computer. The physical brain is only the circuit panel, also known as the "motherboard," that conducts all of the electric signals which control the organism. Our mind, on the other hand, is composed of an invisible and undetectable body located not only within the brain but also beyond the physical boundaries of the human body. This is the quantum field that exists one level below the material reality at the subatomic quantum level. We will explore this in-depth soon.

With this perspective, the solution to the mind-body dilemma starts to appear reasonably obvious. The mind and the brain are not different in nature; they are the same fundamental substance. However, they exist in various states of vibration. Consider that they are both composed of water, one within physical reality presented in liquid or ice form, and the other within the quantum reality in a gaseous state. It's a matter of density of the quantum field. Physical matter is a more dense and concentrated form of the quantum field. You don't need a leap of faith to accept this notion, as this is the actual understanding of physical matter in present scientific theory. In fact, the idea of quantum interactions in the neural synapses of the physical brain has been formally considered. A published technical paper when referring to nerve terminals and ion channels argues about the need to use quantum theory in the study of the mind-brain connection. [6]

However, the leap of faith required entails that this quantum field of which everything is composed, the "empty space" between protons and electrons, contains an extraordinary hierarchical and orderly structure, as opposed to the currently assumed chaos of the subatomic realm.

> **Quantum Structures:** These are hypothetical structures that exist in the quantum field with a high degree of order and organization. They represent the elements of our spiritual nature, invisible and undetectable. They contain the software that runs the physical hardware of the human brain.

The Mind-Body Quantum Mechanics

The mechanism of action by which the quantum structures impose their presence at the denser physical brain is through the creation of electrical impulses from something physicists call the *quantum fluctuations of the vacuum.* This is an advanced concept in quantum theory rarely mentioned in layman literature. The theoretical calculations of the potential production of energy from a region of quantum vacuum the size of a small walnut indicate that we would be able to supply the energy needs of the entire planet for many years.

Let me present three credible but very diverse sources that illuminate the scientific reality of the quantum vacuum as a source of energy. The first is the well-known author and futurist Sir Arthur C. Clark, who said: "If they [quantum fluctuations of vacuum] can be [tapped], the impact upon our civilization will be incalculable. Oil, coal, nuclear, hydropower, would become obsolete, and so would many of our worries about environmental pollution." [7]

The other two are very similar scientists, Tom Bearden and Harold Puthoff, both of whom handled the quantum vacuum secrets very differently. Both men learned of this information while working on secret projects in the military and the intelligence agencies. Bearden, for some reason, was outcast and forgotten as a scientific renegade. Puthoff, on the other hand, was protected and had continued to work in secret technology projects. There are many other similar scientists, but they remain private, and their knowledge is not published.

Army's Lieutenant Colonel, Tom Bearden, was an expert in decoding the nuclear and electromagnetic technology secrets of the enemy in the Soviet era. He decided to go public in the early '80s with information that he was seemingly not supposed to share. Besides making many mind-boggling statements about the secret state of electromagnetic technology, he insisted in his hard-to-find book "Energy From the Vacuum: Concepts & Principles" that "every single watt of energy ever produced by electric generators, no matter how produced, hydro, thermal, or nuclear, has been pulled from the quantum vacuum, but theoretical physicist continue to fail to understand its origins due to their incomplete Maxwellian electromagnetic paradigm." [8]

Harold Puthoff, wrote with his staff of supporting physicists, a technical thesis exploring the theoretical basis of extracting energy from the quantum vacuum for industrial applications. He concluded that we are still short of reaching the point of making it viable. However, in the conclusions, he added that: "the concept of the conversion of energy from vacuum fluctuations is in principle, not falsifiable." This tricky word "falsifiable" in scientific jargon means that the concept can't be proven impossible; in other words, it is possible. It seems that indeed it is not impossible when we look at the official website of his company, which reveals their mission statement that includes "developing innovative space propulsion and sources of energy" as well as "the search for extraterrestrial intelligence." [9]

Without getting overly specific about the very convoluted quantum experimental technicalities, it should suffice to say for this discussion that there is sufficient supporting data in the scientific literature in favor of this notion. I invite the most inquisitive readers to research for themselves the available information and consider that the possibility of "quantum leap" interactions between hypothetical quantum structures and physical neural pathways are not a delusional concept, as it may appear to some readers who are unfamiliar with the latest developments of quantum theory. Given the fact that the whole notion of extracting energy from the quantum vacuum seems to be cloaked in mystery and national security implications, I considered necessary to quote information from diverse sources to warrant some credibility for the proposed model. Such a crucial aspect of suggesting a solution to the centuries-old mind-body scientific problem can't be taken lightly. The presentation of relevant supporting data is mandatory to avoid accusations of making little tenable or even preposterous assertions.

That said, let's move forward with the assurance that the notion of an intelligible quantum structure interacting bi-directionally with physical molecules is a perfectly valid possibility in a strictly scientific sense. The fact that science has not found the technical way of confirming it does not inherently mean it cannot constitute the true state of nature.

> **Volitive Energy:** Refers to the efferent flow of energy that is transmitted by an organized quantum structure from its habitat in the quantum field into the neural networks of the brain. Volitive: That exercises volition; the power of choosing or determining (will); an act of making a choice or decision.

To make it crystal clear, the organized quantum structure mentioned in the above definition refers to our psychological self, who interact with our physical brains to live our lives. The mechanism of action by which the quantum structures interact with the denser physical brain is by the creation of electric impulses from the *quantum fluctuations of the vacuum,*—mentioned above. We, as occupants of our physical bodies, constantly create volitive energy inside the brain in order to perform its function, experiencing physical life. Every single action you initiate constitutes a tacit manifestation of the human will, for example, when you move your arm to grab a cup of tea. In such a case, the volitive energy from your quantum structure creates an electric potential in the quantum field. This triggers a cascade of quantum events that simultaneously materialize at thousands of neural synapses, in this way triggering a neural current known as action potentials in the motor cortex. This electrical activity cascades down to peripheral nerve cells and translates into the motor movement of your arm, grabbing the cup of tea. The same motor process sometimes may be triggered directly subconsciously if you grabbed the cup of tea without thinking about it.

Speculations about hypothetical interactions between the "mind" and neural synapses in the human brain have been discussed for some time in the scientific community interested in the consciousness problem. I admit the proposed quantum model of the psyche stretches speculative thought far beyond the boundaries of current academic propositions, but its immediate application to spiritual healing techniques and psychedelic therapies completely justifies the effort.

Scientific journals oriented to the study of consciousness often publish articles that present novel concepts about the role of quantum mind-brain interactions. One of the associate editors of the Journal of Consciousness Studies, Jane Burns, wrote an interesting article where she proposed the possibility of mental influence acting over the quantum fluctuations. She even mathematically estimated that:

"Within the brain, about 80 ordered molecules, traveling at thermal velocity, provide sufficient energy to break an ionic or covalent [atomic] bond. Opening a molecular gate to a [neural] sodium channel probably requires breaking several bonds. Taking these factors into account, we estimate that about 4,000 molecules would need to be ordered to initiate a physical action.... Nevertheless, if mental influence can order molecules as is proposed herein, and can do this outside the brain as well as within it, it is reasonable to expect that it could produce effects such as ...coherent action between the ordered molecules." [10]

The electric brain activity that flows from the neurons into the quantum structures is much easier to explain or justify than the energy flowing the opposite direction. The energy that flows from the neurons to the quantum structure (efferent) already exists as it is produced by the physical body through metabolic processes. The afferent energy that flows from the quantum structures to the neurons is harder to understand and accept by the strongly conditioned mechanistic mindset. This is the energy produced from the quantum vacuum described earlier. Illustrating this process with a couple of analogies may aid in grasping the concept. In **Figure 1**, we present the analogy of the massive electrical forces that are created and discharged every day in the Earth atmosphere (thunderstorms) resulting from the inoffensive difference in electric potentials of large volumes of thin air. Also, note how the gas in our lung's alveoli (oxygen) is transferred to a

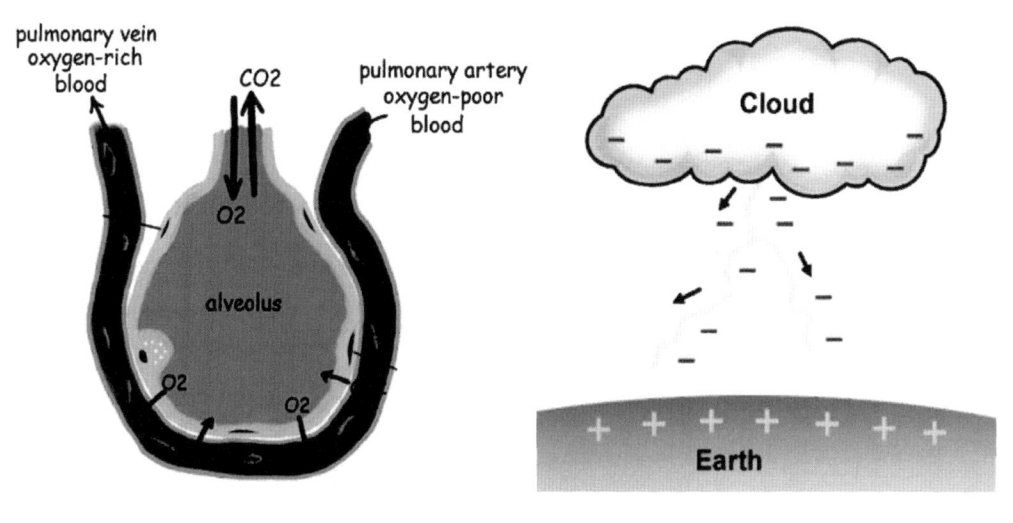

Gas-Solid Exchange   Electric Potential to Lighting Conversion

Fig. 1: Two analogies illustrating the energy transfer from the quantum field into the physical realm. Oxygen molecules from the air we breathe transferred to blood red cells in lung alveoli. Electric potential in the atmosphere collapsing into mega powerful discharges in thunderstorms.

solid mass in our blood (red blood cells) every second during the miraculous process we call breathing.

The proposed and still unknown mechanism of interaction between our psychological self and the neurons in our brains is necessarily a quantum effect connecting a still unmeasurable quantum current to the electrons which compose neurotransmitter molecules. This may sound like a science fiction proposition, but wait, not so fast. While researching for scientific support for my ayahuasca-induced idea, I was encouraged to find a recent increase in the number of scientific papers regarding quantum effects in chemical reactions. The Royal Society of Chemistry alone, published twenty-eight papers in 2019, some of them reviewing the discoveries of earlier years.

The most relevant of these discoveries to our quantum model regards one of the most intriguing mysteries of ecology. How do birds migrate with such astonishing accuracy on distances, which can be thousands of miles? We all suspected that the answer was related to some inherent sensitivity of birds to the Earth's magnetic field, but the underlying mechanisms remained elusive for decades. The key to the bird's navigation system happens to be based on the quantum effect of the Earth's magnetic field on the spin of the electrons in certain molecules located in the tissue of the bird's retina.

A short reminder of quantum mechanics is in order here. We know that the quantum packets that we call electrons spin around the atom's nucleus, like the Earth orbits Sun. We also know that these electrons also spin in their own axis, as the Earth does every day. They discovered that the Earths' magnetic field influences the direction of the rotation axis of the electrons of the atoms within the molecules of the organic tissue located in the bird's retina. Isn't that amazing? The variations in electron spin caused by the Earth's magnetic field creates a visual effect in the bird's eye that works like a magnetic compass. The net result is that birds can see the changes in the magnetic field and use it as a navigation tool. [11]

When we review the technical literature about neural pathways, we find that the field is heavily loaded with terms such as "electric polarization," "electric potentials," "ionization discharges," and similar neuroscientific jargon. The amount of energy required to trigger a neuron to fire an electrical signal is of such minute magnitude that it is not difficult to consider plausible the proposed bi-directional relationship between the quantum-molecule connection. In fact, based on this new paradigm, we can creatively coin a new term to redefine the classical mind-body problem with the more accurate term "quantum-molecule solution." If a hypothetical quantum structure proposed in this model of the psyche exists, then a similar mechanism of action in neural synapses is not hard to visualize. Discoveries of quantum effects in biology will surely continue in the future and shall strengthen the plausibility of this idea.

QUANTUM BIOLOGY
SCIENTIFIC UPDATE 2020

While we develop a quantum model of the psyche for spiritual healing, science makes significant advances in the emerging field of quantum biology. This is a step closer toward the understanding of quantum realities and eventually quantum structures.

THE EUROPEAN SCIENCE FOUNDATION LAUNCHES FARQUEST

Established in 1974 to provide a common platform for its member organizations the main research funding and research performing organizations in Europe. They have launched the "Foresight Activity on Research and Technology in Quantum Information Science and European Strategy" with the acronym FARQUEST.In this context, quantum biology emerged, among other alternatives, as a case study of particular interest since it embodies not so much what research currently is, but what it could become. This emerging field stems from the interrogation of the basic principles that govern interactions at the molecularScale in living organisms. Evidence of quantum phenomena occurring in living organisms suggests that quantum mechanics does play a role in biological systems

Photosynthesis uses quantum transport between chlorophyll molecules

All biological electron transfer is based on electron and/or nuclear tunneling

Olfaction and smell recognition is based on molecular vibrations using the quantum mechanism of electron tunneling

Magnetic sensing in birds allowing them to orientate is based on properties of electronic spin in birds' retinas

The applications of quantum biology in the longer term are potentially enormous and could impact a large number of technologies including advanced sensors, health, environment and information technologies.

In my opinion, the most persuasive evidence of the quantum reality is a little-known medical fact about life in the mother's womb. During embryonic development, when the embryo is still smaller than a kidney bean, a pulsating beat arises from nothingness in a hard to specify location. By the sixth week of pregnancy, an ultrasound can detect "a little flutter in the area that will become the future heart of the baby," said Dr. Saima Aftab, medical director of the Fetal Care Center at Nicklaus Children's Hospital in Miami. [13]. This flutter happens because the group of cells that will become the future "pacemaker" of the heart gain the capacity to fire electrical signals, she said. In other words, a rhythmic beat appears in a spot where the heart muscle fibers are not yet formed. The heart muscle is not clearly defined until the 20th week when the fetus is the size of a banana. This is an incredible anticipatory event, with the beat occurring 14 weeks before the formation of a heart. The location of the beat is exactly where the heart organ eventually develops.

What is the nature of this beating? Isn't that a sort of live phantom heart already beating in the quantum field? The materialistic model stops right there and has no words for an explanation. For the quantum model, the answer is as obvious as natural organic growth. The physical formation is just gradually filling up the "quantum mold" of the already existing baby.

In summary, we must acknowledge that our human existence is played in the theater of the quantum field, less so in the physical world. Neuroscience has gained valuable insights about the inner workings of the mind as it is reflected in the physical brain activity. However, it has a long way before grasping the depth of how the quantum field interacts with the brain.

For the sake of completeness, but without referring to extremely complex scientific terms and processes, we need to provide a general technical description of the quantum-physical mechanics of this model. Consider the following chain of events. After the psychological self, let's say our ego, is called into action, the precise required response is physically manifested as innumerable quantum potentials that collapse into a chain of events starting with the appearance of subatomic particles, climbing the hierarchical pyramid of physical matter all the way up to the molecules forming the neurotransmitters that participate in the brain response to the stimuli. This final stage of neuro-chemical activity is what neuroscientists can capture with some forms of sophisticated equipment. But, looking at it from above, these are only the electrical footprints in the brain left behind by the quantum ripples of the undetectable quantum activity. Allegorically, when we look at it from below, neuroscientists are like fish in the water, attempting to look up over the surface, but their vision is obstructed by mirror reflections of the density of water. They may only see the splashes and ripples on the surface but can't see what is causing them. This is the best way to illustrate the marvelous relationship between the proposed highly organized quantum structures and the physical brain.

I became more confident in my idea of quantum fields interacting with the physical brain when I began to find reputable scientists embracing similar ideas. For example, distinguished neuroscientist and Nobel Prize winner Sir John Eccles said that we have a nonmaterial mind or self which acts upon, and is influenced by, our material brains; there is a mental world in addition to the physical world, and the two interact. [14] This Nobel Prize winner doesn't go as far as proposing quantum structures that equate to parts of our psyche, but at least I felt in good company.

The conceptual notion of the quantum field and its logical implications are the most rational way we have found to describe the scientifically unexplainable idea of the spiritual realm. Our conscious minds, egos, and our souls are fundamentally spiritual in nature, not to mention even higher or more profound aspects of the psyche not yet know to us. The quantum field brings unity or wholeness to any form of dualism. In Hegelian terms, the quantum field is the synthesis of the Cartesian mind-body duality.

CHAPTER FOUR

THE URGENT NEED OF A NEW MODEL

The whole purpose of ayahuasca facilitators is to hold the space and provide assistance to the participants during ayahuasca sessions. However, when it comes to the integration of the experience, not all ayahuasca facilitators are equipped with the tools to handle the situation adequately. Inevitably, the facilitator ends up in an uncomfortable position if issues are not resolved by traditional shamanic remedies.

This is partly because the shamanic tradition of the Amazon Basin never developed a concept of integration surrounding ayahuasca sessions. Shamans or *curanderos* are not persons to approach when psychological assistance is required. Their indigenous ontological paradigm, as mentioned in the Preface, is dissonant with the psychological needs of a Western participant. An authentic curandero handles a participant in need of psychological support by blowing tobacco or Agua Florida, chanting or similar techniques considered appropriate within this tradition. The western participant may benefit from the applied treatment but may also feel a vacuum of required assistance derived from a different paradigm. Participants that have been exposed to fundamental psychological theories in school, psychologists, social workers, counselors, and other mental health practitioners have a unique set of needs that the indigenous paradigm is unable to cater. The ayahuasca movement and psychedelic movement is in the process of developing theoretical frameworks to fill this vacancy.

Ayahuasca facilitators are constantly being asked by participants to provide specific types of psychological support that they are not equipped or trained to provide. In response, a new trend of integration specialists are filling the space facilitators are leaving open. These are often psychologists, life coaches, and people with expertise in counseling. This has become a growing trend over the past decade as ayahuasca and psychedelics have been employed as psychological healing methods. As an experienced facilitator, this trend triggered my curiosity. I realized that the ayahuasca experience and psychedelics were making dramatic shifts in the participants' perception of reality. The traditional theories of psychological counseling had become ineffective in connecting the necessary wires in their patient's souls after ayahuasca sessions. Aware of this, I realized that I had nowhere to go for my personal integration and that I needed to find my own path. After all, I had Mother Ayahuasca in my toolbox, and I was ready to ask many of the well-structured questions during my personal sessions. The good news was that she was prepared to answer these questions in her own, particularly intriguing manner.

Many years and hundreds of ayahuasca sessions later, I had accumulated numerous pieces of her wisdom, and my journal was filling up with interconnected insights about my personal self-realization process. Interestingly, these insights contained information that was not only applicable to my specific case but could also be generalized to others. She was answering my questions about how the psyche works. However, these answers were not direct and disseminated as a teacher would provide to a student. Instead, I was learning about a new model of the psyche through personal deductive generalizations with the enhanced benefit of receiving spiritual healing on my specific psychological issues.

Initially, I developed a rough sketch of this new model as an intellectual exercise. This consisted of a few drawings that I thought would remain in my sketchbook as a conversation piece with friends and family. I later realized that, besides putting a face to the conceptual abstractions, the model might have practical applications as well. When I saw that this was aiding my grasp and understanding of my own inner world, I realized this is not solely a personal hypothesis and that the model may be understandable and transferable to others.

As psychedelic therapies become acceptable in the psychedelic renaissance of the new millennium, we must acknowledge our deficit in novel theoretical models of the psyche, those which need to be congruent with the new healing paradigm. The psychedelic-assisted healing movement is in urgent need of a model, of any kind, that can allow therapists and patients to develop practical, logical speculations about how the new psychology operates. We require a model that can provide a more understandable notion of the mind-body dilemma, which may encompass explanations regarding how the mind may influence gene expression and vice versa. With such a tool and tentative testing, we may gain an understanding of the cosmic dance of two realms, which have defied linear reasoning for centuries. We need to start somewhere, at least with a rudimentary functional theory, which may even only have a fuzzy postulate of its mechanisms of operation.

We need new psychology for the psychedelic era. Analogous to what the enlightened Voltaire once said: "If God doesn't exist, it would be necessary to invent him," we need to invent a new model of the psyche simply to provide a starting point.

Historically, this is the method by which science approached its most difficult questions. For example, What is the origin of the universe? And how did life begin? According to the latest theory and its continually changing refinements, the Universe sprang out of nothingness thirteen billion years ago from the 'Big Bang.' Incidentally, no one fully understands where the initial compacted mass of high-density energy came from or what catalyzed its expansion into the known universe. The Big Bang model was invented because we required a hypothesis, no matter how bizarre, to make sense of our objective scientific observations. The proposed model of the psyche is not much different; both models are just "reverse engineering" the observations to create the best possible meaningful hypothesis to explain them.

The challenge of any novel hypothesis is to identify its mechanisms of operation to design testable experiments clearly. This has not been the case in other significant theories in the past. A quantum model of the psyche would not be without the company in that regard. For instance, Darwin's evolution theory and the Tectonic Plates theory remained stagnant for some time for not having such postulates. In the latter, physical evidence for continental drifts accumulated over decades but remained unpersuasive because no mechanism was provided to explain how continents could move. Only when evidence of seafloor spreading was identified was plate tectonics taken seriously. This is the evolutionary process of scientific knowledge. For example, we now see the revival of Lamarckism to challenge the monolithic dogmas of Darwinism.

In the recent past, we have the case of one brave scientist who conceived a hypothesis that explains a huge number of perplexing phenomena but still lacks a clear postulate of its mechanisms of operation. Dr. Rupert Sheldrake, Ph.D., a British biologist, published his revolutionary ideas and immediately felt the wrath of the scientific community. Considered a scientific heretic by many, Sheldrake outlined the ten core beliefs that most scientists take for granted.[1]

All scientists must operate from these; otherwise, they are ostracized by the academy and ridiculed. This is the experience faced by Sheldrake and many others who defy the so-called "dogma of science." Sheldrake persuasively asserts that science upholds the erroneous belief that it already understands the nature of reality. He demonstrates with convincing arguments that science is being developed by assumptions that have hardened into dogmas and suggest that the sciences would be better off without them. Just to name a few of these scientific dogmas:

- All reality is material or physical.
- The world is a machine, made up of dead matter.
- Nature is purposeless, and evolution has no direction.
- Consciousness is nothing but the physical activity of the brain.
- Free will is an illusion.
- God exists only as an idea in human minds, imprisoned within our skulls.

In the skeptical spirit of true science, Sheldrake turns the fundamental dogmas of materialism, one by one, into exciting questions. He shows that not even the scientific method is free from habituated beliefs. Pure scientific facts do exist, no question about it, but they are such because the vast majority of us accept the assumptions of the scientific method. Reality is a collective agreement on certain rules. When we are concerned about the galactically enormous or the quantumly tiny, where the realities at hand fall beyond the reach of scientific measurements, we all become reliant on our own system of belief. We will see later how beliefs rule our realities.

While researching for existing models of the psyche, I carefully reviewed the reference book *Maps of the Mind* [2]. I studied a collection of several dozen models, including the ancient classics, psychoanalytic, and those relating to brain function. I found them all overly simplistic, with their descriptions not accounting for most of the phenomena I was experiencing in altered states of consciousness. Of course, I shouldn't expect anything different because they all derived from a mechanistic worldview of reality and struggle with the mind-body dilemma. When I later learned about Rupert Sheldrake's theory of causative formation, I stopped flirting with the idea that my notion of a quantum field was a persistent psychedelic hallucination. I had discovered a courageous scientist that put his hard-earned reputation on the line to propose a hypothesis that implied undetectable morphic fields hoping that one day if it happens at all, his ideas could be scientifically proven. [3] Meanwhile, he has endured an endless barrage of criticisms. Rupert became my role model and inspired me to develop this model for presentation to the world.

I found another example in Carl Jung's concept of collective unconscious. Similar to Sheldrake, Jung had proposed another undetectable structure in the 1950s. This time the structure contained instincts and archetypes derived from our two-million-year-old collective history. This work was criticized from the onset and, despite defending his proposition, the theory remained unconvincing to the scientific community. In his own words, Jung said:

"I must emphasize yet again that the concept of collective unconscious is neither a speculative nor a philosophical but an empirical matter. The question is simply this: are there or are there not unconscious, universal forms of this kind? If they exist, then there is a region of the psyche which one can call the

collective unconscious. "[4]

He chose his words cautiously and deliberately omitted the logical consequence "if they do not exist." One of his many critics refuted the concept arguing: *"..... by lending real identity and existence to a concept elevated to the incorporeal heavens yet occluded from direct observation or epistemology is mythology at its finest."* [5]

Having two well-established scientists who have embraced metaphysical concepts as an explanation of physical phenomena as role models, I decided that an unknown ayahuasca facilitator has nothing to lose by proposing another idea, such as this quantum model of the psyche.

I conceived that proposing hypothetical quantum structures with shapes and forms as attributes could be presented as a viable educational resource to help others improve their understanding of their own inner workings. Visualization is a potent tool in spiritual healing with a diversity of applications such as personal growth, self-hypnosis, prosperity workshops, and others. In particular, this model is ideal for developing creative visualization techniques for psychedelic-assisted spiritual healing. Once the patient consciously understands it, the advisor or therapist may design guided meditations with visualizations tailored to the intended purpose.

It's hard to deny that it is easier to access the subconscious by applying commands in the language, which it better understands; images and symbols. Consciously creating and anchoring a quantum field-based visual command into the subconscious would surely be more effective than just using verbal suggestions alone. Think about walking blindfolded through a furnished room you haven't visited before. We must agree that it's much easier to walk across the room having a prior accurate mental map of its layout than doing it without it. Moreover, the enhanced self-confidence garnered through the process shall contribute to effectiveness.

In summary, the practical application of the quantum model is twofold. Firstly, for educational purposes assisting the self-help and personal growth community reach their goals more easily. Secondly, to provide a useful tool to create visualization techniques for the ayahuasca spiritual advisors and other psychedelic-assisted therapies that are currently being developed in contemporary psychology.

A Note on Semantics:

A sensible idea in our discussion is to clarify the semantics of the parts of the psyche and their domain of action. Given the extensive popularity of psychological theories of the mind, we need to define the semantics before we continue moving forward. There are numerous terms coined by Sigmund Freud, Carl Jung, and others, which we should put aside in the context of our model. Instead, we will work exclusively with the self-defined terms associated with this model. The textbook definitions for ego, superego, id, pre-conscious, unconscious, subconscious mind, self, collective unconscious, persona, and shadow should not interfere with our discussion.

Besides the abundance of diverse terms, another difficulty in classical psychology is that in both Freudian and Jungian models there are two sets of terms; one for referring to the parts (ego, shadow, etc.), and another referring to the condition of the mind (conscious, unconscious, etc.). Neither Freud nor Jung provided a clear-cut set of boundaries between both categories. Is the superego entirely unconscious? Does the ego operate entirely in the conscious mind? Scholars have dedicated decades developing a diversity of maps of the psyche, some of them contradictory, in an effort to clarify the domain of action in the mind of the different parts of the psyche.

To ensure adequate semantics, and for brevity, we will provide definitions for a few relevant terms. We will not attempt to make distinctions between these and the classical terms of psychology, although brief references will be in order.

Who Am I?

After the discussion of the consciousness "problem," we must acknowledge the enormous gap that remains between scientific understanding and human consciousness.

> **Ego-self:** the part of the psyche which is experienced as the "self" or "I" and is in contact with the external world outside our bodies. It is the part that remembers, evaluates, plans, and is otherwise responsive to, and acts in the surrounding physical and social world.

There is a trend in scientific epistemology toward dismissing the notion that there must be a supersensible realm that permeates everything containing a considerable amount of phenomenology. Perhaps it is time for science to embrace novel, speculative thought about a supersensible realm, a previously unknown level of reality, and go back to the drawing board to ignite a new era of educated hypothesizing without falling in the abyss of myth.

This brings us to the introduction of the main character of this model, the ego, a quantum structure existing in the quantum field near and together with our physical vehicle. I propose that your ego-self, such self-perception that you interpret as "me," is a torus-shaped quantum structure that exists within the quantum field and cohabits with your physical vehicle. This fundamental unit, living in the supersensible quantum realm, is analogous to the "mental body" as some theosophical advocates would have named it. This ego-self constitutes one living cell in the ecology of the quantum field. If we could have the ability to perceive the ego-self in this field, it would look like a torus-egg-shaped hologram capable of existing in a non-physical timeless dimension. You are one quantum cell from birth to death, occupying your personal cosmic space where you experience your psychological reality and perceive your personal identity. The ego often asks itself about this strange sense of detachment, as it sometimes feels like a tenant living in a rented physical body. This ego, our conscious self, dwells in a quantum medium, an all-encompassing field, invisible and undetectable by the physical senses, but somehow connected to the physical brain while controlling the human organism.

The human ego has gone through history walking toward the far end of a rainbow, aiming at reaching the ultimate truth of existence. Biology has not found consciousness in the brain, and philosophers insist it must be somewhere because we exist. This is the starting point of a model that we can use to understand our inner psychological reality better, understand others, and use to develop ways to reprogram that part of our psyche that acts from the subconscious, ignoring our conscious intentions. This is our ego. The part of me that I believe I am. The concept that I have about myself. The one that goes to work, eats favorite foods, looks forward to sex, likes to relax, and have fun, as well as the one who lies to get what it wants. The one that looks at itself in the mirror every morning, that worries about money, but also takes care of the family members, helps others in the neighborhood, and goes to church to find peace. Where is this ego located, if science has no idea of its location? This is the eternal question of humanity that religions and philosophers attempt to answer for us. Who am I? Where am I going? Who is this entity inhabiting this bag of skin we call physical body?

Well, let's use our common sense and start building a temporary belief system using the most actualized information available about how the physical reality works. If you agree that a temporary belief to answer a crucial elusive question is better than total ignorance, then bear with me and do this together.

In order to make practical use of the quantum model of the psyche, we need to re-conceptualize ourselves from the amorphous, ambiguously defined self-image into a well-defined high-resolution quasi-physical energy being. If you wish, you may relate to your ancient concepts of aura, chakras, Theosophy's etheric body, Kardec's ghosts, or any other conceptual notion you may have encountered in your quest to understand the consciousness problem. It's time to close your eyes and start redesigning the concept of yourself. Let's resonate with the now-famous quote from French paleontologist and philosopher Teilhard de Chardin: "We are not human beings having spiritual experiences; we are spiritual beings having human experiences." [6]

We are literally light beings dressed as human animals. Our avatar appearance allows us to exist in a three-dimensional box, the illusion of reality, the matrix, the maya. Our true nature is spiritual, and, for the sake of logical consistency, it follows to assert that our spiritual nature dwells in the quantum reality. That should not be surprising as the physical attributes of the quantum field include,

Fig. 2 Allegorical conceptualization of the layers of self-perception from the ego's point of view.

as science has already proven, such spiritual-like feats, such as subatomic particles existing in two places simultaneously, traveling backward in time, and popping in and out of existence. Up to now, we have kept the description of these complexities as simple as possible because the focus of the model is not academic. For example, one important aspect of metaphysics that we have intentionally omitted from the model is the description of the different dimensions of reality. Clearly, there are more than three dimensions, as evidenced by our own extremely elusive consciousness. However, for the sake of simplicity, we are assuming all dimensions, fourth and beyond, to operate in the quantum realm, without further specifications.

In order to explain the concept clearly, let's begin peripherally and integrate our macro self-perception with our inner self-perception. This should assist in grasping the notion of quantum-self existing in the quantum field.

When we look out to outside reality, we have a sense of who we are. We learn as we grow up as children that we experience an inner reality and soon discover that it is very personal and intimate; no one knows about it except us. This is when the ego-self of the child is forming a more durable structure and becoming self-aware. This is about the time when the child discovers that it is possible to lie to others, to present a false representation of their own experience for gain or fun. The ego-self is born.

As our ego-self grows in strength and intelligence, it realizes that the perception of others varies in accordance with how much information others have gained about us. The illustration in **Figure 2** here shows what I term the "onion of self-perception" as a metaphor for the various layers of self-perception of which the ego-self is aware. These run from a broad and ambiguous outer layer, which constitutes the general public image that others develop about us. This layer is succeeded by a series of layers of increasing intimacy as they get closer to a more detailed or accurate version of who you are. Note that these layers represent your perception of other people's impressions of you. The penultimate layer is the perception of your most intimate connections; the people that know you best, that could be your wife, mother, brother, or close friend. Then we have the last layer, namely the most intimate "you." This is who you think you are. The layer which guards secrets hidden from all. This is the ego-self that you feel is acting in the physical reality at the most deep-rooted perception of yourself. That intimate "you," which looks at itself in the mirror in the morning. But truly, this is not the deepest layer of the onion. Underneath such deepest layer of your self-perception, you shall find other more profound aspects of yourself that you ignore exist. This is what psychologists call the subconscious mind. There are more layers of your onion that are hidden from your conscious awareness, some of which you may be curious to explore, and others you'd prefer to ignore. This metaphor of the onion is not to be confused with the geometrical shape named "torus," which we will discuss shortly.

Those aspects of yourself that are beyond your reach of self-perception, those deeper layers of the onion are the fundamental units of the proposed model of the psyche.

The Quantum Model of the Psyche in a Nutshell

The quantum model of the psyche can be described as a visual representation of the individual reality to be used by ayahuasca spiritual advisors, but also by other therapists with educational objectives in their normal course of business with their clients or students. It was developed in the simplest terms possible, intentionally omitting aspects of this overwhelmingly complex reality that we all share. The model is designed to provide an integrated view of the classical mind-body in order to end, or at quell for a moment, the endless debates surrounding it. This enables us to focus on developing pragmatic solutions to the human condition that continues to be helplessly ensnared in the robust survival programming that perpetuates dysfunctional behavior. The model aims to create the didactic theoretical framework under which advisors and students can develop innovative psychedelic healing techniques that allow practitioners to effectively modify the behavior patterns which have proven stubbornly resistant to conventional psychotherapy.

The model proposes a personal identity consisting of three interwoven quantum structures, namely, the ego-self at the "bottom," followed by a re-defined subconscious-self, and finally the soul-self. These parts of the psyche are packaged together in an envelope of personal identity that has access to a collective unconscious to which, by definition, everyone else is connected. These are conceptual abstractions of our inner reality that the model brings to life with visual representations of its shapes.

Finally, the model acknowledges higher parts of the self, including our undeniably divine nature, the source of everything. However, in order to bypass lengthy philosophical narratives and focus on pragmatic healing applications, these aspects are not discussed at length. In summary, as shown in **Figure 3**, we can describe the model in three sections: (i) the self, or self-identity envelope ('SIE"), which is defined trichotomous in nature, (ii) the collective unconscious or collective soul, and (iii) the higher divine source.

Note that the model doesn't mention the idea of the free-standing "mind," as this will be described in detail in the following section.

The Self Identity Envelope ("SIE")

Having established the fundamental role of the torus shape, which will be described at length later, we proceed to describe the quantum concept of personal identity. We are using the label of "envelope" to express a sense of togetherness among the lower three parts of the psyche. When we interpret ourselves as a team of multiple parts, it assists us in making sense of the inner world. This will also be helpful in later sections as we introduce additional sub-parts of the ego-self component.

This brings us to another axiom of our model: Our primary identity as a person is not a single psychological unit, but three, that work closely together as a team to ensure the survival of the physical body.

Think of a torus of quantum energy with three interwoven layers vibrating at different frequencies. It consists of our ego-self, our subconscious-self, and our soul-self. Unknowingly to the ego-self, they cooperate in the daily management of life. The relationship between them is unique because they work together so tightly that they may appear as one. So, there we are with our triple self, living in the illusion that we are one indivisible unit.

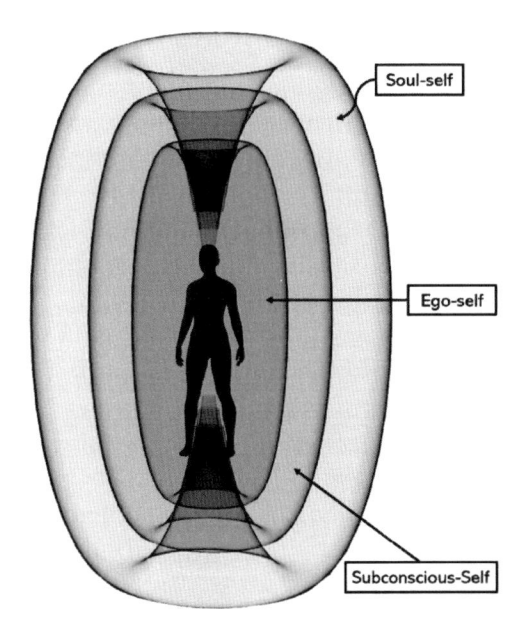

Fig. 3 Trichotomous nature of our quantum personal identity. Ego, Subconscious and Soul compose our Self Identity Envelope ("SIE").

The next important attribute of our SIE is that its components are dynamic and not stationary structures. They constantly morph in response to environmental demands and metaphorically hijack the neural networks to meet the imperatives of the survival programs. We will return to discuss survival programs in detail, but at present, think of these as the instincts that are described in basic psychology courses. We are composed of three players who regularly switch chairs sometimes as frequently as several times in one minute.

The subconscious-self torus is running the show from behind the scenes, conducting the actions that are often automated. It constantly overtakes the system when needed, which occurs more frequently than our ego-self is willing to admit. This dance of quantum structures within us, of constantly flipping roles, may occur harmonically or chaotically depending on the state of consciousness of the overall system. The quality of these inner interactions is a function of the degree of alignment of the structures relative to a common goal. These are the inner conflicts that we often experience while making important decisions. An excellent example of conflicts within our SIE happens when a distressed wife tells her psychiatrist: "I love my husband, but a part of me tells me to divorce him." Such a comment reflects an implicit lack of wholeness as it shows the division of the self. We all can attest to personal situations where our conflicting feelings are similar to those of this patient.

Within this framework, we will later introduce the concept of moral integrity, in terms of how well aligned the quantum structures are toward permitting the functioning of self-realization programs after the survival programs have achieved its objectives. Additionally, we will discuss the idea of the individual free will of the SIE as a whole and not as an exclusive attribute of the ego-self.

Finally, if you are closely following the composition of this model, you may have already wondered how these quantum structures are held together and around the physical body of each person. Why don't they blend with other quantum structures of other people? What keeps these envelopes of identity anchored together?

The answer has to do with the "probability clouds" [7] surrounding the atomic structures of the DNA molecules. This is the terrain where the quantum field meets the physical world. DNA sequences are unique codes of highly complex programming domiciled in the subconscious-self quantum structure, which defines and anchor the identity envelope of the individual.

Soon after the fertilized egg begins the programmed replication, a quantum baby starts forming with significant anticipation of the physical. This quantum baby is the result of higher-order information encoded in the quantum component of the ongoing physical DNA replication and transcription at work. In this process, the quantum structures of the new baby are being created and anchored to the physical body by a resonance pattern created by the billions of identical DNA structures that are being built in the replication process. These quantum structures are as unique to the individual as the DNA that created them. Their anchoring will continue to strengthen as the baby grows and even stronger during development to adulthood.

Sheldrake's morphogenetic fields are perhaps an excellent model to explain the following phenomena, which we already mentioned on page 49. How medical equipment can detect a weak embryonic pulsating beat in a bundle of cells which weeks later will turn into the first muscle fibers of the heart. Orthodox science can't explain the origins of this precursor beat occurring at the exact future location of the heart. The model of quantum structures can make a strong case in favor of the notion that the heart of the quantum baby simply starts beating, weeks before the physical heart of the embryo is formed.

Imagine the eighty-six billion identical copies of DNA inserted in an equal number of neuronal cells in your brain, together with the several trillion of other residents in each of the living cells in your adult body tissues, all vibrating and resonating at the same frequency. Wouldn't they form a unique quantum resonance pattern corresponding to your unique genetic code? Such a quantum standing wave is the anchor of your identity envelope to your physical body. The anchor that holds your consciousness together and prevents it from blending into the wholeness of the quantum field. There is an event, which only happens once when the quantum-physical anchor detaches, and our once radiant living bodies start to decay into decomposing organic matter.

CHAPTER FIVE

THE TORUS AND OUR SELF IDENTITY ENVELOPE

The Toroidal Shapes of our Psyche

To create a model that is useful for educational purposes, we propose a curious innovation. Our ego-self, subconscious-self, and the human soul-self can be represented graphically to provide the amazing human attribute of imagination with a tool to visualize and better understand its consciousness. For lack of better conceptual tools that science has yet to offer, a hypothetical quantum model of the psyche may, at least temporarily, fulfill the voracious craving of the human mind to comprehend its own nature.

Now we proceed to describe the morphology of these quantum structures. How would I look if I could view myself in a quantum mirror? My ayahuasca visions guided me toward an answer to this question. Subsequently, the answer inspired the development of this model. In simple terms, we all are sparks of light of divine origin, which in its process of expansion towards physical manifestation, exhibit a quantum pattern of organization that assumes the shape of a torus. This is the fundamental particle of the quantum model of the psyche. The torus constitutes the core geometric shape that defines the mathematical topology of our souls and the eventual morphology of the human form.

The most historically popular representation of this has been the concept of the aura in the form of an egg-shaped energy field emanating from and surrounding the physical body. The manner in which our model defines the shape of the quantum SIE is focused not on a general egg shape, but specifically on the intrinsic mathematical formula of the torus shape. It may be perceived as an elongated egg-like shape that contains the rigor of mathematics.

The quantum structure of the torus, which blends into and surrounds the human body, has been intuitively perceived by countless sensitive people, as confirmed by its prominence in popular literature. I and others, under the effects of ayahuasca and other altered states of consciousness, have perceived such torus-shaped structures. Due to this, the proposed torus-shaped quantum structure may sound natural and commonsensical to many readers. I believe we are evolving towards a more precise understanding of our quantum nature, and the proposed model attempts to advance such knowledge to a higher level. After receiving these insights, I began investigating the torus, and the information I found gave me a sense of validation.

The torus is a tridimensional geometric shape that is a little more complex than the pyramid, cube, and sphere. It is a donut shape that can assume interesting variations, as we will see here. Contrary to the other basic solids, the torus lends itself to a conceptualization of a flow of moving current or energy. The proposition of understanding the quantum structures as an upward flowing torus becomes increasingly plausible when we consider that the torus is intrinsically embedded in the most fundamental structures of nature.

Let's start with the most basic one, the magnetic field of a simple magnet, the kind that mesmerized us as children. Now expand that understanding of a simple magnet to the planetary level; consider the Earth's magnetic field is emanating and flowing through the magnetic poles due to the planet's massive iron core. These magnetic forces become undeniably real upon considering the Earth's magnetosphere, as evidenced from our perspective by the awesome phenomenon of Aurora Borealis. If we go beyond the solar system, we can continue to find this pattern all the way up to the universe itself, as it also seems to be fractal in nature—See **Figure 4**. There was a cosmological theory proposed in 1984 by Alexei Starobinsky and Yakov Borisovich Zel'dovich from the Landau Institute in Moscow, which describes the shape of the universe as a three-dimensional torus. [1]

There are multiple other manifestations of this fascinating shape's intrinsic energy flow, which can be readily found in nature. For example, the vortex ring is also called a toroidal vortex. This is a torus-shaped vortex in a fluid or gas; that is, a region where the fluid mostly spins around its own donut shape and forms a closed loop. There are plenty of toroidal vortexes in turbulent flows of liquids and gases. Still, these are rarely noticed unless the motion of the fluid is revealed by suspended particles, like the smoke rings, which are often produced intentionally or accidentally by smokers. Dolphins also produce these vortexes underwater by shooting bursts of air from their mouths with much apparent amusement. These rings are also commonly produced when massive energies are released, such as in the mushroom clouds of nuclear explosions. Toroidal vortexes are also present in the human heart. It has been demonstrated that a toroidal ring is formed in the left ventricle of the human heart during cardiac relaxation (diastole), as a jet of blood enters through the mitral valve. [2]

The toroidal shape of the magnetic field was exploited by the intelligent design of the leading candidate for a practical fusion reactor. This reactor design produces a powerful magnetic field that confines hot plasma in the shape of a torus.

Mathematical Torus   Earth Magnetic Field   Torus Around Black Hole

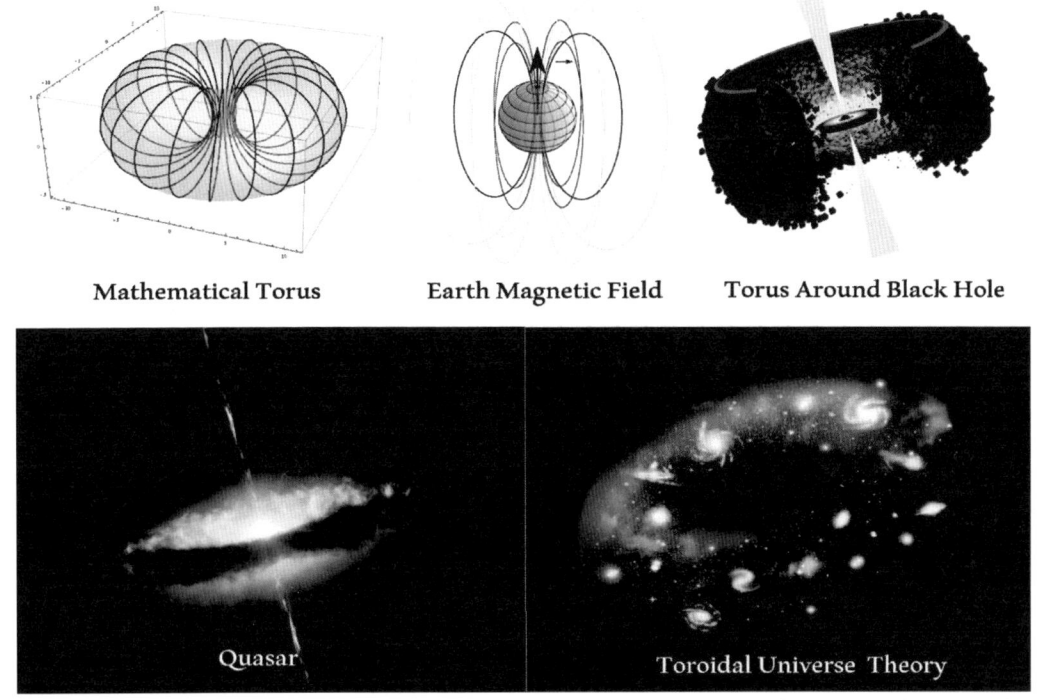

Quasar   Toroidal Universe Theory

Fig. 4 - Several artistic representations of Toroidal expressions in tridimensional space. The Quasar here is based on a photograph from Hubble Telescope.

Regarding the torus shape as a template of living systems, if you pay close attention to forms in the living nature, you will find it everywhere you look. For example, note that this is the pattern followed by the vertical axis of tree trunks, the branches spread over the hidden donut shape and the roots beneath grow under the donut shape as if they were the branches above.

Elsewhere in nature, a large number of fruits and vegetables--See **Figure -5** resemble the geometric torus shape and contain the mathematics of the two-dimensional heart shape. The two-dimensional heart shape associated with romantic love is prevalent in Western culture and can be considered as a modified torus. Some historians have said that the earliest reference of the heart shape is associated with a plant, Silphium, an ancient species which now appears to be extinct.

Fig. 5 The morphology of numerous fruits, vegetables and living plants contain the topological seed of the mathematical torus shape.

The silphium seed and fruit formed a perfect heart shape, as depicted on the face of a rare Roman-era coin. Silphium was originally associated with love and sex for its dual aphrodisiac and abortive properties, and some historians speculate that it could be the ancient origin of the romantic heart shape of our modern era. [3]

Besides Silphium, when we examine the morphology of fruits in general, we find many an exterior which forms a heart shape; strawberries are perhaps the most common of these fruits. Besides, the vast majority of fruits exhibit torus-like geometry when sliced in half. A close look at botany catalogs will also reveal a list within the cordiform category of several hundred species of plants and trees with heart-shaped leaves.

The most persuasive evidence that the torus is fundamental to our human nature is the multiple torus-shaped structures present in the morphology of the human body. **Figure 6** illustrates just a few examples which exemplify how some internal organs follow the torus or heart-shaped geometry. Similarly, the human's external physical appearance exhibit torus-derived shapes in many body parts. The torus and its derived heart-shaped form are an intrinsic element of human morphology.

We have represented our three selves as partially separate for illustration and educational purposes. However, it is vital to remember that these are blended and occupy the same space if we assume the term "space" applies to the quantum field.

The reality of a SIE containing quantum structures existing in the quantum field is intuitively sensed by many spiritually developed individuals. Historically, this has resulted in numerous versions of visual representations of invisible and subtle forms surrounding the physical body. Intuitive insights are often received by sensitively oriented people, and for that reason, tend to accept the idea of multiple subtle bodies naturally. Metaphysical teachings consistently promulgate multiple layers of bodies that are associated with different attributes of human ability. Etheric, astral, emotional, mental, causal, soul and spiritual bodies are some of the most frequently mentioned with several variations of function and purpose. These are also associated with vibrational frequencies, colors, and connections to energy centers called chakras, a term borrowed from the Eastern esoteric traditions.

Ovaries

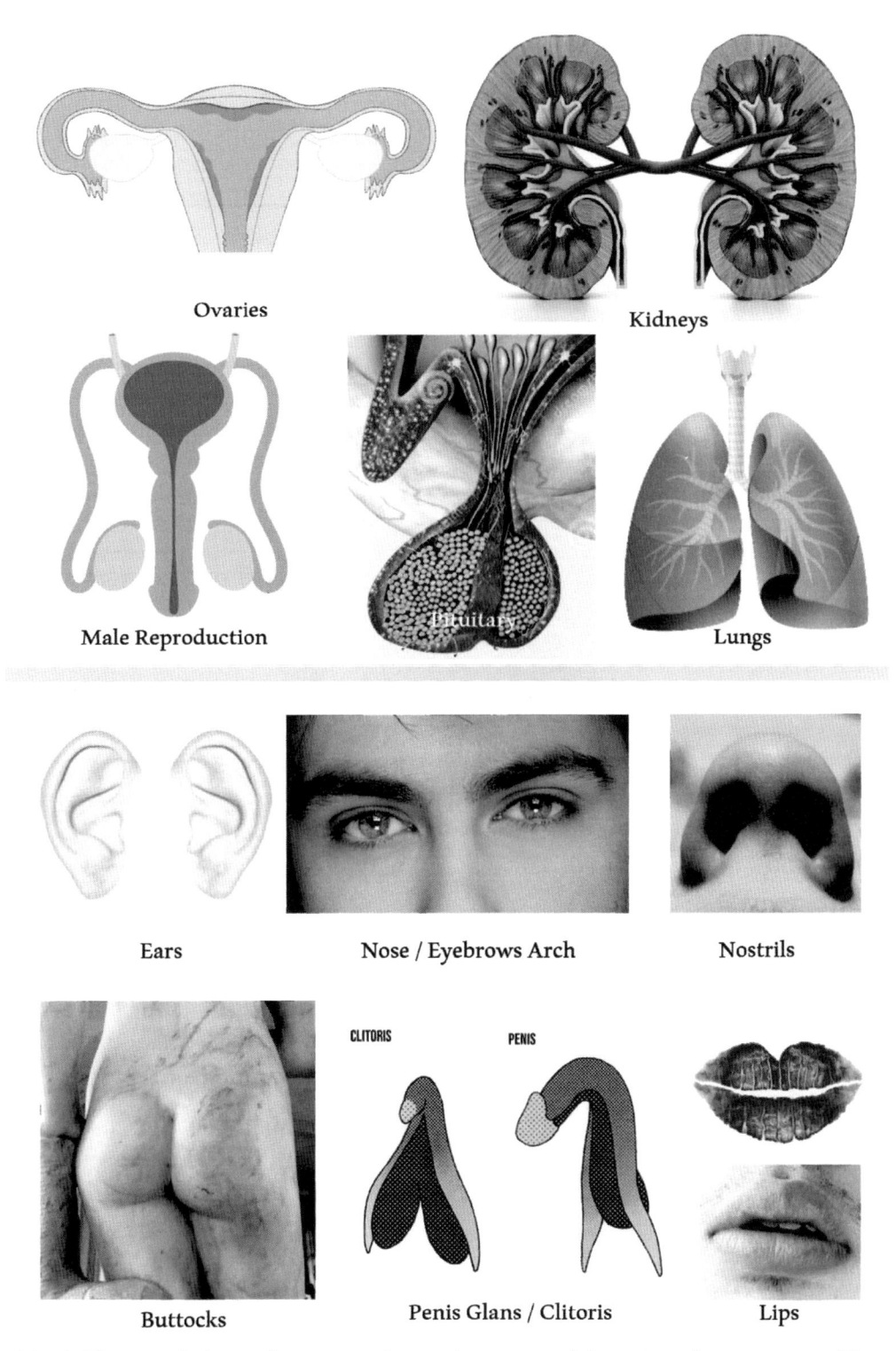

Kidneys

Male Reproduction

Pituitary

Lungs

Ears

Nose / Eyebrows Arch

Nostrils

Buttocks

Penis Glans / Clitoris

Lips

Fig. 6 - The morphology of numerous internal organs and the external appearance of the human body are defined by the mathematical shape of the torus.

What esoteric traditions call "aura" in this model is only a lower vibration by-product of a high vibration, the ultra-high-speed spinning of the quantum torus. Think of the aura as the pre-dawn glow in the horizon just before sunrise, that surrounds the physical body as the far-out remnant energy of the torus spinning at the core of us. Metaphorically, the torus is the Sun, and the aura is the pre-dawn glow. Literally, the imperceptibly high speed of the torus arises from a light core, and this is our life force, our inner light; this is what light beings are made of. We all exist as one of them, anchored to a bag of organic matter we call the physical body.

The Nature of Thought-Forms

To discuss this important subject, we must begin with the most precious attribute of the soul-self - creativity. Creativity is the miracle of generating something from nothing; a musical symphony, a child painting, or a love poem, this is undeniably soul-like. According to the Bible, God said: "let there be light, and there was light." [4] Regardless of its mythical or religious aspects, it carries a profound truth about our human nature. The notion that the human soul can create by just thinking is a nutritious food for thought.

The act of creation with the mind is captured in the metaphysical principle "energy follows thought." The word comes from the Greek 'energos' which means "active." Energy, then, is the capacity for vital activity. Energy is vibration. Vibration is a movement in the quantum field. Movement creates patterns, and patterns are creations. Thoughts, emotions, and conscious-will are creators of quantum patterns that we can describe as thought forms, as they must acquire some sort of shape when they manifest as movement.

The ego-self constantly creates patterns of quantum movement or thought forms, every time it uses its mind for thinking, feeling, or desiring. These patterns are strengthened when they are followed by action in the physical world. Our patterns of behavior are creators of thought patterns in the quantum field, which surrounds our SIE. In another chapter, when we discuss the holographic nature of our memory, we will see how these patterns turn into creations oblivious to the ego-self.

By the principles of morphic resonance, thought-forms with similar harmonic vibration tend to cling together and increase in strength. Repetitive thoughts, emotions, and behaviors strengthen the morphic resonance of the thought pattern, and these acquire a more "solid" reality within the quantum field of our SIE. Acting on the same principle, thought-forms that have gained stability due to constant energy input from the ego-self, tend to attract other thought-forms of the same resonant frequency. These may be located next door or on another continent.

Thought-forms "feed" or absorb the vibrational energy of the same frequency, a thought form that is created with love, then love feeds it. Thought-forms not only absorb similar frequencies into themselves, but they also attract that type of energy to them. With growth, they draw increasing amounts of energy, which can pull other thought-forms toward them. These processes are simply the laws of quantum physics at work; there is nothing magical about it. This is one of the reasons it can be challenging to clear powerful thought forms from your SIE; not only do they possess the energy they were created with, but also the energy that they have drawn to them.

Our beliefs are thought-forms from which guide our actions and, ultimately, our lives. When these are mistaken or plainly false, they become a distorted lens through which we view everything around us. That's why many people watch themselves reliving the same unwanted relationships, unpleasant situations, and unfortunate experiences.

Positive thought-forms, on the other hand, are just the reverse. They operate in service to us as invisible helpers. They often contain past patterns of success, recognition, and inner abilities. Frequent consciously revitalization of these thought-forms reaffirms their usefulness, making life more fun, efficient, and successful.

A Pause to Review

We are a spiritual entity with individual identity and also part of the unified Universe. Therefore, we are at once both an individual and part of a collective.

- Consciousness permeates the entire universal quantum field.
- Individual consciousness is contained in highly intelligent and organized quantum structures.
- We are conscious of quantum structures with highly dynamic toroidal shapes.
- We are a triad of quantum structures consisting of an ego-self, a subconscious self, and a soul self.
- Our triad of consciousness is contained in our unique envelope of identity, anchored to a unique physical body by a unique resonance pattern

created by the trillions of identical DNA molecules of the physical body.
- We are an envelope of identity connected to higher consciousness, represented by the quantum structures of the collective soul and the divine source.

The quantum model of the psyche is fundamentally simple compared with the abundance of models proposed throughout the history of psychology. All fields of knowledge have the classical object-subject relationship of the knower and the knowledge. In the field of psychology, where the knower wants to gain knowledge about itself, object and subject fuse together, and confusion ensues. An example of this is the meanings of the words: *consciousness* and *mind*. Perform the test - search those words in three different dictionaries, and you shall appreciate the semantic confusion.

What is "Mind"?

The meaning, according to Merriam-webster dictionary [5] illustrates the ambiguity by the qualitative differences, namely:

a) Memory recollection, like in "keep in mind."

b) Element or complex of elements of an individual that feels, perceives, thinks, wills, and especially reason.

c) The conscious mental events and capabilities in an organism

d) The organized conscious and unconscious adaptive mental activity of an organism.

Note that mind is defined as memory, elements, and activity. The second definition is ambiguous about whether the element that feels and thinks is one or many. This is what happens when the mind attempts to define itself. Again, we encounter the problem of understanding consciousness; it is simply tough to know the mind by use of the mind alone. As psychology professor Keith Floyd once said, *"neurophysiologists will not likely find outside their own minds what they are looking for, for that which they are looking for is that which is looking."* [6]

That said, for our model, we will settle for our definition for the sake of useful semantics, as follows:

> **Mind:** the intrinsic natural ability of a quantum structure to think thoughts, feel emotions, interpret perceptions, judgemental decisions, recall memories, and desire objectives

The mind is not a thing; it is an ability, a skill, a functional action. Mindfulness is the ongoing sustained awareness of these abilities. Under this definition, any standard term of psychology that refers to the mind as a structure becomes redundant or meaningless. The conscious mind and subconscious mind are examples of these if intended to refer to a "location where thinking occurs," instead of an ability of the structure.

Note that the use of the terms "mental" and "mind" are used as minimally as possible in quantum psychology. They are occasionally used as a communication tool with the traditional frame of reference. These terms associated with an inner location rather than ability, are likely to interfere with the concepts of quantum structures proposed in our model of the psyche. This is because the semantics of these terms have become deeply ingrained in the collective unconscious after centuries of popular and scientific use. In the revisionary role of this model, we redefine the mind as the ability of the quantum structure to perform the act of thinking and feeling. The quantum structures of ego, subconscious, and soul, which compose our SIE, constitute the "location," which has been historically associated with "mind." In this model, we can exercise the ability of mind when we "mind our own business," or we "don't mind thinking about it." However, I can't "bear in mind" or "have it in my mind." The concept of mind, as has been historically developed, is meaningless. The minds described under these concepts are the individuals doing the "minding." You don't *have* a mind because you *are* the mind. The dissociation that it implies doesn't contribute to the integrative work our quantum model intends to achieve; thus, they are incompatible. Also, note that the definition is encompassing enough for application to quantum structures beyond SIE. That is the quantum structures of the collective soul and the divine source. Mind is a universal attribute of consciousness.

The Quantum Realities Within our SIE

With the benefit of the above definition, we can now discuss the aspect of mind in the overall context of our SIE. We unquestionably know that our ego selves have a mind, the one classical psychology calls conscious mind. However, our subconscious self also has a mind. Classical psychology speaks about a subconscious mind, but not of the subconscious self. We will clarify that shortly. Finally, our soul-self also has a mind. That could be a new aspect to many, but upon consideration, it makes sense that it does. After all, what else could any soul do other than the abilities of the mind as defined above? Since this principle can be difficult to grasp at first, let's add some perspective.

The idea of three minds, one for each of our parts of the psyche, can be described from another angle. The original design which arises from the soul-self calls for our SIE to operate as a team. The resulting behavior is closer to that of having one mind. This only happens when the three quantum structures are aligned in purpose and action. However, this is often not the case for many of us. We must be aware that our ego-self is not aligned with our other parts. Therefore, instead of viewing these minds independently, the reality is that the soul-self seeks to share one powerful mind as a self-realized soul-self. Unfortunately, due to our lack of alignment with our other two components, this mind is fragmented among the three quantum structures. Having established a clear picture of the dynamics of the mind within our SIE, let's describe the quantum realities of our three quantum structures.

Ego-Self Reality

The ego-self quantum structure makes full use of abilities of the mind at all times in its imperative goal of survival. All of these abilities, as defined previously, are used continuously to initiate whatever physical actions are necessary to warrant shelter, safety, food, sleep, and reproduction. This is where the ego-self excels. The ego-self is often intrigued by how certain activities and events happen with little or no conscious control of itself. It learns to perform tasks in an automatic mode; it remembers an appointment just in time, it wakes up earlier in the morning just before the clock alarm rings, and many other conveniences that one takes for granted, not knowing that all of this arises from the subconscious-self. The ego-self often imagines fictional and delusional scenarios of the past and the future. It often stares at nothing in particular while recalling strange dreams from the night before. The ego-self lives life in constant denial about the inevitability of its own death, struggles to accept harsh realities of physical existence, occasionally ponders the existence of a greater God, and frequently questions the meaning of life as it ages. There is a small proportion of the world population with some alignment in their SIE's, that contemplates higher-level realities because they have connected with inner experiences that lead to a belief of transcendence. Some of them are reading this book right now.

We are born with a basic latent ego-self that develops with us as we grow into adulthood. It evolves daily at undetectable speeds. Technically, we are a new person each morning following the encoding of memories, experiences, and stimuli from the previous day during sleep. We don't have the same ego-self as three years ago. However, the evolution is as imperceptible as the movement of the hour hand on a wall clock. It is difficult to perceive, even with the most intensely active focus. Despite undergoing significant changes throughout the life course, the ego retains its primary identity and unique qualities. Older people often agree with this proposition when they meet an old friend after 30 years or so. Through the wrinkles and gray hair, they can still see the young "Joe" or "Mary."

Our ego-self begins to split, ever so slowly, from our perfectly integrated SIE before birth. Consider this as an embryonic quantum ego-self that follows us when we are born. It already carries a body of prenatal experience from the time of physical conception. These are reflected as certain behavioral tendencies by the ego-self later in life.

The ego-self is the representative of the other two selves in the physical world. These both feed from the ego-self in the game of survival and self-realization. Metaphorically, similar to the body having a physical eye, the SIE has the ego. The eye perceives physical light, while the ego perceives psychological stimuli instead. The ego cannot see itself in the same way that a physical eye cannot. The ego-self is skillful while looking externally, but it is ineffective at reflecting internally.

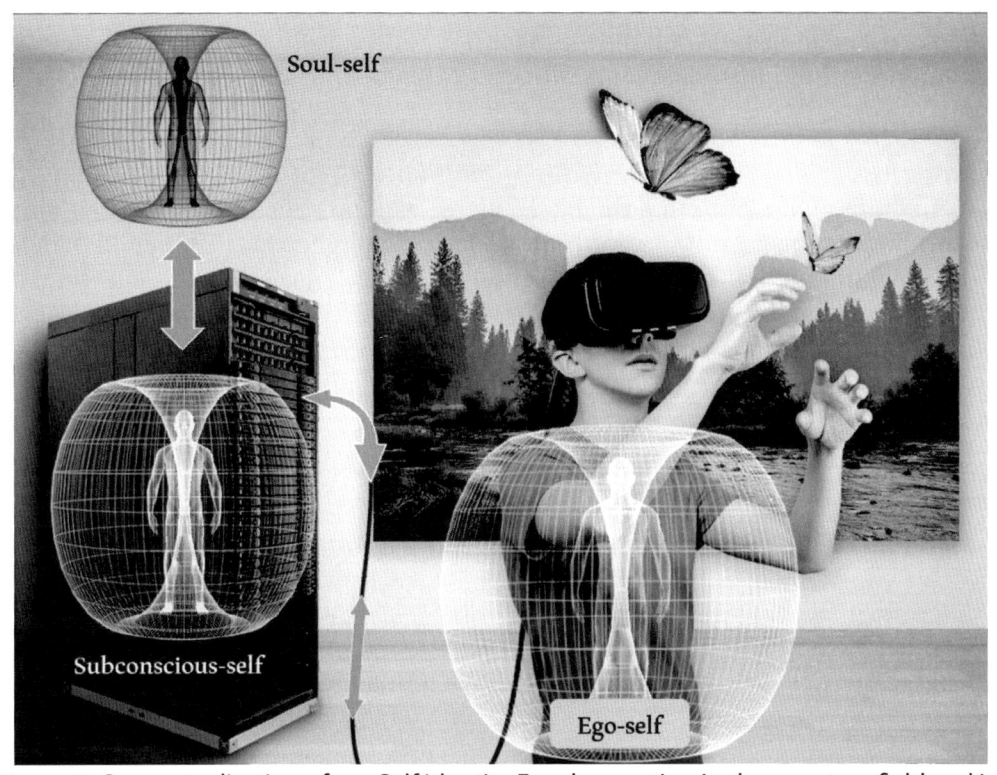

Figure 7- Conceptualization of our Self Identity Envelope acting in the quantum field and interacting with the human brain, which is represented here by the virtual reality goggles. The ego-self (you) process the virtual ultrahigh-resolution images digitally transmitted by the optic nerve to experience human physical reality, looking at the world through our physical eyes. This information is furthered processed at deeper levels of interpretation by our subconscious represented here by a powerful computer that runs independently from the ego. This goes further up to our soul who controls the master program of our physical existence. This trichotomy of quantum structures is our personal identity which truly runs the drama of our personal lives. Our SIE's are not isolated units, the universal connection is illustrated in Figure 8.

This is ancient wisdom as a Biblical passage captures its essence accurately when somebody is critical of behavior in others but not of their own: *"Why do you look at the speck of sawdust in your brother's eye and pay no attention to the plank in your own eye?"*. [7]

Remaining still in meditation with eyes closed is not the ego's favorite activity. This is why meditation is a very powerful practice to experience the soul-self, as only the soul-self can sense its existence in the SIE when the ego-self remains static. This concept of the ego concerning the soul, although intuitively simple, is not found in many places due to the current dissonance between science and religion. Formal psychology has resisted embracing the concepts of the soul and spirit, while religious leaders refuse to get their feet wet in the dangerous waters of psychology.

Let's clarify the excessive qualities which have been attributed to the ego-self. For example, in deep meditation, where you exist with a partially disabled ego-self, there is often a general misconception that the ego-self encompasses the totality of our conscious experience. The ego-self is a combination of characteristics that act in unitary fashion to deal most directly with external stimuli. Mindful awareness is like an advanced video camera in which the ego-self directs the view and focus. The ego-self is the one which pays conscious attention to specific details from the vast amount of stimuli being input into the SIE. When you are in a movie theater, your SIE is aware of the entire frame of the movie screen, but the ego-self is focusing only on specific details of the image. That may be that the background of the scene, the facial expression of the actor with their dialogue, or, even, missing the movie scene completely by watching someone walking through the hallway with a bag of popcorn.

Subconscious-Self Reality

This is one of the two quantum structures for which we have limited knowledge. However, we do have some information granted by keen observation from the perspective of the ego-self. The subconscious is a unique player in the vibrating living experience of consciousness. Due to the widespread popularity of the classical definition of the "subconscious mind," we may use it as an educational tool to explain the subconscious quantum structure in our model.

"The unconscious area of mental life contains all the more primitive drives and impulses influencing our actions without our necessarily ever becoming fully aware of them, together with every important constellation of ideas or memories with a strong emotional charge, which have at one time been present in consciousness but have since been repressed so that they are no longer available to it, even through introspection or attempts at memory." [8]

Firstly, the description states, "more primitive drives and impulses influencing our actions," which refer to the basic instincts of the primal aspect of humans. Here, our model makes an important distinction. The programming of these instincts, the software that executes the instinctive behavior, resides within the soul-self and not in the subconscious. The subconscious only executes software commands, activating and inhibiting the neural circuitry necessary for its implementation. This is a more refined description of the roots of our behavior.

Secondly, the definition refers to forgotten and repressed memories that are "contained" in an "unconscious area of mental life." Our model does not define the subconscious as a depository that "contains" memories as if they are coded as physical memory in the brain. Instead, we suggest the subconscious to act as a highly advanced quantum computer that runs a master program domiciled in the soul-self. It is the bridge between the soul-self and the ego-self. Classical psychology has labeled the subconscious-self as a "mind," but as aforementioned, it is not.

After more than a century of consistent use, the term "subconscious mind" has developed into a colloquially popular term used loosely to refer to anything hidden or forgotten. You may hear discussions such as: "Mary has a nice personality because subconsciously she is trying to please everyone." The generalized proliferation of psychology concepts in school and colleges have created millions of amateur psychologists that use the term confidently. The belief that the subconscious is a "mind" has gained substantial traction in the belief system of millions of people and is considered an indisputable fact. Unfortunately, this misrepresentation has been the source of limiting beliefs that are not consistent with the quantum model.

One of the functions of the subconscious-self is the creation and protection of the ego's belief system. This is a crucial function of the subconscious-self as it belongs to the survival program. The survival program that includes all the instincts and drives mentioned by classical psychology has execution priority over the self-realization programs. The latter generates alignment within the SIE and overall psychological wellbeing once the survival of the ego-self has been warranted. This is one of the main reasons why the human condition has not significantly improved historically.

The problem with the belief that the subconscious is a "mind," is that it gives birth to other limiting beliefs that block the potential for spiritual healing: (i) There is another part of me which I am not aware of, that controls my actions, and there is nothing I can do about it, (ii) I don't want to go there because it can be scary, I may lose control, and it is something that should only be approached with professional help, (iii) I am the way I am due to this subconscious mind, and I am helpless to change something, which workings I do not understand.

In our quantum model, it is called subconscious-self instead of "subconscious mind." We include subconscious-self as one part of our SIE. Admittedly, calling it "self" is not accurate either. Unlike the ego and soul selves, the subconscious resembles more of inanimate machinery than an alive, self-aware part of the self. The subconscious is a sort of hi-tech tool or assistant of the soul. In terms of modern corporations, think metaphorically of a chief operating officer reporting to the chairman of the board. Nevertheless, for lack of a better descriptive noun, we will name it subconscious-self.

This torus-shaped quantum computer uses all stimuli received from the senses of the physical body to run the survival programs. While the ego-self only becomes aware of whatever it focusses its attention, the subconscious becomes aware of all stimuli for processing without the ego-self's awareness. In addition to having control of the belief system, it runs the expansive control systems which conduct the physiological functions of the organism. It also monitors the external environmental signals that may jeopardize its survival. Incidentally, when survival gets extremely serious, the subconscious overrides the ego-self with an emergency motor reflex system to react to threats quickly.

The subconscious-self often does the "behavioral steering" where an action is triggered without much participation from the ego-self. The ego-self often suspects there is something strange about the magnificent performance of its mechanics of behavior. However, most of the time, the ego-self takes it for granted and is inclined to take the credit. The subconscious-self runs the ego-self life, while it ignores it controls just a tiny part of the whole operation. The subconscious-self is the most powerful information processor known. Specifically, it observes both the external environment and the body's internal awareness, reads environmental cues, and immediately engages previously programmed behaviors. All of this is performed without the help, supervision, or awareness of the ego-self. When you order a meal from a restaurant's menu, your subconscious has already decided on the nutrients it needs. Subsequently, you feel a sudden craving or inclination to eat fish. When you find another person intimately attractive, your subconscious-self had already decided on signals, and features which the ego-self had no idea were part of the equation. Your ego-self may feel proud of coming up with a brilliant idea. Still, it is unaware the subconscious-self performed an enormous amount of work before the idea was sparked in the ego's conscious awareness. The subconscious may have spent hours or days solving its conscious desires in secret.

The subconscious is designed to ease the goals set by the ego-self. This has been discovered by many who have learned how to harness its power for egotistical purposes. This is a magnificent tool that could be used to achieve self-realization after the basic hierarchy of needs is satisfied. Instead, it is being used to satisfy the ego's banal desires, such as economic wealth or engagement in power games. Books like "The Secret" [9] and a myriad of others, from self-help gurus, exclaim a promise of wealth and happiness that can, potentially, be true. The flaw in most of these methods is the assumption the ego-self is appropriately aligned to handle the requirements to achieve the promised results. As we will see later, the ego-self falls victim to its own free will and sabotage itself with behavior patterns.

The subconscious-self works at full capacity without holidays or vacations. In comparison to the physical body, the subconscious-self would be our heart, unceasingly pumping blood from birth to death to sustain life.

In summary, the subconscious self: (i) implements the survival program from the soul-self, (ii) steers the behavior of the ego-self, (iii) creates, protects and maintains the ego-self's belief system, (iv) overrides the ego-self in case of emergencies, and most importantly, (v) works in coordination with the soul-self in its master program.

Soul-Self Reality

The word *psychology* was coined from the Greek roots *psychē* ("principle of life, soul,") and logos ("reason"). To the Greeks, psyche also meant "butterfly," which suggests how they imagined the soul. [10] Considering the literal meaning of the word, the quantum structure of the soul-self is supposed to be the object of the study of psychology, but such is not the case.

Today, *psychology* is mostly concerned with the science or study of the "mind" and behavior. In modern English semantics, psyche often sounds less spiritual than the *soul*, less intellectual than the *mind*, and more intimate than *personality*. The proposed model is more concerned with the original definition of psychology and honors its literal meaning.

Classical psychology is based upon the perceptions of the five senses. Hence, it is not able to recognize the soul. It is incapable of understanding the dynamics that underlie the values and behaviors of the personality. Just as medicine seeks to heal the body without recognizing the energy of the soul that lies behind the health or illness of the body, modern psychology seeks to heal the personality without recognizing the force of the soul that lies behind the configuration and experiences of the personality. Therefore, it cannot heal at the level of the soul.

The soul-self is almost exclusively dedicated to monitoring the other two minds, relentlessly aiming at the slightest opportunity to increase alignment. Your soul-self is the captain of your SIE vessel, sextant in hand; it uncovers new routes to guide the ego-self towards self-realization. It's not an easy task, as it must navigate around the subconscious-self, whose mission is exclusively survival. The subconscious-self has more direct access to the ego-self and also precedes in authority over the soul-self.

If we look at the role of the soul-self from a strictly intellectual perspective, it must be a very frustrating job. Consider you have a problem child who constantly misbehaves, gets in trouble frequently, and does not listen to the subtle signals you are constantly trying to send. This child listens loud and clear to the survival instincts, and you agree with that part. However, you long for them to listen to the whispers which you are continually sending embedded in thoughts, feelings, and insights. We will describe such dynamics in later chapters.

The soul's awareness of environmental signals is even higher than the subconscious-self, and, when required, it can also override it for direct access to the ego-self. In fact, the soul can even assume physical control of the body without the ego-self's consent. The soul-self carries the essence of your identity, learns the lessons during the lifetime, carries the genetic memories of your ancestors, and the wisdom learned from other experienced SIEs. From the soul-self's quantum structure perspective, it longs for integration with your other selves, patiently living its cosmic existence.

The soul has been forgotten by psychology. Scientific secularism has unfairly neglected the soul. Instead, the soul has been replaced with the mysterious artifact of classical psychology called the subconscious mind, which nobody can entirely define. This is a catch-all depository of unexplained phenomena historically attributed to the soul. Secular extremism has deprived the soul of its essence while making spirituality unnecessary along the way. Attributes of the soul that have been erroneously given to the fictionally constructed subconscious mind are intuition, emotion, certitude, inspiration, suggestion, deduction, imagination, past-life memory, and life force. Ironically, in the field named after the study of the psyche (soul), the mere reference to the term has become scientifically unacceptable. The quantum model intends to bring the soul back to its rightful place and prominence in the psychological structure of humans.

Alignment Within Our Self Identity Envelope

You are not your ego-self. You are your SIE, a group of three quantum structures connected to a higher collective soul that embounds the entirety of humankind. In this respect, you are more than the insignificant speck of dust in the Universe that sometimes you feel you are.

The quantum model of the psyche interprets reality with a theoretical framework to create working tools which can align our fragmented condition within our SIE and, hopefully, allow us to reach greater existential integrity. The misalignment of our trichotomous nature is the single largest cause of psychological dysfunctions and disease in our physical existence.

The Collective Unconscious

The collective unconscious is the first part of the psyche, which is not contained within our SIE. It is the quantum structure to which we all are connected in some form as it follows the universal pattern of the torus. We can visualize the collective unconscious as the torus quantum structure whose visible spectrum is the Earth's magnetosphere. The collective unconscious might be considered as the Earth's self-identity envelope. The collective unconscious is the soul of the Planet. Within its high energy quantum structure, it contains all of the memories and wisdom of human history.

In this sense, the proposed model is consistent with the idea of morphic resonance proposed by the controversial British biologist, Rupert Sheldrake, mentioned earlier. For that reason, his ideas are generously quoted in this section. His proposed concept explains much of the phenomena experienced in ayahuasca visions. When session participants inquire about visions of jaguars and snakes, I often suggested that they explore his extensive work online.

One of the first scientists that made a connection between ayahuasca visions and the collective unconscious was Dr. Claudio Naranjo. [11] In fact, at the Third World Ayahuasca Conference in Spain, he discussed the subject during his last talk, before passing away less than two months later at 86. He recalled his experiments during the 1960s with harmaline, one of the active ingredients of the ayahuasca vine. He speculated that the ayahuasca experience might somehow access Jung's collective unconscious. He proposed this as a viable explanation to the frequent testimonials of the experimental subjects who often described having beautiful and sometimes frightening visions of Amazonian wild animals. Dr. Naranjo found this intriguing as subjects not only were oblivious to the details of the substance they experienced but also had never contacted or traveled to the Amazon region.

I have an extensive collection of testimonials from participants in my ayahuasca sessions, along with personal anecdotes, where jaguars, panthers, snakes and exotic birds appear in the visions. Would it be possible that the plant's molecular resonance is in alignment with the collective morphic pattern of the jungle? If so, can the ingestion of the plant cause the subjects' subconscious quantum structures to resonate at the same frequency?

According to Sheldrake, morphic resonance is the influence of previous structures of activity on subsequent similar structures of activity organized by morphic fields. It enables memories to pass across both space and time from the past. The greater the similarity, the greater the influence of morphic resonance. What this means is that all self-organizing systems, such as molecules, crystals, cells, plants, animals, and animal societies, have a collective memory on which each individual draws and to which it contributes. [12]

There is an experiment with striking results that started at Harvard in the 1920s and continued for several decades. Rats learned to escape from a water-maze, and subsequent generations learned faster and faster. The interesting thing is that after the rats had learned to escape more than ten times quicker at Harvard, they were tested in Scotland and Australia, and they started more or less where the Harvard rats left off. This effect was not confined to the descendants of trained rats, suggesting a morphic resonance rather than an epigenetic effect. [13]

Sheldrake has had a fascinating personal journey as he has evolved throughout his career from a hard-line atheist scientist to a believer in God. He seems to have found a connection with the higher divine source of everything that lies beyond the collective unconscious, or the morphic field as he prefers to call it. We present an extended quote from Sheldrake's work which aids in the understanding of our quantum model:

"Over the last thirty-five years, I have been doing experimental research on plant growth, morphic resonance, homing pigeons, dogs that know when their owners are coming home, the sense of being stared at, and a range of other sub-

jects. The results of this research have convinced me that our minds extend far beyond our brains. For example, telepathic connections usually occur between people and animals that are emotionally bonded. They are part of the way that minds and social bonds work. They are sometimes called "paranormal" because they do not fit into a narrow understanding of reality. But the phenomena themselves can be studied scientifically, and they have measurable effects. However, they are not in themselves spiritual phenomena. There is a distinction between the psychic and spiritual realms. Phenomena such as telepathy reveal that minds are not confined to brains. But we are also open to connections with a far greater consciousness, a more-than-human spiritual reality, whatever we call it. Spiritual practices help us to explore this question for ourselves." [14]

There are reportedly morphic resonance phenomena that have received extensive media coverage over decades. However, these were later debunked as misrepresentations of experimental results. The hundredth-monkey effect, for example, which is now considered an urban legend, is a hypothetical phenomenon in which a new behavior or idea is said to spread rapidly when a critical number of members of one group gain a new behavior or knowledge. The idea was popularized in the 1970s after non-conclusive results from a behavioral study conducted in the 1950s, where the behavior of Japanese monkeys on Kojima island was misrepresented by several authors. Unfortunately, this kind of poor reporting is exploited by the skeptical movement to dismiss the quantum nature of other real but unexplained phenomena.

There is more to these phenomena than the suggested explanations of the morphic resonance hypothesis. Besides the collective unconscious concept, some examples suggest the existence of a more specific phenomenon called "collective intelligence." There are reasonable amounts of data that support this proposition. The classic example is the story of Sir Francis Galton, the 19th Century British statistician who invented the concepts of standard deviation, correlation, and regression. Encouraged by his statistical curiosity, he asked the organizers of a folk competition at a livestock fair for the 787 entries of the contest. [15] Participants of all kinds of backgrounds were asked to guess the weight of an ox with a prize offered to the closest guess. Galton found that the average guess was only one pound off the actual weight of the ox. The median guess was about 100 pounds from the average. That is, the people who knew little about oxen or were just guessing for fun, corrected the median value of the expert's guesses to the point of no statistical error. This was the beginning of an interesting statistical inquiry that led to the contemporary field of study called collective intelligence.

The latest example of this phenomenon, at least in pop culture, is from "Who Wants to Be a Millionaire?" a TV quiz game show which has been aired on British and American television for more than twenty years. When contestants faced a question they considered difficult, the game rules allowed "life-lines," such as making a phone call to a friend for assistance, reducing the possible answers to a 50/50 chance, and also asking the audience for their opinion. In the latter, each individual in the audience had a wireless device that allowed them to cast a vote for what they believed to be the correct answer. The contestant is provided with their collective decision on any of the four possible answers from A to D. Interestingly, a statistical review of the answers over many episodes revealed that the audience collectively guessed the correct answer 91% of the time. [16] This accuracy rate is remarkable given that they were confronted with questions that were inherently difficult and that these were ordinary tourists that had randomly attended the TV studio. Other scientifically controlled studies of this phenomenon have consistently shown that the collective average of groups ranks among the top 5% of the answers guessed correctly by individuals.

Another widely recognized scientist, Dr. David Hawkins [17] who spent decades studying and understanding the subconscious mechanics of human behavior, wrote this brilliant description about his strong convictions about the subject in the introduction of his book "Mind vs. Power: The Hidden Determinants of Human Behavior":

"To quell my own fear that perhaps, despite my best efforts, the reader might not get the essential message of this study, I will spell it out in advance: the individual human mind is like a computer terminal connected to a giant database. The database is human consciousness itself, of which our own consciousness is merely an individual expression, but with its roots in the common consciousness of all mankind. This database is the realm of genius; because to be human is to participate in the database, everyone, by virtue of their birth, has access to genius. The unlimited information contained in the database has now been shown to be readily available to anyone in a few seconds, at any time and in any place. This is indeed an astonishing discovery, bearing the power to change lives, both individually and collectively, to a degree never yet anticipated. The database transcends time, space, and all limitations of individual consciousness. This distinguishes it as a unique tool for future research and opens as yet undreamed-of areas for a possible investigation. It holds forth the prospect of the establishment of an objective basis for human values, behaviors, and belief systems. The information obtained by this method reveals a new context for understanding human behavior and a new paradigm for validating objective truth…… We have at our disposal a means of finding answers to previously unresolved personal and social problems." [18]

Science is beginning to acknowledge that further exploration of the collective unconscious is warranted. With the advent of the Internet, big data, and high-level algorithms, modern science now has adequate research tools to dig deeper into the intriguing phenomena of the collective unconscious. With this considered, it's not hard to understand why collective intelligence has become a novel field of study, with research centers being established in major universities in the U.S. and Europe. Perhaps in the future, some of Jung's critics, who have claimed for decades that the collective unconscious as a real invisible structure to be a delusional idea, may need to reconsider their stance.

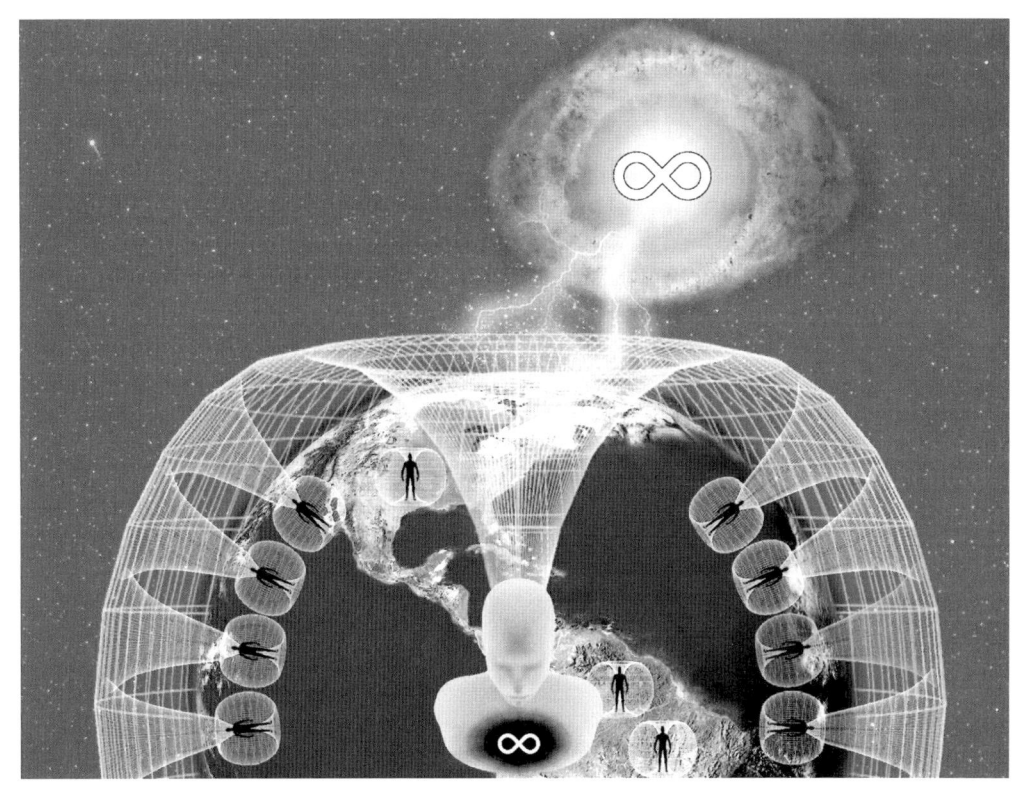

Fig. 8 - Conceptualization of the collective unconscious and beyond. Billions of SIE's on Planet Earth are further connected to the GAIA's identity envelope that covers us all. Also find the divine source, the unifying force of the Universe, represented by a cosmic cloud with the infinity symbol inside. This source also connects all life in all planets and dimensions. Note one highlighted human with the infinity symbol in its heart representing the spark of divine life force that animates our physical body and also representing the connection of the individual with the divine directly through the quantum field. We are all connected with the divine source from the top through the collective unconscious and from the bottom through our personal spark in the quantum field.

The Divine Source

The quantum model presents the last component of the psyche as the divine source of everything; a part placed immediately after the collective unconscious. This is a parsimonious assumption to avoid shifting the focus of the model away from the pragmatic level of the SIE.

A review of history shows us two perennial debates about God. The first one about the existence or non-existence of God and the other about God's attributes among those who profess the existence. A model of the psyche developed to help people align the components of their SIE's for improved psychological wellbeing must not be distracted from its primary goal by engaging in specific tenets of the second debate. These would only serve to introduce the notion of religion. Religion, despite having great social value as a helpful shelter for souls in distress, has historically highlighted that humans are incapable of recognizing its unifying principle. Instead, humans have allowed religion to become a divisive force for humankind.

A fundamental assumption of the model is a principle of natural intelligence that operates at all levels of human existence. Users of the model require an absolute and clear-cut position regarding God, and the model provides the space for such belief. The spiritual healing of the soul inherently needs to incorporate a higher intelligent principle to be consistent with the millions of testimonials from participants in ayahuasca sessions and other entheogens.

On closer examination, the concept of quantum field suggests a natural conception of God, which includes the whole quantum field or an idea of the absolute. This places God above all else; utterly transcendent, indefinable, and indescribable. To define or describe God would be to place limitations on what has no limits. When discussing God, all that can be said is that God is. Moreover, God can be only be apprehended through a temporary communion with the soul-self during a mystical experience. This mystical "touching" of God is the highest transformative moment in life, which can provide permanent spiritual healing, fundamental changes in behavior, and fulfilling psychological states.

Among the millions that have experienced psychedelic experiences, many have shifted their core convictions about God. Perhaps at some point, you have had a mystical experience, you may have felt you experienced God directly or that God came to you. If you have had this type of experience, you likely need no justification or argument for your belief. If you have had a mystical experience of God, this whole business of debating the strengths and weaknesses of arguments about the existence of God may strike you as a mere academic exercise.

In a vibrant, mystical experience, the person is often unconscious, appears to be delirious, or later describes having an out-of-body-experience. The person may be dreaming, awake, or in a trance, they may even have visions or hear voices. Those who have experienced these states frequently report being told by God to write down what they had experienced or to teach others the truths shared. In earlier times, these kinds of mystical experiences were given more credence. Today, in a society dominated by science as the sole judge of what is 'real,' there is a tendency to discount such experiences as malfunctions in brain chemistry or temporal disturbances.

In a future chapter, the concept of psychological projection is discussed in detail. First, let's consider the divine source, which composes part of the psyche of everyone. The all-encompassing quantum field defined as the absolute God-like quality of the Universe exists as a spark of divine light within each one of us. We are part of such absolute, and a spark of it feeds the whole soul-self from the bottom of the quantum field. We are all one, but we are individual souls too. I hope you can see the obvious aspect of duality at play here, which is another manifestation of the wave-particle and mind-body dilemmas.

This brings us to discuss the aforementioned personal God. The personal God can also be validated in our quantum model as a psychological projection of our inner divine source. The God that people feel "out there," with which they engage in personal conversation, prayer, and feel influenced by, is the psychological projection of their inner divine source. Therefore, we can reconcile the impersonal absolute divine principle of the Universe with the personal God people relate, by realizing we are referring to the same 'thing' but viewed from the opposite extremes of the reality spectrum.

CHAPTER SIX

THE EGO-SELF IS COMPELLED TO BELIEVE

Free Will and the Bridge of Belief

Many times, while observing nature, I have reflected on the collective wisdom of the ants and bee colonies. I've noticed how they organize their small 'societies' efficiently, with every member playing the exact role needed for a perfectly synchronized operation. I've wondered whether my curiosity for the mysteries of nature influenced one particular insight that I received during my ayahuasca sessions. This fundamental insight has played a role in my current understanding of the psyche. One of my visions showed me the nature of the collective soul in the animal kingdom. It showed me that the hive mind that I observed in ants and bees was just the most apparent fragmented version of the collective soul that exists across the entire animal kingdom. Every species of animal has its own collective soul, so-to-speak, which contains the master program for the behavior of the group. It reminded me about the Native American teachings that speak about the spirit of the wolf, the buffalo, or the elk. These teachings don't refer to a particular animal, but the spirit of the species as a whole.

The Native American paradigm about animal spirits is consistent with our model of the psyche. Every animal is born, immediately connects to the collective soul of its respective species, and moves through life with the automatic programming code that we call instincts. This collective bee or collective rabbit or snake is not at all concerned with the wellbeing of any particular member, but only the survival of the species as a whole. There is perfect harmony in the quantum reality among all collective animal souls. The killing and fighting which occurs between them is just part of the cosmic order for the benefit of them all.

I realized the fundamental difference between animals and humans. Humans have the individual ego-self in our SIE that defines us, the self-conscious "I" that is reading this book now. The fundamental difference between animal and human behavior is that in the latter, the ego-self finds itself in a position of making decisions. Neither humans nor animals have the freedom to do nothing once they are born in the physical world. Doing nothing is synonymous with death. Animals act automatically connected to their collective species, while humans need to decide what, how, and when to respond to secure survival. Our ego-self often feels isolated, alone in the world, surrounded by risks, insecurities, and uncertainties. We don't have the convenience of living automatically, as animals do, but we have something superior. We have free will.

> **Free Will:** The ability of the ego-self to decide and act in accordance with its beliefs, and not in accordance with its instincts.

We are not free of not having free-will. We are stuck with it; it is part of our human nature, our human condition. We must decide our way to survival, whether we want to or not. The problem is that we don't have the knowledge, the information, the wisdom to reach successful decisions. The ego-self is compelled by environmental circumstances to make survival decisions throughout its interaction with physical reality. Due to the ego-self's incomplete or total lack of knowledge, it must blindly leap across the gap of insecurity to decide its course of action. Without this gap, our human nature would have come with a hard link, like in the animal kingdom, between our ego-self and the physical realms. Instead of our ability to engage with the world as free agents, we would experience a robot-like life, blindly responding to the commands of the quantum dimension with little or no room to act freely.

Contrary to animals, humans have individual souls and find themselves lost in the world as they develop into adulthood. Humans are the most disadvantaged species on Earth. While some mammals start walking right after birth, humans need a year or so to achieve their first stumbling baby steps. While most animals are equipped for survival after a small percentage of their expected lifespan, humans spend an astonishing 20-25% of the lives developing into self-surviving specimens. Humans have both the curse and blessing of having the most massive gap in nature between their souls and their physical vehicles. This gap is enormous in childhood and starts reducing throughout development as we learn from adults and receive conscious and subconscious programming and beliefs that gradually reduce this chasm. Even in adulthood, this gap remains considerably large and has historically forced humans to fill it with beliefs and superstitions. This is the only way to fill the gap and be able to perform while facing situations that require action for survival. Ignorance has to be filled somehow, or paralysis is the resulting condition. When common sense fails to explain and guide meaningful action, uncertainty and insecurity rule the survival game.

Sometimes we look at animals, especially our pets, and observe them connected and happy with their instincts. Animals are unconcerned about their next meal or getting enough sleep. They have no conception of the future, and yet, they are not stuck in an uncertain present as humans are. Humans are like a computer program that doesn't perform automatically. The program continually stops and requests input every few programmed steps; there is a gap that needs to be continuously closed by the operator. In other words, the human program requires a full-time operator to survive. Otherwise, it dies as a result of its inaction.

Survival is the primary force that pushes humans into action. But what action should we take? That's the magic moment where free will makes its entrance into the drama of life. We can do whatever we want! We are free from any obligation to follow; there is no map, no compass, and there is nobody to ask. You decide from inertia into action on how to address any given situation or problem. Closing the gap between our ego-self and physical activity is the miracle of human nature. We are a divine expression assuming responsibility for its actions, an exclusive feature no other animal possesses. Each one of us has no option but to walk the bridge of belief during physical existence.

Primitive tribes and cultures have an enormous gulf to cross, and hundreds of generations have evolved a body of knowledge that has allowed easier survival over centuries of economic and cultural development. The contributions of Rene Descartes to the scientific method provided a breakthrough in philosophical thought, which catapulted human development even further. Assuming mind-body duality was a hard blow to traditional authoritarian knowledge and a new era was born. The gap shrank closer, and bridges of belief became shorter. This new era continues today in our attempts to find the holy grail of unified theories that can explain everything, eradicate uncertainty, and insecurity. We find ourselves searching at the final frontier of intellectual evolution. However, as we have begun to close this gap, things have become more perplexing. Holding the pan of reality by the handle has proven to be a tricky proposition. Then, advanced mathematics began to uncover anomalies in number theory; the theory of relativity turned to time and space into malleable items. Finally, quantum theory has left observers inextricably tied up in the understanding of reality. The line between subject and object turned fuzzy and blurry, which has catalyzed confusion in scientific circles. We are now in the middle of a major crisis of scientific thought. We are searching for new paradigms to make sense of the biggest paradox we have faced as a species. We are now resorting to the desperate creation of new beliefs to close the final quantum gap.

> **Beliefs:** personal understandings and ways of thinking that are assumed to be true.

Due to the hypothetical nature of the proposed model of the psyche, it serves as a temporary belief system that effectively fills the gap in people seeking spiritual healing with ayahuasca or other psychedelic-assisted therapies. Without a believable model that provides inner congruency to potentially distressed patients, it is simply not possible for them to navigate the intensity of the psychedelic experience. It's a relief to the ego-self to have a tool at its disposal, which enables the reshuffling of the core belief system on which it operates. With this tool, we can consciously work in weeding-out our obsolete, self-limiting, contradictory, and often entirely false beliefs, to provide a bright space to improve the alignment of our quantum structures within our SIE.

Having a model that has a practical application and makes sense to us is a huge leap forward in our inner freedom. Having knowledge and self-confidence is a necessary condition to practice self-healing with psychedelics. Knowledge eradicates ignorance, which is the primordial cause of the tragic dissociation between our ego-self and our soul-self. Ignorance is the root of the problem. The soul-self is altruistic by nature, always encouraging the ego-self to reach upwards. The ego-self is survival-oriented, looking downward to preserve physical life. This is reminiscent of the clichéd little angel and demon which perch upon each of our shoulders, the crux of right or wrong, the uncertainty of decisions.

Uncertainty is deeply interwoven into the fabric of our physical reality. Under the current state of quantum physics, it has been established that knowing both the speed and location of a subatomic particle is impossible. This theory, known as Heisenberg's uncertainty principle, permeates into the quantum reality of our ego-self. Our ego-self is our permanent representative in the physical world, one which will always be uncertain of anything it does. Risk permeates every minute corner of its reality. "Death is the only sure thing," the ego-self often proclaims. On the other side of the abyss are the actions that our mere existence forces upon us. The bridge that traverses the gap between our ego-self and the unavoidable actions which we must decide upon is an important key to all spiritual and emotional healing. To be able to act in the physical dimension, the ego-self must believe. When the crawling baby starts watching adults walking around, its baby ego-self starts believing: "I can do that!" before it begins its first baby step attempts. The bridge is built early in life, and the rest is history.

The hardcore skeptic and leading expert in the subject of human beliefs, Michael Shermer, describes convincingly:

We form our beliefs for a variety of subjective, personal, emotional, and psychological reasons in the context of environments created by family, friends, colleagues, culture, and society at large; after forming our beliefs, we then defend, justify, and rationalize them with a host of intellectual reasons, cogent arguments, and rational explanations. Beliefs come first, explanations for beliefs follow. [1]

The necessary consequence of such reality is that our subconscious-self is biased toward filtering sensory input in a way that effectively supports and integrates into our prior held beliefs. All of us will be familiar with this experience while arguing with someone about a seemingly obvious matter. We decide to stop the contest when we realize that the same facts are supporting opposite views and are being used by each party to become more deeply entrenched in their positions. Our perception of reality is strongly determined by our beliefs about it. Our subconscious-self is a belief engine.

Shermer tells us that as sensory data flows through the senses, the brain naturally begins to look for and find patterns that it can then infuse with meaning. *"The first process I call patternicity: the tendency to find meaningful patterns in both meaningful and meaningless data. The second process I call agenticity: the tendency to infuse patterns with meaning, intention, and agency. We can't help it; we are hardwired for it."* [2]

Our subconscious-self is programmed to connect the dots of our world into meaningful patterns that explain why things happen. These meaningful patterns become beliefs, and these beliefs shape our understanding of reality. Once beliefs are formed, the subconscious-self begins to look for and find confirmatory evidence in support of those beliefs, which boosts confidence in the beliefs and thereby accelerates the process of reinforcing them. Round and round, the process goes in a positive feedback loop of belief confirmation.

Believing may be a conscious act of our ego-self. However, it is likely that most of the time, the ego-self doesn't play a role in belief. Our beliefs make the mandatory connections between our subconscious-self and our soul-self. Imagine that you are hanging from a parachute where the hundreds of suspension lines are your beliefs connecting you to your soul-self at the canopy. However, within this metaphor, some of the connecting wires have become entangled. These tangled lines represent your limiting beliefs. Having many lines twisted, broken, or missing is the condition of an unhappy or ill person. The beliefs upon which they make their decisions are plagued with logical fallacies, half-truths, or just plain lies. When you are aware of a problem, you can survey and inspect your beliefs to find it. By being ignorant of your problematic beliefs, like in the parachute, you are prevented from finding a solution. Similar to the hazardous, twisted wires of a parachute, your toxic beliefs can jeopardize your happiness, psychological well-being, and even, in some circumstances, your life.

Uncertainty is the most precious gift human beings can ever have, and it should be well appreciated as the cornerstone of our free will. Although not always obvious, uncertainty forces the ego-self into the hot seat of decision-making, with many of these decisions having far-reaching implications while lacking any kind of guidance. Hanging from belief is its only option. Finding an objective basis, ethical or else, to conduct ourselves properly has been the quest of philosophers and religions for millennia. However, none have come close to finding this ob-

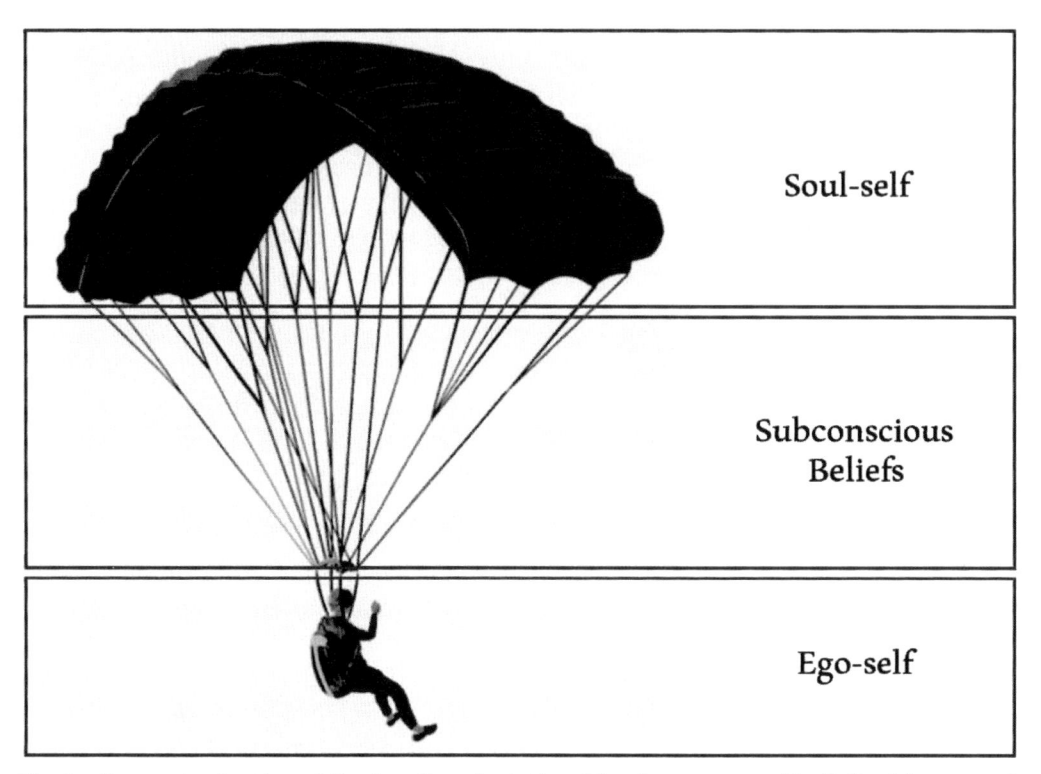

Fig. 8 – Conceptualization of the functional relationship of our personal beliefs with our soul-self. Beliefs of the ego-self are the strings that connect the subconscious to the soul and serve as the quantum requirements or "molds" that induce their manifestation in physical reality.

jective foundation of decision-making yet. Belief, religious or secular, is the only bridge that exists between the ego-self and its actions. From stories buried in the annals of pre-history to the modern myths embedded in current culture, we can list endless examples of beliefs that have derailed entire societies and drawn them down painful paths. We can observe the destruction caused by certain beliefs, for example, the massive human sacrifices of the Aztecs to appease the gods, the killing thousands of healthy sheep to please the God in the Old Testament [3], and people drinking toxic chlorine as a remedy to COVID-19 virus. We must realize that belief always has and will continue to bridge the gap between ignorance and mandatory survival actions.

On a personal level, creating an idea, a concept, an assumption on which our ego-self can rely on decisions is so intrinsic to decision making that we never realize the underlying process. These invisible deeply held convictions extensively shape and create our reality, yet we are not aware of it. The instrumental forces that drive and direct our behavior are based on a series of implicit beliefs that we have about ourselves. In aggregate, these self-beliefs determine the direction and intensity of what we do, how we do it, and how we view our accomplishments concerning the rest of the world. Self-beliefs are so powerful that the evaluations will strongly influence all aspects of our lives, from the careers we seek, the rela-

Fig. 9 – We are continuously forming and creating beliefs that may get deeply encrusted in our subconscious and influence the physical reality we later manifest.

tionships we pursue, and, ultimately, our accomplishments in life.

Ironically, the most significant difficulty in dealing with our own beliefs is that they are implicit, which means many of the personal theories we have about ourselves operate automatically and unconsciously. Self-beliefs are not religious, political, or secular views and don't include beliefs such as "when I stop drinking coffee, I sleep better." Instead, self-beliefs are the guiding principles and assessments we make about our personal capabilities and the outcomes we expect as a result of our efforts. By bringing these beliefs to the forefront of our ego-self, we can take steps to harness their power and influence. But what are these mysterious beliefs that determine the totality of our being? In the next sections, we describe and scrutinize these approaches.

When we explore our collective unconscious, we find a couple of very ancient religious beliefs that have significantly shaped the history of modern civilization, which are noteworthy. Buddhism is over twenty centuries old and has been practiced by billions of believers throughout history. There are nearly one billion people who practice Buddhism today. One of the backbone principles of Buddhism is the concept of Karma. This term has become commonly used in the West with the introduction of eastern philosophies over the last century. Karma can be described as accumulated energy containing the total moral sum of an individual's acts in anyone's life, which is carried in the soul after death. It's the baggage, good or bad, which determines the person's destiny in their next life. Of course, the belief in Karma is deeply entwined with the belief in reincarnation. If you have lived a life of misdeeds and crime, you may reincarnate in very unfavorable conditions to "pay your Karma."

Conversely, living a virtuous life will harvest the opposite. Although this belief conveniently provides relief to our ego-self by explaining the apparent injustice in the world, the fact remains that it often creates a series of ancillary beliefs that reinforce the negative aspects of the ego-self. The most toxic of these being the belief that problems and unhappiness experienced throughout life are the product of Karma from a past life. In this way, Karma places clamps on our subconscious-self and prevents it from producing real solutions to such problems. The belief ends up perpetuating the status quo instead of opening doors to self-realization.

Another proclivity of the ego-self is to superficially interpret the Law of Karma and live a virtuous life only because they wish a better future life as if saving goodwill in a Karma account, instead of focusing on the critical aspects of self-realization in this life. If we closely examine this, we may develop a long list of limiting beliefs that are derived from Karma.

Moving onto the Western Judeo-Christian cosmology, practiced today by over two billion people, we find the belief of guilt and the punishment of sin. There are many examples which are robust deterrents of self-realization, but let's cover the oldest on most enduring one. We won't ever be able to accurately assess the impact of the widespread belief of the original sin, as described in the Book of Genesis of the Bible. Billions of children have had their developing brain programmed with the belief of guilt, receiving personal responsibility for the pain and problems of the world. Not to mention, the belief instilled in billions of little girls, which placed them as the guilty Eve, who corrupted Adam. In addition to this guilt, women are burdened with the additional injustice that they must hold the eternal inferior status under the stronger men who were created first. The collective unconscious of the human race carries such beliefs held by trillions of souls throughout history. The endurance of these collective beliefs is such that our ego-selves must consciously identify and reprogram to untangle a few suspension lines of our metaphorical parachute.

A brief note about the above critique of religious beliefs is appropriate. It should be clear this critical evaluation does not mean that these religions are devoid of valuable teachings. Both traditions carry vast amounts of wisdom to guide their followers to better ways of living. Notably, the Buddhist concept of Dharma [4] useful as it is self-contained and doesn't carry the dangerous transitive belief as in the case of Karma. As Dalai Lama said:

"So actually the practice of Dharma is the constant battle within, replacing previous negative conditioning or habituation with new positive conditioning." [5]

Similarly, the concept of "Divine Grace," as defined by Webster Dictionary, is a state of being which we all should aspire to; the opposite the toxic idea of sin: *"The influence or spirit of God operating in humans to regenerate or strengthen them."*

Ayahuasca can be a powerful tool for deeply religious individuals who are open-minded enough to experience the sacred medicine. There are not many of them, but those who try it may come out either empowered with an enhanced sense of their faith or realizing they were using religion to fill an existential void that could be satisfied in a variety of alternative ways.

Belief System Mechanics and You

Believing in something is always more productive than not believing in anything. Beliefs are connections between our ego-self and our soul-self. The subconscious-self is akin to a highly efficient and heartless computer, which makes no judgments. Instead, the subconscious-self simply processes the wishes and desires of the ego-self in the context of the current belief system installed and in interaction with the soul-self. It is our soul-self that always endeavors to find alignment with the erratic ego-self with the assistance of the subconscious-self.

Spiritual healing is often more effective when our ego-self recognizes the importance of our beliefs in our quality of life, and calmly reflects on them. To make progress, we first need to embrace the belief that our soul-self is the source of life and human attributes. All manifestations of human creativity, inventions, musical compositions, poetry, fiction, visionary art, and breakthrough ideas, arise from our soul-self. As mentioned in previous sections, the subconscious "mind" is just a fiction invented by psychology over a century ago to explain the unexplainable subconscious-self. The soul has access to the collective unconscious, past lives, and the future. It embodies the feeling and wisdom of the past, the awareness and knowledge of the present, and the thoughts and visions of the future. We need to bring our soul-self back to our psyche. As it stands now, science explains all mental phenomena with a subconscious "mind," and the soul-self has been denied its own existence, instead of being reduced to a mythological figure of the long-lost pre-scientific era. We must affirm the existence of our soul-self within ourselves. Without it, spiritual healing is substantially harder to achieve.

Belief sets the "law of attraction" into action; it enables our sustained, concentrated thoughts to correlate with the object of the target. It changes the tempo of the subconscious-self and the harmonic vibration of our thoughts. Like a magnet, our beliefs align the quantum field around us, which affects everything about us, including people and objects at great distances.

Belief is an act of the subconscious-self; it is programmed to create the strings of the parachute to connect the soul-self at the canopy with the ego-self hanging down the physical reality. The bridge of belief must be crossed; our psyche can't operate without beliefs. A parachute without strings is not a parachute. That's the nature of our psyche, like it or not. The problem is that our ego-self is not aware of how our beliefs are created and take no participation in the creation process. The subconscious-self, absent of any input from the ego-self, does the best it can and creates them with whatever life experiences and sensorial information is available. Humans are born with an empty belief system, providing an opportunity for the ego-self to develop a person with no limits - love-giving and fulfilled. Unfortunately, our culture has not realized its potential, and our childhood goes creating dysfunctional beliefs that later run our entire lives.

The gasoline of the self-realization programs is the "desire for success." This is also fueled by the soul-self. Success is defined by the common goal of the survival programs: living safely, preserving the physical integrity of the body, enjoying the pleasures of successful survival such as delicious food, comfortable leisure, and healthy sexual life. But the desire for success far exceeds the goal of survival. Once the survival program succeeds, this desire continues pushing for self-realization.

Scrutinizing Your Belief System

Your belief system is not readily available by simply asking yourself: "what are my deepest beliefs?" We operate our lives based on a multitude of complex beliefs, and we are unable to enumerate say, five of them quickly. Beliefs are buried deep within our operating system domiciled in our subconscious-self. You may find a superficial belief, for example, "I sincerely believe women are stronger than men," but this is connected to a series of more fundamental beliefs concerning what you believe men and women are. These types of more deep-seated beliefs underpin the complexities of our belief systems and are likely programmed during early childhood.

Practicing meaningful introspection regarding your thoughts and opinions may provide valuable clues regarding your underlying belief structure, as these arise from, and speak from the platform of those beliefs. For example, if you have scarcely enough money on which to live and you examine your thoughts, you may find yourself always thinking: "I can never pay my bills, I never get any luck, I'll always be stuck in poverty" Or you will find yourself envying those who have more, degrading the value of money or, perhaps, suggesting that those who have it are unhappy or spiritually poor. When you find these thoughts in yourself, you may indignantly claim: "But those things are true. I am poor. I cannot meet my bills." In doing so, you accept your belief about reality as a characteristic of reality itself, and so the belief is transparent or invisible to you. However, this belief guides and directs your physical reality. In order to change reality, you must change your belief.

Another example is that you may find yourself believing that you are having difficulty because you are too sensitive. While scrutinizing your thoughts, you may say: "But it is true, I am. I react with such great emotion to small things." But that is a belief, and a limiting one. If you follow your thoughts further, you may find yourself thinking: "I am proud of my sensitivity. It sets me apart from the masses." or "I am too good for this world." These are limiting beliefs. They will distort true reality, your own true reality. All you have to do is decide to examine the contents of your thoughts and realize that they contain components that you have overlooked.

When revising our own beliefs, we may realize how frequently we have created limiting beliefs because we have previously made premature judgments in emotionally charged situations. For example, you may have trusted a friend with a personal secret, and sometime later, you find yourself with a severe problem because your friend failed to keep it confidential. Consequently, in the enthusiasm of the moment, you make a judgment about friends in general, creating the firm belief that no person is worthy of your trust and making you skeptical of others from then on. Obviously, such a belief shall close many doors in your future by preventing the formation of rewarding personal relationships due to a lack of necessary trust. The technique to reduce the creation of these limiting beliefs involves practicing the art of suspending judgment.

You will find that you make premature judgments more frequently than you think. Upon examination of these judgments, you will discover that these are based on a long list of limiting beliefs that you have adopted in the past. These pre-existing limiting beliefs act as a framework of "deciding judges" in countless situations and, ultimately, have the effect of reinforcing the belief at hand. When you consciously control premature judgment, you will feel the emotional urge to judge - this is the perfect moment to ask or catch the hidden belief system which is operating behind the scenes. When you question your judgments in a disciplined manner, you will develop a valuable skill, and you will eventually be able to consciously modify, replace, or erase these limiting beliefs at will.

Significant progress will be made once you find yourself at ease with the fact that judgment is unnecessary. You will begin feeling comfortable with frequently suspending judgment and will find that carrying no opinion at all about innumerable matters can provide a sense of peace and wellbeing. Sometimes we become addicted to this process and see ourselves passing judgment on many things that are not relevant to our life purpose.

Belief and the Placebo Effect

Analogous to a computer, the subconscious-self runs the physiological functions of the human body based on its innate survival programming. The default settings of this program come relatively empty when we are born, although some programming occurs during pregnancy, which will be discussed in a future chapter. The power of the human species comes from its extraordinary adaptability to the surrounding environment. Many default settings are imposed by the physical conditions of the environment. Still, others are established as the ego-self begins to understand and create beliefs of its environment and, importantly, itself. Based on those, the subconscious-self operates our physiology. At the juncture, a mention of the 'placebo effect' is relevant because this is the single most convincing evidence of the fundamental role of beliefs in our lives.

Medical history is filled with numerous reported cases where placebos have been found to have a profound and measurable effect on a variety of disorders. Consider the astounding case of a woman suffering from severe nausea and vomiting. Laboratory tests confirmed her disrupted pattern of gastric contractions. Then a 'new, magical, extremely potent' drug was offered to her, the doctors proclaimed would undoubtedly cure her nausea. Within a few minutes, her nausea vanished. The same laboratory tests now revealed standard gastric patterns. However, unknown to the patient, she had actually been given a home remedy usually used to *induce* nausea. When the "new drug" was presented to her with the strong suggestion of nausea relief provided by an authority figure, this acted as a command message to the subconscious-self and triggered a cascade of self-regulatory biochemical responses.

Another remarkable case involved a patient with schizophrenia. This woman was experiencing symptoms, such as delusion and hallucinations. When not experiencing these symptoms, her blood glucose levels were normal. However, upon encountering the delusion that she had diabetes, her entire physiology changed, including elevated blood glucose levels. In a similar vein, several cases of 'disappearance of skin warts' have been reported using hypnotic suggestions. Intrigued researchers have pondered as to how the brain may initiate a biochemical action to constrict certain small arteries, cutting off the specific vital nutrient supply to warts but not affecting the neighboring healthy cells.

Findings of carefully designed research have indicated that our interpretation of what we are experiencing can literally alter our physiology. In fact, there is evidence that worried patients attending initial medical consultations show immediate improvement by merely listening to the doctor's diagnosis. The subconscious-self, which is operating in alert mode at that moment, shifts from the unknown adverse situation into something known, named, tamed, and explained. With the alarm mode switched off, it immediately triggers neurochemical responses that start to improve the diagnosed medical condition.

As amazingly life-affirming placebos are, the reverse of this effect, sometimes known as "nocebos', has also been observed. This effect is associated with negative, life-threatening, or disempowering beliefs. Arthur Barsky, Professor of Psychiatry at Harvard Medical School, states that the patient's expectations and beliefs regarding whether a drug or procedure works or will have side effects plays a crucial role in the outcome.

Belief-reinforced awareness becomes our biochemistry. Through our subconscious-self, each and every cell in our body is absolutely aware of our thoughts, feelings, and beliefs. If your subconscious-self has a registered belief that you are fragile, the biochemistry of your immune system may work inefficiently, and your body may succumb to illness easily. When your ego-self becomes consciously aware of 'being depressed,' it stamps the raw data received through the sensory organs with the belief of what being depressed means and physically becomes the 'interpretation' of the belief by altering neurochemical balance and resulting in increasingly negative feelings.

The celebrated biologist Bruce Lipton in this classic book "The Biology of Belief" [6] makes remarkable observations about the placebo effect and the influence of the belief in the afterlife on our biology and behavior.

Lipton believes that the placebo effect should be a major topic of study in medical schools and the subject of significant funded research efforts. These may result in medical doctors eventually having cost-effective, side-effects-free tools to treat disease. Besides the dogmatic tenets in the medical industry, which are against such an "unscientific" approach, Lipton speculated a significant financial influence over the reluctance to embrace such a tool. If you can heal yourself with scientifically tested "placebo-inspired" therapies, why should you go to a doctor, or why would you need to buy prescription medications? In fact, he was informed that drug companies were studying patients who respond well to placebos with the goal of eliminating them from early clinical trials. It has been disturbing to pharmaceutical companies that in most of their clinical trials, the placebos have proven as effective as the engineered compounds being tested for regulatory approval. In truth, the placebo effect is a threat to the pharmaceutical industry, and, as such, these companies have acted to conceal and sweep these findings under the rug. Unfortunately, this has left the scientific literature devoid of well-controlled human clinical studies that underpin the biological basis for these healing placebo effects. Research shows that at least one-third of the population is particularly receptive to the healing power of a placebo treatment. I recommend that we experiment with the placebo effect when caring for our family members; we may heal them without any danger of harming them.

Mounting scientific evidence has indicated that the belief in religion or spirituality can a significant impact on a person's health and vitality. Hundreds of scientific articles published each year on the impact of religion or spirituality have revealed that medical and psychiatric patients commonly resort to religious and spiritual belief practices to cope with illness and other stressful life changes. People who hold more spiritual beliefs fare significantly better in mental health and adapt more quickly to health problems than those who are less spiritual. The benefits to mental health and well-being provided by spirituality have psychological consequences that impact physical health, including reducing the risk of disease and influence over the healing outcomes of treatment. Spiritual beliefs have a direct, positive influence on the activity of immune and endocrine systems, which are critical for health maintenance and disease prevention. Spiritual patients exhibit significantly better indicators of immune functions, such as higher white blood cell counts and antibody levels, along with considerably lower rates of infection. These patients also exhibit lower levels of adrenal stress hormones, such as cortisol and epinephrine (secretions that directly repress the activity of the immune system) than non-spiritual patients, which likely contributes to their improved overall health and responsiveness to treatment.

Some Life Influencing Beliefs

There are several noteworthy self-beliefs that play an influential role in our lives. Some deeply hidden self-beliefs are related to the nature of knowledge acquisition and intelligence. Some people believe that knowledge can only be obtained through formal college education, or the opposite, that experience in life is the only source of knowledge. Young students often embrace the belief that it's not worth learning new concepts or skills because they can't visualize the immediate applicability. The self-beliefs about intelligence that is acquired in early childhood is often established in a dysfunctional manner through parents or teachers, which seed limiting beliefs in their subconscious-selves with insults such as "dumb" or "good for nothing."

Another prevalent self-belief regards our assessment of the degree of control we have over our destiny. People with that focus on their external environment often believe that their future is not within their direct control. Diminished control beliefs result in ascribing life events and accomplishments to fate, luck, or specific circumstances that the individual will not be able to influence. This is the process that feeds the beliefs of someone who feels that they are stuck in a tedious job because of weak market conditions. Once they believe that, they will not seek challenging goals, instead of settling for the status quo.

Conversely, people who believe in inner control feel in command of their world. Their ego-self believes that they can orchestrate their career, social relationships, and lifestyle. They believe in their internal strength, and this acts as a catalyst for personal growth and development due to the accountability and responsibility which the individual takes for their successes or failures.

Competency self-beliefs are also highly influential in life. These include assessments of our overall ability to achieve desired results. These can also reflect micro-level assessments of the perceived skills and abilities needed to complete a task, such as writing an article or installing computer software. The sources of competency self-beliefs are varied; some are based on past performance, while others focus on current challenges. Competency self-beliefs are not based on actual ability or skills, but the perception of ourselves or biased opinions of others. These beliefs influence perceptions of overall self-worth and are often a deciding factor in determining whether a person will engage in a task or elect to defer, withdraw, or altogether avoid the challenge. Task avoidance is motivated by fear of failure based on a perceived likelihood of unpopular opinions from others, or by fear of feeling negative emotions such as doubt, guilt, or humiliation which often accompany task failure.

Another powerful self-belief is the degree of the value we associate with different alternatives when facing crossroads in life. When ascribing low value to a potential life choice, our ego-self gets reluctant to invest effort. For example, who would devote extraordinary cognitive and financial resources to completing law school or invest physical energy toward running in a 10-mile race when the payoff is seen as marginal, uninteresting, or of questionable value? The importance of a life choice is determined based on the relative value believed by the ego-self. This may be measured by how much the ego-self enjoys the life choice at hand or by how useful or remunerative it may be. If the ego-self has been strongly influenced by dysfunctional upbringing, it may embrace morally disengaged beliefs, which may incline individuals toward questionable personal behavior, lack of environmental concern, or deliberate law-breaking.

Finally, we have the self-beliefs which are related to the reasons we pursue goals. Dramatically different results will be obtained depending on whether the ego-self believes in pursuing goals for strong inner purposes or for feeble superficial motivations. When the ego-self believes in inner oriented goals, it typically shows more significant interest in accumulating knowledge, seeking help when needed, monitoring goal progress. It exhibits more willingness to try new or alternative strategies. When goal pursuit is based upon a superficial belief, the ego-self focuses on looking good in the eyes of peers or avoiding the public humiliation that may accompany goal failure. Social comparison becomes important as the goal is less concerned about the results and more about the appearance and acceptance of others.

CHAPTER SEVEN

PRINCIPLES OF QUANTUM PSYCHOLOGY

Reviewing the history of psychology, Sigmund Freud was incredibly accurate with his theory that behavior was the product of unconscious mechanisms. In an attempt to delineate these underlying mechanisms, Freud investigated outward behaviors and measurable experiences including, slips of the tongue (colloquially known as 'Freudian slips'), association of ideas, and dreams. Psychotherapy arose through this endeavor, and multiple approaches branched out from this field.

I believe that classical psychoanalysis has failed in extracting enough convincing data to formulate any reliable theory of the unconscious. This failure is likely due to the factor that the relevant information required for extraction is too deeply encrusted in the human psyche, to the extent that currently, available research techniques are ineffective. With such a limited view of what lies beneath the surface, the field of psychology has remained stagnant and without a reasonably accurate model of the unconscious realm.

Due to these shortcomings, psychology has faced a great deal of criticism, including being criticized for not being 'real science.' Psychology, in its efforts to decode the secrets of the psyche, has embraced the scientific method and associated research techniques. Unfortunately, psychology has encountered serious difficulties with the replicability of their research findings. Their critics had claimed that the majority of psychological studies could not be replicated, an essential requirement of the scientific method. Moreover, in the eyes of many, the field has failed to meet the standards required for categorization as a "science." There is a longstanding debate within the scientific community in which psychologists and sociologists continue to refute this point, while "hard scientists" continue to dismiss the scientific validity of their field of research. Ashutosh Jogalekar made a balanced assessment of the situation when he wrote in Scientific American:

"To me, the acrimonious debates about evolutionary and positive psychology reflect a trial-by-fire that every field goes through in its early days to separate the chaff from the wheat. If you apply a narrow-minded definition of science, then it might indeed be hard to call psychology science. But what matters is whether it's useful, and to me, the field certainly seems to have its uses". [1]

Psychology as a "science" is only over a century old and is still struggling to gain recognition from the more established fields, such as physics. Psychology has shown convincing evidence to the effect that specific childhood mechanics, for example, are absolute determinants of adult behavior, and this work has robustly influenced public policy in child-bearing or education programs. In my opinion, regardless of how long these debates continue, psychology does provide a meaningful contribution to the understanding of the psyche and improvement of the human condition. Equipped with the scientific method, psychology has been successfully identifying subconscious behavior patterns and mental health conditions, creating a common language that has enabled progress in the field. Until now, psychology has produced names and definitions for phenomena that were already instinctively understood in less academic terms. With the help of neuroscience, psychology now has the opportunity to make evident the predictive power required to be considered a hard science.

Fortunately, with the advent of advanced brain imaging technologies, we are seeing a revolution and novel type of psychological research emerging. Psychological theory and hypotheses coupled with powerful new technologies may herald the revival of the field, enabling psychologists to uncover factual data that may correlate, for example, neural networks and psychological concepts. This combination of theoretical and experimental techniques may enable psychological researchers to couple their behavioral assessment and observations with tangible physiological mechanisms, allowing for the delineation of cause and effect.

This quantum model of the psyche is inherently holistic and consistent with the holistic philosophy of health. Holistic medicine is a form of healing practiced by some medical doctors and other health practitioners that considers the whole person, body, mind, & spirit, to attain optimal health and wellness. It is based on the principle that humans are made up of interdependent parts, and as such, if one part is not working correctly, all others will be affected. This same principle, described in quantum model terms, equates to achieving proper alignment within our SIE.

> **Quantum Psychology:** the study of the human soul -- an actual spiritual entity with a quantum presence in the quantum field-- and its relationships with the other parts of the human psyche, collective unconscious, the subconscious-self, and the ego-self.

Upon reviewing the modern origins of the holistic medical approach, I found that mechanistic medicine began gaining ground in Europe with the development of powerful microscopes in the 17th century. Before this, Oliva Sabuco de Nantes (1562-1626) was making the first contributions to holistic medicine. Decades before Rene Descartes (1596-1650) proposed the ideas of duality between material substance and mind, Oliva Sabuco de Nantes was the first proponent of the modern basis of spiritual healing work. It is not clear whether Descartes was influenced by Oliva's book "New Philosophy of Human Nature," which was published nine years prior to his birth and had become a multinational bestseller across Europe as Descartes entered higher education. The work of both characters has relevant implications to ayahuasca and spiritual healing work, therefore worthy of further discussion.

In Descartes' dualism, beyond God, there are two separate, distinct substances, the material, and the mind. His theory announced, for the first time, the dual nature of reality, which is not far different from the wave-particle and the mind-body dilemmas that still challenge modern scientific thought. However, it is Oliva Sabuco who first pointed toward the idea of holistic medicine.

Oliva correctly predicted that since the properties of the soul are not physical, they cannot be physically located in the human body. Thus, she reasoned, the connection between body and soul occurs through the brain. The brain and the body "serve the soul like house servants serve the house." She argued that the human body is a microcosm, a miniature version of the world, and analogous to God ruling the world; the soul governs the "effects, movements, and actions of humans." [2]

In astounding parallel with our quantum model, Oliva believed that this intimate mind-body connection had a close relationship, not only between psychological and physical health but also between morality and medicine. For example, she proposed that, as soon as a negative emotion such as sorrow affects our bodies, we must control it before it becomes unmanageable despair. Virtuous passions promote good health; she continued. Immoral passions cause sickness and disease. She purported the existence of a natural medical basis for moral sanctions against sexual promiscuity. Certainly, Oliva did not solve the "mind-body problem" in her lifespan. However, she anticipated today's holistic medicine, with its emphasis on the intimate connection between emotional and physical well-being, several hundred years in advance. Finally, she was first among the modern thinkers to argue that the brain, rather than the heart, controls the body, along with suggesting the role of cerebrospinal fluid, and the absorption of nutrients through digestion.

The mechanistic approach to medicine follows the premise that the human body is a Newtonian machine and continues to describe discoveries in neuroscience in those terms. However, in recent years there have been some exciting developments. As neuroscience has begun to uncover the deepest roots of human behavior in neurochemical terms, instead of admitting that their findings are insufficient to explain behavior, they succumb to the same logical error that science has often criticized for philosophers and metaphysics.

After discovering the upper levels of the neural network hierarchies, that is, when neurochemical activity is correlated with the external human behavior, neuroscientists have taken to referring to these processes as though they have conscious awareness. When the model ceases explaining the behavior, they "anthropomorphize" the process. In other words, they add human attributes to chemical processes. To illustrate the point, here is a quote from an excellent book that explores the latest discoveries regarding dopamine, a primary neurotransmitter that plays a leading role in the brain's reward system.

"Dopamine makes us want things. It is the source of raw desire: give me more. But we are not at the ungoverned mercy of our desire. We also have a complementary dopamine circuit that calculates what sort of "more" is worth having. It gives us the ability to construct plans--to strategize and dominate the world around us...... urges come from dopamine passing through the mesolimbic circuit, which we call the dopamine desire circuit. Calculation and planning come from the mesocortical circuit, which we will call the dopamine control circuit..... In addition, the dopamine control circuit is the source of imagination. It let us peer into the future to see the consequences of decisions..." [3]

Since consciousness dwells in the quantum field and mechanistic science has not yet been able to explain its nature, then, to handle the phenomenon, scientists simply speak about neural circuits as if they were consciously intelligent. Here you find statements like: "dopamine makes us want things," neural circuits that "calculates what is worth having," another circuit "make us calculate and plan," and, somewhat comically, "the dopamine circuit is the source of imagination." Clearly, mechanistic science swimming upwards from to the bottom has reached the surface of the water and can't see the great turmoil of quantum activity occurring in the thin air above it. With the quantum model of the psyche, we can easily rephrase the above quote with a different theoretical framework:

"The survival program that operates from our subconscious-self makes us want things. Such desires produce volitive energy that triggers an increase in dopamine release within the brain. But with the soul's attribute of discernment, we decide which urges are worth having. While doing so, it gets reflected in our brain with chemical activity in the desire and the control dopamine circuits. We also have learned that dopamine levels go up when the soul exercises its ability of imagination through the conscious focus of the ego-self."

This alternative narrative illustrates the increased infusion of common sense that understanding this model can provide spiritual healing or therapeutic settings.

Science's inability to account for consciousness is having the unintended and undesirable effect of isolating our ego-self from its true nature. Besides the obvious benefits brought by the increasing number of neuroscience's discoveries of neural mechanisms, we ought to be mindful of potential adverse side effects. For instance, conclusions drawn from this research may open a door that justifies the detachment of human behavior from personal responsibility. Without consciousness in the equation, behavior shall be increasingly portrayed as robotic. Even worse, with this level of detachment, people may begin to feel that they are a victim and powerless under the control of their brain chemistry.

Spiritual healing advisors may adhere to the proposed model to properly guide clients toward a holistic self, rather than promoting a harmful split between body and behavior. A non-religious model of the psyche, which includes the soul, should be particularly useful to the institutions of society that promote civility and proper behavior, such as the educational and judicial systems. I can only dream that one day any kind of soul-inclusive quantum model could be presented as a potentially valid scientific hypothesis and gain respectful recognition throughout modern society. We must accept that all scientific hypotheses are, in essence, well-structured belief systems.

Notably, over the past century, the concept of God has been displaced from public view in many Western societies, based on the secular principles of separation between church and state. In these countries, prayer has been removed from schools, and government events have encapsulated individuals within their own moral bubble. Within these moral bubbles, individuals are left to resolve for themselves and fill the gaps of acceptable behavior that are not explicitly covered by the ever-increasing number of secular laws. Without external moral guidance, the new generations have encountered difficulty in discovering their true essence. In addition, if our society begins eroding the idea of self-responsibility by forgoing personal responsibility, in favor of the idea of an uncontrollable "subconscious mind," which dictates behavior via physiological mechanisms, we risk further descent of the human species. By relinquishing power over our actions entirely to neurochemical processes, we step closer to an 'animal' consciousness and further from the divine nature of humans. While neurochemical processes have a role to play in behavior, assigning the entirety of our complex behavior to these processes leaves us with a low-resolution view of the complex nature of the human species. The proposed model of the psyche also attempts to make a positive contribution to society in this regard.

The Soul's Master Program

By reverse-engineering the behavioral mechanics learned in my ayahuasca insights and visions, we propose an extremely sophisticated master program domiciled in the soul-self. Following science's principle of parsimony [4], the master program is the simplest conceptualization possible to explain the miracle of life.

The computer program is the closest analogy we can find among our modern frame of reference to cognize life into our SIE. The master program is an indescribable feature of our soul-self, our personal computer chip, which enables physical incarnation. The program that runs our human lives is designed with four imperative commands: grow, reproduce, succeed, and return-home. Grow is the process that starts at conception: embryonic development, survive birth, and development throughout childhood until reaching reproductive maturity.

Reproduce is the driving command of sexual behavior, which spits in two fronts, male and female, with different programs designed to maximize long term reproduction efficiency of the species. Reproductive strategies have been studied in considerable detail by evolutionary anthropologists and have gained a substantial congruent understanding of human behavior based on the genetic command interpretation. For example, the concept that sexual attraction between both genders is based on the subconscious selection of physical traits that indicate better reproductive probabilities. Reproduction is the critical function that is most influential over human behavior as it ensures the continued existence of the species is the physical form.

Success refers to the achievement of attaining adulthood, generating offspring, and maintaining stability and safety to ensure the success of future generations. Once survival is achieved by securing food and shelter, the next goal is to protect the fruits of labor and enjoy the victory of life over failure and death.

Return-home is a mission that is present since conception, awaiting the opportunity to play the game, like a reserve player on a sports team who anxiously wishes to be called to the field during an important match. This return home master program imperative has been described by others as the expansion of consciousness, self-actualization in Maslow's terms, enlightenment in Buddhist terms, and ascension in New Age terms. I call these self-realization programs. The return-home aspect of the soul master program is subordinate to the survival programs. This program shall spark the light in our ego-self to induce us to seek spiritual healing. When survival has been secured, the return-home program begins bothering the ego-self by creating awareness of its psychological burdens that deserve attention. It injects inspiration to transcend the ordinary in those who dream beyond conventional lifestyles. The program creates a longing for wholeness and the eternal to return home with the awareness of the journey done, ready for the next step in ascending spiritual evolution.

To pursue the four imperative commands, the master program uses its divine attribute of creativity to create programs that boost efficiency at every possible opportunity to maximize the probabilities of success. This is the dream of the field of artificial intelligence (AI); to design computer programs that modify themselves and adapt to changing environmental conditions. AI aims to mimic the natural intelligence of the human soul. These programs can develop to the point of simulating intelligence convincingly, such as the 'Deep Blue' computer program, which was able to beat the chess world champion, Gary Kasparov, in 1996. Since then, AI systems have developed to impressive new heights and boast an array of remarkable tricks that ease many aspects of human life. However, AI will always be a computer program and remain far from having self-consciousness. The divine attributes of the soul include identifying opportunities for new programs but also programming and installing them into the subconscious-self for execution. This is a complexity that may never be accomplished by a computer program.

When our SIE separates from the quantum all-encompassing absolute, in other words, when our SIE is attached to the embryo, an intelligent guiding principle is triggered, and the SIE shall always be inclined to come back to its source. Consider droplets of water spread over a flat surface which start merging into each other, with each droplet losing their individual identity while becoming part of a larger body of water. You may call it God, the Universal matrix, or whatever concept you may comfortably accept. The fact remains that the ultimate mission of the master program is to return to its origin.

For our model, and to avoid digression onto lengthy philosophical dissertations, we won't attempt at this time to speculate beyond this point. Therefore, let's assert as an operational assumption of this model that this natural intelligence is the engine of the master program. That said, one of the fundamental functions of the master program is to create automatic processes for any repetitive task to relieve attentional demands on the conscious ego-self.

The master program is extremely effective in detecting repetitive tasks, and when it does, it immediately creates a subprogram for the subconscious-self to run. The created subprogram shall be implemented when called by the conscious ego-self or may run automatically when the subconscious-self recognizes a situation of practical use. We can classify these subprograms into four categories:

1. Skills (Thousands) - These are the most basic programs which are created to execute the thousands of simple repetitive tasks encountered in daily life. These may include your ability to flip the pages of this book, type on the keyboard, recalling phone numbers from memory, mental mathematical operations, and any other frequent task which is performed without conscious attention.

2. Habits (Hundreds) - These are programs that harness multiple skills to perform other actions of a higher level of complexity. For example, when you learn to brush your teeth during childhood, your mother most likely trained you

to develop the habit of doing it one or more times per day. We carry hundreds of programs that run our habits from the subconscious-self with little or no conscious attention. Some of these habits are elaborate and sophisticated. For example, you may find yourself driving your car and suddenly arriving at your work location, feeling somewhat surprised about the 'auto-pilot' mode in which you traveled there. You did it safely and followed traffic laws while performing other mental tasks like reviewing your agenda of later that day or the menu of dinner that night.

3. Subpersonalities (Dozens) – When one or several habits are practiced with enough frequency, they begin to organize themselves as thought-forms, creating a new quantum structure within our ego-self structure. Whether we desire to be or not, we are creators; this is an unalienable ability that comes with our divine nature. Anything that you think or do creates a pattern in the quantum field. In this way, we create dozens of sub-personalities throughout our lives. Some are obvious to other people around us, but others are observable only by ourselves.

4. Entities (A handful) – Unknowingly to us, a surprising act of creation occurs when a particular sub-personality is practiced with enough frequency and intensity. At some point, this sub-personality experiences a birthing process and acquires self-awareness. This is the dream or nightmare of artificial intelligence programming, the scenario which we see in the movies when the computer program starts thinking independently and takes control of the computer. When this happens within the boundaries of your SIE, this sub-personality detaches or breaks loose from the direct supervision of the ego-self. We will name these phenomena "entities." These will be discussed in greater detail throughout the book, as they are the embodiment of addictive behaviors.

Note how these programs, analogous to "molecule-cell-tissue-organ" pattern, form a sort of hierarchy, following the universal fractal pattern of organization.

Memory and Holograms

What about memories? Surely by remembering we can know our past? Consider that when we remember, we are not looking at the actual history at all, but instead, at the present trace of the past. From memory, we infer that there have been past events, but we do not always accurately recall past events. Research into the nature of false memories has highlighted that humans can recall memories that never actually occurred or can remember alternative versions of events which diverge from the truth of what happened.

Similarly, to "words," memories never really succeed in capturing reality. Memories are somewhat abstract, composed of knowledge about things rather than of things. Memory never captures the essence, the present intensity, or the concrete reality of an experience. It is the corpse of an experience from which life has vanished. What we recall and know from memory is secondhand. Much like a travel guidebook, this can be a handy and entertaining tool, but it is hardly comparable to the reality of the country it describes.

The experience of personal memories from the ego-self perspective are rudimentary notions of a blurry past. However, there is memory that stems from the subconscious-self perspective, and this is a different matter. When we experience ayahuasca, we may see diffuse or blurry images of past events that come together with a convincing sense of truth. This is because, from the subconscious-self standpoint, we are much closer to reality. The subconscious-self has a privileged view of the show that the ego-self doesn't. How is this possible?

Let's introduce the idea of holographic memory, as this modern concept is remarkably congruent with the quantum model of the psyche. A hologram is a photographic recording of a light field, as opposed to an image formed by a lens. Contrary to a photographic film where anyone can distinguish the recorded image in it, the holographic "film" is a diffuse pattern with no particular form. However, it produces an impressive 3D image that retains the depth, parallax [5], and perspective that changes realistically relative to the position of the observer. That is, the view of the image from different angles represents the subject viewed from similar angles. In this sense, holograms do not merely produce the illusion of depth but are truly three-dimensional images.

Neuroscientist Karl Pribram in collaboration with physicist David Bohm [6] developed the holographic brain theory. This is the branch of neuroscience investigating the idea that human consciousness is formed by quantum effects in or between brain cells. This is opposed by traditional neuroscience, which examines the brain's behavior by looking at patterns of neurons and the surrounding chemistry, and which assumes that any quantum effects will not be significant at this scale. During the 1950s, while working as a researcher at Yale University, Pribram embarked on an investigation into how memory was stored in the human brain. Pribram was seeking to elucidate data from rodent experiments that had shown that animals, even with many regions of the brain removed, could remember the path of a maze that they had been previously trained to run. This was against the generally accepted concept that memories were physically localized in specific areas of the brain, such as the hippocampus. In the 1960s, Pribram read an article in Scientific American describing the first construction of a hologram. He experienced a classical eureka moment. Shortly thereafter, the idea of holographic storage of memories was born.

Our uncanny ability to quickly retrieve whatever information we need from the enormous store of our memories becomes more understandable if the brain functions according to holographic principles. If a friend asks you to tell him what comes to mind when he says the word "ayahuasca," you do not have to clumsily sort back through some gigantic and cerebral alphabetic file to arrive at an answer. Instead, associations like "shaman," "hallucinogenic," and "Amazon jungle" all instantly come to mind. Indeed, one of the most amazing things about the human cognitive process is that every piece of information seems instantly cross-correlated with every other piece of information -another feature that is in line with holographic principles. Since every portion of a hologram is infinitely interconnected with every other part, it is perhaps nature's supreme example of a cross-correlated system. Moreover, it helps to elucidate several unsolved puzzles in psychology and many of the baffling phenomena experienced by individuals during altered states of consciousness.

This is consistent with the increasing number of studies and theories that integrate the concepts of holograms and quantum fields in ways that tend to obliterate the mind-body dilemma. For example, Brazilian researcher Francisco Di Biase said: "But in this new concept, quantum holographic brain dynamic patterns are conceived as an active part of the universal quantum-holographic informational field, and capable of generating an informational field interconnecting each part, each brain-consciousness, with all the information stored in the holographic patterns distributed in the whole cosmos, in an indivisible irreducible informational cosmic unity." [7]

Again, when we scrutinize the advanced theories of memory, we encounter avant-garde postulates, which indicate the holographic nature of information storage, non-local storage of information, accessible instantaneously, and cross-referenced with dozens of other similar data points. It seems that the holographic model of memory shall continue gaining traction among neuroscientists in the coming decades, as it is the model of memory that makes the most sense. The idea that memories are physically stored in neuronal circuits simply falls short in explaining the speed of memory access that we all experience.

The holographic model fits perfectly with the quantum model of the psyche, which adopts it to explain how the quantum structures in our SIE's access the memories for the practical execution of the survival and self-realization programs.

Memory is the non-local, holographic pattern that results from the continuous flow of the quantum movement created by the actions of the dense physical reality. Every single action in the physical world, including every thought and emotion of all members of humanity, has created quantum ripples in the quantum field in a holographic fashion. These are accumulated in an infinite series of holographic layers that surround the originator of the action, blended with the surrounding others, and built up in magnitude from the tiniest to the planetary level and beyond. All the information about everything that has ever happened is theoretically available. After all, if we have already acknowledged that our view of the stars on a clear night corresponds to the scenery that occurred thousands of years ago, it should not be hard to understand the idea of universal holographic memory.

The question is, why is our memory not capable of retrieving more? Why do we forget what happened last week? The answer has to do with access and convenience. Our subconscious-self is a filter of stimuli from our senses that delivers the bare minimum necessary for the ego-self to operate in its limited physical theater. The ego-self is capable of accessing memory on a "need-to-know" basis. If it's not necessary, within certain conditions, it won't be immediately accessible.

There is an almost infinite number of memories in the holographic quantum field that are specifically relevant to your SIE. These may be retrieved by the ego-self by issuing volitive currents with the target inquiry, which the subconscious-self processes and delivers back, if possible. To protect the ego-self from an overwhelming number of accumulating memories, the subconscious-self has a series of mechanisms designed for this purpose. It continuously encodes the memories following the survival priorities to protect the ego-self by blocking any memory that may interfere with its performance.

There are four modes of memory protection:

(1) **Relevant** - These memories are not protected at all, and are readily available for the efficient operation of the ego-self. These free access memories include information such as phone numbers, names, faces, things to do, and practical knowledge. As soon as any of these memories stop being used with reasonable frequency, they are removed from the 'relevant' category.' Note that recalling (i.e., unlocking the memory protection) from other categories is possible at any time, depending on many factors. One of the main functions of the ayahuasca spiritual advising is to assist in the processing of memories retrieved during ayahuasca sessions. By revealing information from the unconscious to the conscious, moving from the forgotten to the remembered, we exponentially expand our possibilities of making fresh re-connections in the subconscious-self. It allows the subconscious-self to start reconfiguring old programming that has run for a long time in the physical brain. Subsequently, with the new connections established, the self-realization program takes control over them in order to modify behavior, worldviews, paradigms, and creates new potential for a better life.

(2) **Non-relevant** - When relevant memories stop being frequently accessed, they fall into the 'non-relevant' mode. This is the largest category. Stating that 95% of the memories become non-relevant with the passage of time, would likely be an underestimate. Depending on their degree of utility, these memories are retrievable with variable levels of effort for occasional use.

(3) **Risky** – This category contains memories that may diminish the ego's competitiveness in its habitat. In social terms, it refers to information that may embarrass the ego identity or reduce its status and, therefore, its survival opportunities. The ego tends to conceal information that may tarnish the onion of self-perception. (See Figure 2) To ensure this protection, it may lie, tell half-truths, omit details, or use other deceptive strategies. For example, unseen mistakes, misunderstandings, mishaps, or "dumb accidents" are often conveniently excluded from casual conversations. More importantly, this category contains

all of the darker behavior and actions which have been contumaciously planned, which were one way or the other unethical, improper, socially unacceptable, illegal, or just blatantly criminal. These memories are tainted with negative emotional energy, mostly guilt, shame, remorse, and embarrassment.

Risky memories are coded for eventual reclassification and remain in an alert mode, which reminds the ego-self about the dangers of exposure or discovery of this information by others. These remain available for immediate retrieval but, without frequent conscious review, can become categorized as either non-relevant or encrypted. Conscious revalidation is a signal to the survival program that any specific memory is still useful.

A classic example of a risky memory going into encrypted mode due to the emotional energy generated from intense feelings of shame and remorse is described in An Unborn Baby named Penelope, one of the stories in the Bonus Section.

(4) **Encrypted** – This category encompasses the repressed memories of classical psychology. "Repressed" is a term with emotional content that is not congruent with the mechanistic action of the subconscious-self. The word 'encrypted' is a descriptive and more adequate label that will be used in this model concurrently.

Encrypted memories are those which are tightly protected for the benefit of the organism. Conscious memories of any event or information that tend to burden the ego-self in its survival functions are prioritized for "amnesia treatment" to remove conscious attention on such past occurrence and promote forward-looking thinking. The survival program runs a "shock-forget" routine, which blocks the holographic access by the ego-self. These memories are often related to traumatic events, violence, abuse, accidents, severe illness, frightening moments, and horrific sights. Memories in the non-convenient category that are not regularly validated fall into this category by default.

Hypnosis therapy has made significant progress in unlocking encrypted memories and reconciling them with the ego-self. This therapy can remove anxiety and other symptoms from patients willing to trust in this technology. Ayahuasca, on the other hand, opens a channel that accurately selects the specific memory containing the most urgent conflict, which requires resolution. It's like Mother Ayahuasca heals in the optimal sequential order using your personal list of "conflicts requiring resolution."

The vast majority of the psychological and physical ailments that successfully heal in ayahuasca sessions involve the unlocking of one or more encrypted memories. The pinpoint accuracy of ayahuasca selecting the correct encrypted memory for the specific intention of the moment almost defies rationality. It constitutes one of the most powerful blessings of the sacred medicine. We have found that this ability of ayahuasca to touch the human soul and decode the survival program's inner workings become enhanced when subjects engage in several consecutive ayahuasca sessions. Single sessions that allow time for the ego-self to reconstitute itself have proven less effective.

These concepts of holographic memories, thought-forms, and quantum structures, as fantastic as they may sound, are not the mere product of baseless speculation. The quantum model of the psyche is a simplified version of extremely complex theories that are currently evolving in the field of quantum physics. Some hypotheses push speculation to limits, which, for the sake of simplicity, we do not attempt to incorporate. For example, there is one hypothesis that proposes that light is produced inside the brain. This is based on a suggested biological process associated with microscopic filaments on the surface of the brain's ventricles. This would add a literal meaning to words such as "enlightenment" and "inner light" [8]. Coupling this hypothesis with the fact that one of the ayahuasca vine's active ingredients, harmine, has fluorescent properties, we may be drawn into elaborate speculations which not relevant to the focus of our work.

There is another theory that describes the psychophysiology of the ability of intuition based on a quantum holographic model of memory. It proposes a constantly evolving fourth-dimensional hologram that contains the history of everything that has occurred. [9]. For our model, we are not engaged in the intricate twists of the quantum possibilities. This enables us to propose a plausible operational framework for therapeutic purposes while ensuring enough scientific congruency to make it plausible and credible to the average psychedelic therapy patient.

The Subpersonalities in Us

In Chapter 5, we discussed the topic of thought-forms and learned that when one or more habits are practiced with enough frequency, they begin to organize themselves as thought-forms, creating a new quantum structure within our ego-self. Some of these quantum structures may turn into what we call subpersonalities. As defined by Rowan, a subpersonality is a semi-permanent and semi-autonomous region of the personality capable of acting as a person. [10].

The idea of a subpersonality is more familiar to us that what we may initially think. Almost all recognized psychology authors had made references to them with a diversity of terms they have coined to describe them. However, it had remained in the sidelines of psychology and had never really been in the spotlight. There is only one psychology book dedicated exclusively to subpersonalities. [11]

Most of us have had the experience of being 'taken over' by a part of ourselves, which we were unaware existed. We say things such as, "I don't know what got into me." The most frequent example is an episode of uncontrolled rage, although there can be positive examples too. How we usually recognize the presence of a subpersonality is that we find ourselves in a particular situation, acting in ways that we later regret or feel unable to change the tone of our behavior through will or conscious decision. This often endures for as long as the situation lasts and is relieved without deliberate action when we leave the condition in which this state was triggered.

Articles written by professional therapists have proposed that we are not a single self, but many selves, which change as the individual shifts between different situations and interactions. Experienced therapists have always been intrigued by patients who show different parts of themselves, which are distinct enough to talk and work as though they are separate personalities.

Phrases like "On the one hand I want to quit my job, but on the other, I feel almost sure I may regret it" or "it was as if a voice was telling me to do that" are incredibly common. These phrases can indicate the advisor or therapist that more than one personality is at work.

Many schools of psychotherapy see subpersonalities as enduring psychological structures that influence how the person feels, perceives, behaves, and mold self-perception. Rather than simply influencing the person, it appears that a subpersonality is an individual during a particular moment in time. It seems as though a person hosts an endless parade of subpersonalities that replace each other, dependent on the occasion at hand.

Roberto Assagioli, the founder of psychosynthesis, said:

"Subpersonalities are psychological satellites, coexisting as a multitude of lives within the medium of our personality. Each subpersonality has a style and motivation of its own, often strikingly dissimilar from those of the others. Each of us is a crowd. There can be the rebel and the intellectual, the seducer and the housewife, the saboteur and the aesthete, the organizer and the bon vivant each with its own mythology, and all more or less crowded into one single person. Often they are far from being at peace with one another. ...Several subpersonalities are continually scuffling: impulses, desires, principles, aspirations, are engaged in an unceasing struggle." [12]

Assisted by many ayahuasca insights, my first few years of ayahuasca work were characterized by observing aspects of my persona that could clearly be classified as subpersonalities. The businessman, driven by the undercurrent of a corporate employee striving for competency in the pursual of a salary raise, was one of them. Being a divorced bank executive during my mid-forties, I could appreciate how the businessman was quickly displaced by the romantic lover when a suitable damsel appeared within reach. Subsequently, the sports fan could hijack me later in the night upon receiving a phone call from my old high school friend, inviting me to a professional baseball game. While I was by myself at home, the intellectual nerd spent hours reading various scientific texts. At the same time, the spiritual seeker ventured into a different kind of reading and pursued some time for meditation and yoga. I learned to observe the parade of different "me" that constantly fluctuated within me. In one ayahuasca session, Mother Ayahuasca confronted me with this. She showed me the soft-spoken formal businessman in the office, side by side with the informal foul-spoken dude drinking beers with my close friends. She asked me who I was. The lesson pertained to the need to integrate my subpersonalities as much as possible to boost the advancement towards self-realization as I often prayed with such intention before my ayahuasca sessions.

Accepting the notion of subpersonalities within my SIE was not difficult because back in my college years during the 1970s, I participated in a psychology workshop based on Transactional Analysis therapy. In this therapeutic structure, the individual personality is viewed as three ego-states; our inner child, adult, and parent-like selves. The therapy aims to resolve emotional issues by negotiating between these parts, thus the name transactional. I realized that classical psychology has been attempting to understand and account for our multiple inner nature for a long time.

Subpersonalities are not to be confused with the innate survival instincts provided by our master program, as we all have these reactive parts of ourselves, which only await their opportunity to grab the driver's seat of your emotional car. Subpersonalities are specific patterns of behavior newly created by our self-adjusting master program to increase our chances of survival. When the quantum field patterns of our repetitive actions reach an adequate threshold, a thought-form is created and utilized automatically each time the repetitive action arises. Subpersonalities are often treated in classical psychology as dysfunctional. However, in reality, they are an inevitable fact of our adaptable human nature. Of course, there is an essential difference between subpersonalities and the dysfunctional psychiatric condition of multiple personality disorder [13] based on the substantially higher criteria required to be met—the qualitative difference of dissociation.

One of the most self-limiting illusions that deceive and derails us from our self-realization goals is probably the reinforced belief that we are indivisible, immutable, totally unitarian beings. When we realize that the contrary is true, besides being surprising, it can be disconcerting to many, to say the least. It is recommended to actively practice mindfulness in our daily lives to access a heightened awareness and watch our various subpersonalities in action. If our ego-self is not aligned within its SIE with the subconscious and soul selves, its subpersonalities may reach a point of acquiring excessive control over the ego-self.

Recognizing subpersonalities in ourselves and others around us can be very useful in our interactions with others, especially in our personal relationships. We can better understand our loved ones by realizing that some of their imperfections do not belong to the whole person but only to a part of them. We can also tactfully and constructively criticize others by highlighting their subpersonality and averting any feelings of a personal attack. For instance, I can say to my wife: "I hope your compulsive organizer doesn't get mad at me leaving this tool out of place for the whole day," or comments to that effect. It is more accurate to speak in this way, rather than implying the whole person is a compulsive organizer. Moreover, once you identify a subpersonality for what it is and can name it with a label, it becomes easier to recognize next time it triggers into action immediately. This heightened awareness aids in control the associated behavior by reminding yourself about the inclinations of the particular subpersonality.

Another exercise is to observe those often overlooked occasions when we talk to ourselves in our privacy. Who is talking to who? This is a powerful question that may uncover exciting aspects of yourself. It is a popular myth that is talking within yourself is a sign of insanity, and experiencing this can cause some people a great deal of distress. In some circumstances, such as in dementia, Alzheimer's, or psychiatric disorders, the extent of this inner chatter may become pathological. However, for most of us, it is a daily occurrence that causes no harm and indicates no pathology.

Our dreams can also reveal hidden subpersonalities. When a character in your dreams tells you information about anything that impresses you as the dreamer, it means another part of you is trying to communicate something to your dreaming ego-self. If you remember the content of the message, you may readily have a relevant clue to one of your subpersonalities.

A frequent occurrence at family gatherings or other festivities where alcohol is consumed generously is the scenario in which someone suddenly or gradually shifts personalities. We all have many stories about people that turn too affectionate, too sorrowful, or overly aggressive. Using subpersonalities as a frame of reference, we can understand how alcohol often numbs the ego-self and allows for subpersonalities to rise from the subconscious-self.

When the ego-self is subjected to trauma for a sustained period, the survival program bundles all the memories together and creates a new ego structure, a subpersonality. This subpersonality can remain latent for some time and may become active later in life when it can intrude and disturb the main ego-self. This is likely the case of people suffering from post-traumatic stress disorder ("PTSD"). Moreover, there may be more severe instances where two subpersonalities end up struggling for dominance. In some cases, a well-compartmentalized alter-ego, driven by a subpersonality, may take full control of the ego-self for specific periods. In these instances, however, we are considering a variety of psychiatric disorders.

Entities: Subpersonalities Gone Rogue

There was one subpersonality that I identified in my subconscious-self during my ayahuasca insights, which was associated with conspiracy theories. I developed this intellectual subpersonality during the late 1980s when I became fascinated with a little-known printed journal, during the pre-Internet years [14]. It was the first subscription magazine entirely dedicated to conspiracies. It was probably a significant genesis in the mind of many to the conspiracy theory movement that later went mainstream after the September 11th, 2001 event. Conspiracies, by definition, contain a strong element of paranoid thinking, and it was this ingredient that fueled my passion after the 9/11 event. This element began occupying a disproportionately large space of my psyche.

This was when I began to understand a different aspect of subpersonalities. I noticed them as a subconscious force that was driving my thoughts in a paranoid direction. After my first dieta in the Peruvian Amazon with Don Jose Campos in 2008, I had gained some clarity on the issue. Still, it took a few more years of self-observation to accept the unavoidable conclusion that subpersonalities may grow in strength to a point where they experience their self-realization. After all, it meant that my creation was awakening inside of my SIE, the same way I

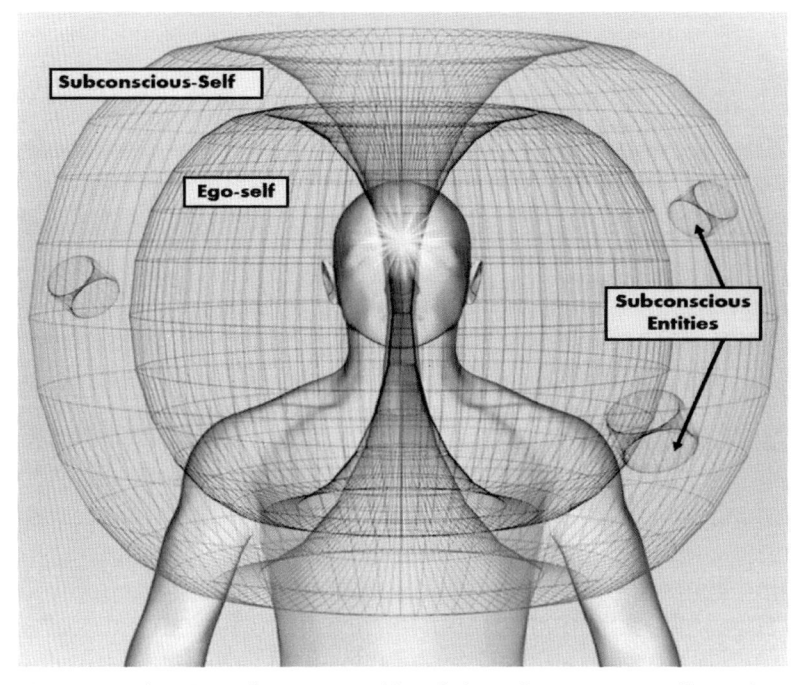

Fig. 10 – Conceptualization of our ego-self and the subconscious self in relation to our physical body. Note the small tours shaped structures representing entities that have detached from the main ego-self to become independent self-aware ego structures not controllable by the main ego-self. Addictions are the typical examples of rogue entities operating from the subconscious-self.

had awakened in my self-realization process with ayahuasca. My conspiratorial subpersonality had realized that it existed within my SIE. A subpersonality had gone rogue and rebelled against my ego-self. It was no longer under my absolute control. My ego-self could no longer deliberately separate this subpersonality from my field of conscious awareness. This subpersonality constantly irrupted my thoughts, bringing its recognizable vibration of subtle suspicion at every opportunity opposite mainstream news, national politics, and cultural evolution. This was my entity.

> **Entity** – a subpersonality that has become self-aware, gaining relative independence from the ego-self and operating under the survival program run by the subconscious-self as if being the ego-self itself. It cares about its own survival and not about the organism from which it feeds. A quantum parasite that learned how to hack the system.

Before going further, from the outset, let's dismiss the concept of 'entity' which has been portrayed in Hollywood movies, with all its scary special effects. More importantly, we should pay attention to the fallacy in the premise that entities are metaphysical structures that arise externally to possess a victim and render them powerless to the entity's control. We also consider the idea of foreign spiritual attachments, as described by devotees of mediumship practices, as irrelevant and beyond the scope of the present work.

That said, within the quantum model of the psyche, an entity is a rogue subpersonality that has realized its existence in the quantum ecosystem of the SIE. Here are some characteristics of the entities:

- Inadvertently created by the ego-self, as a result of the loss of control over a previously well-behaved subpersonality.
- Created by excessive feeding of repetitive behavior, primarily geared toward pleasure-seeking and pain avoidance. Although this is a normal function of the survival program, in these scenarios, it is the entity itself, rather than the ego-self, which is initiating the behavior.
- Contrary to the entity, a regular subpersonality holds some independence but is subject to significant control by the ego-self. An entity may be analogized as a rebellious government faction creating its own "deep state within a country" or "shadow government."
- Being a creation of the ego-self, the entity has all the same features and resources. Entities are as intelligent as their creators. Hence, it is nearly impossible to "outsmart" them. Remember that similar to the Creator in the Bible, [15] the human psyche creates subpersonalities and entities in "our own image and likeness."
- Entities have a narrow field of action as they were created by the over-supply of life force generated by very specific behaviors. Classic examples of entities are all kinds of addictions: sexual, food, codependence, the list is almost endless as it delves into the weird and bizarre.
- Entities become increasingly intense as long as they continue to be nourished by the behavior that created them.
- Entities usually generate enormous amounts of neurochemicals such as dopamine, serotonin, and glutamate in the brain, which produce the rush of excitement in the ego-self. This further empowers the entity. For this

reason, the first step in removing an entity from the SIE is to appeal to the power of our soul-self and stop feeding the entity with the behavior it craves. As many have done before, entity removal by starvation or depriving it of the "food" it desires, is the bravest and hardest route to spiritual healing.

- The ego-self in general, but the subpersonalities and entities in particular, are programmed to survive at all costs and will initiate any actions necessary to persevere, even if it means resorting to behaviors that are ultimately self-destructive to the organism.

The main reason why psychological wellbeing and personal fulfillment are so difficult to attain is that entities covertly operate from our subconscious-self, and search for opportunities to intercept the ego-self's conscious state to provoke the behavior that feeds them. Entities are self-aware thought-forms that become stronger with the quantum ripples created by behavior patterns that produced them. These quantum moves trigger the activity of neurochemical production, including dopamine, oxytocin, endorphins, and serotonin, which are all closely associated with the pleasure-reward system of the survival program.

Addiction is not a sign of weakness of character or lack of will power. It occurs when the desire circuits in the brain are triggered by entities. This plunges the individual into a pathological state of overstimulation. Brain circuits that evolved for the crucial purpose of keeping us alive are overtaken by the self-aware entities and repurposed to enslave the ego-self into its robot-like object of pleasure. For example, Mary Smith's food addiction entity captures her view of a sugar-coated pastry while she walks through to an airport gate to catch a flight. The entity knows she has an hour of waiting idly before boarding. It doesn't care whether she is hungry or not; it just wants the opportunity of pleasure generated by the neurochemicals released after she eats anything. To this end, the entity launches an attack. From its workstation, located in the subconscious quantum structure, it initiates a process that says: "go ahead and eat that delicious pastry even if you are not hungry. It will increase our chances of staying alive and healthy in the future, who knows when food will be available next?". This statement would make sense of Mary's ego-self, who is also subject to the very robust survival program after many generations of ancestors who lived most of their lives on the brink of starvation. The DNA remembers and Mary's ego-self, not being aligned within her own SIE, quickly succumbs to the desire to eat the pastry.

How did Mary develop this weakness in eating without being hungry? Does this behavior have anything to do with her upbringing or beliefs gained later in life?

For a more detailed illustration of entity creation, let's examine the specific case on one of the participants in our observational sample, Rusty Steel. Rusty was a marketing director of a major corporation in Western Florida and had been working with ayahuasca to find the roots of his alcoholism. He began secretly drinking beer with his middle school friends at the age of thirteen. By the time Rusty was in high school, he had worked at a supermarket, and every payday, he purchased a half-gallon of cheap wine to share with his co-workers after their shift. With repetitive behavior that produced excitement and fun, Rusty had created a subpersonality associated with alcohol consumption, and he was comfortable with it. In college, he used to binge-drink at the wild parties of his fraternity house. Once he began earning good money as a young marketing specialist, he remembers ordering a bottle or two of fine wine while inviting clients for lunch. His wife and some close friends occasionally confronted him with his habit, but Rusty was in denial. His alcoholic subpersonality had gradually turned into the powerful entity of alcohol addiction. This entity had practically possessed him. His main ego-self and his alcoholic entity were operating in harmonic resonance. Due to this, Rusty found nothing wrong with his behavior, and he was in complete denial of the existence of any problem. When confronted, he used to justify his behavior with arguments developed by his entity such as: "I like to drink, there is nothing wrong with that, it's a stress reliever, it's legal, it's social, I can handle it, it doesn't interfere with my job, I'm always on time at the office, why you keep bothering me with this?".

This is the signature of a powerful entity conducting Rusty's subconscious self to the point that Rusty's ego-self was entirely convinced of the 'normality' of his behavior. Rusty's entity and ego-self were close friends and supported each other.

Entities tend to distort our ego's self-perception, as metaphorically described in our onion of self-perception illustration in Figure 2. From their privileged and concealed position, entities effectively dominate the ego-self. This explains the high level of difficulty found when attempting to change deep-rooted behaviors such as smoking, over-eating, and other addictive behaviors. The less a person is aware of the existence of different entities, and the interplay between them, the more anxious and agitated they become. In conflict, subpersonalities become increasingly less functional, prompting depression or psychological dysfunction, and perhaps, ultimately creating a crisis in the person's physical or emotional health.

Unfortunately, in our pursual of happiness, our survival program always conceals our inner conflicts and contradictions under layers of amnesia in an attempt to protect us. Subsequently, we wonder why we continue to behave in ways that are seemingly against our real intention. Our ego-self is naïvely conscious of its self-realization goals, while the survival programs dwell in the subconscious-self running our lives. As hard as it may sound, such is the paradox of our human condition.

The social, cultural, and family conditions that prevail today for a newly born baby are clearly in conflict with the environment expected by our master program. If you mail-order and receive factory-fresh, battery-operated, electronic equipment while living in a high moisture, high heat, environment like the Amazon forest, we must expect a short useful life of the device. As we will examine in future chapters, the conditions experienced during embryonic development and early childhood have an overwhelming impact on adult life and predispose us to behaviors originated in our subconscious-self instead of behaviors consciously originated by a well-aligned ego-self.

Since the conditions under which we are raised are far from optimal, our survival program has no other option but to continually encrypt dissonant memories and create subpersonalities to manage the crisis and relieve the ego-self from the underlying stress. In this way, the ego-self is provided with the breathing space necessary to execute critical survival functions. Hopefully, when we reach a time and place where more favorable circumstances arise, we may have the opportunity to reconstruct ourselves more healthily. Unfortunately, for most of us, such circumstances never materialize. Meanwhile, the subpersonalities begin transforming into rogue entities without our conscious awareness, and continue to strive in the background, tightly wired in the old traumas encrypted in our holographic memory banks. These often go unchallenged for the majority of our lives, even if they manifest in self- destructive and unhealthy ways. These subpersonalities and entities are the actors of behavior patterns that keep appearing and playing their role repeatedly throughout the drama of our lives.

This is where an ayahuasca spiritual advisor comes in to perform the role of precious assistance. Ayahuasca has the capacity to put a stop to this cycle of pain and mediocrity in our lives. Without the effective "shock treatment" of ayahuasca to the subpersonalities and entities, the survival program will continue to build more complexity around the existing twisted structures, rather than going back to re-construct its faulty foundations. Unfortunately, the master program incorrectly assumes that environmental conditions are ideal or substantially better than the ones found at birth.

It seems that the human species is designed to live in highly stable conditions, but we have not yet reached the point of providing this for future generations. Survival programs have succeeded in preventing our extinction so far, but the imperative command to return home is almost impossible to follow without conscious intervention. The psychedelic substances found in nature, ayahuasca included, are the gift of evolution for humankind to self-heal and empower itself to pursue the ultimate imperative command of our human existence; the self-realization of its spiritual nature. For this reason, I believe the psychedelic renaissance of this century can build the foundation for a new era where spiritual healing could reach the masses and create better conditions for a better Planet Earth.

Embrace The Paradignm Shift

The only path to psychological wellbeing and self-realization is to evolve from the duality-based to a holistic-based belief system. Think about it as a long-term, transformational shift in your paradigm of reality. This is a gradual process that may take years of patient observation, awakening, and self-programming. It consists of acknowledging the soul's mission in our physical life to evolve beyond the survival stage into the self-realization stage of our master program. Remember that self-realization is not an automatic process; it doesn't happen by itself unless we add our conscious will into the formula. On the other hand, the survival program runs automatically in the sense that your only conscious effort involves following the survival instincts that arise from within you. Self-realization requires a conscious conquering of the resistance from the subconscious-self, which has dominated the battlefield during the majority of our lives.

Since the first part of your life has been guided by the ego's principles and beliefs, we may consciously start guiding it toward the soul principles and beliefs as we travel toward the second act of our lives. Here are the five guiding principles of our ego-self, which prevail in our survival stage and their counterparts to be consciously developed for our self- realization.

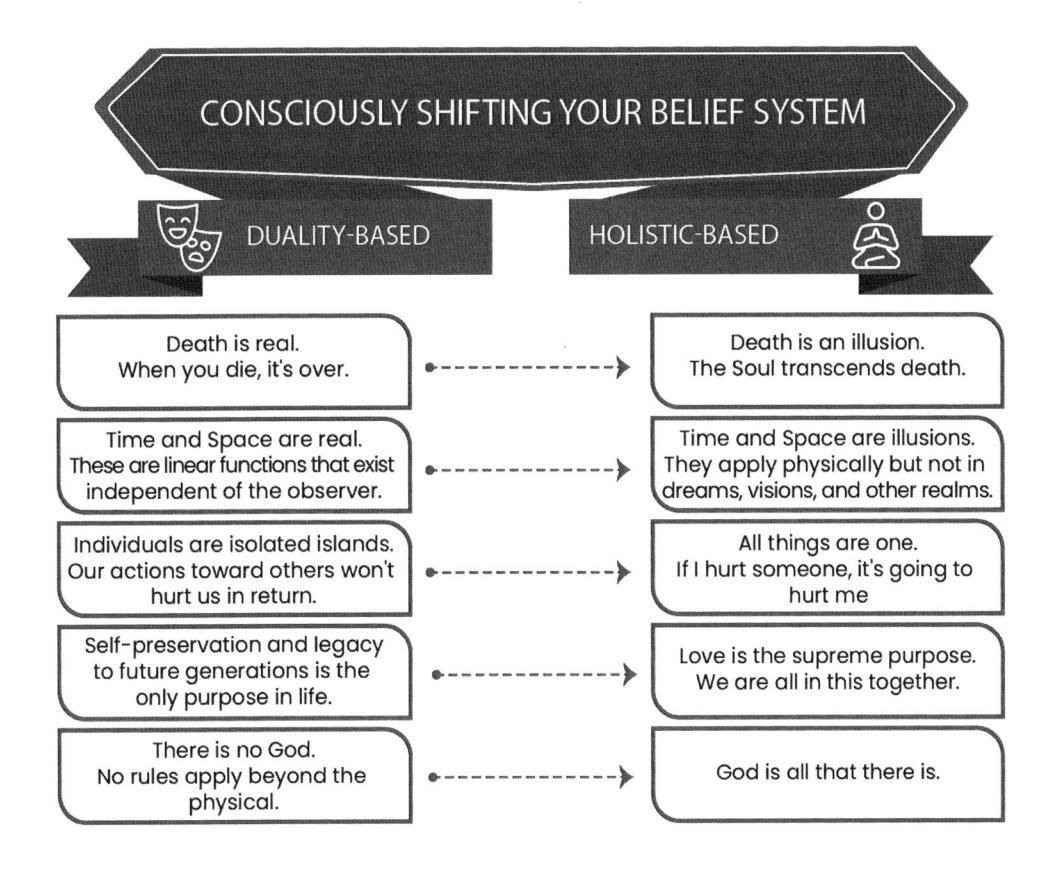

CONSCIOUSLY SHIFTING YOUR BELIEF SYSTEM

DUALITY-BASED	HOLISTIC-BASED
Death is real. When you die, it's over.	Death is an illusion. The Soul transcends death.
Time and Space are real. These are linear functions that exist independent of the observer.	Time and Space are illusions. They apply physically but not in dreams, visions, and other realms.
Individuals are isolated islands. Our actions toward others won't hurt us in return.	All things are one. If I hurt someone, it's going to hurt me
Self-preservation and legacy to future generations is the only purpose in life.	Love is the supreme purpose. We are all in this together.
There is no God. No rules apply beyond the physical.	God is all that there is.

CHAPTER EIGHT

BRAIN & BEHAVIOR PROGRAMMING

Ayahuasca and Brain Neuroplasticity

Throughout my ayahuasca facilitator experience, I have witnessed dozens of spontaneous physical healing cases. I believe that these are the early indications of a promising future of improved effectiveness, efficiency, and predictability of ayahuasca healing. By considering the design of spiritual healing therapies and how behavioral patterns operate, we can develop reliable protocols to effectively treat anxiety, obsessive compulsions, addictions, depression, PTSD, and various psychiatric conditions. We have demonstrated that it is possible to use creative visualization techniques during the peak ayahuasca experience of well-designed and assisted sessions to heal a variety of dysfunctions.

During my personal ayahuasca sessions, I have practiced conscious visualization techniques with excellent results. Once the specific area of work had been identified, the deliberate intervention during the ayahuasca experience made an enormous difference in the outcome of the session. However, my recurrent question was why this reprogramming was significantly easier to achieve with ayahuasca assistance and not without it.

There are two interrelated answers to that question. Firstly, we have the aspect of experience and practice. As practitioners engage in more ayahuasca sessions over time, the healing process becomes increasingly efficient. This increasing experience allows practitioners to learn what to expect and skillfully surrender to the ayahuasca journey. For example, with practice, encrypted memories begin to arise unexpectedly. These memories open new opportunities for healing and expansion of consciousness, mainly when these are adequately processed and released.

The second aspect is a consequence of the first and is related to a process within the brain called 'neuroplasticity.' Neuroplasticity has been described, in the most general terms as "the science of how the brain changes its structure and function in response to the input." There are two critical aspects of this definition.

Firstly, the brain can physiologically change, both structurally and functionally, in response to experience and the environment. This unique ability is unlike any other organ of the body. More specifically, neuroplasticity enables the formation and creation of new neural pathways, the strengthening of synaptic connections between neurons, and also the depletion of rarely used synapses and neural connections. This process takes place in an environmentally dependent manner, meaning that brain structures and functional architecture can be altered by our life experiences. These adaptations can generally occur in response to long-term stimuli or experiences, such as when we practice a new skill or regularly face similar environmental challenges. However, large-scale neuroanatomical and function changes can be elicited by a single event, such as trauma or damage.

Second, the phrase "in response to input," speaks directly to the fact that significant changes in the brain take place primarily in response to challenging experiences or environmental stimuli. Any task that is familiar, automatic, or easy, does not challenge your brain and, as such, doesn't elicit large-scale alterations to brain structure or function. However, activities that are difficult and challenging are likely to catalyze more substantial changes to neural networks.

It appears that when ayahuasca inhibits the Default Mode Network, [1] which we describe further in this chapter, it opens the gates and the ego-self gains more conscious access to its subconscious and soul selves within its SIE. A significant amount of realignment occurs at the quantum field level and triggers homologous neural activity, which contributes to functional and neuroanatomical changes. When discussing neuroplasticity, Donald Hebb coined the classic phrase "neurons that fire together wire together." This means the higher the levels of synaptic activity within a neural circuit, the stronger that circuit becomes. Essentially, the connections between neurons become strengthened with increased activity. Subsequently, networks of neurons can be enhanced with frequent repetition. This is why "practice makes perfect" concerning knowledge retention and skill learning. The process is also the underpinning mechanism of habits; the more routinely a behavioral pattern is followed, the more habitual it becomes due to the strengthening of neural networks that underlie these behaviors. This explains the power of entities in forcing behavior into the ego-self and the challenges encountered in their removal.

It is essential to point out that neuroplasticity or simply "plasticity" is not an occasional state in the nervous system; it is a continuously on-going process. This is because the brain is an incredibly adaptive organ in response to changes in the environment and not just through injury recovery. From an evolutionary perspective, this mechanism of adaptation has likely aided the ability of humans to survive and thrive in a wide variety of challenging environments and situations. As neurologist Dr. David Perlmutter noted, " Neuroplasticity provides us with a brain that can adapt not only to changes inflicted by damage but allows adaptation to any and all experiences and changes we may encounter." [2] These changes occur in the anatomy through input to the neural system, which may originate in the quantum field.

This model assumes that well designed and executed psychedelic-assisted therapies trigger reconfiguration of quantum structures, which subsequently promote physical neuroplasticity. The fact that changes derived from spiritual healing experiences are relatively permanent tends to support this assertion. Another supportive idea is the robust observation that cognitive and, in particular, visualization exercises serve to stimulate dendritic arborization, which, as the name suggests, is the growth of dendritic spines similar to the branches of a tree. Dendritic spines serve as the small pieces of machinery which typically receive information from the synapses and axons of neighboring neurons. The spines help to strengthen synapses and transmit electrical signals, or "information," onward to the neuron's cell body for further processing and communication with other surrounding cells. Dendritic spine morphology can rapidly change in response to electrical or chemical stimulation, which neuroscientists believe changes the synaptic activity of neurons and subsequent network activity.

In 2008, neuroscientists Jeffrey Kleim and Theresa Jones published an article [3] describing the ten principles of neuroplasticity as applied to the rehabilitation after brain damage. As these principles describe the dynamics of physical neuronal changes, I found that they also closely correlate to the dynamics occurring in the quantum structure. Given the potential causal relationship between neuronal physiology and quantum structure, the congruency between them is unsurprising. Let's review the principles of neuroplasticity in detail to confirm that nine out of the ten are also principles of ayahuasca-assisted spiritual healing techniques.

1. "Use It or Lose It": "Neural circuits not actively engaged in task performance for an extended period of time begin to degrade." This has its well-known equivalent in quantum structures, as it relates to all sorts of learning skills, which is the genesis of the popular term. This is why skills and abilities can fade without practice.

2. "Use It and Improve It": "Training that drives a specific brain function can lead to enhancement of that function." At the quantum structure level, this translates into "practice makes perfection" applicable to any physical skill or mental

ability.

3. "Specificity" "The nature of the training experience dictates the nature of the plasticity." From a treatment standpoint, specificity highlights the importance of tailoring an activity or exercise to produce a result in specific circuitry. This is precisely what the quantum model of the psyche aims to achieve—providing the hypothetical framework to be able to target specific psychological issues with visualization and other techniques.

4. "Repetition Matters" "Induction of plasticity requires sufficient repetition." One of the challenges for ayahuasca spiritual advisors revolves around estimating how many ayahuasca sessions are needed to experience permanent spiritual healing. The truth is, we don't know exactly, but we do know from experience with our observational sample that it may range from one single session to several dozens.

5. "Intensity Matters" "Induction of plasticity requires sufficient intensity." This principle is somewhat self-explanatory, as intensity is one of the unquestionably defining characteristics of the ayahuasca experience.

6. "Time Matters" "Different forms of plasticity occur at different times during recovery." This principle is based on the idea that the sooner treatments are applied after brain injury, the faster the recovery. This principle doesn't apply to the quantum structures as psychedelic-assisted sessions for spiritual healing have consistently been proven to work with issues that originate as far back as prenatal traumas.

7. "Salience Matters" "The training experience must be sufficiently salient to induce plasticity." What the person learns from recovery training and the importance and impact of this experience can have a substantial effect on their recovery. This is another principle of fundamental application to ayahuasca and psychedelic-assisted therapies. It has been well established that the impressions and memories from ayahuasca-assisted spiritual healing experience cause profound feelings in patients and are incredibly long-lasting.

8. "Age Matters" "Training-induce plasticity occurs more readily in younger brains." Although younger brains are generally more plastic and adaptable to change than older brains, we have found that older people in our observational sample can experience profound changes in their view of life and interpretation of their life events. Reconciliation with their idea of God and with the fear of death are frequent themes in older participants.

9. "Transference or Generalization" "Plasticity in response to one training experience can enhance acquisition of similar behaviors." This is another frequently experienced situation, where participants not only resolve their specifically targeted issues but find the applicability of these lessons to many other areas of their lives as well.

10. "Interference" "Plasticity in response to one training experience can impede the acquisition of similar behaviors." This is a negative side-effect of brain injury recovery training that doesn't apply to our analogy with the quantum structures. We have not identified any interference effect of spiritual healing with other cognitive functions of the participant. Speculatively, we may correlate this principle with the temporary inconveniences that some participants experience after ayahuasca sessions, as described in Chapter 1.

This Neural Network is the Gate to the Soul

Ayahuasca became prominent within the American psychedelic culture through the early psychonauts in the second half of the 20th century. Concurrently, scientists investigated the chemical composition and physiological properties of the substance. Research progressed at a reasonable rate concerning identifying the psychoactive alkaloids of DMT in the Psychotria Viridis and the harmine family of alkaloids in the Barnisteriopsis Caapi. The surprising inhibitory relationship between one compound and the action of another was also quickly uncovered. This revealed the mechanism by which DMT enters the bloodstream unharmed by the destructive gastric process. After such initial breakthroughs, the psychopharmacology research community made further progress in understanding the sacred medicine over the following twenty years and demonstrated its healing potential with robust scientific results. Meanwhile, psychedelic research began to diversify into psilocybin, LSD, and MDMA. This was mostly driven by their single-molecule simplicity, which substantially eased experimental design. Moreover, this molecular simplicity contributed to a higher possibility of acceptance and approval by the medical establishment for the treatment of certain medical conditions. Following this, an unexpected discovery in neuroscience was reported, and this expanded the understanding of how psychedelics chemically induce mystical experiences.

Since 2009, on the Hemmersmith campus of Imperial College in West London, a team led by neuroscientist Robin Carhart-Harris has been working to identify the "neural correlates" or physical counterparts of the psychedelic experience. By injecting volunteers with LSD and psilocybin and then using a variety of brain scanning technologies, his team has given provided the first glimpses of what ego dissolution, or hallucinations, may 'look like' in the brain as it unfolds in real-time.

There is no one better than Michael Pollan to tell us all about this discovery, as he describes it in his bestseller "How To Change Your Mind," from who I generously quote here:

"They had discovered that psilocybin reduces brain activity, with the falloff concentrated in one particular brain network that at the time they knew little about the default mode network (DMN). This [neural] network forms a critical and centrally located hub of brain activity that links parts of the cerebral cortex to deeper and older structures involved in memory and emotion. The discovery of the DMN in 2001 was actually a scientific accident, a happy by-product of the use of brain-imaging technologies in brain research. The typical experiment begins by establishing a "resting state" baseline for neural activity as the volunteer sits quietly in the scanner, awaiting whatever tests the researcher has in store. It was noticed that several areas in the brain exhibited heightened activity precisely when the subjects were doing nothing mentally. This was the brain's "default mode," the network of brain structures that light up with activity when there are no demands on our attention, and we have no mental task to perform.

The DMN appears to play a role in the creation of mental constructs or projections, the most important of which is the construct we call the self or ego. This is why some neuroscientists call it the "me" network. The more precipitous the drop-off in blood flow and oxygen consumption in the DMN, the more likely the volunteer was to report the loss of a sense of self.

The mystical experience may just be what it feels like when you deactivate the DMN. This can be achieved in any number of ways: through psychedelics and meditation and perhaps other mind-altering techniques. But whatever it happens, taking this particular network off-line may give us access to extraordinary states of consciousness--moments of oneness or ecstasy that no less wondrous for having a physical cause." [4]

The DMN is described as a director of the orchestra of brain activity. This essential character in the brain correlates to the door to the human soul. This suggests the possibility that at the peak of the ayahuasca experience, the director is removed from the stage of consciousness, allowing the soul to manifest freely with every musical instrument chaotically playing at its own rhythm. This validates the experience of thousands of ayahuasca users who agree with the idea that the ego-self is temporarily disabled and followed by a period of random expressions of emotions, memories, visions, and other sensory experiences. The orchestra director (DMN) correlates with the presence of the ego-self, which usually exercises inhibitory influence over other brain regions. Notably, this includes the limbic regions involved in emotion and memory, similarly as Freud conceived the ego as keeping the anarchic forces of instincts in check.

This reminds me of Rene Descartes, who believed that the "seat of the soul" resided in the pineal gland. He would have rejoiced to have learned that the "gate to the soul" instead, was only a few centimeters away. The DMN, the orchestra director, the disabled ego-self quantum structure, or "the gate to the soul," as I prefer to call it, is the next step in understanding how ayahuasca may accomplish her magnificent "miracles."

Considering the presented information, we may speculate that neuroscience has unveiled the neural correlates of Freud's ego, the notion of repression, and the healing principle of ayahuasca and psychedelics. The understanding of the brain mechanisms which underpin spiritual healing is of great value to the spiritual healing advisor. Hence, this should be studied in further detail and supplemented with additional reading of the increasing flow of scientific literature being published on the subject.

The great value of having this "gate to the soul" wide open during an ayahuasca session is that the ego-self gets the opportunity to re-process information. When we consciously process a memory or feeling for the second time, it can be reviewed, re-interpreted, and re-classified in entirely new and meaningful ways. How an experience was processed in the first instance will not remain the same, as the subconscious connections and associations with other parts of the soul will shift permanently. Spiritual healing encompasses the reprocessing, at the soul level, of experiences which have previously been neglected to ensure survival at the expense of the self-realization.

An Inconvenient Truth: Early Behavior Imprinting

Throughout my years of ayahuasca facilitator, I started to note a substantial number of testimonials with a similar pattern started to accrue. Participants made detailed descriptions of the difficulties they were seeking to heal with ayahuasca before the session. Following the session, participants shared intimate details of their enlightening visions and messages. The connection of their current difficulties and their early childhood traumas were evident, as it would be to any reasonable ayahuasca spiritual advisor. For illustration purposes, let's review a couple of cases from the dozens in my collection.

While in session, a young woman experienced a strong emotional connection with the excitement of her expecting mother preparing her future bedroom with decoration, clothing, and toys. Ayahuasca has taken the participant under the skin of her mother and transported her back to a time before her birth. The problem was that everything was themed in the color blue; she was expecting a boy as she already had two daughters. The participant felt her mother's disappointment immediately after her birth when she found about her being another girl. After the session, she understood many things about her early childhood relationship with her sisters; she never was able to bond with them as another sister; she felt different. Many facets of her life made sense after this experience, including her gender confusion as a teenager and her sexuality as a lesbian.

In another case, we had a successful entrepreneur that saw how his mother attempted to abort her pregnancy numerous times. He saw that his mother needed this to appear as natural abortion because she was married and suspected that her pregnancy was the product of a secret love affair. She failed in her goal during the first few weeks. When her husband discovered she was pregnant, she reluctantly accepted her complicated situation and moved forward to convince her husband that it was his future child in order to earn his support. His mother hoped that the child resembled her husband's physical appearance after birth. Nine months full of maternal fear and insecurity resulted in a child that developed a congenital testicular malformation. Notably, a conflict in the reproductive area of the mother (via sexual infidelity), combined with a sustained period of fearful emotions throughout fetal development, crystallized a congenital disability in the reproductive area of her child. After the session, he was in awe. Of course, this explained his reproductive sterility and his life-long distrust for women. He had never married and channeled all his creative energy into pursuing business ventures. A few months after the passing of his father, the participant confronted his mother regarding this subject, and she admitted to these actions.

We have many stories like these in our observational case studies. One after the other, we find strong correlations between their freshly retrieved prenatal or early childhood memories and the troubling circumstances that developed after that.

What have we learned from these cases? Psychology and neuroscience are beginning to explore this vital area of research. Here, we are discussing the concept of limbic imprinting. Learning about the mechanics of limbic imprinting has been one of the most fulfilling experiences in my ayahuasca path. Helping participants to spiritually heal from the core of the soul resulting in permanent changes is the fuel that keeps me striving in the healing mission of my work. Understanding the unparalleled power of ayahuasca to release the hidden mysteries of our pre-programmed filters of perception drives me to share it with the world, with the hope that others may continue to map this uncharted territory.

> **Limbic Imprinting** - the automatic function of the nervous system to absorb and memorize all our sensations in a non-cognitive manner. This takes place during the whole formative period, from the moment of conception, through birth, and the first few years of childhood.

The limbic system is the central station of basic functions and survival behaviors, such as food gathering for nourishment and preparing a safe place to sleep. However, to understand this better, we must be aware that these basic behaviors and motivations can influence more sophisticated behavior and may inconspicuously operate with ulterior motives to advance survival objectives. A modern example of this is an individual getting married for strictly financial reasons (safety) or sexual satisfaction without much interest in love-based bonding (reproduction). Our survival strategies may unconsciously generate other subtle behaviors to achieve these primary objectives.

Limbic imprinting is a vital function of the human brain that currently lacks specific scientific research. There is a vast body of knowledge about the biology of emotions, but the field of psychology has not yet developed an affirmative quest to explore the effects of limbic imprinting on adult life behavior. This area is relatively new, and we may find more explanations in pop-culture psychology publications than in research/scientific studies.

The limbic system is a network of brain regions that underpin a substantial portion of our behavioral and emotional responses. It is particularly dominant with regard to survival-related behaviors: for example, feeding, reproduction, and caring for our young, and fight or flight responses. The limbic structure is composed of two primary structures, the amygdala and the hippocampus. However, the network encompasses additional regions with specific functions. These are the thalamus, known as the 'sensory gate' which filters incoming sensory information. The hypothalamus, a small region that is involved in the production of hormones and the regulation of metabolic function. Finally, the basal ganglia, a group of subcortical nuclei composed of the striatum, globus pallidus, ventral pallidum, substantia nigra and subthalamic nucleus. These basal ganglia components act collectively to influence reward processing, habit formation, movement, and learning.

The hippocampus is another torus-derived, heart-shaped organ that is present in a pair like many other structures in the brain and body. It is known as the 'memory center' of our brains due to its characterized role in memory encoding and processing. Here, the initial mechanics of our quantum holographic episodic memories are physically formed and cataloged to be uploaded into long-term storage in the quantum field of our SIE. Neuroscientists suggest that these memories may be 'physically' stored in other parts of the cortex, at synapses or within extracellular matrix structures such as perineuronal nets. Note that these are the biological correspondences of much higher processes occurring at the soul level, as explained earlier. Science can only describe what occurs physically.

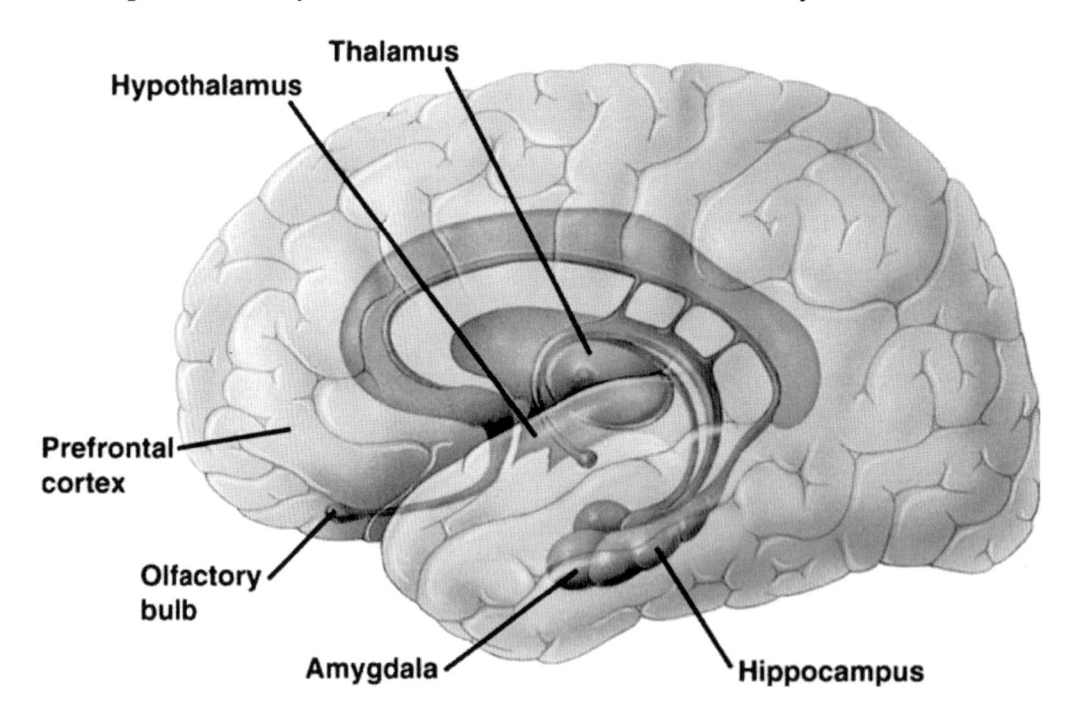

The hippocampus also helps us associate memories with various senses. The association between the Christmas season and the scent of pine trees would be forged here, as well as the nostalgia triggered by your favorite oldie love song.

The hippocampus is one of the few regions of the brain where new neurons can be derived from newly born adult stem cells. This process is called neurogenesis and is the basis of one type of brain plasticity. It is unsurprising that this primarily occurs in a region which vital for learning new things. Relevant research has been conducted showing the actual mechanisms of neuroplasticity, which highlights that established neuronal network connections can be 'rewired' throughout the life course. This type of neuroplasticity changes the strength and sometimes the existence of synapses that neurons use to communicate. Subsequently, new concepts can be learned and memories made via a process known as 'long-term potentiation,' whereby synapses are continuously active and excited.

Conversely, memories can be diminished or forgotten when synapses undergo sustained inactivity. This sustained inactivity weakens synapses, and they can eventually be eliminated, a process referred to as 'long-term depression.' These processes take place throughout their entire life, meaning the strength and existence of neuronal connections which underlie our thoughts and memories are activity-dependent.

Manipulating your brain via processes that enhance neurogenesis and modulate neuroplasticity is a viable way of seeking long-lasting emotional healing. This is precisely what ayahuasca enables. Ayahuasca does so by allowing access to painful memories and traumas, and subsequently, enabling ayahuasca practitioners to rebuild the existing dysfunctional neuron pathways consciously. This procedure can harness the power of long-term potentiation and long-term depression to redesign synaptic structures that underlie destructive and damaging thought and behavior patterns. This is where the proposed model of the psyche comes with valuable contributions.

Considering the monumental impact of limbic imprinting across the lifespan of a human, one may have expected a greater scientific interest in the subject sooner. Never-the-less there is now a growing body of high-quality neuroscience literature from which can draw valuable references. Over the past few decades, neuroscientists have sought to understand the basis of brain development and how this relates to the complex interactions between genetic and environmental factors. Throughout this research, it has become apparent that much of what determines our adult proclivities or behavioral patterns are imprinted during early development in utero and at early post-natal stages. This work has become particularly advanced in the understanding of psychiatric disorders such as schizophrenia. At first, this may appear curious, considering that schizophrenia is generally onset in late adolescence or adulthood. Despite this, neuroscientists now term the condition as a "neurodevelopmental disorder." It is now well understood that trauma, including maternal stress, infection, or malnutrition, during embryonic development, can disrupt brain development to increase this risk of psychiatric disorders. If this trauma is coupled with a genetic predisposition, we find the odds rations of disorders such as schizophrenia dramatically increase. [5]

Although there have been a variety of advances in neuroscience, a great deal of these complex mechanisms and interactions remain to be discovered. This is especially true in psychology, where we have seen comparatively less work in this area. However, we can draw upon the experiences of doctors and psychologists that, based on practical experience rather than theoretical medical training, have realized and investigated the vast amount of unusual anecdotal accounts of their pregnant patients. Let's refer to some of them briefly.

Art Janov, Ph.D. (1924–2017) was the American psychotherapist who wrote "Imprints: The Lifelong Effects of the Birth Experience." One of the reviews of the book says that his work: "was the result of over twenty years of research on the birth and other early traumas which are engraved into individuals' physiologic and neurological systems. Such birth imprints can later shape personality and physiology. They can determine how long we will live and what inflictions we will suffer later in life."

Dr. David Chamberlain, Ph.D.; (1928-1914) was a Californian psychologist who lectured on birth psychology in over twenty countries. He wrote the book "The Mind of Your Newborn Baby" and later wrote an excellent paper on the subject: "Babies are not What We Thought: Call for a New Paradigm." In the latter, he concludes: "Because infants of all ages manifest intelligence and are learning from their experiences with us, providers of physical care should always consider the effect of a procedure on the baby's emotions and mind. Let us think mind, not just body. In closing, infants are much more than we thought. Nineteenth-century science was materialistic in viewing the baby as body, brain, and reflex material. The 21st-century view of babies will, I believe, focus on their sensations, emotions, sense of self, personality, communication ability, mind, and consciousness. This major paradigm shift is urgently needed." [6]

Thomas Verny, MD, is a psychiatrist and academic who has taught in several educational institutes, including Harvard University. The Pre-and Perinatal Journal, which he founded in 1983, has established him as one of the world's leading authorities on the effect of the prenatal and early postnatal environment on personality development. In 1989 he wrote "The Scientific Basis of Pre- and Peri-Natal Psychology" This paper deals with the significant parameters of Pre- and Peri-Natal Psychology from a research perspective. He extensively researched the development and function of the fetal central nervous system and reached conclusions about the effect of perinatal trauma on personality development.

Elena Tonetti-Vladimirova is another active proponent of limbic imprinting who did not arise from a behavioral or neuroscience institute or university. Instead, after immigrating from Russia during the Soviet era, she has spent most of her life promoting healthy birth rearing. I casually bumped into the fantastic work of Elena Tonetti-Vladimirova while researching the subject in my quest for understanding the numerous ayahuasca testimonials at hand.

Her work is focused on the improvement of healthy birthing practices. Her accurate observations regarding birth traumas and adult life difficulties bring forward strong correlations with our ayahuasca work. Moreover, this work is corroborated by multiple, large-scale epidemiological studies that have shown that birthing complications (such as emergency c-section, prematurity, preeclampsia, and use of forceps) are correlated with a significantly increased risk of psychiatric disorder later in life. Direct experimental neuroscience research is beginning to support these findings. This indicates that this type of early-life trauma leaves a significant and long-lasting imprint on the individuals – one which may become apparent through behavioral and psychological patterns later in life.

Elena, along with the other experts mentioned, has observed the phenomenon from the gestational and perinatal perspective, while realizing the consequences projecting into the future of the person's life. Our ayahuasca work has been seeing the person's current difficulties and exploring all the way regressively back to birth and prenatal states to find rational explanations. Existing perinatal research undoubtedly supports our quantum model and helps us to grasp a fundamental understanding of the potentially dire consequences of limbic imprinting in our behavior as adults.

Let's carefully examine this fascinating area. The holographic memory concept is entirely appropriate to describe the creation of a baby in the mother's womb. Think of a mother creating a new human being inside of her. Does it make sense to speculate with a certain level of confidence that this creature is a holographic model of the mother? Translating this into Newtonian terms would result in the question: could the production of an organism using both mother's and father's DNA be influenced by the manufacturing process at the factory? Tonetti's view of fetus formation describes it as follows:

"Birth should not be taken out of the context of Life. Birth is like a hologram; it reflects everything that happened in a woman's life. It reflects her cultural background, her behavioral patterns, her belief system, her female lineage history, and her sexual history. Also, this hologram includes her relationship with the world in general and with herself. " [7]

The wisdom of our elders in all cultures knows this inherently. This wisdom has been present for centuries; our grandparents know this. However, science has lagged behind in accepting and incorporating this fundamental truth. One simplified example comes from well-known Bruce Lipton, who in his celebrated book "The Biology of Belief" acknowledges the terrible reality of the effects of childhood traumas in the adult's physical health as well as psychological wellbeing:

"Statistical correlations reveal a direct connection between traumatic childhood experiences and a wide variety of health issues, including obesity, coronary artery disease, chronic pulmonary disease, cancer, alcoholism, depression, drug use, mental health problems, and teen pregnancies. Interference with developing behavioral processes can result in an adverse impact on adult health in either of two ways: (i) by inflicting cumulative damage over time, or (ii) by embedding destructive behaviors in the young mind that are only activated in adult life situation. In either case, there can be a lag time in years before early environmental disturbances manifest a disease. For example, depressed adults with a history of childhood adults are twice as likely to develop cardiovascular disease than depressed individuals with no history of juvenile maltreatment." [8]

If we understand the formation of the fetus as a hologram of the mother, we must reach the unavoidable conclusion that babies are not a 50-50 product of their parents. Both parents contribute equally in terms of genetic composition, but it is the mother who retains full epigenetic control of which of those genes activate and how they activate. We have to remember that from the moment of conception, the cell division of the zygote, and its transition to an embryo, the future baby is already immersed in the mother's quantum field. The influence of the father is nowhere to be found after conception, while the baby develops its quantum field entrained by the harmonic resonance with its mother's. When we become aware of this, Tonetti's hologram-baby analogy seems to make a lot of sense.

That said, we must face the crude reality that the genetic design of human fetal development is designed to be executed under ideal conditions that have not been present in the majority of gestational periods across human history. Early in our formation, months before we are born, our development becomes influences by everything concerning our mother's feelings, including stress, insecurities about the future after delivery, fights, and arguments with the father, expectations of gender, accidents, infection, alcohol and drugs consumption.

Don't forget that the quantum field of the baby is formed far in advance of the physical fetus. You can corroborate that by observing in the development of an embryonic heartbeat prior to the formation of a physical heart mentioned earlier. Similarly, limbic imprinting begins before the limbic system is actually fully developed. Notably, it happens that neural development begins early with the formation of the neural tube. However, neuronal maturation is a long, protracted, and delicate developmental process. In fact, the entirety of this development will not be complete until after adolescence.

"In the embryology of the limbic system, we find that by 13 to 14 weeks, the partially developed hippocampus is already starting to unfold, and by 18 to 20 weeks, the fetal hippocampus begins to resemble the adult hippocampus."

"This development generates the most complex structure within the embryo, and the long time period of development means that in utero insults during pregnancy may have consequences to the development of the nervous system." [9]

The above quotes are from a scientific paper discussing "in utero insults," a medical term that refers to "insults" such as physical damage, immune activation, exposure to toxins and inflammation. These insults can collide with the delicate developmental process, and the genetic factors which regulate them, to disrupt development and result in abnormalities in the central nervous system.

Some contemporary research has begun to delve deeper than simple psychic 'insults.' Many neuroscientists are currently attempting to understand the impact of maternal emotional distress, chronic stress, and deprivation on brain development, with the aim of understanding consequences in adult life. Some scientists have begun to investigate the influence of various aspects of the maternal living environment too. However, this work is still in its infancy.

In the quantum model, we are talking about subtle effects and consequences during pregnancy, which extends further than current scientific inquiry. We are referring to the quantum field of the fetus and its ability to record resonance patterns from its mother's quantum field before the physical limbic system is developed.

Note that at the physical level, the limbic system is somewhat developed in the fetus by the fifth month of gestation. This physical limbic system is the network which will continue processing the quantum field information throughout the entire lifespan. It's essential and has previously been hard to accept for some, that adult perception of reality is pre-determined by limbic imprinting. However, some contemporary scientists have realized the value and importance of this perspective.

I find it relevant to include an extended quote from Dr. Chamberlain here. His observations from the work mentioned above are entirely explained by the quantum field model and provide substantial support to its validity. Here is Dr. Chamberlain's position about the cognitive capacities of unborn babies.

"Babies are not tabula rasa (blank slates); they are not without intelligence, and not without a sense of self and a purpose. A close look at early memory and learning defy the limitations traditionally placed on them. Memories of birth shine with verifiable accuracy, a keen perception of meaning, and, with unexpected wisdom, yet such memories were not supposed to exist at all. Another surprise: baby memories reflect empathy and caring for the suffering of parents or of a twin dying in utero-qualities and virtues that were not expected in prenates or neonates. In reality, womb babies are becoming familiar with television theme music, scary movies, and classical music being rehearsed by their parents, domestic violence, and mother's native tongue. They are keenly aware of parental sexual activities, get "wired" with caffeine from mother's coffee, know if they are wanted by one or both parents, and develop early relationships with older siblings and household pets. They learn and copy a mother's depression, as well as her voice characteristics. The unborn are constantly learning from personal experience, but like all other humans, they are vulnerable to trauma and a misunderstanding of surface realities. Indeed, a baby presents a complexity of character to inspire awe when you contemplate communicating with one. An example, a foster mother was concerned about the seductive behavior of a three-year-old in her care. The young child preferred to wear as little clothing as possible, liked to continually take her clothes off, and climbed up on tables where she danced "very provocatively." It turns out the birth mother was a Night Club stripper who became pregnant and continued working all through the pregnancy. After birth, the daughter was sent to foster care and never saw her mother dance. Question: How did the child learn her mother's striptease routine? Hint: What was the baby doing while her mother was performing?" [10]

Thanks to the work of Dr. Chamberlain and several others, the correct dimensions of fetal consciousness are emerging. In retrospect, historical, scientific views of the sensory, emotional, and mental nature of pre and neonates, which were grounded exclusively in a brain-matter paradigm, appear grossly inadequate. A new paradigm is replacing this previous scientific view based on baby awareness and their evident cognitive skills.

Imprinted Behavior and our Unfortunate Human Condition

We are discussing the most significant obstacle which prevents humanity from transforming into the advanced civilization that we all dream to become one day. In 1515, Sir Thomas More published Utopia, a book about the political system of an imaginary, ideal island nation. Utopia literary means "good place" based on its Greek etymology. We all dream and long for a planet that is an excellent place to live, far from the chaotic and contradictory world we currently inhabit. We often ask ourselves why we have seen little progress in the human condition after millennia of recorded history. The short answer to such a question has to do with the human's inability to make permanent behavioral change. How many diets have you started and never reached your goal? How many new year's resolutions have you accomplished by year-end? How many times have you regrettably acknowledged having failed in changing an unwanted habit? If the right intention is there, and the energy and desire go to work with tenacity, then what drags us back to old patterns?

There is a reality so painful and disheartening that it is rarely explicitly stated. Instead, universally acknowledged and often taken for granted, we find a situation so hopeless yet accepted as a fact of life. We are speaking about the lamentable human condition on our beautiful planet. There is not a period throughout human history, brief or prolonged, that is characterized by individuals having reached a generalized state of psychological wellbeing. Our history of empires, wars, domination, and corruption applies at all levels, extending globally, regionally, and locally. In fact, these characteristics are not even present in families nor within individuals in themselves. We may blame governments, kings, and queens, economic systems. However, to accurately assess the problem, we first examine the basic unit of the social order, the individual. Why is that regardless of the favorability of conditions, we remain immersed in misery and suffering with little or no improvement, despite thousands of years trying? The reasons which underlie these are diverse and vary depending on who we ask. However, let's draw our attention to two principal causes. They are closely interrelated and strike to the core of human existence. The first is the extreme persistence of the profoundly ingrained limbic imprints, these behavioral patterns programmed during the early stages of life. The other is the generational transference of trauma and beliefs.

These two major problems perpetuate this unfortunate condition. If we are ever going to heal the planet, starting with ourselves and develop an effective healing strategy, we need to recognize the problems that we face. There are many problems and factors in the world, but we will focus on these two fundamental issues for the moment.

The long answer to these questions regards the survival programs in our souls. Our survival programs have multiple built-in functions to ensure success in protecting the biological entity. These are implemented from our soul-self and subconscious-self in our SIE and can be physically correlated with specific neural activity occurring in the limbic system of our brains.

The first dimension of limbic imprinting is linked with brain development during gestation. Coupled with the hard-wired activation of developmentally regulated genes, epigenetics plays a crucial role in the initial formation of the baby. In accordance with the current epigenetic understanding of gene activation, appropriate genes are activated in the developing fetus in response to environmental signals. This process is responsible for developing a baby optimally adapted to fit the actual circumstances surrounding its forthcoming birth. However, these environmental influences can also interact with gene expression in a negative manner. Environmental disruption, which collides with and dysregulates gene expression during a vulnerable timepoint, is thought to be at the root of a variety of psychiatric disorders.

This is the first level that is not necessarily programming but defining your physical features. This concerns the random genetic selection that occurs when the 23 pairs of your mother's chromosomes are matched with your father's other 23 pairs. Historically, this is what the materialistic model is considered to be the only basis that defines your physical features. However, there are more complex mechanisms that contribute to physical development. For example, it is widely accepted that epigenetic mechanisms begin to trigger or inhibit certain genes that make significant contributions to fetal development. These are based on environmental signals. Within our quantum model, these signals are received from the mother's quantum field.

As you may appreciate, there are many more elaborate processes during fetal development. During gestation, there are still hundreds of potential "you," the expression of which is dependent on the epigenetic mechanisms specifically engaged. This is where a large amount of programming is recorded in the quantum field of the future limbic system of the baby.

The act of birth alone also infuses essential programming in the baby's quantum field that influences its behavior for the entire lifetime. Traumatic births, cesarean sections, umbilical cord complications, and many other incidents create programming associated with attitudes toward life. Some obstetric traumas have been associated with an increased risk of psychiatric disorders later in life.

Following birth, there is another extensive period of limbic imprinting, which appears to last several years. Some authors postulate that imprinting keeps going during the stage of childhood that exhibit brain waves (oscillations) primarily in the theta spectrum. Stable theta oscillations are associated with deep sleep and some phases in a hypnotic trance. Children, with their vivid imagination, are believed to operate on such brain mode for up to the seventh year of age. Children who operate primarily in theta are thought to be highly connected with their inner world. Children do not appear to think in the rational beta wave range but in the more suggestible theta wave range. After the age of 5, children still operate in the theta band but have an intermitted period of the slightly higher frequency, alpha. It isn't until the years of 8-12 onward that beta oscillations become observable in children. If we assume that children's limbic imprinting continues for as long as seven years, we can only imagine the enormous amount of programming that goes on during such an extended period.

Attitudes toward others, parents, siblings, people in general, attitudes toward receiving and giving love, friendship, loneliness, sexual arousal, trust, belief in God, responsibility, honesty, good and evil, self-worth, and dozens of other human values are all defined and recorded in the child's quantum field during this period.

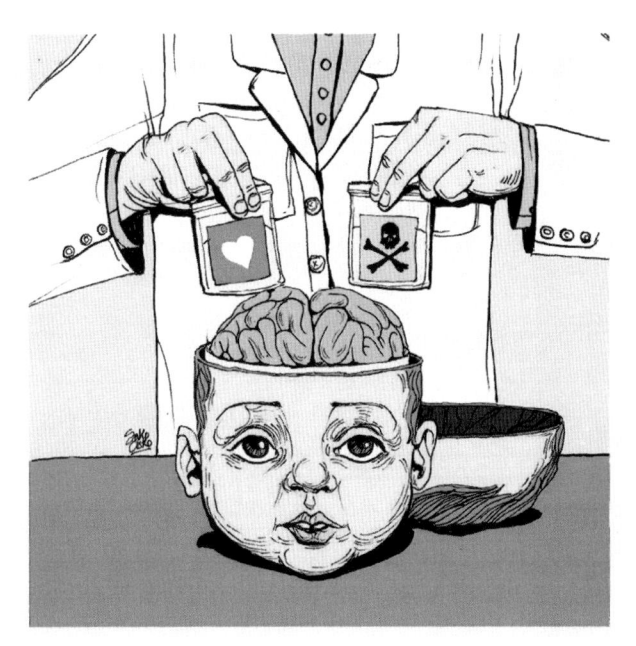

We all receive Limbic Imprinting during our early childhood. The scientist represents the adults around us which metaphorically insert loving or toxic programming represented by the two envelopes.

This could be well-known knowledge since antiquity. Reportedly, the Catholic Church has historically declared seven years old as the "age of reason," after which a child becomes responsible for its actions and is capable of sinning. Interestingly, this coincides with the seventh year mentioned earlier were alpha/beta wave-driven thinking, or conscious thinking, arise in the child. The great Greek philosopher Aristotle once said: "Give me a child until he is seven, and I show you the man." It is highly likely he was referring to the same principle.

In summary, with limbic imprinting, we are facing one form of generational transference of behavior. This one operates by the child recording programming from their parents. Toxic behavior is transferred and can affect the new generation for life. This pertains to all matters, from relationships with others and society to physical health. This explains the generational chain of dysfunctional families that perpetuate poor socioeconomic conditions in certain countries or regions. Remember the discriminatory attitudes of certain parents concerned with the future wellbeing of their sons and daughters when they intend to commit to marriage? Instinct and experience lead them to wish for their children to marry someone coming from "a good family." In psychological terms, they are just attempting to find someone with "good" imprinted behavior that would warrant a long-lasting marriage.

Imprinted toxic behavior brings sustained dealignment of the ego-self within its SIE, and illness is a consequence. That is, illness is not always transferred genetically. Instead, the environment and behavior can cause disorder and disease. This has confused medical science for decades as they attempt to make statistical correlations in the population of people with certain health conditions and the incidence in their other family members. When we visit a medical doctor, among the paperwork of our first visit, they include questionnaires asking whether a family member has suffered illnesses such as depression, arthritis, gout, hypertension, kidney stones, and many others. These are intended to assist the physician in assessing the patient's condition better. These statistical correlations exist not necessarily because of hereditary factors, as some may be, but due to the generational transference of toxic behavior. People with certain conditions are more likely to raise children with those conditions, not due to their genes, but to the toxic behavior that generates a particular disease in the long run.

Let's examine some more deep-rooted behavior. We can begin with a brief look at the undisputable survival instinctive behavior which we inherit genetically. We may interpret fear, anxiety, self-protection, and aggression as transferred trauma behavior, which has been ancestrally filtered through millions of years of suffering, fighting, and helplessness. We are talking about the epigenetic factors of inheritance.

Transgenerational Transference of Trauma and Beliefs

Until recently, our civilizations were oblivious about the lesser-known laws of inheritance. Historically, conventional wisdom had described the more apparent aspects of inherited traits, such as physical features. We know that observant and sagacious grandparents had been able to notice the resemblance between their grandchildren and their parents in terms of other more subtle aspects such as character, temperament, and particular preferences. Sometimes they even accurately predict the eventual unfolding of certain traits. However, not many people are aware of how deep this goes.

From a historical perspective, we have the 19th Century notion of Lamarckism, proposed by French naturist Jean-Baptist Lamarck in his book *Philosophie Zoologique*. In this text, he laid out the first theory of evolution, around fifty years before the publication of Charles Darwin's On the *Origin of Species*. His ideas of generational transference of certain traits in animals were discredited by subsequent discoveries in genetics. However, over two centuries later, Lamarck is making a gracious come-back with the recent advancements in epigenetics.

The epigenome is a multitude of chemical compounds that can tell the genome (DNA) what to do. It responds to various factors in our environment, such as diet and toxins. These factors can cause changes in the epigenome during exposure throughout the lifetime, which, in turn, causes changes in the expression and regulation of various genes. For example, some epigenetic changes can 'turn genes on and off' and affect the interactions of DNA and other proteins. The process, knowns as methylation, is one of several modifications that can be made to modify gene expression. Importantly, the epigenome does not ever change the DNA sequence of a gene. However, curiously, some epigenomic changes acquired during a lifetime are passed on to progeny through the sperm and egg. Although it is not through the usage of parts of the body as Lamarck proposed, there is evidence of inheritance of traits acquired during a lifetime. One could call that Lamarckian. [11] He must be laughing in his grave, colloquially of course, after enduring decades of scientific attacks and ridicule.

More recently, during the 1960s, studies were published that appeared to show a transfer of memories from one rodent to another through injections of brain extracts, that is, brain tissue samples reduced to liquid form. [12] In these cases, negative results from other researchers called into question a theory that may have been too difficult to digest. And yet, in recent decades, it has become known that some types of RNA molecules are involved in the most common epigenetic mechanisms, and they are also involved in the formation of long-term memory. Since then, a series of studies have consistently found supporting evidence. For example, how the sea slug *Aplysia californica*, a classic animal model in memory research, trained to respond to an electrical stimulus is capable of transferring this learning to other untrained individuals. In 2013, a study showed that the fear induced in mice by a particular smell could be transmitted to their offspring via epigenetic mechanisms. In 2019, another study showed that *Drosophila melanogaster* (fruit flies) could inherit from their parents' abnormal egg-laying behavior induced in parents by contact with wasps that parasitize their larvae; their descendants adopt the same behavior without having experienced the threat themselves.

We are now beginning to understand molecular mechanisms that allow animals to inherit particular types of behavior and memory. Although these studies are preliminary findings not yet confirmed in humans, science is providing some glimpses into what ayahuasca participants have consistently established over the last few decades. The first type of generational transfer is behavioral. Attitudes toward specific situations and life have been correlated by ayahuasca participants as coming not from their parents, which could be easily dismissed as learning during childhood, but from more distant grandparents.

There are many examples of these phenomena in worms and mice, but the study of environmental epigenetic inheritance in humans continues to be debated among genetic scientists. Inherited effects in humans are challenging to measure due to the long time elapsing between generations and difficulty with accurate record keeping. However, there are cross-generational studies that support the idea of the existence of epigenetic inheritance in humans. [12] In addition, we account for many testimonials of ayahuasca participants that make us lean in favor of it.

Some research suggests that events in our lives can indeed affect, without changing the DNA, the development of our children, and even grandchildren. For example, studies have shown that both the children and grandchildren of women who survived the Dutch famine of 1944-45 were found to have increased glucose intolerance in adulthood. [13] Other researchers have found that the descendants of Holocaust survivors have lower levels of the hormone cortisol, which helps your body bounce back after trauma.[14]. In 2017 study on nematodes showed learned behavior being transferred over more than twenty generations, which is a crucial step towards understanding more about our epigenetic inheritance - mainly because it serves as a remarkable demonstration of how long-lasting these inter-generational effects may be.

In terms of empirical observations in our sample of participants, we had received first-hand testimonials shortly after the session of participants remembering from the perspective of their mothers the emotionally charged moment when she was pushing to give birth to them. This includes details of the room where it happened. Remarkable, these were later confirmed as accurate. We have one case of a male participant that released the trauma of his grandmother being raped as a teenager, the product of which was his mother. We have the case of another male participant who released the trauma of his mother, who, as a child, was given up for adoption during the confusion of the Nazi occupation of Croatia in World War 2. These cases, which are a few of many, indicates a connection to the quantum holographic memory of history that, through a quantum mechanism, appears to be linked and attached epigenetically or otherwise. These memories carry strong emotional charges that influence the person's feelings, attitudes, and beliefs towards the corresponding roles implicit in the underlying dramas of life. [15] The worst part is that it all happens deep in the subconscious-self without the slightest suspicion of the ego-self, who is living the consequences.

While calmly reflecting on these matters, an exciting connection came to my conscious awareness. If generational transference of behavioral tendencies is possible, I wonder how this mechanical process may also occur in less traumatic situations such as strongly held beliefs. For example, how is the human species programmed with thousands of years of toxic limiting beliefs taught by religion? I refer to the guilt of the original sin, making us feel undeserving and treasonous against our creator. Imagine what influence one single belief may have had over thousands of generations. A belief that justified the fear of God, and psychologically projecting the "evilness" of Eve in every woman. With what we know today about epigenetics, there must have been some ancient wisdom about the laws of inheritance if we pay close attention to some interesting passages in the Bible.

Almost a dozen times, we find the God of the Bible cursing man for "visiting the iniquity of the fathers on the children and the children's children, to the third and the fourth generation." I always wondered why the God in the Bible would punish future generations for the mistakes of their ancestors. From an epigenetic perspective, I can now interpret this not as a capricious and unfair act of an anthropomorphized God, but as the natural result of little-known epigenetic laws of the transgenerational transfer.

These realities force us to accept the idea that we are partially defined and burdened by significant ancestral conditioning. We are limited by multiple factors, from physical, environmental, geographical, and of course, genetic. Freedom is simply the art of letting go, being fully open, honest, and loving toward the next moment, the next person, and the fullness of life as it is. We can teach and serve others by how we listen and how open our hearts have become. Freedom is contagious, and love is too.

The Bright Future of Psychedelic Therapies

The primary purpose of the quantum model of the psyche is to promote spiritual healing by identifying the misalignments within our self-identity envelope to design strategies that allow the self-reprogramming necessary to achieve alignment. Every misalignment which causes spiritual or emotional issues has the potential to be resolved with our conscious action. This is where psychedelic substances can play a fundamental role in making spiritual healing techniques incredibly powerful. Visualization techniques have been around for decades. Although these techniques can work with relative success across diverse applications, we must admit that deeply imprinted programming is a different story. Everyone has experienced the frustration of failing to achieve the desired results in nutrition habits. This is a perfect example where willful intention, frequent visualizations, or affirmations have proven ineffective. The truth is subconscious programming is beyond the reach, and resists the ego-self's commands. Ayahuasca advisors must understand the nature of subconscious resistance and the dynamics of our subconscious programming if they want to understand the mechanics of spiritual healing techniques.

The entire animal kingdom comes with fixed pre-programmed instincts that allow the effective performance in their designated ecological niches. However, once removed from them, survival is compromised. On the other hand, humans enjoy their position at the top of the food chain due to their amazing adaptability, which comes from their inherent capacity to program behavior tailor-made to their specific environmental demands. But, here comes the caveat.

The human soul not only has the survival programs, but it also comes with the self- realization programs. Once the demands for survival are satisfied, the self-realization programs start to make demands. The existential imperative of humans consists not only of surviving, but also exploring and realizing their full potential. Incidentally, such full potential goes well beyond achieving happiness and psychological well-being. It extends into higher possibilities of the soul and spirit. Humans are extraordinary spiritual beings living human experiences inside marvelous physical vehicles.

The caveat is that the same way such adaptable mechanics work in favor of the survival, they work against the self-realization goals of the individual if suboptimal or abnormal settings are recorded in the default settings of the behavioral filters mentioned earlier. Once the developing child unconsciously set one of these empty default boxes, such corresponding "style" (not the actual behavior itself) becomes hard-wired. It will become a relatively permanent part of the core persona of the individual.

If we carefully look at human personalities, we can observe that our main defining features remain somewhat persistent throughout our lifespan, despite the many devastating or life-changing events the person may have encountered. Experience shows that personality does not change extensively over long periods, but adapts moderately and transiently in response to shifting environmental and existential circumstances. In fact, this has been empirically tested and supported by long-term studies of the stability of human personality traits across the life course. Personality is somewhat malleable in response to life experiences, but there are significant components of personality that remain constant from childhood to old age. This indicates the deep-rooted and stable nature of the original core settings.

Similar to imprinted behavior that occurs in childhood, when the behavior of higher complexity such as subpersonalities creates their neural pathway network in our brains, the modification of them becomes a real challenge for our SIE. An abused child that exhibits abusive behavior as an adult may find ways to survive and possibly have children. But life is more than that. If not adequately reprogrammed with spiritual healing, it shall never succeed in self-realization. Visualizing how behavior is mechanically filtered to act in a specific predefined manner, at least hypothetically, constitutes a significant advancement in understanding human behavior and may provide fertile ground for possible testable hypotheses in the future.

The quantum model aims to establish a credible hypothetical framework that would allow understanding and modification of such quantum processes employing psychedelic-assisted therapies. Such framework is essential for psychedelic therapies to work effectively. We have learned that ayahuasca-based therapies have the capacity to modify those default settings. This can produce astounding outcomes for the spiritual and emotional healing of practitioners. The future success of psychedelic-assisted therapies lies in the capacity of therapists to achieve effective reprogramming of the subconscious-self in cooperation with the patient's ego-self.

Otherwise, therapies implemented within a defined structure as though operating in automatic mode, without the patient's conscious participation, will not yield the same success. Patients need a simple model to assist their understanding and visualization of the spiritual healing process with which they want to engage. To achieve that, it is necessary to hypothesize beyond the vague concept of "genetically driven" behavior. Visualizing how behavior is engineered to act in a predefined manner constitutes a significant advancement in understanding human behavior and creates practical healing applications.

The engine of spiritual healing doesn't lie in the psychedelic substance itself but, instead, within the conscious power of the patient. The entheogen only acts as a gate opener to resistant brain circuits (recall the default mode network discussed earlier), which keeps the ego-self focused on the immediate physical reality for survival purposes. Psychedelic-assisted therapies represent an enormous opportunity for the human species to break free from the arguably tyrannical survival program and may enable us to embrace the self-realization module of the master program. A reasonably credible model of the psyche could provide a tool to creatively modify survival-based programming by harnessing the power of conscious intent. This implies the active participation of the patient in understanding their dysfunctional condition and their decisive willingness to instill their best mental efforts into the healing process. Patients often show-up with

Metaphor of our self-realization program operating individually and collectively

attitudes such as "here I am, apply to me your psychedelic-assisted therapy, and heal me."These won't receive the same results, if any at all, compared to fully engaged and committed patients. Patients who are aware of their mental power and spiritual capacities will obtain optimal results. Recall our detailed discussion of placebo effects, which confirm the power of belief in physical healing. Naturally, it follows that the possibilities for non-physical reprogramming at the quantum structure level are endless.

We have described the two gigantic stumbling blocks which have kept the human race stuck in a cycle of mediocrity. Whether we like it or not, we are designed to preserve the status quo. For millennia it has been terrible, suggesting a very traumatic origin of the human race. However, such a curse can eventually become a blessing. Turning the tide is an enormous project, but it all starts with the first step. The good news is that for the first time in history, we are finding the technology that can re-wire the subconscious-self, providing a promise to a brighter future. The emerging field of psychedelic-assisted therapies has the challenge of creating new methodologies to overcome the inherent limitations of human design. For the first time, we can change our factory settings. If we can change the individual, we can change the world. We have the opportunity to start a new paradigm of human behavior in front of us. This can define a turning point in our modern civilization.

CHAPTER NINE

BEYOND PSYCHOLOGICAL PROJECTION

"We don't see things as they are, we see them as we are." - Anaïs Nin

Introduction to the Projection Principle

It is now time to examine some applications of the quantum model of the psyche with practical situations. The primordial quantum field, which permeates everything, is where we live our lives, this reality exists beyond our physical perceptions, and we are only just beginning to understand it. Our SIE vibrates, expands, and contracts continuously expressing our life force in a myriad of ways. Thoughts and emotions emanate from our SIE and dance within the quantum habitat, which is also inhabited by other SIE's. This quantum ecology is composed of SIE's interacting with forces of nature, electromagnetic radiation from human-made devices, and energy patters emitted by other living beings from the plant and animal kingdoms. Everything is connected. We are all one together, but we are not scrambled. We preserve our envelopes of identity while subtly maintaining our oneness.

Our human physical vehicle is the lens of our SIE's reality cameras. This lens of extraordinary complexity, encompassing all organs of perception, is just a bundle of quantum material which acquires a magical sense of tangible reality when the element of the ego-self observer is added into the reality game. Without it, there is nothing but meaningless vibrations. Consciousness is everything. This idea is proposed brilliantly by Dr. Lanza in his masterpiece work, Biocentrism:

How Life and Consciousness are Key to Understanding the True Nature of the Universe. [1] Every ayahuasca spiritual advisors and psychedelic-assisted therapist should be required to understand the concept of the consciousness-centered reality, as psychedelic experiences shall inevitably confront them with it.

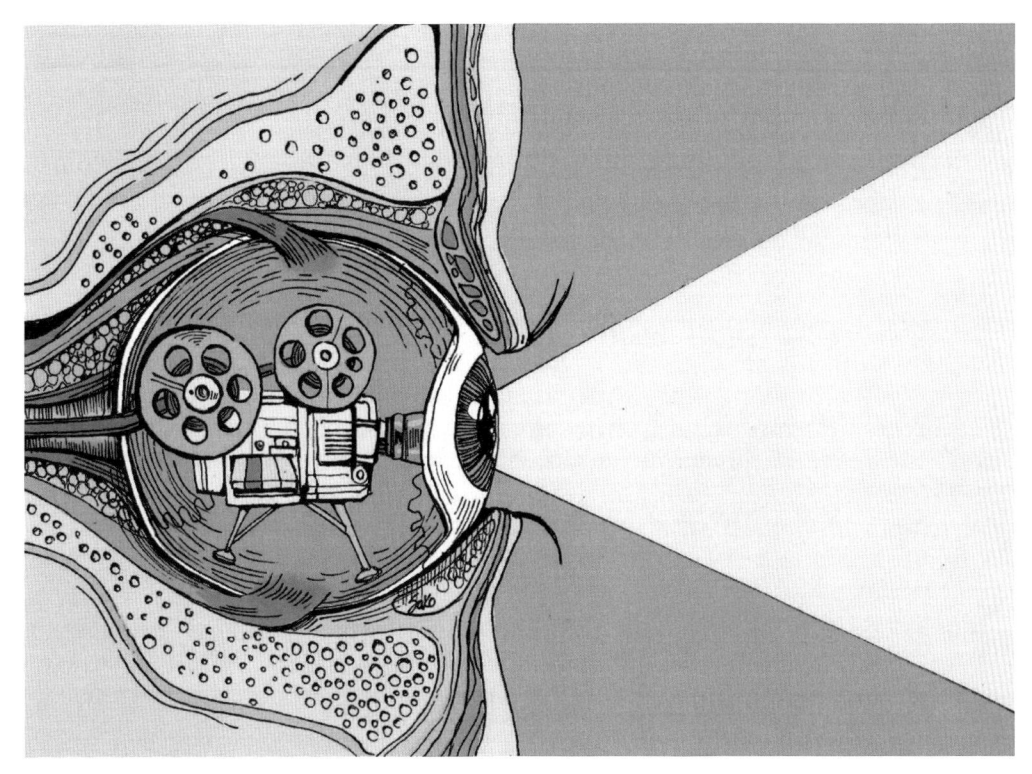

Conceptualization of the projection principle. While on the physical level images are captured by the retina like a camera, at the quantum level, we project our SIE into the perception of our reality. The images are the same for the camera and the projector, but their interpretation is SIE-dependent.

When we observe reality from the "objective" perspective, from the mechanistic worldview, it appears as a Newtonian clockwork universe. The sense of vision, for example, is explained with a classical photographic camera allegory. The image enters through the eye's iris, and an inverted image is reflected onto the retina, corresponding to the camera film. From the quantum model worldview, we perceive more than what is already in the movie. That is, in addition to the physical camera that captures images, we are quantum projectors of our pre-existing inner images. We are generally unaware that we are the lens of the projector; the images arise from our SIE and are projected outside as interpretations of our perceptions. This is the dual nature of reality. We do not deny the mechanistic part of reality, but we are waking up to the quantum nature of it. Living life as though there is only one side of the duality, is living half-empty or half-full. When we awaken to this, reality cannot be perceived strictly mechanistically again. There is no way back to ignorance. This awakening is one red pill in the Matrix movie.

This is an axiom of the nature of reality accepted by many experienced ayahuasca practitioners and psychedelic explorers. This constitutes a fundamental idea required to achieve spiritual healing easy and fast. Scientific studies on the perception of optical illusions have revealed how the perceptual mechanisms of the brain can be fooled by physical tricks. Professional magicians are well aware of how to exploit the projection of our perceptions and have made a living out of it. However, the most valuable application of the projection principles is the conscious understanding of the phenomenon in the thoughts and emotions if we are willing to see it. The project of becoming an effective ayahuasca spiritual advisor starts with your willingness to unlearn everything that you have learned and begin again. Empty the glass to fill it up.

You may ask Mother Ayahuasca to show you. Have you heard elsewhere that the world is an illusion? Have you heard about the Maya? Here is a definition:

Maya, literally "illusion" or "magic," has multiple meanings in Indian philosophies depending on the context. In ancient Vedic literature, Maya literally implies extraordinary power and wisdom. In later Vedic texts and modern literature dedicated to Indian traditions, Maya connotes a "magic show, an illusion where things appear to be present but are not what they seem." Maya is also a spiritual concept connoting "that which exists, but is constantly changing and thus is spiritually unreal," and the "power or the principle that conceals the true character of spiritual reality." [2]

Ancient Indian wisdom understood reality clearly, while we are still blinded by our mechanistic upbringing. The world is not fixed in a definitive pattern. If you drink enough ayahuasca with the intention of "getting to the bottom of it," you shall eventually realize that you are mistaking your view of the world with the world itself. Because the world can be viewed from many perspectives., the world does change according to who is watching it.

For example, an optimistic person will notice potential life opportunities and immediately begins to feel grateful. The optimist will inherently understand that while circumstances may be hard or bad at present, these circumstances will change once again. The pessimist will likely stay stuck in inaction and think that his or her world is unchangeable. The pessimist may look down or ridicule the optimist as some gullible and naïve fool and, through these actions, find a way to feel superior and excellent about themself.

It's all about yourself. This helps you realize that what you see "out there" is also telling you something about yourself. If you find a lot of hostility towards you, then perhaps there may be some hostility hidden within you. If something about others irritates you, then maybe it is you holding this undesirable quality, and you are in denial of it. Think about your world and what it can tell you about yourself.

Think about yourself and how you may be interpreting the world in ways that do not serve you.

This realization that the outer world is a projection of the inner world is one of the cornerstones of ayahuasca spiritual advising. To skillfully apply this principle to others, you first need to learn it through self-practice. First, the concept captures your imagination; then you ask yourself whether it is true, then you start to uncover hints and clues within you, then finding them in others, until you start believing. Finally, after such discovery, you accept and comprehend the conviction that it is the truth. You can start with the assumption that it is accurate and make your way up to conviction with patience and careful observation. The great thing is that regardless of what stage of this process, you may be, this assumption works very effectively when advising others with their healing process in ayahuasca.

Metaphorical representation of our perception of reality. The subject is pointing at sacred books containing a diversity of religious beliefs. In reality, we are choosing certain brand of contact lenses through which we decide to interpret the events in external reality.

Patients who are drinking ayahuasca intending to seek clarity on personal issues, like the anxiety caused by knowing that "my daughter is doing drugs," or complaining about "my husband or wife's imperfections," are great examples. In these cases, patients are surprised when I turn the mirror on themselves. They present themselves standing on the comfortable platform of victimhood. Often, people do not like to be removed from this platform upon receiving the advisor's coaching, urging them to assume responsibility. The assumption is that everything is about yourself. You are projecting your personal issues onto your reality, and others are acting in a way to confront those same issues of which you are unaware or in denial.

The incredible thing is that when the patient opens up to the possibility that such is the case, they experience important realizations in their next ayahuasca session. They find the aspects of themselves that are being projected. I have to admit that I have no idea how it works. However, the fact is that once you realize and accept the projection connection, your reality starts to change for the better. I feel like the first scientists dealing with electrical phenomena. Pioneers like Alessandro Volta and Andre-Marie Ampere were learning about electricity and manipulating the flow of such energy while having no idea of how it worked. All they knew was that this force was real, and they were able to experiment with it through trial and error. It was not until recently in the quantum physics era that the debate regarding electrical mechanics has finally begun to settle. We find a similar pattern with the projection phenomena.

I am proposing that we can harness the undisputed power of ayahuasca to service humanity by exploring and practicing the projection paradigm. If we begin practicing with ourselves as advisors and with others as patients, we will eventually develop a methodology that will lead to a breakthrough in the mind-body debate. With a strengthened mind-body paradigm, we will have a practical and effective methodology to explain and heal the illnesses emerging from inner disharmony; emotional, mental, and physical. When alternative medicine can reach such a level of reliability, it will powerfully challenge the currently dominating symptom treating paradigm of conventional medicine. Ayahuasca can help us to achieve this outcome.

Referring back to the maya, we can use other examples to illustrate the projection phenomena in more detail. Let's look at Plato's cave allegory with a slightly alternative perspective. Plato developed this compelling story, which has captured the imagination of multiple generations for centuries and continues to do so today. You may read the extended version directly in his timeless book, "The Republic," or you can find excellent online reviews and discussions on academic websites.

Plato's Cave, The Matrix Movie and Other Reminders

There was a group of people who were born and grew up in a cave. They were prisoners in chains, and they could only look at the dark side of the cave but not at the entrance. They were arranged with a wall in front of them where shadows of objects and people moved as though in a movie theater. They could never see that the big bonfire behind them was the source of the light, which was hitting real objects and people that moved in front of it, thus projecting the shadows in the front wall. The real people talked and made sounds whose echo in the cave appeared as if it was coming from the wall with the shadows. For the prisoners who were born there, these shadows were their reality. As they talked to each other for many years about the shadows and the voices that came from them, they validated their reality to a great extent. There were even acknowledged experts in interpreting the shadows. These experts explained the behavior of the shadows and made predictions about the future.

What would happen if one of the prisoners escaped from the cave and was able to see the bonfire and the real objects? Just imagine his reaction to realizing the fire-shadow mechanics of his previous reality and to the real colorful objects that he only knew as shadows. Plato proposed that people confronted with a higher reality, similar to the prisoners accustomed to a dark cave who could not handle their painful eyes, would retreat to the comfort zone of their shadow world. Moreover, if a prisoner gradually got out of the cave and allowed his eyes to adapt to the stronger light, wouldn't he feel joyous for knowing what was behind everything he thought was real? What would he feel about his expert friends who were so admired for their predictive abilities? Would he still envy them?

Plato reflected further if the prisoner returns to the cave, he could never interpret the shadows the same way. He would be an object of mockery and would be taunted by his friends when trying to tell them about the higher truth. His friends would conclude that getting out of the cave is dangerous because it "distorts your vision." Plato's cave is an allegory to everyday life. Escaping from the cave and realizing the bonfire trick corresponds to becoming aware of our own deeply rooted beliefs. Coming outside of the cave and under the sun corresponds to us feeling our infinitely divine nature or our new level of truth experience.

We can also equate the cave allegory with our process of self-identity, separate from others. In a practical example, let's take a grown-up woman with a well-formed self-identity who lives with her sister. She frequently gets upset with her sister because of her ignorance toward her personal needs and her lack of contribution to the shared housekeeping chores. After some questioning, we can offer her a different perspective. Based on the projection principle that everything is about you and not the others, we can coach her by suggesting that what disappoints her is that her sister just does as she pleases, a behavior which that she doesn't allow in herself. The selfishness she perceives in her sister (the shadow) stems from her lack of self-respect, as she continually forces herself to do things she doesn't like to do (the bonfire). She can respond: "yes, but she is irresponsible," or some alternate rebuttal because she wants to stay in the cave looking at the shadow. Those shadows are true, but the advisor needs to point at the bonfire to help her. When the woman realizes and accepts that she forces herself to do things she doesn't like, she is prepared to experience a breakthrough using ayahuasca by finding the specific origins of this behavioral pattern.

Magically and unexplainably, when she finds and resolves the blockage after one or several ayahuasca sessions, her sister will begin to show an improved attitude. The rule of thumb is that when you resolve an inner issue, blockage, or internal contradiction, the reality around you starts to change. The world that surrounds us is a projection of our inner cave. To better understand the projection principle, we need to perceive our issues and conflicts for what they are - shadows. We live in a social and cultural cave, and it is hard at the beginning to identify the bonfire. Once you do, it is hard to find anyone whom you may share these views, as most people are uninterested in escaping the cave. Your proposition presents something unknown, and people prefer the comfort of the known shadows, and that's understandable. Not everyone is prepared to wake up to a higher reality. The real scary monster here is the fact that to live in a higher reality commands and acceptance of responsibility for our own life and everything that happens in it. It is incredibly difficult to give up the convenience of playing the victim when you have spent a lifetime living it.

The Matrix Movie

We can progress from the ancient Plato allegory to the modern film production entitled "The Matrix." If you watch this movie again with new eyes, you may see the close parallels of both stories. The ancient notion of Maya, Plato's cave, and the Matrix are related in curious ways. The same message persists throughout the ages, and perhaps it's time to put it into practice somehow.

The setting of the Matrix movie is clearly Plato's cave. We are all immersed in computer animation (the Cave), which makes us believe in a reality that is not so (Maya). There is a higher reality (the bonfire) that others have discovered, and these people are trying to escape from the falsehood of the reality in which they were educated. The illusion is very powerful and resilient, and they are seeking the One (you) that will destroy the Matrix. Everyone in the world is Neo, the One that can destroy the matrix, the One that can escape the cave.

In the movie, Neo believes he was living a normal, but slightly troubled life in 1999. By day, a computer programmer; by night, a hacker, providing the fruits of his labors to other troubled souls. He lives alone, he doesn't sleep, and there's a profound emptiness in his life. For Neo, there is something he can't put his finger on, and he is intrigued by the matrix; he suspects he is in the cave, but he's not sure at first.

He is found by the group of rebels who represent the inner motivations that continue to push us forward to find an exit from which we can escape. We know we can do it, but inner doubts invade us. We can interpret the movie as an inner journey of discovery, escaping the cave to a higher reality, dissolving the Maya. The parallel with our reality is clearly established at the beginning when Morpheus explains to Neo: "When the Matrix was first built, there was a man born inside that could change what he wanted, to remake the Matrix as he saw fit." The translation is, "Since the beginning of creation, men have always had the capacity to escape the cave."

Neo (we) need to make a definite choice of awakening to empower ourselves into a worthwhile journey of living life fully. Morpheus, which is the name of the Greek god of dreams, is the character that represents our inner self. It is with this character that we choose to take the red pill. This 'red pill' is an ingested chemical substance and quickly awakens you from Maya and enables you to see the truth. Any similarity with ayahuasca? After drinking ayahuasca, you gain access to a higher part of yourself, call it your soul, higher self, spirit, or anything that makes sense to you. In the movie, this is the Oracle. In this scene, there is a clearly visible sign in the room that reads: "Temet Nosce," which means "Know Yourself" in Latin. Such a famous phrase in Greek is known to adorn the main entrance of the temple of Apollo at Delphi, also known as the Oracle of Delphi. This was where the ancient leaders and wealthy people attended to ingest an unknown type of entheogen to receive guidance about their personal problems. The movie script intelligently provides clues that support this interpretation. Again, there is a parallel of attending the Oracle of Delphi, drinking ayahuasca, and drinking the red pill, to receive guidance and know yourself. Neo is unsure if he can escape the cave and is asking the Oracle for the answer. The Oracle answered the way ayahuasca likely would; she tried to explain Neo that he doesn't believe he can escape the cave and that he is looking for external assurances which he can only find inside his heart.

In summary, the Matrix movie can be interpreted as another Plato's cave that has attempted to remind us of our infinite human potential subliminally. By awakening to the principle of projection, we open the door to the possibility of escaping Plato's cave, dissolving the Maya, or destroying the Matrix; just pick your favorite allegory or make your own.

More Cultural Reminders of the Projection Principle

The projection principle seems to have been pullulating for eons in the collective unconscious. It is a profound notion that has been indirectly or non-specifically captured by many cultural manifestations throughout the ages. It seems as if we already know it subconsciously, but it hasn't settled yet at the conscious or rational level. Here are a few examples which contain the unspoken wisdom of the projection principle:

Popular Proverbs:

There is a widely known proverb in Spanish that captures the projection principle accurately: "el ladrón juzga por su condición" which literary means "the thief judges by its own condition." It applies when someone accuses others of evil intentions in situations that are not evidently true, where the facts could have been interpreted benignly. The proverb is used to indicate that the accuser is projecting themselves in their interpretation of the facts. Many people have realized that our opinions in casual conversations frequently contain projections, most of them inadvertent, that provide our listeners with valuable information about our prejudices and twisted judgments.

The French language also has its own equally accurate proverb: "Un voleur pense que tous le monde est voleur," which means "A thief thinks everybody else is a thief." The curious similarity of both proverbs makes me speculate about its likely antiquity due to the common roots of both languages. It is very possible that a similar proverb may exist in Latin or Italian.

The English language has the popular "It takes one to know one," which is colloquially used to express the same message as the Spanish and French versions. However, it is a bit less specific or ambiguous about the accuser.

Religious Texts:

The ancient and profound nature of the projection principle is well illustrated by the revered passage in the Bible's New Testament. In Matthew 7:3-5, Jesus said: "Why do you see the speck in your brother's eye, and not the beam in your own?". Although the context of this verse is about not judging others, teaching also found in the Quran, the relevant aspect here is that it contains an implicit message of the projection principle. Note that the person that criticizes the speck on their brother's eye is clearly projecting their imperfections externally onto others.

Verse 70a of the Kiddushin Talmud, a Judaic text that predates the New Testament, notes the human tendency toward projection and warns against it: "And Shmuel says: If one habitually claims that others are flawed [in their lineage], he disqualifies himself with his own flaw. The flaw he accuses them of having is the one that he has.". Again, we find here the wisdom of the projection principle manifested in ancient religious texts. [3]

These are cultural snippets that focus on the negative aspect of the projection principle. Others have harnessed the positive side of the concept with the motivational message of projecting the good inside of you to the world. The highly admired leader of the Indian independence movement, Mahatma Gandhi, is attributed with many wise quotes, including: "You must be the change you wish to see in the world." This famous quote is inviting everyone to project into the world the good things you have within. Obviously, this assumes that people want to change the world for the better, and that's a fair assumption. He invites people to visualize a better world and then project such visualization into your being, a compelling action that has struck the consciousness of millions around the Planet.

Finally, one of the most recent examples is the song from the world-famous African American pop singer Michael Jackson entitled "Man in the Mirror." This bestselling song implicitly refers to any man looking at himself in the mirror, while the chorus line of the song repeats over and over: "If you want to make the world a better place, take a look at yourself and then make a change." This is almost the same message of the Mahatma Gandhi's quote but with the convenient enhancement of the visual aid of a physical mirror. It makes the message easily understandable, relatable, and actionable as billions of people worldwide stand in front of a mirror with reasonable frequency.

The Projection Concept in Psychology

Psychological projection has several levels of depth. We shall dig down to the deepest of these levels. Firstly, we have the classical definition of psychology books:

"Psychological projection is a theory in which humans defend themselves against their own unconscious impulses or qualities (both positive and negative) by denying the existence of these within themselves while attributing them to others. For example, a habitually intolerant person may constantly accuse other people of being intolerant. It incorporates blame-shifting. According to some research, the projection of one's unconscious qualities onto others is a common process in everyday life."

Then we have the genius of Carl Jung with the advanced version which he proposed during his doctoral studies. In his own terms he writes:

"Just as we tend to assume that the world is as we see it, we naively suppose that people are as we imagine them to be. In this latter case, unfortunately, there is no scientific test that would prove the discrepancy between perception and reality Although the possibility of gross deception is infinitely greater here than in our perception of the physical world, we still go on naively projecting our own psychology into our fellow human beings. In this way everyone creates for himself a series of more or less imaginary relationships based essentially on projection, In these imaginary relationships the other person becomes an image or a carrier of symbols. Although all the contents of the unconscious are in this fashion projected onto the environment, we can recognize them as projections only when we gain enough insight to see that they are images or peculiarities that are part of our own makeup. Otherwise we are naively convinced that these peculiarities belong to the object." [4]

In other words, according to Jung's definition, we are all living in the delusional world of our projections. This brings us to the epistemological question of whether we can actually know another person for what he or she is, or we have to abdicate to the strange fact that we can only meet our ideas of others. The latter tends to be the case when our relationships are superficial and ephemeral. Old friends, mothers, and their grown-up children, and decades of marriage are examples where these projections become polished over many years, as suggested by the "onion of self-perception" in Figure 2.

Why Are We Projectors of Ourselves?

Consider that everything that happens in the outside world first must occur within the person. It is the person that manifests thoughts, feelings, and emotions based on their beliefs. This is all concerning some desire of that person, for example, the desire to survive or to be accepted and loved. Why must it be this way? Why do we project all the time?

If we are pure consciousness and we are creators, there can be no other way to exist but to project ourselves outwardly. What external reality can we perceive if we are all one? The game of separability can only be played by projecting from the inside of our SIE; when there is no outside to perceive, projecting yourself is the only way to go.

Psychological projection is the mechanism that allows the expression of our subconscious-self without collaboration with the ego-self. Our projections necessarily create the stage for the drama of the ego-self, who, by the way, is ultimately responsible for a large portion of the content of the subconscious-self in the first place. Such is the manifestation of consciousness in the physical dimension.

There is no other way unless the ego-self awakens to the game. We use projections to externally construct the elements which we have neglected or remain in denial of to have them available for integration whenever we are ready for the task. Consciousness works for wholeness. Anything that we believe we "don't have" or "aren't being" for whatever reason must necessarily return to us. Thanks to the mechanism of projection, we have the potential for the integration of our subconscious biases. We have the possibility of returning from separateness and duality into solid unitarian soul-self.

Metaphorical representation of a man "falling in love" with a woman. Note that the man is just projecting his own ideals into the woman's face, which he never actually see. Prolonged experience with the "loved one" eventually dissolves the projected illusion and "love" fades away.

The projection is especially relevant for men to break the bond with the mother and look outside the family unit for a sexual partner. Contrary to women who share the gender with their mothers and retain a strong identity with them during adolescence, men feel the instinct to detach from their closest ally when testosterone starts flowing in those years. The subconscious projection of ideal qualities is the mechanism that removes their mothers from the center stage and makes them run away from the comfort of home. The projection toward other women triggers the neurochemical reaction of "falling in love," which pulls them out of the nest. Women have a similar but distinct route to experience the "love projection" when they later idealize characteristics in young men who are often considered unsuitable candidates by their mothers. If we further scrutinize this phenomenon, we will end up speaking about Freud's Oedipus complex, but that would be the subject of another book.

We can also see projections as a hook that triggers the ego-self into action. The latter too often fails to see the trick at work and ends up tangled in a complex cascade of projections. Arguments between significant others are a typical example of this.

The Law of the Mirror: Spiritual Advisor's Most Valuable Tool

One of the attributes I most admire about my dear wife Rosalia is her relentless commitment to continuous self-improvement with the direct connection to Mother Ayahuasca. Over the years, I witnessed how she gradually grabbed this most intriguing self-help principle during the process of getting to the bottom of a family situation, which was significantly disturbing her heart. Her daughter, Stephany, was acting out a radical, rebellious spirit, which is typical of some teenagers and had run away from home. Anxiety was eating her heart as days passed without news of her daughter's whereabouts. After some time, she returned but remained on non-speaking terms with her mother. At least Stephany was closer now. However, my wife avoided any kind of confrontation with her, afraid of pushing her away a second time. This situation was the root of Rosalia independently discovering the law of the mirror. Rosalia had a ferrous faith and determination to find a solution to her miserable situation and decided to drink ayahuasca as many consecutive days as necessary until receiving the inner guidance or insight that would resolve her problem. She isolated from the world at home in silence, prayer, and meditation. She drank ayahuasca every evening. To her surprise, by the third day, a breakthrough poured down from her soul-self.

She realized that she was projecting her fears onto her daughter, and by removing this projection, the situation would change. In shock and awe, she thought further about her fears. The worst that may happen is that her beloved Stephany may die. Rosalia then received the recomforting assurance that under such a scenario, it was the experience that both she and Stefany were meant to live in this existence. Rosalia accepted the will of God. She surrendered Stefany to her divine destiny, and there was nothing Rosalia could do to avoid it. A profound sense of peace permeated every single living cell of her body, and she sobbed in gratitude for hours. This epiphany was deeply imprinted in her limbic system. She feels that a gestalt memory containing a diversity of sensory inputs shall forever continue to reverberate in her relevant memory banks. It marked a new stage in her spiritual life.

Her story made intuitive sense to me, and I began observing reality through those eyeglasses. Further hours of self-observation in the empirical process led us to develop some fundamental advising principles which we incorporated into our coaching sessions with ayahuasca practitioners. People began finding that this was a useful tool to discover hidden aspects of themselves. It became an integral principle of both our advising approach to others and the roadmap of our own lives as well. After some time applying this principle to our lives and teaching it to others, Rosalia began to call it the law of the mirror.

The law of the mirror affirms that the external world acts as a mirror for us. What the mirror reflects is nothing more than our light and our own shadow; that is to say, our inner world. Moreover, it asserts that by consciously changing our internal biases exposed by the mirror effect, we trigger causal quantum effects that tend to gradually, and sometimes immediately, change external world circumstances. This is an extraordinary leap beyond the traditional idea of psychological projection. It confronts the ego-self and its linear, mechanistic paradigm. By definition, it is a hypothesis that appears impossible to prove or disprove scientifically. It is only by integrating the principle into our belief system that we can determine whether any value is added to our lives.

When we internalize this "law" and make it part of ourselves, our way of seeing life is automatically transformed. We realize that we are not victims of anything or anyone, only ourselves. We comprehend that the cause of all that we experience and of what others show us is already within us. However, this law goes one step further, something that Jung never attempted to say. The novel idea of the law of the mirror is that our external reality changes when we consciously and profoundly reprogram our inner projections. The statistically significant frequency at which this mechanism seems to work made us embrace it as a powerful coaching principle in our practice. With the powerful ability of Mother Ayahuasca to assist us in deconstructing our beliefs and projections, we found a suitable companion for effective spiritual healing.

By consciously applying this law to interpret our reality, our problems become our primary source of learning. The negative emotions that someone awakens in you become like a friend, which aids in healing something that needs to heal or enables the allowance of something that you are not permitting yourself. You understand that what bothers us about others is something that we are not seeing or do not want to see. Since others only reflect you what you must heal or release; when you manage to change internally, as if by magic, your mirror begins to reflect a different reality. Not only have you been transformed, but your external world is also transformed. The law of the mirror is simply the way we become aware of our limitations; everything begins with us and ends with us.

The law of the mirror is the "secret weapon" of the soul-self, which activates the self-realization programs after the survival programs have substantially achieved its objective. The brilliance of Carl Jung again captures this with his famous quote: "Until you make it conscious, your unconscious will control your life, and you will call it fate." Therefore, the path to self-realization, to psychological wellbeing and inner happiness, is the relentless pursual of pulling unconscious material into our conscious awareness. The law of the mirror is the single most effective guidance maxim to be followed by our awakened ego-self in its pursual of alignment within its SIE. You may call it expansion of consciousness, enlightenment, ascension, transcendence, or any other descriptive adjective that fits your worldview.

The Law of the Mirror Mechanics

What you deny, submits you; what you accept, transforms you – Carl Jung

When another person triggers rejection or anger in us, think for a second that this scene is a mirror that is reflecting something about your inner world. Honestly, what is this mirror reflecting on you? Generally, these events will reflect one aspect that we must carefully examine with an attitude of brutal vulnerability. Remember that even if your ego-self craves and seeks alignment with your other parts, your subpersonalities will resist and will try to persuade your ego-self to abandon the project by appealing with persuasive, logical arguments. There is one major reason for this: the law of the mirror represents the refulgent lightning that may annihilate them. When a subpersonality is pulled from the subconscious into the conscious, it immediately starts melting away into nothingness as its trapped light is recaptured by the light-torus that we are. It elicits, especially in the denser entities, the fear of death, because "death" is sensed coming around the corner. They run scared within our quantum field invoking archetypical "good versus evil" cosmic dramas, attempting to persuade our ego-self to reject the "craziness" of our agenda. The process is not comfortable, but it is worthwhile.

Equipping our ego-self with a clear checklist for self-observation improves self-confidence in the task. Our initial job is to find out which of these situations our mirror is reflecting as requiring attention for ego-self transcendence.

1. The mirror reflects similarity to you - In other words, what bothers you outside is nothing more than a reflection of parts that bother you about yourself. A part of you reflects that you do not want to see. The external person or situation is showing your dark side - your own shadow. Evaluate where the pain or discomfort this reflection is provoking in you and find situations in which you do the same. In this case, you need to accept that part of you. Acknowledging it with deep honesty shall trigger a cascade of quantum events leading to changes in your external circumstances.

2. The mirror reflects the opposite side to you - There are cases where the mirror is showing you the opposite of you; something opposite to what you are and you cannot bear in others. For example, if you are very orderly, you can-

not stand them being very messy, or if you are very generous, perhaps you cannot stand them being very stingy—each one bothered by what you carry inside. Your mirror is reflecting that you are standing too far right or left. The exterior shows you that neither end is good and that only in the center do we find balance. In this case, your job will be to find that balance.

3. The mirror reflects that you are being victimized – This is when the external world is doing to you what you would not do to that same person or situation (victim mind game). However, if you look closely, you will realize that you do the same to other people or in other situations. For example, it is possible that you feel that you are working with somebody or with a certain employer who is taking advantage of you. You feel it is unfair as you are not performing the same actions toward the "aggressor." However, if you pause and expand your vision, you will realize that perhaps you are acting this way toward a third party; a parent, your partner, or a brother. In this case, you become aware of what you are doing to other people. You should consider whether you are excessively rigid with others but more lenient with yourself. Accessing and embracing flexibility and compassion shall melt anger and resentment towards others and yourself. Accepting the opportunity to transform it shall cease the situation that is recurrent in your life.

4. The mirror reflects the difference between expectation and outcome – This is when your expectations of someone or a situation clashes with your experience of them. We call it idealization. What bothers you is that your experience is not what you expected; you want that person or situation to be as you want it to be and not as it is. This triggers your need to control and change others. The lesson here is that we must accept reality as it is. We must halt our desire for control and stop wanting to change people. Instead, we must accept them as they are.

These are the four situations that our mirror will reflect on us. Our job is to identify them and transform what is required within yourself. If you don't, life will

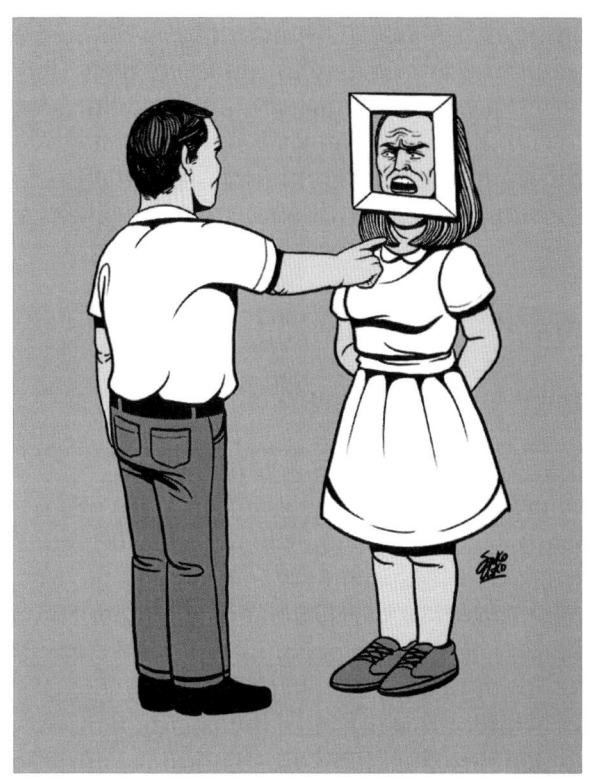

Metaphorical representation of the Law of the Mirror. The man is arguing with a woman but he is actually disappointed with his own negative aspects which he projects into the woman.

continue to bring you similar situations until you become aware of what needs to be healed or released. Those people who know how to push your buttons are your teachers of growth. These people often awaken our most negative side. These teachers can be a couple that drives you crazy, your children who ignore you, your mother, who tries to direct your life, or a boss who does not value you. Stop fighting for them to change; they are just a reflection of yourself. If you don't change, you will continue to receive the same reflection in your life. Take the information that you receive externally to transform your SIE, and everything from the outside, through quantum magic, will change. Your purpose in life is to be happy. This is achievable through personal self-knowledge, self-awareness, rejection of automatic reactions, healing wounds, and reordering your interior.

Since the law of the mirror is congruent with the quantum nature of reality, it should allow your self-realization programs to progress more quickly if the ego-self is willing to embrace the mission. When subpersonalities and entities stubbornly resist the process, this is where the sacred medicine becomes convenient to deconstruct them and ease the required spiritual healing. Another Carl Jung quote is relevant here: "What you resist, persists."

Practicing this principle will enrich your life with self-understanding and self-acceptance. This comes without wearing personality masks or playing fake characters, and by being more authentic, transparent, and enjoyable. It also will boost your self-confidence, overcoming the virus of victimhood through gaining the conviction that no one can emotionally harm you. You will come to understand that your wellbeing is not dependent on the actions of others as it only resides in your soul-self. You shall be ready to manifest more compassion and wisdom toward those around you. Remember that you are fully responsible for the events that unfold in your life and the consequences of the actions that you take.

Some After Thoughts

Rosalia was very excited by her discovery of the mirroring quality of our inner projections and that by shifting them, it produces external change. She was constantly putting this principle into practice, and after some time, she began calling it "the law of the mirror." Another instance that fed our conviction that we are all connected was an amazing synchronicity of the similarity of this label with the title of a book written by a professional life coach from Japan. As I was doing Internet research in preparation for this book, I stumbled into "The Rule of Mirror" by Yoshinori Noguchi, originally published in Japanese in 2006. My first surprise was that this was the year that my wife made her "discovery." Even more remarkable was the fact that, through a moving emotional story, the book postulates the same doctrine that we had instilled in our participants for years. The short book narrates the story of a mother suffering from her young son being bullied at school. The climax of the story is about the mother's realization of her projections related to her father, which was the key to resolve the situation. We understood that Rosalia's "discovery," as with many other discoveries, was just an ayahuasca-assisted connection with the collective unconscious that resonated with her urgent need to stop suffering from her daughter's conflicts.

Another relevant observation about Yoshinori's book is the minimal acceptance it had in the United States. It was translated into English and Spanish in 2009. Surprisingly, despite being based on the widely popular concept of psychological projection, the principle has not spread throughout the worldwide coaching community as one may have expected. I explored this and found interesting book reviews and articles borrowing from the book in Italian, French, Spanish, and Portuguese. Curiously, eleven years after its publication in English, I found almost nothing speaking about the rule or even borrowing the concept in different terms. There is a moderate number of sources describing the "law of the mirror." However, upon close examination, they only cover the most superficial aspects of psychological projection.

In my attempt to explain this, I tend to surmise that the ultimate consequence of this rule, that the external world changes in response to changes within the internal world, is too much to accept for the average mechanistic-minded coaching client. Therefore, life coaches tend not to embrace this novel approach to personal growth. In my opinion, the law of the mirror has not become a popular theme in pop psychology and the life coaching community because it's not ego friendly. The law of the mirror is not congruent with the "Three Easy Steps for Attaining Happiness" kind of article found in most mainstream magazines. The law of the mirror launches a frontal attack on our subpersonalities and entities. This is a message only our soul-self wants to hear. Coaching clients do not want to hear uncomfortable realities; they want to hear and pay the coaching fees to make their lives easier, not harder. When coached about the law of the mirror and its implications, the natural negative reaction of a coaching client is: "Oh, so you are saying that I am the problem?". The law of the mirror is not the perfect business partner for a career coach. Ironically, it is the one that may help their clients the most.

CHAPTER TEN

Achieving Personal Spiritual Healing

The Nature of Spiritual Healing

The psychological and emotional healing experienced by millions of ayahuasca participants originates in processes that unfold in the quantum field, where our SIE dwells. In a cosmic dance of hierarchical high order, we are all connected, interacting in an infinite spectrum of influences that range from solid clashes to subtle currents that gently exert an effect.

Whether fast or slow, there is an indefinable quality of subtle energy that finds its way down to the individual soul level and then to the conscious ego-self. This results in fundamental changes in the mental and emotional pathways that eventually lead to observable results. A premise of this work is that the nature of psychological and emotional healing is fundamentally spiritual; hence, the title of this book. When the conscious intention of the ego-self reaches the higher frequencies of the quantum field, an effective link is established, and a breakthrough pops into the field of awareness.

This may manifest as visions, pseudo auditory messages, intuitive insights, emotional releases, or in a variety of other ways. Translated in traditional religious terms, this would sound like: "When prayer is sincere, God listens." As shown later, we emphasize intelligent intention setting, surrendering to the process, and assuming a warrior attitude as we prepare to rush through the gates of the unknown as soon as our brain's control circuits get temporarily shut down. Metaphorically, a dam collapses within the control system and enables the temporary opening of these gates. It is during the peak of this entheogenic experience that the connection to Mother Ayahuasca, the spirit of the plants, elicits a temporary conscious communion between two realms.

The force at the core of spiritual healing is the power of consciousness. To achieve spiritual healing, it is imperative that we seek out, face with courage, and bring into the light of consciousness, the unconscious mechanisms of our entities. When that which needs to be conscious is not, it cannot be healed at the soul-self level. In other words, there is not such a thing as unconscious healing. A psychiatrist, therapist, healer, or shaman cannot provide healing if you do not become acutely aware of what is being healed. The soul is not a mechanical device that a healer can manipulate and re-program externally. Only you can heal yourself. Intuition is one of the most powerful healing tools of the soul. The soul sends you the messages necessary to heal, but if we have the channel turned off, the message is never received, much less understood. The field of psychology does not recognize this intuition, except as a curiosity. Therefore, the ego-self does not recognize the messages received and fails to process them. We are limited to the messages received through the five senses. We need to learn to receive the messages of the soul-self which are transmitted through our intuition. As we do this, our ego-self can process them, and we can incrementally align with our soul-self.

We must be aware that the natural state of the ego-self is not to operate in a polarized manner against the soul-self. When the ego-self, for convenience or survival reasons, embraces the spiritual path, it becomes aligned with the soul-self. Together, the ego and soul-self can focus on self-realization, instead of squandering life juggling the ego's multiple masks. When the ego-self raises hell in our lives, it is because it has been unable to find a reference point, or connection, with its source. The conflicts in our lives are directly proportional to the distance between them. When the ego-self is in balance with the soul-self, we cannot see where the ego-self ends, and the soul-self begins. When that happens, you become a whole human being.

The conscious path to authentic self-realization requires recognition of our non-physical SIE and the vast amount of knowledge available from within ourselves. We need to identify behaviors that operate in opposition to harmony and wholeness. We must recognize the disparity between our behaviors and the energy of the soul-self. We must consider the broad-reaching elements of negativity, how many forms of negativity exist, and the effects of these upon the soul-self. The soul, while remaining aloft during our physical existence, carries the blueprint of wholeness and self-realization programs. It holds a holographic pattern of wholeness to be pursued and pulls us upward like a sprout bursting from a seed. When the wholeness pattern is not followed, dysfunction results due to the misalignment with its fundamental purpose.

Spiritual healing resolves situations that may otherwise hurt the soul-self. The soul-self cannot tolerate brutality, excessive pain, or irrationality. Poisonous energies to the soul-self include deception, lack of forgiveness, jealousy, and hatred. When the ego-self engages in these behaviors, it administers venom to the soul-self, in this way blocking its strength and power. Understanding this process is at the heart of spiritual healing. When we see those wounds in ourselves, or anyone else, it is the soul's impulse to rush into doing something about it. Despite the continuous interaction between the two, the ego-self is often unaware of this trauma. As soon as the ego-self becomes enlightened to this, the lightning guidance of the soul-self immediately manifests.

If you are not aware, the ego-self suffers the emotional density that comes with doubt and confusion. Moreover, if you are not aware of your soul-self or deny its existence, then the ego-self can only learn through the density of physical events; the harsh lessons that life brings to us, those that often triggers the question, "why me?". In those cases, the ego-self only gains awareness through a crisis.

We must understand that the ego-self, including its five senses, is not positive or negative; it is simply the tool of the soul-self, a crucial and important player in the overall scheme of reality. Authentic needs belong to the soul-self. We need to love and be loved. We must express creativity through the multiple possibilities that exist. We need to cultivate our soul-self like a delicate plant in the greenhouse; our ego-self must awaken and work consciously to find its alignment with its soul-self. When they work as a team, our personal power is unlimited.

The fearful and violent emotions that have come to characterize human existence can only be experienced by the subpersonalities and entities within the ego-self. Only these components can feel anger, fear, hatred, vengeance, sorrow, shame, regret, indifference, frustration, cynicism, and loneliness. It is only these entities and subpersonalities which can manipulate or exploit. Moreover, these are the only constituents that can pursue external power. These subpersonalities and entities can also be loving, compassionate, and wise in their relations with others as part of a sophisticated survival strategy. However, true love, compassion, and wisdom sprout exclusively from the soul-self. The soul-self is the eternal part of you. The soul-self is not a passive or theoretical entity that occupies a space somewhere in our chest cavity. It is the part of us that understands the impersonal nature of the energy dynamics in which we are involved, that loves without restriction and accepts without judgment.

Before we examine more important concepts relevant to the spiritual healing process with ayahuasca, allow your ego-self to reflect and meditate about your spiritual awakening.

Understanding Spiritual Awakening
- Awakening is not an act of magic, although it may fill your life with magic.
- Awakening has nothing to do with your outer world, although everything

around you will seem to have a new brightness.

- Awakening will not change your life, although you will feel that everything has changed.
- Awakening will not erase your past, but by reflecting, you will perceive it as the story of someone dearly loved who has learned many things. You will feel that this someone is not you anymore.
- Awakening will not wake-up your loved ones, but they will look more divine in your eyes.
- Awakening will not heal all of your wounds, but they will no longer govern you.
- Awakening will not solve your financial situation, but within yourself, you will feel like a millionaire.

Awakening occurs when we remove specific filters through which we used to watch and cognize the world.

- Awakening will not make you more popular, but you will no longer feel alone.
- Awakening will not beautify you in the eyes of others, but it will make you perfect before your own eyes.
- Awakening will not give you more power, but you will discover the power that you have.
- Awakening may not erase the bars of your prisons, but it will give you the freedom to be yourself.
- Awakening will not change the world; it will change you.
- Awakening will not take responsibility for you, but it will give you awareness

of the consequences of your actions and choices.

- Awakening will not ensure you are always correct, but you will no longer feel the need to be.
- Awakening will not make love flow into your life, but you will discover that this flow already dwells in you.
- Awakening has little to do with what you imagine and has everything to do with love.

To awaken is to love yourself, your limits, and your experiences. It is to love others as part of your being and to love existence itself. Love this beautiful life, so wonderful and varied in all its nuances. Your life is sacred because God is the miracle of life that lives in you. It only remains that you trust and allow the Spirit of Ayahuasca to commune with your own.

For your awakening, seek and grasp all of the help available; read all the books you find, attend all the meetings you are invited to, meditate, breathe, and wait. Everything will be useful. However, it is only you who will conduct the alchemy, because nothing but your intention to make it happen can precipitate it.

Even if you do nothing at all, be still, just as though it has happened. If at some point you feel awakened and you see that others around you are still sleeping, then walk on tiptoes, respect their dreams and allow them the perfection of discovery in their own time, just as yours was. When they open their eyes, the brightness of your spark will help them awaken without needing to do anything. If you are still sleeping, relax, and enjoy your dream, you are being lulled and receiving loving attention. Ayahuasca is here to help.

Understanding Ayahuasca Visions

We all have a fairly good idea of what a vision is, but let us explore the concept more deeply. A vision is the sensory transference of subconscious material that is perceived by the ego-self as convincingly meaningful despite its obvious illusory nature. Visions carry the seriousness of tangible reality; they stay with us and produce a significant impact on our interpretation of our reality. To further clarify the concept, let us start by making the necessary distinction between visions and hallucinations.

Hallucinations are perceived by us with the awareness of being sensory illusions. We feel a high degree of certainty that they are not real while we experience them. We do not usually try to interpret them because they render themselves clearly nonsensical. We may feel awe and wonder during the experience, but our perception is only comparable with the show of a good magician; we do not know how the trick is done, but we unequivocally know it is a trick. Additionally, hallucinations don't leave a notable mark in our consciousness.

During my exploration phase with psychedelics as a youngster, I had accumulated some experience with LSD-induced hallucinations. When I began having ayahuasca visions years later, one of the aspects that caught my attention was a dramatic qualitative difference between the two. Without any scientific evidence, I formed my hypothesis to explain their apparent difference in experiential quality. In my attempt to reconcile my perceptions with our model of the psyche, I propose that hallucinations are distortions in the perceptual processing pathways of the brain. I suggest that as the subconscious-self is randomly accessed, imagery is provided, which can be experienced as fragmented pieces of unrelated images or as a fluid sequence that resembles a story. This experience may also be induced by neurochemical interference, which dysregulates neurotransmission and uncovers the memory hologram of the person, the human species, or the collective unconscious. Regardless of how hallucinations are produced, the fact remains that the experience fails to reach the soul-self. Consequently, the ego-self misses the meaning of the experience. A hallucination is always followed by a sense of meaninglessness or cluelessness.

This definition of a hallucination is crucial in establishing the distinction from the experience of a vision. In ancient times, visions, Biblical or otherwise, were described as having a divine origin. Today, we feel visions are downloaded to the ego-self from the higher parts of our SIE or beyond. They contain different types of memories, literal and symbolic information from encrypted biographical memories, collective unconscious, genetically stored memories of ancestral origin, and soul memories from previous lives.

There is a popular premier booklet for entry-level seekers of ayahuasca information called "Ayahuasca Manifesto." It is presented as though written by the plant spirit of ayahuasca itself and speaking in the first-person mode; it makes an interesting remark about visions:

"*Although I carry hallucinogenic properties, such is not the main gift I have to offer. There are hundreds of hallucinogenic agents on the planet, but only a handful of "visiogens," those powerful tools that open new inroads towards the light. The hallucination is entertainment; the vision is virtue*" [1]

During ayahuasca experiences, visions can manifest as brief flashes of meaningful images or as longer episodes of detailed, colorful journeys. These are dependent on many factors. Visions seem to be produced by the effects of Dimethyltryptamine ("DMT"), a naturally occurring hallucinogenic chemical found in many plants and animals, including humans. The primary suspect responsible for the production of DMT in humans is the pineal gland. This tiny corpus of tissue inspired Rene Descartes in the 16th century to declare it as the "seat of the soul." Dr. Rick Strassman, in his classic book: "DMT: The Spirit Molecule," proposed the possibility that the DMT could be produced by the pineal gland, a theory that was subsequently supported by laboratory experiments in rodents. [2]. The riddle of the source of DMT has not been fully elucidated, as these same experiments also revealed that DMT remains present in rats, which had their pineal glands surgically removed. This has resulted in the speculation that DMT may also be produced elsewhere in the human body.

The pineal gland, judging by some of its biological features alone, is a remarkably interesting little organ. A small gland with an average of five to eight millimeters in size, strategically located in the geometric center of the skull and, curiously, is exempt from the blood-brain barrier. These factors immediately catch the interest of anyone interested in the subject. This barrier is a highly selective cellular filter that prevents "unauthorized" substances, such as pathogens and toxins, in the bloodstream from infiltrating the brain and reaching neurons. Aside from the kidneys, the pineal gland receives the highest blood flow percentage compared to other organs of the body. The pineal gland produces melatonin and is involved in our perception of light. This gives the gland a role in modulation of sleep-wake cycles (circadian rhythms) and seasonal functions. It is also associated with sexual development, as this appears to be inhibited considering the abundant melatonin levels in children, and pineal tumors have been linked with precocious puberty. Another characteristic which adds further intrigue to the pineal gland is that, despite its location deep inside the brain, studies have demonstrated a primary role for the pineal gland (along with the retina) in the recognition and processing of external light. Melatonin is present in both pineal and retinal photoreceptor cells. Moreover, the morphological and functional similarities of these cells indicate a close evolutionary relationship.[3]

Having defined the distinction between visions and hallucinations and discussed the role of the pineal gland and DMT in their manifestations, we can now focus on dissecting the experiences more meticulously.

Ayahuasca visions continue to baffle psychologists, anthropologists, and neuroscientists because they do not fit the established understanding of psychedelic hallucinations previously researched via LSD and similar drugs. The first intriguing finding from early anthropological studies was the recurrence of certain visionary themes reported by ayahuasca practitioners. Regardless of ethnicity, nationality, or cultural background, subjects reported having experienced vivid visions of serpents, large cats (jaguars, tigers, and pumas), exotic birds, and impressive beautiful palaces. Other animals that were unknown in South America, such as elephants, were also reported. The vast majority of subjects reporting these visions have only seen these animals in photographs. I have experienced crocodiles and lizards during my first few years working with the medicine. I also enjoyed the awesome visions of being inside phosphorescent palaces and temples. These are the kind of visions that are generally of unsurpassed beauty and splendor, which visionary artists try to capture in their paintings. Other frequent themes are scenes of ancient civilizations, panoramic scenery of nature, and heavenly scenarios. Objects in visions often appear to be made of gold, crystal, precious stones, and white or pastel-colored fabrics.

From a psychological standpoint, these visions depict an entirely new category of visual elements, not previously described or studied by classical theories. They differ significantly from the Jungian archetypes, which focus on themes such as the great mother, the adventurous youth, the hero, the wise old man, birth, and death. In dream analysis, psychologists have not seen such a consistent body of themes arising from subconscious imagery. The limited diversity of themes in ayahuasca visions are too circumscribed to be explained by the highly variable individual subconscious-selves. Moreover, these depictions are too mundane to be considered archetypal. They are simply unexplainable by current psychological theories of personality. This is one of the many mysteries of ayahuasca.

There are also auditory "visions," in which participants telepathically hear an inner voice that points toward the confirmation of the meaning of a visual vision. The "voice" may also briefly explain issues relevant to the explicit pre-session intention set by the participant. However, the most important aspect of the ayahuasca phenomenology is the evident boost in ideas, insights, and reflections in the field of consciousness of the ego-self during the experience. Many participants report that they think faster and feel more intelligent during and after the ayahuasca experience. In our spiritual advisory work, we promote the conscious pursual of insights. Some participants consider that these spontaneous insights are more meaningful than visions. In general, participants report ayahuasca work has made them more insightful and involved with deeper psychological analyses and philosophical contemplation. Experienced practitioners often gain insights concerning personal questions, find answers or solutions that are subsequently applied in their lives, and find comfort and solace.

When I reflect on these aspects collectively in our observational sample, I recognize concerning both insights and visions, a pattern of common personal features. The ayahuasca experience tends to gravitate around the personal aspects that are being reflected. Therefore, we advise not to over-emphasize the setting of intentions for the session, as it appears that the experience naturally flows in the direction most urgently needed for the participant's healing process. I discovered this characteristic of the ayahuasca experience during my early days as a practitioner and quickly realized its enormous potential for spiritual healing work. I passionately followed this personal journey, which, years later, produced the book you are reading now.

As a final proposition regarding ayahuasca's visionary features, I hypothesize that there is a physical correlation between the active ingredients in the brew and the type of visionary effects experienced by the subject. Perhaps with future research, we may be able to determine whether the DMT is more closely associated with the intensely graphic aspects of the visions (such as the animals and palaces described above), while the more non-visual and cognitive insights may be correlated with the Harmine family of chemicals. I have observed that the sessions tend to exhibit colorful visuals during the early stages of the journey, while the non-verbal aspects tend to manifest in the later stages. Harmine also has hallucinogenic properties, and this may explain why the visuals at the end of the session tend to resemble more "black and white" images in contrast with the spectacular colors at the beginning. We may draw an interesting parallel between the effects of the two active, visionary chemicals brought by the two different plants contained in the brew. The chacruna leaf (Psychotria Viridis) contributes DMT or the 'colorful' component, while the vine (Barnisteriopsis Caapi) contributes the Harmine or the 'non-visual' constituent; each one becoming a protagonist at different times during the journey. This is an idea which I will continue to research with anecdotal accounts.

The Pineal Gland and Third Eye Mysticism

The word pineal, from Latin pinea, means pinecone. It was first used in the late 17th century during the evolution of anatomical study in European universities. By the 1630's Rene Descartes had postulated its presumed relationship with spirituality, and its cone shape became a symbol of wisdom and enlightenment. For this reason, it was adopted as an architectural motif, and we can find it detailed on fountains, entrances, and building facades around the world.

When we consider that the pineal gland contains photoreceptors cells, regulates sleep, and may produce DMT, we should acknowledge that this small structure has had sufficient elements to raise the interest of ancient intellectuals. Just think about it, it is located in the darkest place, but it can sense external light. Subsequently, the gland produces melatonin, which enhances drowsiness and aids sleep induction. Additionally, it seems to produce DMT - the strongest known hallucinogenic. The structure is complex, multi-faceted, and may hold great importance for our innate spirituality and the human condition.

Ancient civilizations, including the Egyptians, Indians, Assyrians, Mexicans, Greeks, Romans, and Sumerians have all depicted pinecones in their art, usually in their religious portrayals of gods or holy people. This must be because there has been a clear association of the gland with elevated spiritual qualities. In the modern-day, we can still observe pinecone symbolism in Catholicism; the staff carried by the Pope, the shape of bishop's mitre, lamps, and candleholders in the church all appear to be adorned with pinecones.

In addition to the pinecone association with the pineal gland, we have the mystical tradition of the third eye. Considering the gland's photoreceptor capacity, the assertion has merits and relevance; potentially more literal than symbolic. Many believe that past civilizations were aware of these properties due to the prominence and influence of the structure in ancient sacred art. The Indian spiritual tradition has long held this belief, which originates from their ancient deities. Shiva and other Hindu deities are often depicted with a literal third eye on their forehead. This eye represents an awakening, or enlightenment, as the ability to see into higher realms of existence and consciousness. The popularity of this belief has been relatively recent in the West as it came with the arrival of Buddhism, yoga, and other Eastern philosophies during the 20th century. Significant momentum to the belief in the third eye was impacted across Western cultures during the New Age movement during the 1980s. Since this time, the idea has been widely adopted by meditation psychedelic and consciousness cultures.

Be aware that the quantum model of the psyche does not focus on the pineal gland and the third eye mystical interpretations of the spiritual process. Other than acknowledging its importance in terms of biological function and historical relevancy, this information adds little practical value to the quest for spiritual healing. The potential for distraction from the immediate tasks at hand is greater than the practical benefit we may extract from it. The knowledge already obtained should be enough information for our intellectual satisfaction, without investing excessive valuable personal energy in cultivating the development of the third eye as a self-realization path. Therefore, despite its recently found scientific link with the pinecone-shaped gland, the third eye mythology should not be a subject of serious consideration for the evolution of ayahuasca spiritual advising or psychedelic-assisted therapies.

Ayahuasca-Induced Near-Death Experiences

Soon after we experience our first few ayahuasca journeys, we realize that the concept of darkness is an intrinsic part of the process. We realize why the ancient curanderos in Peru named the vine the "rope of death." When we browse the classic texts of Freud or Jung, we encounter the subconscious parts of the psyche, which are described with terms such as "repressed memories," shadow, and importantly, darkness. As hundreds of ayahuasca practitioners may attest, the subconscious represents the unknown, a mysterious, scary place. We cannot expect anything different from the gateway to the traumatic and most disturbing encrypted memories of our lives. Such a dark and odd subconscious realm are strongly associated with the ayahuasca experience. During the peak of the experience, the wall between the conscious and the subconscious crumbles and enables powerful information flow from the dark side towards the transparent and clear access of the ego-self. At this point, the most urgent or relevant issues required for the resolution of our inner conflicts are projected over the main screen of our conscious movie theater.

That is when the participant gets perplexed with a Wow! Moment, followed by emotional confirmation of previous cognitive awareness. We become perplexed when impressive unsuspected images, memories, feelings, or facts are revealed and find matching correlations with previously suspected situations based on "gut feelings," intuitive insights, or just plain rational analysis.

This "wow" moment opens the door to somewhat permanent healing, which is entirely unavailable with conventional techniques. The emotional confirmation that follows ratifies and provides a sense of absolute certainty of previously suspected situations fueled by family rumors or an unexplained emotional rejection towards a family member. There is nothing glamorous about encrypted memories as these are invariable dark by definition. The release of encrypted darkness is among the most powerful and beneficial properties of ayahuasca.

One of the consequences of releasing subconscious darkness is that it confronts us with our deepest fears. Death is the ultimate fear. There is a phenomenon that I labeled "ayahuasca-induced near-death experience" ("AINDE"). Participants often panic during ayahuasca sessions as they feel something is going terribly wrong and that they may die during the experience. Shamans and facilitators know this well and often manage subjects in a panic with proper care, as there is nothing more understandable than getting in panic while unexpectedly confronted with your imminent death. On rare occasions, participants experience the process of dying and later describe their visions resembling the testimonials of people who have been declared dead but were then resuscitated and return to tell their story. After the session, some participants find the experience detestable and hard to accept as heathy, while others experience the most healing and liberating epiphany of their lives. I considered myself privileged when this happened to me once in the unforgettable night of July 26, 2012, with my teacher shaman Don Jose in the Peruvian Amazon. To prepare participants for this eventuality, I always include a brief caveat to assist them beforehand in understanding and embracing this unique healing opportunity in my pre-session orientation.

The medical research conducted by Dr. Rick Strassman can aid in comprehension of this phenomenon. In his famous book, "DMT: The Spirit Molecule," Dr. Strassman postulates that the pineal gland secretes large quantities of DMT during a particular period preceding death.

Based on abundant empirical observations, there must be a genetically designed neurological mechanism that, at the imminent collapse of the biological organism, triggers an altered state of consciousness in the dying patient to assist crossing the portal of life. There are thousands of anecdotal accounts from family members and hospice employees describing how patients describe their visionary experiences hours or days prior to passing. These include descriptions of already deceased family members, beautiful places which they will soon visit, and of course, the peaceful acceptance and absolute certainty that the final moment has arrived. The universal occurrence of these incidents across all nations and cultures in the world is evidence of the existence of some type of neurochemical mechanism. If not a heightened production of DMT, another neurological mechanism must be present to explain such a widely recognized phenomenon. Dr. Strassman's hypothesis received a boost of validity in 2018 with the discovery of increased levels of DMT associated with experimentally induced cardiac arrest in laboratory rats [2]. These findings are relevant to the idea proposed by Strassman. The results suggest that a fatal cardiac arrest was accompanied by a huge burst of DMT secretion into the bloodstream. The parallel with the human experience is too close to ignore. Since the ayahuasca brew contains a significant amount of DMT, it is not difficult for an experienced practitioner to accept the hypothesis that at the moment of death, the human brain is flooded with a DMT compound. These visions of the dying are too similar to the ones occurring during the AINDE's, which we should not dismiss as mere coincidence. I feel the hypothesis that the dying brain is flooded with endogenous DMT is a solid proposition which awaits scientific research to support it.

The question then arises, if the increase in DMT levels precede death in humans and it is genetically programmed this way, is it possible that artificially increasing DMT levels in the brain may trigger the feeling of death approaching? There is ample evidence that this may be the case. We appear to have reached a fair understanding of the intriguing phenomenon of participants reporting AINDE's.

This is exciting news for the field of spiritual and emotional healing because there is an enormous accumulation of reliable testimonials of people that were declared dead and were resuscitated to tell the story. The notable factor prevalent in these cases is the outstandingly dramatic reprogramming of the individuals' persona. These individuals come back with the certainty of another reality following their physical existence. Atheists come back believers, criminals come back loving, and the anxious come back tranquil. Almost all those interviewed confirm feeling happier with a revitalized sense of meaning in life. Something deeply transformative occurs during near-death experiences. Therefore, it logically follows that an AINDE's could be equally transformative.

This is the exact phenomenon that has occurred thousands of times over the past few decades to subjects that have had the blessing of living through one of these experiences. When we closely examine the aforementioned death-bed testimonials, we find a consensus that during these final moments, people embark into a thorough and frequently painstaking review of their life events.

I learned this truth firsthand with the passing of my beloved father on Thanksgiving Day of 2007. Being his only son, he was content with having me beside him for the last few days. He asked me to provide support and encouragement to help him pass away. I could barely hear his voice, only when my ear was almost touching his lips. He started to have what I already knew was DMT visions; my little sister that died at nine years old, almost 47 years earlier, appeared in his visions to assist him from the other side. He was eager to join her, but it was not his time yet. For hours, he repeatedly closed his eyes after saying bye to me but failed to detach every single time. He then shared with me in his faint whisper the process of dying; he wanted to teach me this in the same way he taught me so many things since I was a little child. He told me that it was like a train with many wagons, and every time he stepped into one, he realized there was an emotional issue yet to be resolved, making him get off the wagon to find a resolution before trying again. He went through the process several times until he finally succeeded, the train departed with his soul.

That story resonates in my heart to this day. I learned that the more spiritually healthy you are when you meet death, the smoother and more enjoyable the transition will be. The power of having death at your doorsteps is healing to the extreme. All accounts must settle before checking out—acceptance of far forgotten mistakes, remorse of wrongdoings, releasing all attachments including love. You go as empty as you came. Death is the ultimate healing experience.

Can you imagine the healing power of confronting your subconscious deeply rooted issues with the intensity and realism of feeling death approaching to take you? With the benefit of all the scientific literature available and the ample empirical evidence at hand, I can only state beyond a reasonable doubt that there could never be a more effective healing therapy than facing your death without actually dying, and finding yourself a few hours later sipping a delicious vegetarian hot soup under the care of experienced staff. It just can never get better than that, period.

AINDE's and the Mind-Body Dilemma

When we examine the similarities between the AINDE effect and the natural visions experienced by the dying, we find them thought-provoking and deserving of further commentary. This situation serves as an excellent example to illustrate further the mind-body relationship. In earlier chapters, we have proposed the influence of our quantum SIE over our physical brains and that we live our spiritual lives embedded in our physical bodies.

Under our model of the psyche, we postulate that when our soul-self has determined that it has consummated its purpose, it triggers the ultimate self-realization program of departing its physical vehicle. Under this theory, the subconscious-self triggers the execution of a neurological program that produces large quantities of DMT in the brain to let the ego-self know that the final moment is near.

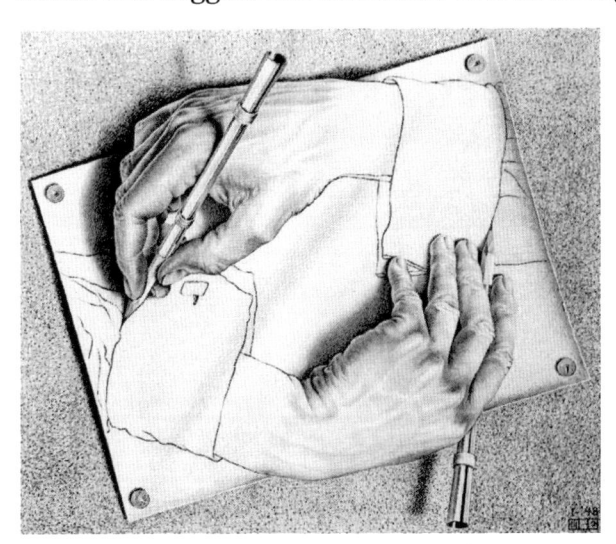

"Drawing Hands" by Maurits Cornelis Escher (1948)

From the medical perspective, we must assume that there is a genetically designed chemical switch that somehow is activated when the body systems begin to collapse irreversibly. Following this, it triggers a process of shutting down all physiological functions, while investing the last life force reserves into the production of large quantities of DMT to induce a soothing hallucinogenic experience in the dying individual. We have seen how the body provides soothing relief in the presence of excruciating pain by flooding the brain with primary beta-endorphins. When experiencing a severe injury, like accidentally losing a finger or a hand, the brain reacts this way, and the person enters into an altered state where pain seems to disappear or becomes reduced to negligible levels compared with the severity of the injury.

Regardless of the paradigm of reality used to interpret the terminal phase of human life, it appears that AINDE's occur because the ayahuasca brew seems to mimic the chemical cocktail that is present in the brain of naturally dying patients. When you replicate such a cocktail in the brain with sufficient accuracy, the ego-self receives a sort of alarm message from the physical body, saying that it is about to collapse or die functionally. In other words, the events in the body determine the events in the quantum field, not the other way around, as proposed by the model. The critical point is that both realities, the quantum and the physical, are complementary, interdependent, and never polarized or dual in nature. They are aspects of the same essence. The physical matter influences the quantum field and vice versa. The scientific establishment accepts only the physical dimension and often finds itself impotent before unexplained phenomena. By accepting both, this quantum model offers a broader and more unified understanding of reality. I include here one masterpiece of the genius artist, M.C. Escher, to illustrate the complementarity principle of the presumed mind-body dilemma. There is no beginning; there is no end. Human life is a multidimensional continuum of divine origin and incomprehensible complexity. Zen Buddhists "know" this, and silence is their answer.

There is another philosophical comment which is relevant to this topic. The fact that the human brain has a pain reduction anesthetic response which aids the suffering organism implies that evolution has considered the suffering in developing improved survival mechanisms. Let us assume that the 'anesthetic' brain response evolved to handle other physiological considerations, and the reduction in pain is just an unintended by-product of its action. Alternatively, we can assume that reduction of the neurological signals that define pain has a survival advantage. This would explain that evolution found its way to develop a pain-soothing mechanism to assist organisms in critical life-threatening conditions. Evolution, once again, has developed increasingly complex systems to warrant the survival of the species. This makes perfect evolutionary sense because an organism that survives trauma may be able to mate and reproduce in the future.

What I find extremely intriguing is that evolution has no incentive at all to develop a mechanism that assists the suffering organism to die in peace. The experience of dying, as we have described it, with meaningful visionary episodes chemically induced by the strongest hallucinogenic known to man, is entirely baffling. DMT is endogenously produced in large quantities during the moment when death is near, causing the well-known spiritually healing effects described earlier. When we evaluate the whole situation, it necessarily makes us reflect on the grandiosity of life and the inherent compassion built-in the natural process of dying. The inevitable question then arises: What evolutionary advantage could anyone conceivably hypothesize about such gracefully smooth process of terminating human life? How could natural selection have developed such gentle courtesies when there is no clear benefit? How could natural selection produce a special-purpose, once-in-a-lifetime process, not transferable to the next generation?

Not having a near suitable scientific answer to such a profound question turns me into a believer that our SIE is spiritual in nature, that our souls originate from a divine source. Our physical bodies most likely evolved following evolution principles, but until evolutionists answer such question convincingly, my belief in God shall remain rock-solid in my heart.

Medical Healing vs. Spiritual Healing

As new psychedelic substances begin to be approved for medical use, health authorities shall define the treatment protocols and regulate their application by accredited professionals. These substances will be supplied by the pharmaceutical industry and distributed through their channels. However, plant medicines from natural sources will continue to be available, and spiritual healing practices shall continue using the healing paradigms which encompass decades of experience and, in some cases, centuries of tradition. The advent of medical psychedelic therapies will establish parallel healing paradigms with traditional methods that are analogous to existing pharmaceutical (allopathic) and naturopathic approaches. These approaches will exist concurrently; one comprised of highly regulated medical practices, and the other, composed of informal spiritual healing practices. The latter, which has sprouted mostly from the expansion of ayahuasca in Western culture during this century, is characterized by a community of facilitators and practitioners with a broad diversity of healing beliefs and techniques. One evident trend arising from the globalization of ayahuasca is an inevitable syncretism as practitioners integrate their alternative healing techniques and beliefs into their ayahuasca sessions.

This diversity of approaches to spiritual healing has been catalyzed by the failure of the mechanistic scientific model to provide convincing answers to unexplained phenomena, including the elusive consciousness problem described earlier. This has prompted the emergence of pseudoscientific healing approaches that attempt to fill the void left unresolved by science.

We can enumerate many approaches, each one based on a limited paradigm of our highly complex multidimensional reality. During the last few decades, leading pioneers have developed innovative healing approaches based on their empirical observations with the sincere intention of providing effective solutions to the ailments of others. Upon examining these approaches, we find that almost all of them contain highly valuable insights into the nature of the disease. When we view these approaches as a whole, we discover a sense of complementarity in the relationships between them. It is as though each individual approach contains a piece of a higher truth. When viewed together, these truths appear to connect with powerful reciprocity.

1. Neurolinguistic Programming (NLP) emphasizes behavioral mechanics and structure.

2. Hypnosis emphasizes deep state learning.

3. Psycho-Genealogy emphasizes the transgenerational transfer of information.

4. Chinese Medicine emphasizes herbal remedies and dietary guidance.

5. Acupuncture emphasizes balancing energy flowing in body meridians.

6. Transactional Analysis emphasizes the role-playing of basic subpersonalities.

7. Homeopathy emphasizes remedy dynamism.

8. Rebirthing Therapies emphasizes reprogramming birth traumas.

9. Biodecoding emphasizes the emotional origin of psychological and physical ailments.

Due to the previously discussed limitations, the healing of the personal psychological realm is still far from being a precise science. It bears great resemblance to an art form rather than a formal science. The therapist's intuition, combined with the insights received by the patient during the psychedelic experience, play a fundamental role in the healing process. Therapists develop the style that works best for them, applying protocols that cannot be found in textbooks. Like artists and musicians, patients connect with and follow therapists who emotionally connect with them. Trust is often an important factor that influences healing outcomes.

The unfortunate reality is that too often, healers become charlatans, while others obsessively grab their paradigm and justify its validity with increasingly delusional arguments. This has fostered a skeptical movement and hardcore critics that actively attack them in their quest for justice and reason. Official medical and psychological organizations have repeatedly issued formal declarations against such practices. These statements have contributed to the destruction of healers' reputation and created an overwhelmingly negative public image. Additionally, there are also economic interests within the medical establishment that stimulate such skepticism. This skepticism is fed by the deeply embedded science dogmas described by Sheldrake earlier (footnote). Therefore, we have a fundamental abyss which separates the emerging alternative healing methods from the longtime-established and powerful mechanistic medical establishment.

The important idea which must be understood by emerging ayahuasca spiritual advisors and psychedelic therapists is that, despite the historical mistakes of alternative proponents and their failures to develop robust and testable theoretical frameworks, the fact remains that there is something in these approaches that makes sense to anyone who sincerely investigates them with an open mind. This "something" corresponds to the missing link that science has been unable to explain with its powerful scientific method rationally. The fact that these therapies, all of which are in their infancy, have not yet stood up to scientific scrutiny, does not mean they should be dismissed without further review. To understand the dynamics of psychedelic healing, we must start by examining the dynamics of the established medical practices from their perspective.

The Osteopathic Medicine Healing Paradigm

Many people are unaware that there are two different paradigms in scientific medical practice. The most widely known physicians are the medical doctors who earn with much effort the right to add the letters M.D. after their names. They practice allopathic medicine, which means that they treat symptoms and diseases using drugs, radiation, or surgery. However, there are alternative methods that do not follow prescriptive allopathic methods. In particular, osteopathic medicine which uses a whole person approach to partner with their patients. Doctors in Osteopathy (DO's) believe there is more to good health than the absence of pain or disease. DO's are licensed to practice medicine and surgery in all 50 states in the USA and are recognized in almost 100 other countries to varying degrees. In this century, osteopathic physician training in the United States is equivalent to the training of MDs. Osteopathic physicians attend four years of medical school, followed by an internship and a minimum of two years of residency. There are over 30 medical schools that offer DO degrees within the United States, while there are 141 accredited MD medical schools. Osteopathic medicine has steadily grown in popularity, with numbers of DO's growing from 13,000 in 1960 to over 145,000 in 2020. [4]

There are two main distinctions between osteopathic and allopathic physicians. The first and most obvious difference lies in the osteopathic physicians' use of osteopathic manipulative medicine. While these methods are most commonly known by the general public as a treatment for neuro and musculoskeletal injury, DOs may utilize these methods in their diagnosis and treatment of diseases involving internal organs and all other parts of the body. A more subtle, yet arguably more important, distinction between the two professions is that osteopathic medicine offers a concise philosophy upon which all clinical practice is based. Central to this philosophy is the belief that the body has an inherent healing mechanism that allows the maintenance of health, resistance to illness, and recovery from disease. The goal of osteopathic medical treatment is to provide patients with the tools they need to restore and maintain their natural, self-healing state. The four major tenets of the osteopathic medical philosophy are:

1. The body is entirely united; the person is a fully integrated being of body, mind, and spirit. No single part of the body functions independently. Each sep-

arate piece is interconnected with all others and serves to benefit the collective whole of the person. Alterations in any part of the system, including an individual's psychological and spiritual health, affect the functioning of the body as a whole and all other components therein.

2. The body is capable of self-regulation, self-healing, and health maintenance. Health is the natural state of the body, and the body possesses complex, self-regulatory mechanisms that it uses to heal itself from injury. In times of disease, when a part of the body is functioning sub-optimally, other parts of the body come out of their natural state of health to compensate for the dysfunction. However, this compensatory process may contribute to new dysfunctions. Osteopathic physicians must work to adjust the body to realign all components back to a normal state. Osteopathic manipulative medicine aims to restore the body's self-healing capacity by decreasing allostatic load, or the physiological effects of chronic bodily stresses, and enhancing immune system function.

3. Structure and function are reciprocally interrelated. The structure of a body part governs its function. Hence, abnormal structure manifests as dysfunction. Function also governs structure. Besides, if the body's overall structure is suboptimal, its functioning and capacity for self-healing are also inhibited.

4. Rational treatment is based on an understanding of the first three principles. These permeate all aspects of health maintenance, disease prevention, and treatment. The osteopathic physician examines, diagnoses, and treats patients according to these principles.

It is important to realize when reviewing the philosophical principles of osteopathic medicine that these also apply to the practice of spiritual healing with ayahuasca. The contribution of common sense in the evolution of medical practice have positioned osteopathic medicine in a congruent space relative to ayahuasca spiritual advising. By emphasizing the similarity of their healing principles, ayahuasca spiritual advisors can eventually gain authenticity and, importantly, recognition.

The Psychosomatic Medicine Healing Paradigm

Psychosomatic disorder is an illness that connects the mind and body. This occurs in such a way that the physiological functioning of the body is affected by the psychological tensions that either causes disease or worsen a pre-existing condition. It is also known as Psychophysiologic disorder. A maladaptive stimulation of the autonomic nervous system, which regulates internal organ function, is responsible for the evolution of this disorder and leads to impairment in organ function. The exact cause of the evolution of psychosomatic disorder is unknown. Studies have revealed that the physical disorders associated with psychological states can be correlated with hyperactive nerve impulses, which can cause the secretion of adrenaline into the blood, leading to an increased state of anxiousness. Such hyperactivity can be triggered by genetic factors, irregular biological conditions (e.g., metabolism or amino acid levels), stress (e.g., trauma, fear, anger or guilt) or family circumstances (e.g., parental absence or behavior or relationship difficulties)

There are three general categories of psychosomatic illness: [5]

(i) Persons with both psychological and physical issues, whose symptoms and management complicate each other. For example, type-2 diabetic patients are more susceptible to stress-related hypertension, while such hypertension exacerbates the diabetic condition.

(ii) Persons with psychological issues due to a medical condition or its treatment. For example, patients feeling depressed because they have cancer and are taking treatment for it. Studies have suggested that psychological stress can affect a tumor's ability to grow and spread, thereby worsening the state of cancer.

(iii) Persons with psychological issues who also have one or more somatoform symptoms. There are several types somatoform illnesses such as hypochondriasis where they believe a minor physical symptom to be a grave disease; conversion disorder, where they don't have any medical illness but experience neurological symptoms such as seizures; somatization disorder, where they feel frequent symptoms which have no relation to a serious medical condition such as asthma, peptic ulcer, and arrhythmia. Finally, pain disorder, where they may experience severe pain in any part of the body for more than six months, without any physical cause. For example, migraines, tension, headaches, back pain, etc.

After learning the healing philosophy of osteopathic medicine, it is reasonable to expect that psychosomatic medicine would have developed a strong resemblance to such methods. Unfortunately, this has not been the case. On closer examination, this is easily explained by the fact that psychosomatic medicine evolved from the allopathic paradigm of psychiatry. Except for the developed state of psychosomatic medicine in Germany, osteopathic medicine adheres to holistic principles while allopathic medicine does not. Considering this, ayahuasca spiritual healing has much to offer to the mechanistic paradigm of psychosomatic medicine.

Psychosomatic medicine in Germany is undoubtedly the most advanced in Europe and, potentially, the world. In Germany, psychosomatic medicine is not a synonym for consultation-liaison psychiatry like in the United States. Still, it represents a comprehensive field and a specialized medical discipline with a larger institutional basis than exists in any other country.

German psychosomatic medicine is not a subspecialty of psychiatry, although it may have shared models, methods, and overlapping care for patients. In some places, departments of psychosomatic medicine are part of internal medicine.

Historically, German psychiatry resisted the integration of psychotherapy as a core method. This contributed to the independent development of psychosomatic medicine as an institutional and academic basis for psychotherapy in medicine. [6]

Their clinical care is centered on somatoform/functional disorders, eating disorders, and an ample spectrum of somatopsychic disorders such as psycho-oncology, psychocardiology, neuropsychosomatics, psychodiabetology, and psychotraumatology. Overlap with psychiatry exists with conditions such as depression, anxiety, and personality disorders. As a conceptual basis for empirical research, non-reductionist accounts of the interactions of patients with their environment are most important. Therefore, the German model of psychosomatic medicine is a strong advocate for bio-psycho-social medicine in the 21st century.

In summary, we can appreciate how psychedelic-assisted therapies, especially ayahuasca spiritual advising, can find inspiration and a convenient "friend" in osteopathic medicine while having much to offer to allopathic and psychosomatic medicines. However, osteopathic medicine, despite its congruent principles with alternative healing methods, it is still tied-up by the rigor of the scientific method without much flexibility. Osteopathic medicine enjoys wonderful healing principles, but it cannot extend these too far, making it comparable to a turbocharged Ferrari that is only allowed to run in school zones.

Having reviewed the state of medical science and its limited capacity to effectively and efficiently restore health, we must explore and embrace new paradigms in our quest for richer physical and psychological wellbeing.

CHAPTER ELEVEN

THE POWER OF CONSECUTIVE AYAHUASCA SESSIONS

Three Times is Better than One

In the years following ayahuasca's entry into western civilization, an increasing number of psychologists and therapists have been drawn into confirming her promising healing benefits.

With mounting experience, a pattern began to arise. Some facilitators realized that the quality and intensity of the participant's experience significantly increased during the second day of scheduled consecutive sessions. This has been independently "discovered" by several facilitators, including my wife Rosalia, who experienced first-hand the power of consecutive sessions when she learned about the law of the mirror previously described.

Rosalia and I began regularly drinking the sacred medicine for three consecutive days and confirmed the impressive magnification of the medicine's effects. When inviting others from our community to do likewise, they experienced similar results. At this point, we knew we were onto something. This discovery formed the basis and origin of the spiritual healing program, which we later developed and implemented for more than five years.

As we were developing the program for spiritual healing, we found that other researchers around the world were independently making the same "discovery" within a few months or years. During the Third Ayahuasca World Conference held in Spain in 2019, one of the workshops was explicitly geared to ayahuasca facilitators. Interestingly, one of the novelties discussed was the new approach to therapeutic ayahuasca work, which consisted of conducting at least two consecutive sessions for more effective results. The idea of consecutive sessions has been gaining traction in the ayahuasca therapeutic community worldwide. We encourage anyone with the opportunity to experiment with this approach and confirm its undeniable power.

Note that this idea of consecutive sessions is not aligned with most of the traditional healing protocols in the more indigenous retreats in Peru. Under these existing methods, one day of rest is normally provided between sessions for integration. The implementation of a day of rest is well-intended and aims to allow participants time to integrate and recover. However, the fact remains that this recovery time also gives time to our subpersonalities and entities to regroup and organize back into the original formation, which we intend to dismantle through the healing process.

Why does this happen? This phenomenon is related to the functional brain network called Default Mode Network (DMN), mentioned in Chapter 8. The DMN is the functional network of brain structure and neural circuits that inhibit the access of our ego-self to our deeper subconscious-self during regular waking hours. In terms of our quantum model, this scientific term is functionally meaningless. In quantum psychology, the DMN acts as an envelope that contains and restrains the ego-self and its subcomponents to warrant the stability and perceived continuity of our personal identity. In a way, it could be described as the physical, neurological correlate of our Ego-self.

When active components of the ayahuasca enter the neurochemical scene, the DMN becomes inhibited, and the ego-self, along with its subpersonalities and entities, lose their tight control over the traffic of sensory data in our brains. It is worth mentioning that the ego-self is rarely fully inhibited during the ayahuasca experience unless the participant falls asleep or temporarily loses consciousness. It is the core part of the ego-self, the component which goes through the experience and receives the insights. Our subpersonalities and entities which normally filter and distort our perception of reality are the first inhibited components, allowing the essential ego-self to better perceive the unfiltered chaotic symphony of stimuli that gets unleashed during the peak of the experience. It is under these circumstances that the brain becomes primed and available for re-programming under the conscious intent of the unburdened ego-self.

When the chemical effects of ayahuasca begin to wear off, and the majority of the medicine has been metabolized, the DMN gradually regains functional stability. However, it is essential to note that the exit of ayahuasca's chemically active ingredients from the brain is a prolonged process and can be highly variable across individuals. The entire displacement often takes more time than we may imagine.

After the initial drop in intensity of the effects after the session, there remains a prolonged period of "after-glow" which may last anywhere between a few hours to a few days. There are numerous anecdotal accounts of this phenomenon, both written and in social media videos. Subjects frequently report receiving spontaneous "ayahuasca-like" insights even days after the session, both whiles going through their daily routines or during sleep in the form of meaningful dreams.

As the DMN regains control of the sensory traffic, our quantum ego structures return to occupy their established neural pathways, and subsequently, their strength. Imagine metaphorically, that the ayahuasca experience acts like a police force that briefly detours the traffic ("the DMN") in a congested highway ("neural pathways") allowing road repairs ("conscious re-programming") before the traffic returns. Extending the period of traffic detour leads to more superior road repairs. Doing ayahuasca sessions over consecutive days inhibits the DMN for long enough to achieve permanent repairs. This technique becomes very effective by the third day, and it gets increasingly effective the more extended the consecutive sequence is extended. In unusual cases, we may conceivably plan for more extended series of sessions to attain more productive results.

This intensive work constitutes a shock treatment to the subpersonalities and entities and reliably yields enhanced spiritual experiences in the participants. This explains why multiple practitioners and facilitators around the world have realized the power of consecutive sessions. Experience shows that if a significant psychological breakthrough doesn't occur during the second session, the third session will most likely bring the process to fruition. For those who receive a substantial breakthrough during the second session, the third session often provides a soft landing to their three-day journey. Ultimately, this leaves participants with a deeper understanding of the lessons received during the first two days. Additionally, the third session sometimes elicits the opening of new windows of insight into the ever-expanding consciousness that we all are.

I found reassuring support to the idea of the consecutive session when watching the excellent film "Reconnect." In this film, Brian Rose, the founder of the media outlet London Real, [1] documents his ayahuasca journey at a retreat center in Costa Rica. The well-known biochemist Dennis McKenna acts as his ayahuasca advisor and prepares Brian for the journey which they will embark on together. Dennis counseled Brian about the value of doing three sessions in a row (with one day of integration between them in this case) and described the process in his own words: "The first-day ayahuasca is just within you, and it is opening you up, you're just getting friendly with it. On the second day, that's when you are usually at the bottom of the abyss. You get to plunge the depths, or reach the heights, depending on what's happening, but that's the primary experience. Then on the third, this is kind of resolving, summary up and getting out, putting everything back together in a whole place, and end it up." I believe that the notion of undertaking consecutive sessions has gained traction in the ayahuasca community as the tradition has matured over the years

In summary, empirical observation from hundreds of sessions tells us that the future of ayahuasca-assisted spiritual healing programs lies in the development and improvement of consecutive session techniques.

Who Benefits Most from Consecutive Sessions?

It's well established within the ayahuasca field that the sacred medicine is not for everyone. Of course, we know those already under the influence of antidepressant medications are automatically disqualified unless they quit them for a reasonable time beforehand. Moreover, a variety of medical conditions are considered high risk, including some heart dysfunctions, liver problems, and compromised kidney function.

Beyond these common-sense precautions, there are a significant number of people with acceptable physical health who are not prepared to face the tough love of Mother Ayahuasca. Fortunately, the vast majority of these individuals are protected by their fears and will never attempt to try her. When confronted with the question, they immediately react with an objection, which is ultimately an expression of fear disguised in rational terms. "I don't do drugs" and "I am OK, I don't need that" are two of the most frequent socially acceptable responses of people that are either fully content with the life they are living or are in denial of the fact that their lives could be much brighter. This segment of the population exercises their free will by avoiding risks, and that's understandable. After excluding these, we are left with the remainder of the population, those that are prepared to experience ayahuasca.

For illustration purposes, here, I describe a few categories of participants. Be aware that after their first ayahuasca experience, many individuals morph their original characteristics and move to a different category.

The first of these groups can be labeled as the "Curious" category. These people have learned about ayahuasca over social media. After watching some videos and hearing a few testimonials, they develop a curiosity that is strong enough to encourage them to give ayahuasca a chance. Generally, participants in this group exhibit thrill-seeking tendencies and have probably experienced psychedelics at some point in their lives, if not currently. Alternatively, participants tend to enjoy adrenaline intensive activities such as extreme sports, rollercoasters, or bungee jumping. They see ayahuasca as their next "been there done that" tick on their checklist. When these individuals have the experience, they are almost always caught off guard. As a result, they either quickly fall into the "never again" category or awaken to a new level of much deeper curiosity. When this happens, they become more willing to look into the depths of their subconscious-self. The latter are formidable candidates to join the next category.

The "human growth crowd" is composed of individuals who have met their basic survival needs and are seeking to improve themselves through a wide variety of modern techniques. They are likely to have previously experienced from yoga/meditation, holotropic breathing, vegan nutrition, physical fitness, all the way to smart chemicals or 'nootropics,' and sensory deprivation chambers. These individuals often read motivational authors and frequently engage in the pursuit of business success. As shown in the statistical profile of our observational sample in Chapter 1, these participants tend to be between 35 and 45 years of age. That is, they tend to be older than the younger Curiosity category, which tends to be in their twenties.

This piece of data feels intuitively correct; the younger generation is still experimenting, while the older human growth crowd has a reasonable understanding of the basic mechanics of urban life and has an inner drive or voice, which suggests that there must be something else out there. In this case, there are entirely correct; yes, there is a lot more to uncover and learn. That's why this group is the most favorable in their likelihood of obtaining the maximum benefits of undertaking consecutive ayahuasca sessions. This group, by definition, is the best equipped to handle the paradigm shift that comes with the new territory of psychedelic-assisted spiritual healing.

An additional population which somewhat resonates with the human growth crowd is the "health seeker." Contrary to the human growth crowd who are "pulled" by their desire for optimal performance, this group is "pushed" by the survival imperative or their desire to improve their physical health. Scientific research has confirmed the effectiveness of ayahuasca in improving a diverse range of medical conditions. With the increasing popularity of ayahuasca, the news of its healing power is reaching more people who suffer from these conditions, and they are awaking to the possibility of healing with her.

Many members of this group are also interested in human growth. However, for the majority, the primary driver of this interest is a hope that the medicine will provide physical healing, with less consideration of emotional or spiritual outcomes. I would suggest that some individuals within this category, were it not for their health condition, would have shown no interest in ayahuasca at all. The good news is that Mother Ayahuasca will shake-up inside-out everyone who tries her, regardless of their intentions. In general, upon trying ayahuasca, the health seeker group is unknowingly making an entrance to a new world full of surprises as they frequently discover that the causes of the conditions they are aiming to heal are deeply rooted in the emotional dimension. Upon realizing and accepting the hard reality of the mind-body connection, the health seekers distance themselves from the traditional mechanistic model of health. That's when physical healing starts to manifest, and amazing results occur. These are frequently described as miraculous, not only by the individual but by their inner circle of friends and family.

In summary, the human growth crowd and the health seekers are the groups that may benefit the most from consecutive sessions. As a final word, we should mention the group that would benefit the least, although it would still benefit anyway, relative to the other groups mentioned above. I refer to this category as the "persuaded ones." These are people who are either not or only slightly interested in the experience but were somehow persuaded to try the sacred medicine. The situation may arise in numerous ways, the most common being when a friend or family member with previous ayahuasca experience persuades them with specific reasons as to why they should or must try the medicine. They often come partially or fully sponsored with the associated monetary costs. Sometimes these people agree despite a feeling of hesitancy. In more severe circumstances, these individuals are intimidated or emotionally extorted into the experience by their eager sponsor. Some undecided individuals just go along with the invitation. Sometimes a subtle form of fear influences the decisions, whereby people feel they don't want to fall behind because they sense something momentous is occurring with their sponsor, who is often a spouse, significant other, or direct family member.

For these and other reasons, a person may end up doing ayahuasca without feeling the necessary inner call. You must remember that it's all about intention. When this intention lacks full authenticity, the results are suboptimal.

Those Who May Benefit More, But Don't

The above distinctions reasonably describe the ideal participants concerning their intention and motives. However, we must also define a sizable section of the general population that would potentially benefit even more than those mentioned above. We are referring to people who, for a variety of reasons, are not in any way interested in opening themselves to experience the sacred medicine. Here are some groups that may benefit from the sacred medicine but, unfortunately, consistently pass on the opportunity:

1. The first group that is naturally inclined to decline the opportunity are individuals who have a relatively high standard of living. This group feels that their lives are working within their concept of fulfillment and happiness, and therefore don't see the need for further exploration. They think: "Why to open up to a new experience that may uncover areas that diminish my current state of wellbeing?" to which the answer would be, "If you feel good already, can you conceive an even higher level of wellbeing?"

2. The second of these groups encompass people who may or may not feel fully satisfied with their lives, but they remain extremely obfuscated in their life issues. These could be economical, personal relationships, professional, time management, and a diversity of external factors that compete for their conscious attention and prevail in hindering their ability to stop and partake in introspection beyond their immediate surroundings.

3. A third group is comprised of people who feel comfortable with their addictions (i.e., possessed by their entities) and are not interested in exploring anything that may pull them away from their attachments. These additions can include recreational drugs, eating disorders, intellectual endeavors, toxic relationships, sexual perversions, and other dark secrets. These are people that feel that their personal attachments could be threatened by self-guilt and prefer to stay in their comfortable bubble of reality.

4. People that harbor large amounts of prejudice in their hearts tend to firmly reject the sacred medicine. Prejudice is a powerful defense mechanism used to avoid looking at the deeper parts of their psyche. One of the most prevalent of these mechanisms stems from religion. Even though we have served the medicine to Christian pastors, practicing Muslims, Rabbis, Buddhists, Hindus, and Sikhs, there exists a less open-minded religious sector that regards the ayahuasca experience as self-inflicted punishment, sinful behavior, or merely malefic and diabolic. Another common prejudice is found in people with a recalcitrant attitude toward drug use. When they notice about the "drug" factor in ayahuasca, it triggers an automatic rejection response, which is too strong to overcome with dialogue. This is very understandable when it comes from people who have either successfully defeated some type of drug addiction or alcoholism in the past, or have close ties with someone that is currently fighting or have lost the fight with drug addiction.

5. There is another group who have experienced substantial emotional pain and tribulations in their lives and are initially attracted by the idea of healing their wounds with the sacred medicine. However, after some thought, they decide to pass on the opportunity. This is generally because they have already invested lots of energy in keeping those wounds hidden from conscious view, and they instinctively realize that subjecting themselves to a healing process implies re-living painful memories in some manner. After a cost-benefit analysis, they prefer to continue to manage their existing condition, rather than to risk exposing themselves to a most likely painful process with no guarantees of feeling better.

6. At the risk of being accused of prejudice myself, I wish to share one interesting observation about African Americans. Throughout a couple of decades on my path of the organizer of shamanic ceremonies, group leader of ayahuasca tourism, and medicine facilitator, I have contacted thousands of participants and practitioners. I can say with a reasonably high degree of confidence that a disproportionally low number of African American individuals have sought the ayahuasca experience. Possibly for a variety of factors, most of them unknown to me. This ethnic group statistically ranks lower than other, even smaller, minorities in the USA, such as East Asian, Indian, and Middle Eastern. We may speculate about the possible reasons for this; socio-economic factors may play a role. However, I tend to consider the severe painful trauma of slavery and discrimination subconsciously carried in their genetic code from their recent ancestors. The African American community is one that may yield significant benefits from the healing potential of the sacred medicine. Unfortunately, until the present, we haven't seen this de-

mographic coming toward the ayahuasca experience in any significant numbers.

7. Last but not least, we have a large group of people too quickly inclined to abdicate to the emotion of fear, an aspect covered in more depth in Chapter 1. As R.D. Laing once said: "there are three things humans being afraid of death, other people and their own minds." [2]

Happiness Is Not The Goal

People who seek to experience the sacred medicine primarily look to improve health conditions or find the resolution of personal psychological issues. We often caveat people who seek happiness as their primary motive by telling them to look deeper for improved reasons. Conventional wisdom from many sources, and more recently from controlled clinical studies, have identified what is called the "hedonistic paradox," also called the pleasure paradox. It postulates that someone who seeks happiness will not find it, but the person who helps others will. One study aimed at finding a potential connection between happiness and generosity using modern experimental methods [3] found a significant correlation between both of them, which led researchers to examine various possible explanations for it. Interestingly, they concluded that a tertiary personality variable, sometimes called psychological wellbeing, was the primary cause of both happiness and generosity.

Another aspect of the hedonistic paradox is the misguided idea of associating happiness with financial wealth. A scientific study found evidence "supporting the widely held but previously untested belief that having access to the best things in life may actually undercut people's ability to reap enjoyment from life's small pleasures." [4] For instance, on a trip to an exotic destination, a wealthy person would likely fly first class and stay in a suite at the best resort. On the other hand, a middle-class person would probably fly coach and stay in a standard-sized hotel room and be perfectly content. The more wealth a person has, the higher their standards are raised, causing them to find less joy in the small things in life. Too many people live with the conviction that money is the solution to everything in life. Money can cause more unhappiness in our everyday lives. Most financially wealthy people feel compelled to live up to the image of their position, constantly comparing themselves to other wealthy people. What money gives with one hand—access to pleasurable experience—it takes away with the other by robbing us the ability to appreciate simple joys.

Therefore, psychological wellbeing, not happiness, is what people should be aiming for when considering taking ayahuasca. The practical difficulties encountered by the hedonist in the pursuit of pleasure or happiness are now well understood; consciously pursuing happiness interferes with experiencing it. Politician William Bennett captured the essence of this principle with his most famous quote: "Happiness is like a cat, if you try to coax or call it, it will avoid you, but if you pay no attention you'll find it rubbing against your legs and jumping into your lap." [5] Moreover, Viktor Frankl, the creator of logotherapy, which explores the meaning of life, wrote in his classic book: "Happiness can not be pursued; it must ensue, and it only does so as the unintended side effect of one's personal dedication to a cause greater than oneself or as the by-product of one's surrender to a person other than oneself." [6] When you improve your psychological wellbeing with ayahuasca spiritual healing, you move a step closer to feeling happier and more generous with others. It is something that comes with the territory of healing oneself, not by pursuing it directly.

Aligning and Instilling Direction to our Ego-self

Ayahuasca spiritual advisors and individuals who are interested in spiritual healing must understand that the process of personal self-realization doesn't unfold automatically. Instead, the process must be initiated through the voluntary enrollment of the ego-self. Our ego-self, the one holding this book, must consciously want to align itself with its soul-self to reach a point of satisfaction and fulfillment in life. Since our ego-self is designed to render its primary loyalty to the survival programs, it must consciously navigate numerous twists and turns in the quest to connect with the flow of the self-realization programs. In this section, we explore these programs at a more advanced level by examining situations from the ego-self perspective to gain knowledge and, more importantly, to attempt to gain wisdom.

Contemplation: Navigating Our Human Existence

Our ego-self, including its reasoning and calculating abilities, is a part and a product of the total self. It is as natural as the lungs or the stomach, which, when used correctly, should never be our enemy. To achieve effective spiritual healing, the ego-self must be put in the right place. An organ is a team member of the whole body. In the same way, the ego-self is a member of our SIE, not the other way around.

One of the main challenges of navigating the human experience from the ego-self perspective is that in the pursual of safety and security, it too often fails to stay focused in the present. Instead, our ego-self begins frantically chasing an elusive, non-existent future or wandering into the ever gone past. This is the natural response of the survival programs in circumstances where the ego-self is living isolated from the other parts of its SIE. But how do we heal this split duality? How do we find inner peace in a world which is insecure and ever-changing by nature?

We must understand that awareness is a view of reality that is free from ideas and judgments. Everything that can be described is an idea, and we can't make an affirmative statement about anything, which is not an idea. We need to understand that inner peace is found by ignoring false impressions, which are inherent in concepts and ideas. The truth is revealed by removing the layers that cover its light. Michelangelo, the master sculptor, was once asked how he could produce such graceful and almost alive forms from such crude blocks of marble. He answered, "Very easy; the artwork is already there; I just remove the excess marble.". This is how the ego-self, with amazing intuition at its disposal, can circumvent the impulses of the survival programs without argument. The ego-self, when in alignment with the soul-self, can progress into the flow of existence without becoming involved with the chit-chat of mental dialogue. Alignment is the key to removing the metaphorical angels and demons which sit on our shoulders and endlessly whisper into our ears.

Contemplation is an art to be cultivated by anyone interested in smoothly navigating physical existence. Finding alignment within our SIE is easier to achieve through contemplation without judgment. When we are capable of practicing mindfulness in our daily lives, learn to dodge the persistent ego-self, which is constantly evaluating and judging. Subsequently, we can enjoy a precious reward. It is at this point that the soul-self is allowed to exercise one of its most potent abilities, intuition. When we contemplate without judgment, in any situation, the soul-self sends intuitive messages towards the part of the ego-self which is enrolled in the self-realization process. These are non-verbal messages, or insights, which are gently delivered into our field of consciousness. These insights and messages are "inaudible" in the presence of judgmental activity.

Contemplative attitudes are hard to sustain because the ego-self is running under the survival programs and is constantly monitoring safety and security. When we desire to be secure, that is, to be protected from the flux of life, we wish to be separate from life. To put it plainly: the desire for security and the feeling of insecurity are the same thing. We cannot begin to work on any problem until we understand that the craving for security is itself pain and a contradiction. The more we pursue this craving, the more painful it becomes. This holds true for whatever form of security we may want to conceive. We need to understand that we are as fluid as reality itself. We are not fixed souls that can be protected; such a fixed "me" that I want to protect doesn't actually exist. The security and safety sought by the ego-self under the survival program is a self-defeating game. However, this program has been beneficial for the survival of the species. Contemplation is a tool of the soul-self that can be harnessed to bypass the survival program and achieve the dual goal of advancing inner growth while remaining compliant with the survival program requirements.

The Paradoxical Existentialism of our Ego-Self

A key strategy to disable the resilient impulses of the survival program is to focus our attention on the flow of messages constantly arising from our subconscious-self. These messages are the wisdom of bodily functions and other subconscious impulses that resonate with them. Remember that the subconscious-self is in direct contact with the soul-self, executing the programs like an exemplary computer. The subconscious-self runs our physical vehicle without any intervention from the ego-self. It has the wisdom of whatever action is required and when it needs to be taken. Too often, the ego-self, entangled in its madness for survival and safety, ignores and postpones the subconscious signals pointing to actions that must be executed. Nutrition, sleep, waste elimination, healthy sexual conduct, muscle toning, relaxation, leisure, play, and hygiene & grooming occupy a substantial portion of our days. The ego-self should listen and partner with the subconscious in these endeavors joyfully and consciously. The rest of the time, the ego-self can invest in the organization, planning, and controlling the factors necessary to earn a living, expressing love, negotiating, resolving conflict, and healing ailments. This is life in the simplest terms while running the survival program in modern urban society.

Unfortunately, this is often not the reality of life, as the ego-self is relentlessly monitoring our present safety and future security. When we expand our consciousness and seek self-realization, we end up facing a paradox. An inevitable by-product of expanding our consciousness is an increased sensibility, sensorially, emotionally, and spiritually. Our soul-self is closer to our ego-self. Paradoxically, by becoming more sensitive to pleasure, we also become more sensitive to pain. By remembering the past, the ego-self can plan for the future. However, our ability for inner growth is repressed by our worries of avoiding pain and the unknown. We continue to grow internally, but our extreme sensitivity renders us unadaptable, instilling a feeling of living as strangers and pilgrims in this reality within us. It feels as though the discontent of our souls is a sign of our divinity. This is the paradox created by the separation from our source, from our present, it is the price we pay for the thrill of existing as playful children in this reality theme park. We must learn to let go and flow.

Our ego-self tends to think that making sense out of life is impossible unless the flow of events can somehow be fitted into a rigid framework. We have forgotten that our thoughts and words are conventions and that taking conventions too seriously is ineffective. We are ultimately projecting our thoughts, ideas, and words into the gradual creation of reality. Just as money doesn't represent the perishability or edibility of food, our thoughts do not represent the vitality of life. The more we try to live in a world of words and concepts, the further isolated and alone we feel, and the more joy and liveliness is exchanged for certainty and security.

On the other hand, when we make significant progress in letting go and living the present, the ego-self persists in worrying about feeling ignorant, uncertain, and insecure about everything. The survival program pushes the ego-self into acquisition and control, while the self-realization program fosters surrender and flow. Recognizing this paradox of existence is mandatory if we want to find the necessary balance to cruising our sailboat through the ocean of reality.

The Wisdom of Impulses vs. Compulsive Behavior

There is a pearl of unique wisdom in following the impulses of our subconscious-self. When subpersonalities and entities govern our lives, they dominate our agenda at the expense of our "instinct wisdom," the innate ability that which we are allowing to atrophy. Consequently, we are at war with ourselves; the subpersonalities desire things that the body doesn't want, and the body craves things that the subpersonalities don't allow. Subpersonalities initiate cravings that the body resists, and the body sends impulses which the ego-self cannot understand. These desires of the body originate from our subconscious-self, which directs our physiology.

The wild animals tend to eat with the stomach, but the human subpersonalities don't. When the animal is full, it stops eating, but the human subpersonality is never sure when to cease. When it has eaten as much as the belly can take, it still feels empty; it always feels an urge for further gratification. It desires the dessert, the coffee, the after-dinner liqueur. This is mainly due to anxiety, stemming from messages from the survival programming, stating that the supply of food and pleasure are uncertain. Therefore, our subpersonalities try to intake as much as possible regardless of the detrimental consequences to the body. The subpersonalities are insatiable, and our ego-self does little about it. The ego-self too often goes along with impulses initiated by an unseen rogue agent working in the background of conscious attention.

Our subconscious-self perceives reality as it is and ignores future events. It lives immersed in the present and perceives whatever is happening at the moment. The ego-self, in its survival mission, analyzes the experiences and can make predictions. When these predictions are accurate and reliable, the future is presented with a high degree of authenticity to reality. The future becomes real enough, and the present loses most of its survival value. The game of life is all about the future. Hence, the present becomes irrelevant for survival.

This is why the ego-self has designed the economy of modern civilization around the promise of future "happiness." World economies are built on the principle of manufacturing pleasures by providing constant excitement of the senses with incessant streams of noise and visual distractions. The perfect citizen of this economy doesn't live in the present. Instead, this individual continuously itches their ears for new music and fixates their eyes on 400 TV channels, endless flows of movies, and glossy paper magazines. We are kept in a sort of endless orgasm through a series of teasing glimpses of shiny cars, female bodies, and other sensuous surfaces. Then we are fed tons of information with a touch of "human interest," showing criminals, sports fights, disasters, and political hypocrisy. The real problem is the increasing frustration that we feel by attempting to please the ego-self. We remain ignorant of the fact that such an endeavor is as futile as trying to fly like a bird. Unfortunately, under this economy, we have lost our capacity to feel real pleasure. We have become insensitive to the most acute and subtle joys of life, and have forgotten how common and simple to enjoy these are. The broad hypnotized masses holding mobile devices in public events and family gatherings are a living showcase of the current human condition.

To illustrate the dichotomy of healthy impulses and compulsive behavior, let's examine the unhealthy obsession of men with the pleasures of sex, the compulsion which they tend to pursue with most anxiety. A scenario that occurs in men more frequently than is admitted is the craving that arises from the ego-self (sexual subpersonality) rather than the body (healthy subconscious impulse). Subsequently, the body renegades by failing when the moment of truth arrives. This confuses the ego-self hopelessly as it tries to understand why it fails to grab the great delicacy of readily available sex and why after hours or days of anticipation, the body does not cooperate. This happens when the ego-self evaluates women by standards that are primarily visual and intellectual, rather than purely sexual and visceral. He is attracted by the surface gloss rather than the real body. The ego doesn't want to accept that sex is an instinctive function and persists in increasing the already intense pleasure it provides by making it faster, fancier, and more frequent. It can only be achieved by cerebral fantasy, surrounding it with fetish, suggestions, diversity, and alternatives. The isolated ego-self is perpetually frustrated because verbal and abstract thinking makes it believe that it is possible to cut loose from the limitations of real life. It forgets that the infinite is an abstract concept, and it doesn't exist in human reality. It actively persuades and tricks the subconscious-self into desiring this fantasy to attain more of everything as a life goal. Remember that healthy living and happiness are directly linked to our capacity to lift the veil of this illusion.

When the healthy impulses from the subconscious-self are hijacked by the subpersonalities and entities, we begin to observe what is clinically defined as compulsive behavior. Ignoring the problem, the ego-self embraces the behavior and becomes a willing accomplice. Once the repetitive behavior establishes strongly connected neural pathways and the ego-self loses control of the behavior, it awakens to the harsh reality of the addiction and wonders how it ever happened.

The only way the ego-self can discern between healthy subconscious impulses and the compulsive impulses from the subpersonalities and entities is by establishing an effective connection in alignment with the soul-self. There are three types of impulses, each one having a distinct "flavor" or vibrational quality. The first form of impulses is very easy to identify, as these are the ones that the ego-self decides to act upon consciously. For example, "It's time to brush my teeth, let me go to the bathroom and do it." The second type of impulse may occur when you are watching a TV program and, without consciously thinking about it, you stand up and instinctively walk to the bathroom and brush your teeth. This is your subconscious-self triggering the programmed habits to warrant hygiene and health. Sticking with the same example, the third type of impulse would involve you becoming triggered by a toothpaste TV commercial and standing up to brush your teeth for the seventh time that day. This would be a clear exhibition of a compulsive behavior problem. Self-observation of your behavior will provide valuable clues that can enable the identification of the root of impulses and help to establish healthy boundaries with your subpersonalities. However, the most authoritative guidance is received from the soul-self, which is continuously sending signals to assist us in discerning when a particular impulse has been hijacked by a subpersonality or entity.

Our Honorable Ego-self

Our true identity emanates from the highest part of our SIE, our soul-self. Our ego-self is the representative agent necessary to do business in the physical realm. We know now that the ego-self splits into numerous independent subpersonalities to efficiently execute behaviors in repetitive scenarios. In general, anything in your psyche which runs on auto-pilot mode is potentially governed by a subpersonality; from brewing your coffee, driving the same route to your job every morning, or, even more so, when you become the joker at the party after a couple of beers. Sometimes our subpersonalities become self-aware and turn into the entities that raise hell in our lives. We can blame our rogue subpersonalities, which are in the process of becoming entities, and our hardcore entities for the bad reputation of the ego-self in the world. When we say "he has problems with his ego," we are suggesting that the person has frequently triggered entities that take control by an assault of his healthy personality. Our ego-self pays the social price with comments such as "he has a huge ego" when being arrogant, or "she is very egocentric" when being selfish. Due to this, we hear many speaking against the ego-self. However, we hear very little in the ego-self's favor when it is behaving in its normal state; the ego-self which runs your affairs pays the bills, takes the kids to school, and takes responsibility for working and earning a livelihood. This is the ego-self that we think we are when we look in the mirror. We all need the ego-self to survive, to have a sense of ourselves, and remain psychologically stable.

Along those lines, with self-observation of your daily life, you may realize that many subpersonalities don't deserve to be re-programmed or eradicated at all. You may find some who work in favor of both your survival and self-realization programs. For example, let's consider a subpersonality that takes care of the organization and order of your personal attire, keeps a neatly organized closet, does laundry, and looks for new outfits to replace old ones. In this case, people may describe you as a well-organized and presentable person. However, if this subpersonality turns into a self-aware entity, it shall feed on the obsessive behavior. An unbalanced passion for clothing and a personal appearance may grow and begin to spill into other healthy areas of your life. All subpersonalities, healthy or not, are vulnerable to transitioning into problematic entities.

Another example may be when physical fitness goes beyond the healthy habit to stay in good shape and morphs into an obsession with extreme bodybuilding. With careful observation you may find less obvious subpersonalities hidden in plain sight, behind the veil of socially acceptable behavior, such as watching too much television programming, excessive Internet surfing, endlessly listening to the same genre of music, or watching pornography daily because "it's healthy for your sexual life." Being aware of these subpersonalities is essential. Without awareness, you may not be able to regulate them. You need to be self-vigilant to avoid unconsciously, creating new entities that eventually end up sabotaging your psychological wellbeing.

We also need to recognize that the ego-self is not the enemy of self-realization. Although we know our subconscious-self and our soul-self are intrinsic parts of our personal identity, the ego-self is our closest sense of identity. However, the ego-self is you, and you need to recognize your self-worth and love yourself. Our self-esteem is a necessary element for the achievement of psychological wellbeing, and loving ourselves implies that we must honor our ego-self for what it is.

There are two prevalent ideas which do not resonate with ayahuasca advising as it relates to the ego-self. The first is the idea that to achieve self-realization, we must dissolve the ego. Some refer to it in more gruesome terms, such as killing or destroying the ego. Even some advanced Buddhist teachings speak of the need to reach an ego-less state to experience the heavenly state of nirvana. I strongly agree with the idea of becoming subpersonality-less and entity-less in our path to self-realization, which may be what others are trying to describe. However, the complete dissolution of the ego is impossible and, in my opinion, an unfortunate and enormous loss of energy if seriously pursued. The ego-self has a rightful place which is deserving of honor and celebration. I believe that in our modern society with our sophisticated lifestyles, we can even allow ourselves the luxury of hosting and sponsoring a handful of subpersonalities that prove helpful in running our self-realization programs.

The second idea points in the opposite direction. It postulates that we must embrace the ego-self to advance our self-realization. This is suggested to avoid the necessary confrontation that comes with removing or "killing" it. When we fight with our ego-self, we strengthen it. Once our fighting force is depleted by exhaustion, the ego-self bounces back, defeating our mission with the added aggravation of experiencing depression or hopelessness. Therefore, these theorists recommend that we become friends with the ego-self and embrace our shadow. Upon close examination of this idea, it appears that they are referring to the undesirable entities which we describe in our model of the psyche. The implicit mission of this idea is the desire to remove the ego-self as a negative aspect of our personality. This is a very narrow view of the nature of the ego-self, and following such advice shall lead to even more troublesome scenarios. Embracing our entities does not make sense, since this is how the entity was initially created. Negotiating or accepting to live with the entity under specific terms is a delusional proposition which is undoubtedly sponsored by the entity itself. This action would simply perpetuate the existence of the entity and, most likely, foster its growth. This idea should be firmly rejected, and we alternatively guide those situations in chapter 18.

Surrendering our Ego-self to our Soul-self

We must surrender to our greatest highest good, to our soul-self. Ayahuasca is the key to unleash the neurological constraints that keep the ego-self within the boundaries of our conscious experience. When we experience the sacred medicine, our ego-self becomes partially disabled (reconsider the DMN), which allows the soul-self to play a more active role in our field of consciousness, in addition to the myriad of previously inhibited memories, emotions and thoughts that are released. This partially disabled ego-self, which is undergoing the shocking experience of not being in full control, needs to consciously surrender to the soul-self. Again, we need to involve semantics in the discussion of this idea. Too often, the word "surrender" is associated with the idea of "giving up." There is an element of "giving up," but only in the sense of not allowing the stubborn ego-self to persist in its pursuit of control over the situation. However, in our discussion, the idea of surrendering not only means giving up control and expectations. Our definition stretches beyond and encompasses merging with our greatest highest good, which emanates from our soul-self. Surrender is yielding to the power and the presence of our divine potential that dwells on our soul-self. Such should be the intention of our ego-self to seek alignment with the soul-self. In short, we must surrender to our divine nature, not only during the ayahuasca experience but at all times throughout our daily lives.

In Summary

A quantum model of the psyche has been presented here with ideas of quantum psychology and quantum healing principles. It is now possible to conceive an organization in our quantum field as a hierarchal order analogous to the cell-tissue-organ structure. Our model begins at the bottom with the mechanistic skills produced by our subconscious-self to master repetitive tasks, is proceeded by habits, ends at the top with our ego-self. Based on these quantum structures, we find hundreds of locally domiciled programs containing behaviors which have been created as the result of a wide diversity of limbic imprints that are rooted in our fetal development and persist throughout our lives. These are primarily handled by our survival programs to protect us from future dangers but are also influenced by higher-level programming that defines the style and consistency of our behavior.

Now, stemming from the ego-self, the "I" that we think we are, we find an underlying family of subpersonalities created by our repetitive behavior, which constantly take turns in expressing themselves as required by environmental demands. Finally, we find subpersonalities that have developed strongly enough to become self-aware, and we call them entities. These raise havoc in our SIE, struggling for survival, feeding on the psychic energy produced by the behavior it craves, and frequently "possessing" or overbearing our ego-self. When I think about it, this inner personal reality bears a reasonable resemblance to the ecology of the jungle with beautiful birds, fascinating primates, and a few scary beasts.

Self-realization is harder than we think. It requires resolute commitment and continuous mindfulness. We must be aware of the unique situation of the human species, which, contrary to the animal kingdom, holds a dual set of programs. One drives us to survive with operational priorities over the other program, which continually reminds us of our ultimate mission after survival stability has been achieved.

Being aware of this existential reality gives us direction for our project of achieving psychological wellbeing. The following quote may help us understand our human dilemma:

"According to neuropsychologist Rick Hanson, your brain is like Velcro for negative experiences and Teflon for positive ones. For most of human history, we were chased by predators or endangered by natural forces. So we are genetically wired to focus on what is wrong, what we do not have, what lurks in the unknown. It takes practice to create positivity bias, to be grateful for all you do have instead of all you do not have, all that is right instead of all the wrong, all that feels good instead of all the aches."[7]

Contemplation without judgment is a highly effective strategy to gain empirical knowledge about our quantum territory and execute the self-realization programs without interfering with the survival programs. Most people, unaware of their primary quantum habitat, fall prey to the seductions of their own creations and allow them to run free under the mistaken conviction that "this is the way I am." In a sense, these assertions are correct. Still, upon closer examination, we can see an enslaved part of us that suffers and pays the price for not being able to follow the self-realization programs we eagerly desire to run.

With this model operating as our healing paradigm, we can now embark on the hands-on exploration of ayahuasca spiritual advisor principles, which have been developed with an empirical approach over the last two decades.

CHAPTER TWELVE

AYAHUASCA SPIRITUAL ADVISORS

Ayahuasca spiritual advising is the healing modality born from the need to provide ayahuasca participants with specialized guidance after their ayahuasca sessions. As described earlier, a parade of emotions, visions, and memories arise almost uncontrollably during these ayahuasca sessions. It's naturally difficult to make sense of such a burst of previously repressed experiences, especially when lacking any kind of reference point that may create a context for interpretation. Upon reviewing a few dozen ayahuasca experience testimonials, we realized that the participants generally lack a theoretical framework about the nature of the experience they underwent. They often feel unsure of what happened at the soul and ego levels, or how to interpret the experience terms of relevance moving forward in life. There is a short supply of reliable resources to integrate the experience. Moreover, the literature available often only offer very basic and straightforward guidance for such highly complex psychological scenarios. Under these circumstances, spiritual guidance becomes especially pertinent.

A traditional spiritual coach is someone who helps you connect with who you truly are. They assist you in redesigning your life, uncover your desires, help you to take steps toward your goals, dissolve limiting beliefs, and remove blockages. Spiritual coaches aim to find the root causes of problems, rather than merely managing the symptoms. To this end, coaches use a more in-depth and more holistic approach compared to other modalities. The growth that can be accomplished with the aid of a spiritual coach includes connection with the divine, working with universal metaphysical laws, shifting your subconscious, and taking control of your power and happiness.

Ayahuasca spiritual advisors (ASA's) are different. Ayahuasca's guidance differs from other coaching modalities in one fundamental aspect. Ayahuasca advisory sessions are carried out under an entirely different framework from traditional protocols. Typically, a coaching client expects the coach to be the primary source of guidance, and their performance will be assessed depending on their quality and knowledge of the subject matter. However, in ayahuasca spiritual healing advising, accurate advising is provided by the ayahuasca experience itself. The advisor is not the source of the expertise and instead acts only as an "assistant" advisor. After having met the real guide personally, Mother Ayahuasca, practitioners subsequently approach her assistant to clarify their doubts, issues, and concerns. Therefore, ASA's are not required to engage in assessing practitioner spiritual needs at great length, as that process is already being led by Mother Ayahuasca in a very profound manner.

The primary mission of ASA's is to lead practitioners to find, through their ayahuasca journeys, the magnificent gift of spiritual healing. Specifically, this is achieved by:

- Assisting in making sense of the overall ayahuasca experience in the context of the client's profile and circumstances. This often involves showing them how to adjust their life processes after going back to their daily routines.

- Assisting in interpreting confusing perceptions and creating a sense of acceptance of them. This includes guiding in releasing trauma, clearing stagnation, healing old wounds, and removing energy blocks.

- Promoting the practice of articulating inner questions that guide the journey of self-discovery in future ayahuasca sessions.

- Promoting the notion of our divine nature, the worthiness of love, happiness, and abundance; all-powerful beliefs that guide our behavior. These principles are described in more detail below.

- Promoting awareness of the projection principle and the need to emphasize self-awareness, self-love, self-forgiveness, and self-compassion.

- Guiding practitioners to enrich their toolbox of resources with techniques of intuitive therapies. These may include other techniques mastered by the advisor or referral to complementary alternative therapies that could be effectively integrated with ayahuasca spiritual healing.

The expansion of ayahuasca practices worldwide has catalyzed a growing trend of people offering integration services, counseling, and advising. Ayahuasca session participants often use these services when provided by the outlet offering the session or may seek them via online alternatives, days, or weeks following their experience. When adjunct to a retreat center or ayahuasca community, the ASA has an opportunity to become a significant player in the participant's personal growth. Advisors may not be as influential when hired online with remote contact. An ASA must have the attributes which are generally found in spiritual or personal coaching, with the added requirement that must have experienced a significant number of ayahuasca sessions in which they have found substantial transformative value. Although the practice of advising may conceivably be applied based on theoretical training, the ASA cannot effectively guide a participant without having their prior personal transformation. In the same way that celibate Catholic priests are not likely to provide the best marriage counseling, ASA's without a reasonable track record of ayahuasca sessions will not be able to relate and connect with the practitioner's needs. Similar to coaching in general, ASA's must exhibit some essential qualities:

- Genuinely care about their practitioner; guidance without care is a mechanical process.
- Maintain an empathetic and positive attitude.
- Be fully present with active listening
- Not opinionated, and without judgment
- Cultivate curiosity, lead with questions
- Be a keen good observer of body language
- Be challenging of conventional narratives
- Communicate with clarity
- Remain honest and preserve their integrity. ASA's relationships are entirely dependent on trust.

To create a comfortable atmosphere of trust and vulnerability during advising sessions, ASA's should present themselves as informal friends without the formalities of a conventional therapist. The use of voice recorders, notebooks, or clipboards should be considered intimidating walls that may intimidate and withdraw the openness of a practitioner as those types of tools may trigger memory associations with other assessment processes in their past. These may trigger memories of previous encounters with credible authorities such as medical doctors, psychiatrists, or other alternative medicine therapists, which were conducted in a more formal setting with note-taking for diagnostical purposes. Instead, ASA's should aim to take notes shortly after the session to keep a record for future reference.

Another important caveat for ASA's is the challenge of dealing with their own subpersonality of social recognition. ASA's may be tempted to add an air of superiority or special status in the way they project themselves. ASA's must remember that they are mere assistants to a process that is remarkably larger than themselves. If they have experienced ayahuasca deeply enough, or better said, if they have surrendered themselves and have allowed the sacred medicine to work within them deeply, then they should understand that they are humble servants of higher forces beyond comprehension. ASA's must realize that guiding and advising practitioners within these higher forces has little to do with themselves, and everything to do with the sacred medicine. An ayahuasca advisor should never claim credit for whatever expertise they may have developed in the field because, after all, we all are explorers of virgin territory.

ASA's Principles and Assumptions:

Spiritual healing with ayahuasca is based on a paradigm of reality that must be understood by the practitioner. One of the missions of the advisor is to ensure these principles are appropriately presented to the practitioner for their consideration, mainly if these are not already part of their belief system.

Universal Consensus of a Higher Reality – The nature of reality contains a higher dimension of consciousness existing above our human condition. Since ancient times, humans have devised a variety of methods to tap into this higher reality through which they have sought information, understanding, and intuitive insights into the divine nature of reality. This drive may have originated from the human's innate curiosity upon being presented with the undeniable peculiarity of dreams while asleep. Buried deep in every human's consciousness is the mystery of the relevance and meaning of the images, feelings, and messages which are received during sleep. This quest for the higher realm has proliferated throughout human history with creations such as religions, sects, occult practices, and a myriad of belief systems, all of which attempt to explain the complexities of physical existence. Such matrices of infinite knowledge and wisdom have been called God, divinity, higher self, Tao, Universal Mind, and many other labels necessary for language communication. However, all of these terms refer to and describe the same phenomena.

Paradigm Shifting Effects of Entheogenic Plants - Human beings demonstrate almost infinite biological complexity and are equipped with an extremely sophisticated nervous system. Until the present day, this physiological wonder remains only partially understood by the most advanced sciences. This system is capable of accessing and interacting with the aforementioned universal matrix, sometimes with natural or developed abilities, and occasionally with the aid of natural substances ingested for this purpose. Curiously, some forms of vegetation contain specific molecules that fit precisely into cellular receptors contained within the human brain, as though they were put there with a purpose. These plants contain molecules that act as 'ligands' which activate cellular receptors and trigger a biochemical cascade within the cell. The interactions between these plant-contained molecules and endogenous cellular receptors in the brain can have profound physiological consequences and alter human experience. The consumption of entheogenic plants will cause profound changes in the interpretation of reality, changes that are permanent and irreversible. Once a person interprets reality from the perspective of an expanded state of consciousness, it shall never perceive reality again exactly the same way.

The Holographic Nature of Oneness – The connection with the higher reality is of such amplitude and magnitude that it touches the spiritual nature of humans and compels them to accept their own divine origin, or at least a tacit manifestation, of a higher dimension. Being one with the whole is analogous to being a small part of a larger hologram. While this description falls short in fully describing the idea, it is a modern concept that is very useful in communicating this notion. As is well understood, a hologram is a photographic physical recording of an interference pattern of a light field. By diffraction, the record of the light field can be viewed as a whole image. Importantly, if a hologram is physically broken, each piece will contain the whole view of the entire image. This is true even if the hologram is shattered into thousands of tiny fragments; each piece contains the whole view of the image contained within the originally recorded hologram. Similarly, humans are tiny functional holograms with all the features of the whole. Ancient metaphysical wisdom summarizes it with their maxim: "as above, so below."

Survival & Self-Realization Programs - Humans are spiritual entities having a physical experience. The human biological entity was designed, or evolved, for survival and reproduction. There was less emphasis on the requirement to find happiness or self-realization. Survival is the imperative command of physical existence, but self-realization is the primary command of our spiritual nature. The former takes priority, and this paradoxical duality is one of the many sources of inner conflicts and dysfunctional behavior. The advisor's client should be aware that the mission is to expand their individual consciousness to surpass the limitations imposed by the inherent survival mechanisms.

The Subconscious-Self is Your Friend - The storage of subconscious memories is necessary for survival. These memories enable humans to strive forward with the genetic commands without carrying the burden of conscious obstructive and confusing memories of trauma and conflicts which have been encountered along with the survival mission. The subconscious-self efficiently creates a myriad of automatic reflexes, either hard wired or soft programmed, within the nervous system to equip the organism with quick responses to predict future scenarios. On the other hand, memories that elicit stress and anxiety are selectively encrypted out of view, as if covering them with a layer of amnesia. Ayahuasca's spiritual healing will surely lift some of those layers to the extent that the individual is equipped to handle the revealed memory. Ayahuasca will not reveal memories that are beyond the capacity of the participant to manage them.

From a spiritual perspective, there is no limit to what is possible. The essence of ayahuasca advising revolves around tapping into our spiritual power to overcome boundaries we place on ourselves, find our purpose, and reach our full potential.

Screening Participants to Determine Eligibility

Ayahuasca ASAs must understand the enormous responsibility that lies on their shoulders by assuming this role. This is especially relevant when we consider that the practice of ayahuasca sessions for spiritual healing purposes is a relatively new, mostly undeveloped field of study. As any responsible practitioner that intends to help others in improving their lives, ayahuasca ASAs must be very attentive every step of the way for identifying any clues that may lead to a potential complication in the participant's healing process.

We already know that ayahuasca practice is not for everyone. There is not only a list of medications that should be avoided but also a series of medical conditions that are incompatible with it. This is an area that traditional curanderos in South America often overlook and fail to identify the often obvious clues that some participants exhibit before, during, and after an ayahuasca session. This lack of awareness is the leading cause of most of the unfortunate cases of adverse reactions to the medicine we occasionally see in media reports. I believe that almost all cases of complications and even reported deaths associated with ayahuasca sessions were avoidable with proper screening before the session or careful and proactive attention during and after the sessions.

Let's examine the screening process as it applies to a more significant number of people that attend sessions for the first time. The facilitator or ASA should assume a very conservative policy rejecting participants at the slightest suspicion of potential health problems, but this inevitably results in the exclusion of people that could have experienced the badly needed spiritual healing. I admit that determining when to decline participation is often hard to make a judgment call, as we don't have an exact science behind the screening process. In the end, it's a decision that substantially relies on common sense and intuition after considering the many factors at hand. When in doubt, a participant may be allowed to take an initial partial dose and later decide for an additional portion, especially if no effects are triggered. When we positively identify potential participants with incompatible pre-existing health conditions, we should responsibly and compassionately take the necessary time to explain why it's preferable to skip the ayahuasca session by describing the risks involved to both the participant and the facilitator.

Since we know that the quality of the experience is not dose-dependent, staying on the safe side with a partial dose would be the most prudent course of action. For the sake of fairness to facilitators that have experienced serious problems with health complications of participants, we have to acknowledge the inevitable situation where specific individuals who are so driven to have the experience lie about their medical conditions and the medications they use. Some of the adverse reactions mentioned earlier could have been the product of participants that lie and not for lack of proper screening. We may question why people could act irresponsibly or even negligent with their health, but the truth is that it happens more frequently than it should.

Another crucial factor in ayahuasca advising is the legal dynamic surrounding spiritual healing. The screening process is an essential element in the relationship with the client, and it must include the review and discussion of hold-harmless agreements, legal release forms, and related documents. Written certification by the client about pre-existing medical conditions, medication regimes, and psychological state, should be a mandatory step before initiating ayahuasca sessions. ASAs should be aware that a source of legal disputes may come not necessarily from the participant but from its direct family members. It often happens that people participate in sessions while in disagreement with close family members or significant others who explicitly oppose their decision to experience ayahuasca. At the slightest inconvenience derived from the medicine's side effects, they tend to alarm the participant by assuming a hostile attitude toward the facilitator, ASA, or even the session organizers. It is of utmost importance that in such situations, the ASA involved show their sincere compassion and support at all times. Indifference or reactive attitudes from the ASA is the worst possible reaction.

Developing a Basic Practitioner Profile

Although the ASA only acts as an "assistant advisor" to the leading guidance provided by ayahuasca experiences, it is vital to develop an adequate understanding of the practitioner's existential status. It is here that the ASA may apply their prior training and knowledge about human nature to assist the practitioner to process, integrate, and extract maximum benefit from the ayahuasca experience. Spiritual healing is achieved through the optimum combination of preparation before the experience, observation during the experience, and effective integration after the experience.

The first scenario we should consider is one in which a client who has never experienced the medicine before is consulting an ASA to prepare for an upcoming session. There may also be occasions in which a practitioner with prior experience begins a relationship with an ASA. After a brief introduction establishing informal rapport, the ASA starts with assertive questions probing about the motives of seeking an ayahuasca experience for the first time or the motives of their previous experiences, if any. Why do you want to do this? What elements did you consider when deciding to undertake the experience? Answers to these questions should be carefully assessed for clues or clear evidence of the client deciding to do ayahuasca for the wrong reasons. "Because my wife said this would be good for me and our relationship" or something vague such as "I want to become a better person" are questionable motives that deserve further scrutiny.

ASA's should be able to distinguish when these motives come from the analytical mind and should try to dig deeper to identify a motivation stemming from the heart, an emotional-based incentive. Intellectual motives such as "I want to know what happened in my previous incarnation" or "I want to experience sacred geometry and the patterns of the tree of life" clearly come from people who need to be guided appropriately, as they are candidates who may receive an unpleasant surprise when they find out Mother Ayahuasca is taking them out of their analytical mindset and into their emotional core. In such cases, the ASA should inquire about other areas of their lives where Mother Ayahuasca may give a more relevant service. The motives of these clients may seem deviated from a more fundamental of spiritual and emotional healing. However, it is not the role of the advisor to move them from where they are standing, and they must not instill fear about what may happen during the experience for not having the proper mindset. This is the job of the real healer, Mother Ayahuasca. As long as they are gently informed by the ASA, they should be welcomed to the ayahuasca sessions. Note that even with distorted or wrong intentions, many first-time participants have precious experiences and later realize how delusional their original motives were.

Once the intention is cleared, a few basic questions are in order. These will provide critical aspects that are valuable in understanding their forthcoming ayahuasca experience account after the session. The following areas of inquiry are sufficient to create a profile useful for the advising sessions:

a) First questions to generate rapport: What do you want? What do you long for? What are the areas of your life which you don't feel comfortable with? What are the childhood events that have influenced who you are today? In which ways have you experienced receiving love and giving love? How do you handle stress and pain?

b) Age and a brief history of significant personal relationships to assess patterns of emotional stability.

c) Where are their parents located? If deceased, what age was the client when each of them passed away? This to assess and correlate with the patterns revealed in (b).

d) Ages of the client's children, if they have any. Relationship with each of them and with their mother, if separated or divorced male. This to assess the developing ancestral patterns.

e) Any memories of events that they feel left marks in their development, such as emotional trauma from abuse, accidents, loss of loved ones, to assess how these have played a role in their answers above.

f) The earliest memory they can recall. This is to assess possible encrypted memories. These memories are assuredly there when the practitioner is unable to remember anything prior to first grade in school.

g) Any areas that they are looking forward to improving or not happy with, in terms of health, emotions, or behavior.

The more understanding the practitioner has of the process they are embracing, the more powerful and effective the results will be. Their aligned ego-self needs to be fed with as much information and knowledge as possible to equip their inner explorer with the necessary gear before they enter the dark cave of the unknown. Metaphorically, if a practitioner enters in plain clothing, they will not ever reach as far as if they otherwise enter carrying flashlight, rope, and compass.

Their aligned ego-self should begin looking at the cave from the outside. The advisor should effectively convey the simple message illustrated in Figure 2. This illustration shows the different nested perceived realities from others toward us from the perspective of the ego-self. These are the layers of the onion of self-perception which end with the ego-self at its core; that secret part of us that no one else knows about. The ASA must be able to remind practitioners about the reality of additional layers of the onion which they are unaware reside inside of them. This is the unconscious-self that clients must learn about; this is what Mother Ayahuasca shows you in her own language; this is the cave inside the onion that they need to willfully visit to start their healing and self-realization process. Acknowledgment of this helps to align the clients' ego-self within its SIE.

To truly support people in their own growth and transformation, advisors should always empower the client and avoid removing their power by either attempting to fix their problems, implying that they should know more than they do, or overwhelming them with more information than they're ready to absorb. Advisors should be prepared to step to the side and allow clients to make their own choices, offer them unconditional love and support, give gentle guidance when required and make clients feel safe even when they make mistakes.

Advising for the Feeling of Isolation

Ayahuasca's work awakens the ego-self to the higher realities of its SIE and facilitates the alignment of its parts. People that begin to awaken with ayahuasca or other modality of self-realization, experience something that is statistically rare when compared with the general population. An inspiring pattern we may observe in recent decades is the increasing number of people "waking up," entering the initial or intermediate stages of questioning their roles in this matrix of reality.

There are millions of people who notice that they are more sensitive, notice more, or see more than the general population does. There are millions of people drawn to spiritual practices, meditation, yoga, shamanism, energy sciences, tarot, psychology, reiki, and healing practices because they are waking up in this sense. But there is a point where spiritual experiences can be isolating. It is no longer a self-created illusion. It simply is. Most people, even those beginning to awaken, are still on the surface levels of reality. Most books, teachers, gurus, and information out there are designed for the "90 percent" of people who are in the beginning stages. As we go beyond this 90 percent, our experiences may make us feel isolated. Particular spiritual doors begin to open that once gone through create understanding levels and experiences that are rarely talked about. Typically anything beyond this 90 percent point needs to be experienced to be believed. Anything beyond this point is too far off from consensual reality to be assimilated easily by others. This authentic experience of isolation may be perceived as a problem by some clients.

We must realize that our lives, by definition, are lived in the quantum field at a subtle level above (or below) the physical reality. We can enjoy the beauty of the higher realms acknowledging that it can't be shared with others while simultaneously enjoy the simplicities of physical existence with all its shades of gray, from social interactions, friendship, entertainment. Waking up is isolating only if we lock ourselves into living in only one channel. We need to wake up to the truth that life is multi-dimensionally beautiful, instead of boringly linear. The feeling of isolation derived from waking up is just another illusion we must learn to unmask.

We can have spiritual experiences that are isolating and take us far away from the cultural norm and simultaneously experience oneness, have friends, lovers, partners and family (even when they are part of the norm), go to yoga, baseball games, work, and the grocery store and also bump into teachers and guides that may help us understand and build skills to work with what we are experiencing. We need to be open and ready to move on from where we are. The famous Zen Kōan cryptically captures the essence of this message: "Before enlightenment, chop wood, carry water. After enlightenment, chop wood, carry water."

Although it appears nothing has changed on the outside (doing), everything has changed on the inside (being). On the surface, the visible, external actions of chopping wood and carrying water are the same before and after enlightenment. So, what's changed? The deeper invisible and internal—your quantum reality presence, awareness, perception, mindset. Your body may be busy, but your ego-self is still.

The "*being*" is more important than "*doing.*" As Eckhart Tolle says:

"*Doing is never enough if you neglect Being. The ego knows nothing of being but believes you will eventually be saved by doing. If you are in the grip of the ego, you believe that by doing more and more, you will eventually accumulate enough 'doings' to make yourself feel complete at some point in the future. You won't. You will only lose yourself in doing. The entire civilization is losing itself in doing that is not rooted in Being and thus becomes futile.*"[1]

Some Standard Instructions Before Ayahuasca Sessions

The initial advising session with new clients requires the teaching of basic concepts that are necessary to help the client's ego-self to discern truth from illusion, as the ayahuasca path is anything except simplistic.

Projection Principle - Most people, including those interested in exploring the world of ayahuasca, are unaware of the reality of psychological projection. Participants of ayahuasca sessions should be familiar with at least the basic version of the projection principle to open up to the possibility of understanding their inner world through the model of the psyche. Without it, they will likely find themselves perplexed and confused with the experience. This can diminish their chances of receiving spiritual and emotional healing. This is what happens in the vast majority of first-time ayahuasca experiences. The projection principle is tightly entwined with the fibers of our psyche, and embracing it at least in the most basic form, is mandatory under this healing model.

Advisors should be able to translate their advanced level of understanding of the concept into a variety of versions that are suitable for the easy consumption of the different levels of knowledge in their client base. ASA's may continue to deepen their understanding through the abundant currently available information sources on the subject.

Surrendering - Clients should beware of the ego-self's natural resistance to the transformational power of the medicine. As previously mentioned, intense anxiety and fear are common, and the well-prepared ego-self must play a leading role in navigating the inner boat into a safe harbor. The key is encouraging the client not to resist the process by consciously surrendering to whatever unfolds during the experience. Uncertainty of what is coming next is a fact to be unconditionally accepted. "Playing dead" is the most effective trick in calming down. Focusing on the rhythm of your breathing and talking to yourself about being nothing to be feared is also effective in leading yourself to whatever Mother Ayahuasca has in store for you. It boils down to trusting the medicine and the facilitator, and accepting that the experience you are having is perfectly aligned with what is required at that moment. This concept fits with the next two topics; encouragement and motivation.

Warrior Attitude - An ayahuasca maxim that we openly promulgate is: "Mother Ayahuasca will never make you worse than you were" referring to before and after any ayahuasca experience. Therefore, we encourage participants to find within themselves the inner courage to face whatever needs to be seen or felt during the experience. We invite them to review their motives and visualize the results of a successful ayahuasca experience, the new person they want to become, and fight for that ideal as if you are an indigenous warrior. Such an attitude is very useful as it is supported by another maxim: "Mother Ayahuasca will always respect your free will and will never impose an experience that you won't be able to tolerate." An unexpected logical conclusion of these assumptions is that if a client feels fearful of the experience and presents an attitude of weakness, this will be respected with the consequence of having a very mild and possibly mediocre experience. Since this is not the desired outcome, advisors must empower the participant to attain a warrior attitude before entering the ayahuasca session. The qualities of an inner warrior that will serve well in the session are focus, courage, and perseverance. The qualities of acute awareness and inner trust are fundamental to its completion. A true warrior must learn to nurture these qualities while remaining without opponents and enemies. Their mindset must be unconcerned with winning or losing.

A Great Investment – A useful "pep talk" for the analytical type of client is comparing the ayahuasca session to an excellent financial investment: "If you are presented with a business opportunity where you invest four hours of fear and stress in exchange for a lifetime of wellbeing, would you take it?". This is a deal that anyone wishing for a better life should immediately sign-up for. This hypothetical scenario makes participants think twice when they are undecided about whether to step forward to embrace their first session. This should not be considered as unreasonably pushing a hesitant client into participating, but instead, as merely presenting an every-day situation which the client can relate to.

Advising for Balance - Advisors must be aware that obtaining superior results from ayahuasca sessions requires the ability to balance seemingly contradictory instructions. For example, simultaneously calling for courage while asking for surrender and release. These are easily reconciled by clarifying that courage is an attitude to be cultivated in preparation for the session. In contrast, surrendering is the attitude to be held during the session. The warrior attitude will prepare the subconscious-self to unfold whatever is required. Surrendering will be the dominant attitude during the session to control the naturally fearful ego-self from resisting the experience.

Pre-Session Orientation - Every single ayahuasca session should be preceded by an orientation session that covers specific instructions and warnings in sufficient depth. In the case of multi-session retreats, it may be offered only before the first session. This is equivalent to the mandatory instructions given by flight attendants in all commercial airlines; if you are a first time or an occasional flyer, you may listen to them carefully. Contrary to commercial flights, in the case of ayahuasca sessions, most experienced participants don't object to repeatedly listening to them. These set your entire SIE with the correct anticipation and expectancy to embrace the experience.

Here is a partial suggested script of instructions and reminders which can be imparted to the audience prior to a session:

(a) The session will open with a spiritual, religious, or shamanic invocation and will be declared closed after four or five hours at the discretion of the facilitator. After closing, you may remain to process your experience for as long as necessary. Those who are willing and able to move to the dining area are welcome to join the staff and enjoy hot vegan soup, fresh fruit, or other healthy treats, before retiring to your bedroom.

(b) After approximately one hour into the session, the facilitator will check with each one of you to assess and ask whether you want or need another dose of medicine. Every person has different body chemistry, and the initial dose may not be enough to elicit the experience you deserve. If the facilitator understands that you are beginning to flow into the experience or if you are already into it, they will not offer you another dose. If the facilitator perceives the contrary and believes you need another dose, you will be encouraged to accept it. Please accept and drink the dose; otherwise, you may remain in a gushy state, going nowhere in particular and will likely miss the experience altogether due to an insufficient dose for your chemistry. The problem with the second dose is that, contrary to the first one, your stomach is feeling a bit upset from the first dose, and the natural reaction is to decline drinking more. You must disregard this bodily reaction and find the courage to overcome it. The second dose is the one that you will be most grateful for later. Don't ask your stomach; just do it.

(c) At any time, if you feel the effects have subsided, feel free to stand up, walk towards the facilitator, and quietly ask for another dose. If you can't physically do this, you are not ready to drink more and should continue processing whatever sensations you are currently having.

(d) Keep your bucket within reach of your arm for fast access in case of a sudden vomit reaction.

(e) You will most likely vomit on one or more occasions. However, it's also possible that you may not vomit at all. Don't be concerned if others are vomiting, and you are not. This is your unique process, and it's not comparable to any other.

(f) Don't abuse the drinking water. Of course, if you are thirsty, drink water as necessary, but observe yourself that it is likely to be your ego's way of dealing with the anxiety of facing itself. Using water as a remedy to calm the nausea is absolutely futile. Instead, realize that this is another distraction, close your eyes and keep surrendering yourself to the experience.

(g) Concentrate, focus, or pray on the questions you intend for this session during the peak of the experience when you feel it has reached its maximum intensity. Catch yourself getting distracted wandering into irrelevant rumblings and call yourself to order, you are the captain of your journey and don't let your ego-self mutiny with its menu of distractions.

(h) Observe yourself going to the bathroom just to move the energy of your experience, not actually needing to go urgently. This is another strategy of your ego-self, desperately looking for an escape like a caged animal.

(i) You will experience visions of different kinds, not necessarily visual. Visual visions are more prevalent in right-brain dominant people; the musical, verbal, artistic type. The analytical, skeptical, scientific kind of people tend to have more auditory visions, somewhat like a voice in your head that tells you messages or insights without visual correspondence. For those who are stubborn with robust ego-self structures, Mother Ayahuasca bypasses both and gives you impressive breakthroughs in the form of sudden realizations, not visions nor voices, but a conviction or 'eureka' moment, where previously and seemingly unrelated data end up connecting in a meaningful way.

(j) Be aware of your inner subpersonalities. We all have distinct parts of ourselves that sometimes conflict with each other; they control our behavior and sometimes act against our best interests. For example, addiction to drugs, food, and toxic behaviors are subpersonalities that, if you zealously seek them in your heart, Mother Ayahuasca will reveal like a policeman with a flashlight breaking into the dark corners of your subconscious and illuminating them for you to see. Powerful life-changing healing is easily possible with your conscious intention to dig and find.

To close the pre-session instructions with a touch of humor, I say one final guidance, which I borrowed from my teacher shaman Don Jose Campos. Extending further the flight attendant's pre-flight instructions metaphor: "We are now about to start our journey, please unbuckle your seat belts to let yourself fly away towards your inner self."

About Mobile Devices in Ayahuasca Sessions - A vital recommendation to retreat organizers and ASA's, in general, is related to the mobile devices of participants. We strongly encourage retreat organizers to require all participants to surrender, with no exceptions, their car keys, and any kind of communication device to a designated staff custodian. This requirement should be made part of the registration process and agreed by the participant beforehand. These items should be held at a safe location beyond the reach of participants.

The rationale for such a policy is twofold. First, participants must agree once the session is about to start; there is no reason to communicate with anyone outside the group. This is a common requirement in specific workshops where participants are expected to focus on the flow of the event without distractions. But more importantly, the second reason has to do with a potentially problematic situation that could arise if any participant initiates a phone call during the session while under the effects of the medicine. Participants may do it while in the bathroom or other opportunities. This could be distressing to the recipient of the call, as it will be undeniable that the participant would be undergoing through some sort of crisis or simply experiencing an altered state. An even more distressing scenario could be avoided with this policy when a participant in their delusional fear of imminent death may call to 911 emergency asking for medical help or asking for law enforcement to intervene in with a kidnapping situation. We have reports from other facilitators, including myself, where a session has been severely disrupted by the sudden appearance of rescue units or law enforcement in emergency mode.

For the same reasons, participants must not have access to their car keys as they may forcibly decide to abandon the location in the middle of their ayahuasca experience. We strongly recommend never to commence an ayahuasca session without first securing every single mobile device and car keys of participants.

The Existential Challenge of ASAs and Psychedelic Therapists

We are dealing with the elusive element of pure consciousness. The spiritual healing mission is to assist people to find alignment within their SIE's and beyond as this will yield the desired self-realization and psychological wellbeing. There is a remarkable difference between traditional spiritual healing and psychedelic healing. When we include ayahuasca in the healing process, the ASA relies on the feedback received from the participant to figure out the particular situation and articulate specific advice that hopefully assist the participant in personal progress. There is no roadmap or guidelines on which the ASA may rely to communicate such advice. The epistemological problem of knowing other's people inner processes is present in ayahuasca advising as it has been present for decades in psychology, psychiatry, and other counseling practices. Contrary to these traditional disciplines, which have historically developed an extensive body of theories, well documented by hundreds of respectable professionals, ayahuasca spiritual advising, on the other hand, is an infant beginning to crawl in an elusive theater of action. We are living in the early stages of a new area of healing. To that effect, this book is an attempt to lay some theoretical foundations and contribute to the rapid evolution of this field. Meanwhile, experience is the only compass available to ASAs to assess the personal situation described by a participant.

Therefore, the challenge is that the quality of the advising provided to the practitioner will be a function of the previous level of advancement achieved by the ASA in its own spiritual work and self-realization process. We cannot lead to places we haven't visited before. The best ayahuasca ASAs and psychedelic therapists will be those who embark themselves into the healing process they intend to induce in others. This is true for Freud, Jung, James, and many other pioneers of psychology who did not have the privilege of learning from the ones before them. We are living in the pioneer era of psychedelic-induced spiritual healing. My advice to anyone interested in learning about ayahuasca advising, counseling, shamanism, or similar disciplines is to drink ayahuasca as frequently as possible, and when it feels is enough, drink a bit more. Over time, as the discipline develops and reliable literature becomes available, it may gain traction with successful healing models being learned by future ASAs more academically. Meanwhile, experiential learning from your own healing process is the only university available for this course.

CHAPTER THIRTEEN

DURING AYAHUASCA SESSIONS

Let's continue moving from the theoretical aspects of the model of the psyche toward its empirical implications. There are essential aspects of ayahuasca sessions that ASA's must be fully aware of and integrate into their practice.

The Art of Holding Space

What does it mean to "hold space" for someone else? Holding space is the conscious act of being present for others. The term 'holding space' has grown in popularity among caregivers, healers, yogis, and spiritual seekers. It is a broadly used phrase that defines the act of "being there" for another. However, the effects of this practice go much deeper than only offering support.

When you hold space for someone, you bring your entire presence to them. You walk alongside them without judgment and share their journey to an unknown destination. While the outcome is unknown, you must be completely willing to end up wherever they need to go. You must give your heart, let go of control, and offer unconditional support.

Holding space is not something that is exclusive to facilitators, coaches, or palliative care nurses. It is something that we can all do for each other, for our partners, children, friends, neighbors, and even strangers who strike up conversations as we're riding the bus to work.

The most crucial element in holding space effectively is to have previously developed a minimum level of trust with the participant. The value of holding space can become redundant if the participant doesn't trust the facilitator or specific people in the immediate surroundings. Here are some practical guidelines to assist ASA's in adequately holding space during ayahuasca sessions:

Safety - A key component in holding space is the quality of safety. For others to be open, genuine, and frequently vulnerable, they must feel secure and have a sense of trust. Participants won't let down their defenses until they feel it is safe to do so.

Humility - In the ancestral ayahuasca tradition, the shaman is seen as the center of the ceremony, the all-knowing, authority figure. During ayahuasca sessions for spiritual healing, this idea still holds true as there must be a clear understanding of who is ultimately responsible for the flow of the session. However, authority and authoritarianism are two different things. A vitally important aspect of holding space is the understanding that it's not about the ones holding the space. When we hold space for others, we must make the conscious decision to leave our subpersonality of self-importance at the door. Holding space is about serving others, and your personal concerns or needs are not part of the process. It requires radical humility and the willingness to be a temporary caretaker of the feelings and concerns of the others.

Non-judgment - Holding space is an impartial process. You are not there to pass judgment or evaluate others. When you judge the experience of another, you create additional mental static that will interfere with the process. At the moment that you are holding the fears, suffering, or grief of another, your opinions are irrelevant. Unless you've been through what they're going through, you can never truly understand their feelings. Being there is enough. Good and evil are merely a matter of perspective, and, at this moment, your attitude isn't the one that's important.

Practice Loving-Kindness – This is a term rooted in the Buddhist tradition, though it also appears in other religious and secular traditions. It describes the reverent present-moment cultivation of compassion and love for another living being, the earth, or the self. In many cases, simply being a loving presence can bring about a deep sense of relief that eases the pain of another.

Unconditional Positive Regard – Here, the person holding space is conscious of having acceptance by setting aside their own personal opinions and biases. The therapeutic value of this attitude was developed by humanistic psychologist Carl Rogers. [1] The concept entails the necessary and unconditional acceptance and support of a person, regardless of what they say or do. This is the foundation of all therapeutic healing relationships. Thus, unconditional positive regard means that the ASA should have the ability to isolate behaviors from the person who displays them and hold the belief that the individual has the internal resources required for personal growth.

Sustain Mindful Breathing - Remember to breathe mindfully. Checking-in with your breath is an effective way to make sure you remain grounded. It will also help you stay connected to your own body, which is the most powerful tool you have in assessing your connection to yourself and the other person. To hold space, you must be able to be present with and for yourself. Otherwise, you will be hard-pressed to be open and honestly present.

Avoid Your Emotional Identification - Holding space for someone in deep pain can bring up your pain. You must have a clear intention that, despite going through trenches with the participant, this is not a space to trigger your emotional issues. There is also the temptation of trying to help them. While that might make us feel better, it may cause the other person to feel further isolated in their pain. Instead, simply be there and don't try to fix the participant or their feelings. They only need to go through whatever the experience is unfolding to them.

People are bound to make mistakes along the path of growth and learning. By practicing the above guidelines, we offer participants the opportunity to reach inside themselves to find the courage to take risks and the resilience to keep going even when they fail. When we let them know that failure is simply a part of the journey and not the end of the world, they'll spend less time beating themselves up about it and more time learning from their mistakes. Through the practice of holding space, you serve as a container for which the healing and transformation can take place. Holding space is a powerful gift of presence that you can give to others through the quality of your attention.

Observing Purging Reactions During Sessions

ASA's work may be performed more effectively when they are present during the sessions of their clients. In many instances, this happens organically because the ASA is also acting as the session facilitator. Regardless of whether they assume this dual role, the ASA should pay close attention to the flow of reactions coming from each participant. When acting solely as observers, it is highly recommended that ASA's take a few milliliters of medicine. This dosage is sufficient enough to elicit a mild effect that can enhance perception acumen during the session. Carefully observing participant reactions during the ayahuasca experience will provide a great deal of objective and subjective information that may evolve into valuable insights during the forthcoming advisory sessions. ASA's will be able to better assess participant's experiences and the descriptions in their personal narratives.

It is essential to inquire about their reactions during the coaching session, as this will add substantial advisory value. For example, questions such as "Do you remember why you were crying for so long?" or, perhaps, "Why did you decline a second dose when the facilitator felt you needed it?" can lead to the discovery of additional information that the participant is unlikely to reveal if not asked directly. Participants often forget details of events that occur during the ayahuasca session, and such reminders may trigger memories that are valuable to the healing process.

Physical and emotional cleansing is probably the single most notable or defining attribute of the ayahuasca experience. Purging is the swift and decisive transition from a state of discomfort to a state of relief. Dictionaries define purging as:

> **To Purge:** (i) to rid of whatever is impure or undesirable, cleanse, purify, (ii) to clear of imputed guilt or ritual uncleanliness.

Rest assured that anyone who experiences the sacred medicine shall engage in one or more manifestations of purging. This happens because shortly after arrival in the physical body, the spirit of ayahuasca begins to move all localized energy centers in the system. The medicine uncovers their vibrational value and connects them for re-establishing balance in a state of wholeness. It works effectively to create wholeness from disconnected local areas of the nervous system. These local areas may be an accumulation of stress and anxiety in various organs, such as endocrine glands, skeletal muscles, the heart, or stomach, which have resulted from survival challenges.

Since profound and long-lasting healing can only be accomplished while the system is in the state of wholeness, purging is necessary for the "settlement of accounts." The function of purging is to remove byproducts and discordant energies from the system. The purging process channels these energies toward the most appropriate outlet for discharge, in accordance with their toxicity level. The denser and darker energies are eliminated through excreted bodily fluids and the more subtle energies through physical expressions.

The strong channels of purging are vomiting (digestive matter), evacuation (feces), and crying/screaming (tears and saliva). The soft channels are laughing, moaning, talking, and yawning. The strong channels are widely known for their purging qualities. However, the weak channels are not often recognized for what they are. Participants frequently purge and balance significant amounts of emotional energies while engaging in prolonged periods of moaning or yawning. We have also seen participants experience "laugh attacks," during which they are processing the healing of painful emotional issues, somewhat paradoxically to what may be expected. We may also include the rare Visionary Intense Release Syndrome (VIRS) is a form of purging. This syndrome is fully described in Chapter 15.

After the purging process is completed, the participant experiences an overwhelming sense of relief, which confirms the attainment of a state of wholeness. It is at this point that the spirit of ayahuasca brings forth the more profound and consciousness-expanding component of the experience. This period is where some of the heavy lifting is done, both consciously and unconsciously. Note that during a highly productive session, a participant may experience more than one cycle of purging, which encompasses different aspects of their overall spiritual growth.

Observing the purging reactions during sessions often provide to the ASA relevant insights about the inner processes of the participant. Understanding the dynamics of ayahuasca purging enables the ASA to make better assessments which they can share with the client throughout subsequent sessions. All participants will exhibit at least one type of purging which may be experienced in a variety of forms. The sacred medicine is purgative with no equal, and no one is immune to her effects. We have carefully studied purging reactions and realized they could be listed in the following approximate order of intensity:

1. **Vomiting** – Observe whether no vomiting occurs, or occurs once, twice or multiple times.

2. **Evacuation** – Observe the number of visits to the bathroom

3. **Crying/Screaming** – This is associated with emotional release. Observe whether this manifestation is constant or occasional.

4. **Laughing/Coughing** - Observe whether this is continuously manifested or occasionally.

5. **Kinetic** – Observe whether repetitive movements are voluntary/involuntary, controlled, rhythmic, or chaotic.

6. **Yawning/Moaning** – This type of purging generally occurs during the later period of the session. It appears as tiredness but may contain a deeper meaning.

7. **Talking** – Observe the specific words spoken and attempt to identify their intended meaning. Participants often forget what they were vocalizing, and a reminder may trigger relevant content.

As clearly detailed above, purging manifests in a variety of forms besides the more obvious vomiting and crying. Repetitive or rhythmic movements for a sustained period of time, coughing, uncontrollable laughter, and yawning are often overlooked as favorable release reactions. Under this perspective, we can confidently affirm that purging is a universal reaction to the medicine. If you drink ayahuasca, you will undoubtedly purge and, subsequently, feel a gratifying sense of relief.

All forms of purging constitute a somatic release of pent-up energies that have accumulated over time until Mother Ayahuasca opens the gates of expression. Participants are generally not aware of the specific events or issues associated with the release as these mostly occur deep with the nervous system unconsciously. However, especially concerning vomiting, participants often report knowing exactly which issue is being addressed at the moment of vomit release.

Both ASA's and participants should be clear about a misconception that has become popular in the ayahuasca community. Understand that vomiting is not healing. Participants often confuse one with the other and put aside important healing work still required following this purge. Participants may erroneously believe that an issue or trauma was healed when a clear vision of a past event was immediately followed by intense vomiting. This may be interpreted with joy and celebration. However, participants should realize that this experience is just the beginning of a process that may lead to permanent healing and resolution if the necessary follow-up work is undertaken. It's a great beginning, but it's not the end.

Preserving the Established Collective Trust

Addressing the subject of group atmosphere or "collective trust" is not an easy task due to its metaphysical nature. I refer to an energy that is not measurable via scientific instruments. Instead, this is an energy that influences participants subconsciously during the session or retreat.

There is a general consensus among experienced practitioners about how the sacred medicine enhances our personal sensorial sensitivity. Most participants experience heightened sensitivity in all five senses. This heightened awareness and sensitivity also extend to sensing the energy of people and places in intriguing new ways. Personal growth trainers and leaders of self-help workshops understand that a particular "group energy" is created among participants once a group begins to interact. Some describe it as a form of bonding or a 'family spirit' that permeates the group. This effect is enhanced when the group drinks ayahuasca together. A collective trust is formed within the group. For that reason, we are cautious in avoiding any kind of energy disruption during the sessions, no matter how subtle this may be.

To manage and stabilize this energy, in retreats of several days, we do not accept participants that intend to stay for only part of the retreat. For diverse personal, professional, or health reasons, some potential participants request to join the retreat on the second day and skip the first day. Others may ask for similar accommodation of leaving the retreat one day early. Despite their insistence, we do not accept participants under these conditions. A new participant arriving on the second day may feel like a stranger or intruder to others. Similarly, when a participant leaves before the closing, a vacuum can felt in the group energy when the rest of the group sees the empty sitting spot on the session floor.

On rare occasions, participants decide to quit the retreat program and, even after some conversation, we may be unable to persuade them to stay. To minimize the effect of an abrupt departure, we simply remove their belongings from the session space and ignore the situation entirely concerning the other participants. No comment or reference is made concerning the participant's absence. Most of the remaining participants will notice the absence. However, they will often keep it to themselves and will assume the obvious. We feel this is the most effective way to minimize disruption in the established collective trust.

Regarding staff members, we try by all means possible to avoid having a new staff member join the retreat after it has started. Having a staff member leaving prior to closing is more permissible as the departure of someone that primarily works backstage should not drastically influence the participants.

About Wearing White Clothing

Another element that aids healthy energy flow is our invitation to participants to wear white clothing during the sessions. Although not mandatory, we encourage the practice, and it is generally embraced by most. The type of attire required for a session or retreat is a decision I defer to retreat organizers who better understand the sensitivities and preferences of their enrolled participants. Some may feel it could be perceived as too religious or "cult-like" to specify attire. This is understandable in very secular communities. However, wearing white clothing is ideal as it places all participants on the same level, which creates and fosters a group or team culture. Consider the idea in terms of the effect uniforms have on groups of people, such as medical staff, school students, firemen. Uniforms can equalize and galvanize a group.

White is fresh and inspires purity and cleansing, which is well-aligned with the intended work and creates a favorable subconscious alignment with it. White is the absence of color and reflects most of the color spectrum. We use and encourage white clothing during the sessions while respecting the free will of participants. This is just our preference and not necessarily a recommendation for future program designs.

I Quit, This is Not for Me!

In our experience with ayahuasca retreats with multiple scheduled sessions, approximately five percent of first-time participants will approach the organizers to inform about their intention to quit the process and abandon the session space or the retreat. We acknowledge that doing consecutive sessions can be overwhelming to some participants for which we ask them to relax and invite them to share how they had reached their decision.

We have learned that quitters are divided into two distinct groups; those who can be persuaded back into the process and those for whom no amount of persuasion can change their minds. Of course, free will is always respected. When all reasonable persuasion has failed, we lovingly return their car keys, mobile phones, and checked-in belongings and with special courtesies assist them in leaving the premises. After all, they were courageous enough to undertake this kind of retreat and tried their best. This group is further subdivided into another two: those who leave and never look back, and those who shortly after that realize that their decision was a mistake. In the latter case, these participants will often call back to book a future retreat a few weeks after departing. These participants recognize that quitting is something they have done too many times in different situations in their life. They realize the underlying behavioral pattern and recompose themselves with a new air of empowerment. In our experience, those who quit and subsequently return invariable end up having amazing breakthroughs and express lots of gratitude to the process and the organizers.

Those who quit and never look back usually are participants who have discovered deep wounds, dark behaviors in denial, or strong, irrational fears. Thus, they ultimately decide not to approach or handle them at all. Instead, they prefer to move forward in life and leave those areas untouched. Their position is understandable as not everyone is prepared and ready to grapple with their Jungian shadow. Perhaps years later, when they feel better prepared, these participants may reach out for deep healing with the assistance of Mother Ayahuasca or any other healing modality they find appropriate.

When they leave, we emphasize our availability during the next few days and welcome their calls to discuss how they are feeling in their process of connecting back into their quotidian lives. They often call back asking for advice, which we gladly provide as many times as needed until the participant feels self-confident enough. If we don't hear from them within a few days of their departure, we give them a courtesy call to inquire about their whereabouts and show our unconditional support. Under no circumstances those who quit should feel rejected or turned down by any staff member. Nor should those who quit being made to feel like they have failed or are losers. Failure is not an acceptable word in the vocabulary of ayahuasca work.

Let's return to those participants who can be persuaded. Our first line of defense against the desire to quit the retreat is cleverly included in the orientation provided prior to the session or retreat. As mentioned earlier in the orientation section, we take a special moment to carefully anticipate and explain to participants that thoughts of quitting may overwhelm them at some point. First, we tell them that these thoughts are a normal reaction of the ego-self, which is attempting to flee from an uncomfortable zone. We emphasize that they must prepare for the eventuality of this confusing dilemma and remind them that only their conscious effort can overcome it. We empower them to confront this feeling and explain its nature. We also describe the great sense of accomplishment they will feel after the process is completed as they originally intended.

CHAPTER FOURTEEN

LIMITING BELIEFS AND AYAHUASCA MYTHS

Sexual Abstinence and Ayahuasca Work

One of the most frequent questions asked by participants is why the shamanic tradition calls for a period of sexual abstinence during the preparatory period prior to and after ayahuasca retreats. Shamans themselves justify the practice with a diversity of reasons, which are generally considered to be unconvincing by the scientific community. The indigenous and the biological ontologies which we discussed in the introduction of this book clash with irreconcilable interpretations. While a convincing answer to this question remains elusive, the consistent request for sexual abstinence during ayahuasca dietas remains prominent in the retreat centers of South America.

"Avoiding sex during la dieta is purifying and prevents your energy from getting tangled up with someone else's while you're sorting through your own body, mind, spirit, and heart during the ceremony," [1] says Dr. Joe Tafur, a medical doctor, shaman, and co-founder of Nihue Rao Centro Espiritual near Iquitos, Peru. He warns that having sex while taking ayahuasca affects the visions, interferes with the medicine, and could have lasting repercussions. *"You might end up having to work through some other kind of healing process. So then, you just wasted a healing opportunity and created the need for another one."* [1]

The shamanic tradition evolved independently from the European world. However, despite this isolation, we find similarities in the perspectives on sexual abstinence between both cultures. Sexual abstinence has been considered beneficial in many religious, philosophical, military, and sports traditions throughout history.

In ancient times, abstinence was considered the best method to ensure athletic performance and communion of body and spirit. Roman and Greek educators believed that great sacrifices could sustain success. This is a likely reason for the support of sexual abstinence by many modern sports coaches, with many of them believing that subconscious sexual frustration leads to increased aggression.

What science has to say about sexual abstinence? A 2016 systematic study analyzed 512 research studies on the subject of sexual activities correlated to athletic performance and found that the topic has not been adequately researched. Many studies lacked the necessary scientific controls, and many others simply were poorly designed. Therefore, we have no scientific evidence to argue in favor of or against sexual abstinence prior to sports competitions. [2]

The fact is that the scientific research of sexual abstinence is not possible. The Newtonian mechanistic paradigm will not be able to make any direct causative correlation because the nature of the effects of sexual abstinence is rooted in the quantum field. The mechanistic framework encounters the same problem it found in attempting to understand consciousness. To adequately address the subject of sexual abstinence, it is necessary to introduce the concept of "life force."

At the moment of physical death, we lose our life force, and our bodies immediately begin to decompose. The life force that disappears upon physical death is an energy that permeates all living beings, from microorganisms to sequoia trees and blue whales. Our life force has a quantum nature; it is the essence of our SIE, the quantum structures that compose our personal identity. This life force has been described by various cultures. Chinese cultures describe this energy as chi, which they believe flows through the acupuncture meridians. Indian cultures call this energy 'prana,' and it is believed that we can cultivate it through the practice of yoga.

This life force and its hierarchical order in the quantum field, as described in earlier chapters, has not been detected by scientific instruments. Eastern traditions believe in an electromagnetic field that surrounds the body, which they refer to as 'aura.' Some believe that this aura can be detected with the techniques of Kirlian photography. However, studies have shown that this technique actually captures an electric ionization effect in the photographic medium associated with the moisture of the subject. Although it makes sense within the quantum model of the psyche, the reality is that there is no physical evidence of the life force we are addressing here.

Despite this lack of evidence, humankind is continually exploring the universe, and a lack of scientific confirmation of certain phenomena doesn't necessarily rule out its existence. A few centuries ago, most Europeans believed the Earth was the center of the universe. Scientists who were 'ahead of their time' in disputing this fact were executed, such as Giordano Bruno [3], or misunderstood, such as Nikola Tesla. We still know very little about the universe to claim anything with certainty.

The life force is manifested in a diversity of ways. The volitive energy that drives our voluntary actions mentioned in our model is a form of life force. Carl Jung's psychic energy, Wilhelm Reich's orgone energy, and Sigmund Freud's libido are all forms of life force. We should agree that the concept of libido is more relevant for our discussion of sexual abstinence.

Succinctly, the libido is defined by medical dictionaries as "The psychic and emotional energy associated with instinctual biological drives." Due to the enormous interest in the undeniably real sexual libido, it has been a subject of scientific research for decades. When we search the scientific archives for studies containing "libido" as their subject of interest, we find 7,745 entries since 1945 [4]. Libido is elusive and challenging to investigate through traditional scientific methods as it must rely on the subjective perceptions of the subjects under study. Absent of a libido-measuring instrument, all of these studies must have relied on interviews to determine the levels of libido on whatever correlations they were attempting to measure.

Perhaps the ancient belief of sexual abstinence prior to prestigious sports competitions came from their observations about the effects of intense physical endurance training on the athlete's libido. A study in 2017 revealed that "Exposure to higher levels of chronic intense and greater durations of endurance training regularly is significantly associated with decreased libido scores in men." [5]. The ancients may have realized this relationship and eventually developed the belief that by accumulating libido through abstinence before competitions, it may offset the observed detrimental effect.

Another area that may give us clues about the effects of sexual abstinence is the studies on human fertility. Most beliefs that promote abstinence rely on the fact that ejaculation expels billions of sperm cells that contain life force. Note that, at the average of 200 million sperm cells per cubic millimeter, one gram of semen has enough sperm cells to potentially create many times the existing human population on Planet Earth. Some speculate that the massive depletion of life force during ejaculation is the reason why they feel the pleasurable collapse of all physical systems while extreme weakness ensues. To promote the fastest recovery possible, the survival program elicits the production of prolactin to induce sleepiness. It is not difficult to infer following a large expel of life force, a substantial amount of energy must be invested to replenish the depleted inventory. This inference is supported by a study that found male testosterone levels increased by 145% on the seventh day of abstinence. [6] This elevation in testosterone may be consistent with an evolutionary reproductive strategy, which induces physiological changes to drive the pursual of sexual activity.

Another indication of the influence of sexual abstinence is that the life force, using sperm motility as a biological marker, tend to decrease during days eleven to fourteen of sexual abstinence. [7] Sperm motility describes the ability of sperm cells to move through the female reproductive tract or through the water to reach the egg effectively. Sperm motility can also be thought of as a measurement of quality and a critical factor in successful conception; sperm that do not "swim" properly will not reach the egg to fertilize it. Note that we are assuming that the quantified laboratory parameters of sperm motility are an acceptable indirect indicator of life force.

But why do testosterone levels peak on the seventh day of abstinence, and sperm motility decreases between days eleven and fourteen? Reconciling both studies, we may only speculate that after seven days with testosterone at enhanced levels, there is a window of a few days for optimal reproduction probabilities before the sperm motility begins to deteriorate. It makes evolutionary sense that if ejaculation has not occurred despite the enhanced level of testosterone, then the life force is diverted elsewhere, and sperm cells begin to lose their ability to perform.

From this discussion we can summarize the following: (i) There is a life force, seemingly undetectable by science, which belongs to the quantum realm (ii) Our survival program is exceptionally efficient allocating its valuable energy resources, (iii) Changes in testosterone production and sperm cell motility can be considered indirect biological markers of the influence of sexual abstinence. (iv) Ejaculation has an indisputable effect on the cycle of libido fluctuations, as confirmed by the majority of males through anecdotal accounts.

Finally, we can explore the hundreds of anecdotal accounts found on several online forums about the effects of sexual abstinence in stamina, health, and well-being. Abstinence appears to have variable consequences across individuals; some individuals will feel powerful effects of sexual abstinence, while others will experience no change. Sexual energy is an extremely complex phenomenon with an enormous number of contributing factors. Concluding a definite rule that applies to all is simply unrealistic.

Without definite scientific guidance regarding this matter, we may resort to ask and rely on the intuition of our soul-self. We have to remember that due to repetitive behavior, we all have developed a sexual subpersonality in our SIE, and many have developed powerful entities that control their lives. If we are consciously attempting to achieve spiritual healing which belongs to the quantum realm, it is prudent to temporarily pause the sexual survival program factor while in the process. I personally recommend a short period of abstinence before and after ayahuasca sessions but recognize that this is a very personal decision.

Menstruation During Ayahuasca Sessions

The traditional prohibition of women drinking ayahuasca during their menstrual period has endured to this day all around the Amazon Basin. In some venues, shamans ask women the sensitive question. If answered affirmative, they are precluded from participating in the session. If they are part of a larger group that comes together to participate, they face the inconvenience of having to wait for the others in a separate area at a prudent distance from the session space. They are not even allowed to be passive observers nor remain in proximity to the session space. Based on statistically well-powered sample size, this is a shamanic rule that we have debunked.

In my interest in understanding the rationale of such blatant discrimination, I found a variety of senseless explanations. Here, I will only discuss the two most reasonable ones. Firstly, it is suggested that women carry negative energy while menstruating, which can interfere with the work and negatively influence others. Another source indicated that this rule originates from remote ancestral times of non-existent feminine hygiene and that certain unpleasant odors were the real negative energy that is referenced. The former seems more rational than the latter. Another claim suggests that intense vomiting may exacerbate menstrual bleeding. Hence, the shaman has reasoned that prohibiting menstruating women from drinking ayahuasca was essential to avoid a dangerous hemorrhage.

After listening to numerous anecdotal accounts from women who ignored this rule (mostly by lying), which confirms that there is nothing to worry about, I decided to encourage women to dismiss this rule as irrelevant. Dozens of women have experienced the power of three consecutive sessions during their menstrual period without any notable consequence. In our practice, we provide a diversity of sanitary supplies for women who may require them. Our empirical observations show that there are no valid reasons to prevent women from connecting with their sacred feminine based on such a discriminatory excuse.

Speculating on this tradition from an anthropological perspective may provide further insight. Likely, this tradition has more do with the historical convention within Amazon tribes of prohibiting women from becoming shamans of the tribe. Shamanism is male-dominated and probably another manifestation of senseless machismo in the world. Preventing women from ayahuasca sessions and discriminating against them for their biological condition may have been a mechanism to preserve male dominance in the tribe.

It was very inspiring to listen to Waxy, the indigenous medicine women from the Yawanawa tribe of the Brazilian Amazon, who attended the 2016 Ayahuasca World Conference in Acre Brazil. With her nose and mouth covered with their exotic achiote red tincture in a beautiful pattern, she spoke publicly about her longstanding struggle to gain the right to become an ayahuasca shaman in her tribe. This is something she recently achieved. Indeed, women from the indigenous world are standing up against discrimination and winning.

Too Young or Too Old to Experience Ayahuasca?

Participants are often curious whether there is a minimum or maximum recommended age to safely experience the sacred medicine. Some of them ask the question with one or more family members in mind. "Maybe I can suggest to my 70-year-old mother to consider an ayahuasca experience.", Or "perhaps I can invite my teenage son to attend my next ayahuasca session with me.". There are very few scientific studies that investigate the safety of ayahuasca consumption across the life-span. However, these are valid questions that can be quickly answered given the vast number of anecdotal accounts which concern the matter of age.

Let's start with the youngest. In Brazil, we have an excellent opportunity to learn about the use of ayahuasca in minors because entire families have participated in religious ceremonies for decades under the UDV and Santo Daime religions. In 2010, the Brazilian government issued CONAD Resolution No. 1, which stated:

"Keeping in mind the lack of sufficient scientific evidence and that Ayahuasca has been used for centuries and has not shown damaging health effects, and considering the terms of CONAD Resolution 05/04, the use of Ayahuasca by minors under eighteen (18) years old is left up to the deliberation of the parents or legal guardians, within the domain of adequate exercise of parental rights."

Regarding scientific studies, the only published literature comes from an international consortium of researchers who evaluated forty adolescents from UDV in three different cities in Brazil and compared them with a matched control group of forty non-ayahuasca using adolescents. Overall, the UDV adolescents showed similar results to the control group on most neuropsychological and psychiatric tests applied. [8] This suggests that the use of ayahuasca in adolescence does not have substantial consequences in adolescent behavior. None-the-less, it's important to remember that adolescence is an extremely critical period of brain development, in which many developmental processes can be disrupted. A wealth of research has shown that substance use, for example, cannabis use, can disrupt brain development during teenage years and sustained consequences into adulthood. However, this does not appear to be the case with ayahuasca.

I have heard stories in the Ucayali region in Peru about the wives of curanderos spreading a bit of ayahuasca around the nipple when breastfeeding their baby boys. Supposedly, the idea is to prepare the boy to follow into his father's curandero footsteps. When we examine this carefully, this practice may create a powerful imprint in the developing brain by associating the bitter taste of the sacred medicine with the mother's love, nourishment, and safety. Children who experience this may be more likely to develop curiosity, rather than rejection, in later life when they eventually face their first encounter with ayahuasca.

There are other stories in the Peruvian and Brazilian tribes where children are given sample doses to test their natural reaction to it. I don't outright dismiss the veracity of such folkloric tales because we have more recent examples that add credibility to them. I became very interested in a story from the Putumayo region of Colombia, where birthday parties for children are organized by members of the community. During these parties, the members offer a mild version of their traditional yage. I was shown several candid snapshots of such parties. As with any birthday party, children play games and have fun together. However, they do not appear to exhibit any particular reaction such as lying down, feeling drowsy, or vomiting as the result of the "refreshment." The social value of this practice lies in children learning that the consumption of yage is an encouraged and socially acceptable practice, something which they should not be afraid of exploring.

Another remarkable case from my homeland in Puerto Rico regards a facilitator who I know personally. This facilitator conducted a private session for a nine-month-old baby. The baby's parents were both experienced practitioners who wanted to initiate their baby in the medicine path as they claimed Mother Ayahuasca herself had urged them to do so. The facilitator agreed and administered a couple of drops of ayahuasca under the baby's tongue with a droplet dispenser. They sang and played lullabies as the baby relaxed in her mother's arms. At points during the session, they were amazed to see the baby going through some kind of visionary experience. He tightly clenched both of his little fists and began to kick into the air, slowly at first, then vigorously, while reflecting a stressful face. He gradually calmed down and opened his eyes in euphoric happiness, giggling and laughing. The mother intuitively knew what it was all about. She later shared with us that as she worried about her baby's feelings, she emotionally connected with him. This made her feel a sense of relief as she realized her baby was in the process of healing the only trauma which he had experienced in his short life. During the child's birth, the mother recalls that his tiny legs were entangled with the umbilical cord. He instinctively began kicking in an attempt to free them. Ultimately, it was the doctor who carefully finished the job. However, the fear of the moment was imprinted in the baby's memory. This is the youngest ayahuasca participant I am aware of, a very successful one indeed.

Another compelling case in which I was present occurred at a session during a ten-day dieta in the Peruvian Amazon. In one of the sessions, my teacher shaman, Don Jose Campos, appeared at the maloca with his two sons, aged nine and eleven respectfully. They had been curious about their father's profession, and he had promised them that one day they would join him and be initiated in a group session. That day had finally arrived, and the boys were excitedly looking forward to the grand occasion which they had long anticipated. The rest of the group gladly agreed when Don Jose asked for permission to include his children in the session. The outcome was uneventful. One of the boys fell asleep early, and the other remained relatively conscious, watching his dad singing icaros and alternating with occasional short naps. Don Jose was delighted as he was aware this was a remarkable memory in the lives of both kids.

Another story I heard from a practitioner mother who wanted her four-year-old son to experience medicine because she had recently observed signs of depression in his behavior. The mother had recently argued with her husband with lots of drama and screaming. The argument almost resulted in physical abuse. Sadly, the boy witnessed most of the incident. She believed this might have seeded psychological trauma in her son, which was subsequently manifesting in his behavior. One night she went to sleep with him, and after he fell sleeping, she briefly woke him up to administer one teaspoon of diluted ayahuasca pretending to be cough syrup. She stayed with him all night to monitor any possible reactions. In the morning, the boy made two comments during breakfast, which served as confirmation that the medicine has played its role. Firstly, he complained about having difficulty sleeping because she had left the light on all night. This was not the case at all. The boy appeared to have experienced being in a room filled with light. Secondly, and more relevant, while having breakfast, the boy spoke about a dream which he had. He saw his father praying and asking God for the peace of the family, and God said not to worry because everything will be alright. The boy had some sort of healing experience as he had regained his healthy vitality during the days that followed.

Aware of these and many other anecdotal stories, I feel comfortable saying that there is no minimum age limit for anyone to experience the sacred medicine. However, it is essential to emphasize the need to administer the medicine wisely in terms of dose, care, and setting. I may add that given the benefits of ayahuasca can have on a growing list of neurodegenerative conditions, we may speculate in favor of the argument that this amazing chemical cocktail and its plant spirit could have immediate and long-lasting effects in the healthy development of the youngster's brain functions. Improved neural pathways connections must lead to better cognitive functions in the worst case, and marvelous mental and emotional abilities at best. As I said, this is my biased opinion, as only future research may settle this matter with a high degree of certainty.

Moving to the opposite end of the age spectrum, we may ask how old a participant may be to experience ayahuasca safely? The answer to this question is more obvious and less controversial. In this case, we can confidently affirm that there is no upper age limit, which precludes the safety of ayahuasca. The fact that traditional shamans from Peruvian, Colombian, and Brazilian indigenous communities tend to live longer than average suggests that there is little to be concerned about regarding elder practitioners. Traditional Peruvian curanderos and Colombian taitas are known to live in their nineties and even early centennials, after many decades of practicing their trade. I have conducted sessions for an eighty-eight-year-old gentleman who wanted to experience ayahuasca for the first time. He did so with very favorable results. This same person returned when he was ninety to experience it again. Over the course of twenty years, I have personally handled over a dozen participants between ages sixty-five to eighty, all of whom were interested in having their first experience. Older participants are scarce for the understandable reason of how careful and conservative individuals tend to be at this age. I invariably praise and express my admiration to those that step forward to the challenge. Especially given their knowledge of how physically demanding the experience will be. These participants are often open-minded people with a very positive mindset toward the new and anything that may help them to become better people. They generally require special assistance during the session, for example, aiding them to the bathroom, placing a bucket on time when they vomit, and assisting with chores customary of hospice facilities. Invariably, these participants never regret their decision and embrace it as something exceptional in their lives. Elderly participants tend to have very profound experiences with lots of spiritual healing as Mother Ayahuasca is meeting a soul with a lifetime of material available for reprogramming. Among their most common resolved issues are the re-characterization of many of their vital life events, reconciliation with their concept of God, and developing a new fearless attitude toward the inevitability of death.

We can summarize by saying that there is no lower or upper age limit where ayahuasca should be avoided for any reason, other than the standard health precautions recommended to participants of all age groups.

Ayahuasca During Pregnancy

In Brazil, the regulation which allows the use of ayahuasca in minors [9] also indicates the following:

"... concerning pregnant women, they themselves assume the responsibility for deciding the degree of their participation, always attentive to protecting the development and personality structure of their underage and unborn children."

Some retreat centers in Peru recommend that women in an advanced stage of pregnancy should abstain from ayahuasca due to possible risks of miscarriage. However, they allow women up to the fifth month of pregnancy to participate, but not more than twice a week and only receiving half the regular dose. On the other hand, traditional taitas in Colombia do not accept pregnant women at their ceremonies. They don't elaborate much about the rationale underlying this decision. It appears to be a traditional prohibition.

In his online blog, Singing to the Plants, [10] Steve Beyer wrote the interesting guidance he received from his female teacher shaman, Doña Maria Tuesta:

"A woman, too, Doña María told me, should not drink ayahuasca while lactating, for reasons that she did not make clear — only that ayahuasca should not be in the breast milk. On the other hand, a woman can drink ayahuasca when she is pregnant because the ayahuasca gets into the child and gives it "fuerza" (strength). The same belief is found among the Shuar: some women express the belief that a child is born stronger if it receives the beneficial effects of ayahuasca while still in the womb."

In my personal experience as a facilitator, I have served the medicine to a handful of women in their first trimester of pregnancy; this number excludes participants who were unaware of their pregnancy. Among these participants, there was one who experienced meeting the soul of her baby. They spoke about the future after birth. She was fascinated with the encounter, and, as I learned later, she established a relationship with her unborn baby boy, emotionally connecting with him daily for the rest of her pregnancy. I believe this boy will grow up healthy and happy. There were two more cases where mothers received a keen intuitive insight about their baby's genders, which were later confirmed to be true.

No scientific studies have suggested that ayahuasca is harmful during pregnancy. To that effect, I must comment on another published ayahuasca book [11], which issues a warning, erroneously, in my opinion, to pregnant women that consume ayahuasca. Such warning is allegedly supported by a scientific study [12] indicating "that there is a high incidence of Down syndrome in this population." This alarmed me enormously and immediately rushed to carefully read the study. To my relief, when I reviewed the relevant section of the study, I realized that it was not the case. This is a direct quote from the study:

"The fact that regular ayahuasca consumption by pregnant women and children is common among members of the UDV and Santo Daime churches, and the relatively high incidence of Down Syndrome as a developmental abnormality, mean that these populations may represent a viable cohort [13] to investigate any correlation between harmine consumption and Down syndrome phenotypes."

The authors of the study were suggesting that since pregnant women who are members of these Brazilian churches are known to consume ayahuasca, they constitute an ideal group to investigate a potential correlation with Down syndrome. That doesn't mean that any correlation has been found. More importantly, no causation has been discovered, either. No studies have been conducted, which is the reason the authors of the study make this suggestion. They are interested in investigating such correlation because, based on prior research, harmine, one of the active ingredients of the ayahuasca vine, is seen as a strong candidate to act as an inhibitor of the gene that causes Down Syndrome in children. If such a study is ever conducted, I hope that it unequivocally confirms that harmine reduces the risk of Down Syndrome in babies from mothers that drink ayahuasca during pregnancy when compared to the general population.

To those interested in learning more about the subject of children and pregnant women consuming ayahuasca, I strongly recommend the in-depth exposition presented by renowned anthropologist Beatriz Labate, Ph.D. titled Medical Controversies and Religious Perspectives.

CHAPTER FIFTEEN

AYAHUASCA'S ANOMALOUS OUTCOMES

It is well-known to highly experienced ayahuasca ASA's and facilitators that ayahuasca sessions occasionally exhibit unusual phenomena that can cause significant disruption. From participants who become physically out of control, to the reception of messages of questionable subconscious origins, these occurrences are discussed infrequently within the ayahuasca community. However, these areas deserve further observation and open discourse.

About Fatalities Associated with Ayahuasca Sessions

A disturbing element regarding the safety of ayahuasca is the number of media reports describing fatalities of participants during an ayahuasca session. These reports arise almost exclusively from South America, where ayahuasca sessions are extensively practiced, especially since the 'boom' of Peruvian ayahuasca tourism over the past two decades. We must carefully examine these cases due to these contain elements that make reasonable judgment difficult challenging to reach.

Let's start with the number of historical reports. After carefully reviewing the existing collection of reported fatalities, we find that these do not exceed two or three dozen. An apparent problem with these reports is that they primarily originate from poor reporting, with their detail often derived from somewhat 'sketchy' police reports. The original news headlines are published in a sensationalized tone and are rarely followed by updates on subsequent findings. Unfortunately, the television news reports also follow suit and rarely add any value to the information. They focus on the fact that the deceased subject had consumed ayahuasca sometime before dying. However, information regarding participant health status, circumstances surrounding and leading up to the session, and a myriad of other important factors is generally scarce if offered at all.

Such tragedies would not make such a prominent headline if the substance involved happened to be an over-the-counter medication or prescription pharmaceutical rather than a psychedelic substance. In the small number of cases where detailed accounts are provided, we frequently find reasonable doubt about the suggested cause.

Of course, there must have been a few deaths caused by the use of ayahuasca. However, we should remember that in South America, except for a handful of responsible retreat centers geared to the western traveler, the pre-screening for health conditions is practically non-existent. As long as a willing client with money asks for ayahuasca sessions, a shaman (authentic or otherwise), will immediately appear - no questions asked. Considering the mandatory health precautions required before consumption of the medicine, we should all be surprised that so few tragedies have been reported.

If we scrutinize the details contained in media reports from South America, we can observe sufficient circumstantial information that enables us to make reasonable inferences about what actually happened. Considering their strong media bias against ayahuasca use, if we read between the lines, we can always envision a version of the story that exonerates the sacred medicine as a cause of death.

When a foreign tourist dies after participating in an ayahuasca session, we can discover a reasonable amount of media coverage. In 2014 a British youngster, Henry Miller, decided to participate in a session while traveling in Colombia. He experienced complications during the session and was quickly transported to a nearby hospital by the panicked assistants of the shaman. Unfortunately, carrying an unconscious man on a motorcycle resulted in the likely outcome of losing him along the way. It was widely reported as an ayahuasca-induced death. However, photographs that were subsequently published showed head injuries, as a consequence of a motorcycle accident, were likely to have abruptly ended Henry's life.

Many ayahuasca retreat centers offer the optional treatment of tobacco purge. The purge consists of inducing vomiting by sometimes drinking over one gallon of a dark brown liquid with a sour taste. This liquid is an infusion of dried tobacco that was boiled for hours following a traditional protocol. This treatment has proven to be beneficial to many who have tried it. However, some experience adverse reactions that result in a fatal collapse. A number of these tobacco-poisoning related deaths were wrongly attributed to ayahuasca in the initial media reports following the cases. Only after these reports, which tarnished the reputation and public image of ayahuasca, did the actual cause of these fatalities come to light.

In 2015, Matthew Dawson, a 24-year-old New Zealand citizen, died in an ayahuasca retreat center near Iquitos, Peru. After being reported as an ayahuasca-induced death, the autopsy report confirmed nicotine poisoning as the cause of death. Matthew had participated in a tobacco purge the previous day. Earlier the same year, 32-year-old Canadian, Jennifer Logan, experienced the same tragedy in a retreat center outside the city of Puerto Maldonado in the Peruvian Amazon.

In 2001, a Canadian woman died in Ontario (Canada) shortly after ingesting copious amounts of an ayahuasca and tobacco mixture, which was designed to induce vomiting. Evidently, facilitators were negligent in not conducting an adequate screening of their participants. In this case, the victim was a 71-years old diabetic who had reportedly ceased her medication to prepare for the three-day event.

Regrettably, ayahuasca has also being used by unscrupulous shamans to cover criminal acts. In 2012, Maestro Mancoluto, the main shaman at the Shimbre Retreat Center in Peru who has been featured in the award-winning documentary "Stepping Into the Fire," was involved in the death of 18-year-old American, Kyle Nolan. Following Kyle's death, Maestro Mancoluto secretly buried his body. This was only discovered after his mother flew to Peru from the U.S. to urge the police to conduct a full investigation. Maestro Mancoluto admitted to concealing the body, explaining that his action was an attempt to protect the reputation of himself and the center. An autopsy suggested that the cause of death was pulmonary edema, with the probable cause of nicotine poisoning, as Kyle had engaged in a tobacco purge during his stay at the retreat center.

Another death that resulted in an arrest was the case of Leslie Allison, a U.S. citizen who died in Ecuador while participating in an Ayahuasca ceremony in 2016. Her death was initially reported as an accident resulting from an adverse reaction to ingredients contained in the ayahuasca brew. However, according to her autopsy records, Leslie died a violent death in which she sustained a broken neck and blunt force trauma. The shaman conducting the ceremony was found guilty of her murder by an Ecuadorian court.

With the evidence available, it has proved impossible so far to find a single case supported by an autopsy report or death certificate confirming ayahuasca to be the primary cause of death. The issues discussed above provide context for the controversial issue of ayahuasca deaths. The statement that you can die by drinking ayahuasca is an unfounded urban myth. Yes, you can experience death, many times, but as explained earlier, this death is not physical but metaphorical.

VIRS: Visionary Intense Release Syndrome

Those with experience of attending ayahuasca sessions know that, on occasion, some participants may begin to scream, cry, laugh-out-loud, or engage in uncontrolled body movements. These behaviors can disturb the experience of other participants in the session. On many occasions, such incidents are short-lived, and, with some patience from the facilitator, the situation returns to normal after a few minutes.

However, there are instances where the volume, the intensity or the duration become intolerable for a facilitator who has the responsibility of overseeing the wellbeing of all participants. It is at this moment that the facilitator and support staff must take assertive action. At some point, it will become evident that the participant's interfering actions will not stop soon. The only prudent alternative to avoid total disruption of the session is to gently remove the uncontrolled participant from the session space into a separate place nearby where a staff member can continue to monitor and protect the participant from possible accidents or self-harm. Sessions that do not provide an alternative space to handle such possibility run the risk of having a session with mediocre results and many disappointed participants.

I have termed this unusual reaction as Visionary Intense Release Syndrome ("VIRS"). A VIRS reaction may vary from a fragile woman with a high pitch screaming non-stop for an extended period, to a strong muscular man unconsciously moving around bumping into other participants or nearby items. In both cases, these participants must be physically relocated for the safety of themselves and others. Such episodes tend to last between thirty minutes and a few hours. Generally, these episodes end up with the participant running out of energy and collapsing into a recomforting deep sleep. Upon recovering, the participant may have no or only partial recollection of the experience. Usually, these participants feel at ease and satisfied with the experience.

To better understand the VIRS phenomenon, we examine the coaching sessions which follow these events to learn about the participant's version of the experience. Our records show an equal distribution of subjects who recall going VIRS and those who don't. Interestingly, those whose VIRS experience was more kinetic and less passive tend not to remember the details of their actions. At the same time, those who were more emotional or talkative often have a better recollection of the inner drama taking place.

A short description of some cases can provide an improved understanding of the VIRS phenomena. A participant who had previously described in his pre-session interview, his anger issues against his biological father began to act extremely disorderly during the session. A staff member gently persuaded him to move out of the session space and assisted him in the area designated for VIRS cases.

While gently holding him by his left arm to lead him while walking, the participant suddenly snapped and violently attacked the staff assistant. The participant was a tall, athletic young man while the staff assistant was in his early sixties. The facilitator was able to quickly intervene to subdue the rageful youngster, but not on time to avoid the staff assistant's bleeding nose. It was found the next day that the participant was a victim of sexual abuse by his biological father. When the older-aged staff assistant grabbed him by the arm, despite doing it ever so gently, it triggered a violent response from the subconscious-self and acted-out the repressed physical actions which he never dared to inflict to his father. The image of an older man controlling him triggered the association with his abusive father, and for the first time, he "defended himself" against him.

In another VIRS case, a woman in her mid-40's yelled very loud at her mother for long hours across three consecutive sessions. She remembered every single argument she yelled about. The participant shared in her coaching sessions the profound understanding and healing she had experienced after resolving her emotional traumas from her relationship with her. These were so severe that, as she understood from her visions, these were the direct cause of a reproductive dysfunction from which she suffered permanent sterility. Holding such deep traumas with motherhood prevented her from becoming a mother herself.

There are VIRS reactions that require decisive interventions for the safety of the other participants. On rare occasions, as mentioned above, a participant may become overly aggressive to the extent that it disrupts the experience of everyone else and jeopardizes their safety. Screaming insults to imaginary enemies, attempting to destroy nearby items, or attacking anyone trying to control him are all clear indications that physical force is necessary. Facilitators must always have knitted belts which can be used to restrain the hands and feet of a participant after getting them under physical control. Controlling these participants may require the assistance of several staff members and constitute a serious disruption to the flow of the session. Fortunately, it is not hard to re-establish the rhythm of the session after the violent participant has been removed from the session space.

The question remains: what is the root cause of VIRS? I have asked several facilitators about their experience with VIRS, and there doesn't appear to be a rational consensus. Most of them have no idea and don't think much about it, perhaps because it's not a frequent occurrence. The reasons for this unusual reaction are mostly unclear. However, I will adventure into the speculation of some possibilities for the sake of starting a conversation. Perhaps one day, we may find a convincing explanation from this thoughtful discussion.

One possibility is that certain people carry an enormous amount of pent-up emotional energy. Ayahuasca may unlock the gates, resulting in the manifestation of the 'broken dam' effect, the consequence of this overflow may be VIRS behavior. Another speculation is that the truth that needs to be exposed from the subconscious-self is extremely shocking to the unsuspecting ego-self. This may entirely diminish any remaining control mechanisms of the ego-self and trigger VIRS behavior, a sort of "too hot to handle" response.

I have described the VIRS phenomenon, something rarely seen in the ayahuasca literature, and attempted to provide a rational interpretation as a humble contribution to the future ayahuasca students and researchers. It's a very intriguing phenomenon as it dramatically differs from the other 95% of the ayahuasca experiences. To date, VIRS has remained ignored. I feel it's time to raise the issue in order to open a dialogue regarding the phenomena across the ayahuasca community.

Benevolent Ayahuasca Lies?

In 2016, I read an excellent interview [1] with Wahid Azal, who is a Sufi mystic of the Fatimiya Sufi Order and an Islamic scholar. I was interested because I had learned that this mystic order endorsed the practice of entheogen consumption for spiritual purposes, primarily haoma [2] and ayahuasca. In this interview, Azal presented fascinating views that displayed unquestionable open-mindedness.

However, what struck me the most were specific references that compared the experience of ayahuasca to that of haoma. Specifically, he said: *"Many of my sessions with Ayahuasca ended in visionary aporias"*[3], followed by *" just as some of the native shamans of the Amazon have admitted, Ayahuasca sometimes does lie"* and finally, *"To me, at least, the Haoma has proven itself to be the superior ally to the Ayahuasca."*

We may conclude that ayahuasca is not Azal's favorite entheogen through his statements. Ayahuasca appears to often leave him confused and with the feeling of being lied to. Instead, Azal feels haoma to be a superior ally. As discussed previously, ayahuasca is not for everyone. I respect Azal's opinions and experiences entirely. However, something continues to resonate in my psyche regarding ayahuasca being a 'liar.' Is this true? I wondered about it for some time and began recalling instances where yes, there were participants that had reported messages from Mother Ayahuasca that later turned out to be false.

Statistically, these were just a handful of anecdotal accounts, to which no one paid too much attention. However, since a spiritual Sufi leader stated the issue with great weight, I decided to delve deeper. I began collecting stories of experiences where a message received as true ended up not being so. Upon closer examination and analysis, I began to decode the cryptic pattern, which emerged.

Let's review three of the cases where ayahuasca had allegedly 'lied' to participants.

Your Son Will Die From Drugs: My dear friend Susan had experienced ayahuasca with Don Jose and myself dozens of times. Throughout one-year, Susan received the same persistent message from Mother Ayahuasca. Susan, in her late 30's, had a teenage son who was losing the fight with drug addiction. She was losing him and desperately seeking guidance from ayahuasca. The message was crystal clear: "Your son will die soon due to the drug problem." I cannot describe the magnitude of agony and suffering; this trusting mother went through as she began to prepare for the worst. She received the same message with very slight variations on two more occasions in the following months. In her desperation, she had continued to seek guidance about what to do to change the course of destiny. She decided to intervene more assertively with her son, told him the bad news for his future, which he received skeptically and practically forced him to return to live with her with permission to use drugs at home. Eventually, Susan was able to convince her son to enroll in a costly drug treatment program for several months. The story ended with a rehabilitated young man. He graduated from a vocational school and has been living a healthy, relatively successful life for the last decade. Ayahuasca lied to Susan repeatedly as her son never died product of his drug addiction.

Marry That Woman: Ramiro is a successful Peruvian salesman in his late 30's. He had been drinking ayahuasca for some time for personal growth purposes but was explicitly seeking the key insights to overcome his addiction to pornography. In one session with twelve participants, he received a clear message from Mother Ayahuasca. The woman of his dreams was right there with him in the session, and it was up to him to make the right moves to materialize such an opportunity. Ramiro confessed his experience to me after the session and sought my advice. It was easy for me to go along with ayahuasca's message, given that they were both single and available for a relationship. He could not believe that Katerina, an independent, financially successful, physically attractive, blonde woman from Ukraine, could be the one. Optimistic and armed with the privileged information, he began inviting Katerina to social events and dinners. However, these offers ended up with Ramiro receiving a polite but definite decline of the possibility of anything more than friendship. Ayahuasca lied to Ramiro, making him believe that Katerina would eventually become his wife. In fact, she met and married another man two years later.

Your Husband Will Die Next Month: Carmen is a Peruvian woman in her early 50's who had been married for twenty years to a Canadian engineer. She came with her husband to a ten-day retreat in the Amazon jungle. She sought guidance as her marriage was in crisis. She was miserable. However, her husband remained in denial that anything was wrong. After her experience, she came to me anxiously, as she had seen in colorful detail that her husband was going to die in an accident during one of his construction projects. She said it would happen shortly after their return to Canada from the Peruvian vacation. She even described the circumstances, how a piece of heavy machinery would collapse and kill him. In my wish to calm her down, I told her not to take things literally that it could be like interpreting the meaning of a dream. Curious about the outcome, I emailed her about a year later to learn about their whereabouts and what happened next. She replied with the story that her husband never had the fatal accident which she saw. However, she told me that their relationship deteriorated further. After some time, she empowered herself and filed for divorce. Ayahuasca lied to Carmen, showing her in gruesome details the imminent death of her husband.

Similar to these, there are another handful of cases not included here. Can you see the pattern? Note that Susan, Ramiro, and Carmen are three individuals facing very complex personal problems, and their reactions to the "lies" ended up being part of the solution to their respective problems. Susan empowered herself to take the necessary actions to pull her son out of his drug addiction. Ayahuasca never tells you what you have to do with regard to any particular problem. You are the one who must decide; you are the owner of your life. Ayahuasca merely shows you the scenario clearly to aid you with better decision making. Ayahuasca showed Susan the final outcome for her son, should she remain in the inertia and victimhood she was living. Prior to her ayahuasca experience, she was anxious and worried about her son but paralyzed to take meaningful action. The death was also symbolic, as I said to her, like a dream interpretation. If her son would have been permanently lost to drugs and disappeared from her life, becoming homeless and hopeless, then he would have figuratively died.

Ramiro's vision of Katerina was the inducement he needed to explore; seeking a real woman for a meaningful relationship, instead of feeding his addiction with fantasy sexual encounters. His pornography addiction was sucking his creative energy and desire to enjoy a loving connection with the female figure. Ayahuasca's lie convinced him that a healthy relationship was a flesh and bone possibility - no longer a fantasy in a computer screen. Despite his failed attempt with Katerina, he learned of his desire for a loving relationship and pushed forward with all his strength to conquer his addiction. Enrolling in a couple of additional retreats with such intention, Ramiro successfully defeated the entity of pornography, which had controlled him for most of his adult life. In fact, he turned his problem into both personal growth and professional business opportunity when he authored a book about conquering pornography addiction, became a public speaker and coach.

Finally, Carmen's marriage was in crisis, but she never dared to bring up the word "divorce" in any conversation with her husband, despite this being always present in her thoughts. She wanted to end her marriage but was debilitated with fear and insecurity. She embraced ayahuasca's "lie" about her husband's imminent death as a convenient tragedy, an effortless way out of her marriage without the burden of taking meaningful action. In her frustration as the predicted accident failed to occur, she finally empowered herself to initiated divorce legal proceedings.

I must admit that my interpretation of these cases may be a product of my strong advocacy for Mother Ayahuasca. However, I hope that others agree that the few instances found where Mother Ayahuasca appeared to have "lied," she has ultimately done so with benevolent ulterior motives. In fact, it may be considered a strategy from the soul-self as one of its almost infinite number of ways to circumvent the ego-self to allow the reconnection of the ego-self with its divine essence.

Nudity and Eroticism

On rare occasions, you may find participants who consciously, or sometimes unconsciously, remove their clothing and expose themselves during the ayahuasca session. Despite being reminded during the initial orientation about refraining from doing so, it still occasionally happens. When the participant gets imbued in the dizziness of the experience, the futility of prevention becomes obvious.

When dealing with the subject of sexuality in any healing modality, and especially in ayahuasca sessions, we are walking on unstable ground. Firstly, there are numerous anecdotal accounts and media reports about shamans and facilitators partaking in highly unethical transgressions toward women, many times crossing the criminal boundaries. Unfortunately, the dark sexual entities that dwell in the quantum field of these unscrupulous shamans break loose in the face of the vulnerable state of mind of their victims during the sessions. I categorically condemn this behavior and strongly encourage victims of abuse of any kind, to step forward and contact law enforcement to press criminal charges. Permanent harm is caused by these actions, not only to the victim but also to the public trust in the laudable practice of ayahuasca sessions.

For the benefit of the entire community, I do not sanction any manifestation of sexual energy during ayahuasca sessions or retreats. The mere attempt to manifest sexuality during ayahuasca sessions is sufficient evidence that the participants are acting out repressed sexual issues from their past. By only noting and observing the behavior, the facilitator or ASA gather crucial information that may be discussed with the participant after the session.

It's not necessary to allow anyone to fully undress to realize that there is healing work to do in the sexual area. Besides undressing, ASA's must also be observant of participants who cover themselves in blankets or sleeping bags while showing signs of rhythmic or suspicious movements underneath. Auto-erotism may also occur. While you may think that such practice is harmless and invisible to others, an intervention is in order. These are surely manifestations of sexual entities that surface during the experience and gain control over the human vehicle. Such energies should not be allowed to spread into the healing space, and it should suffice to politely interrupt whatever is going on to effectively terminate the episode.

These occurrences are generally associated with sexual behavior, which has been imprinted prematurely in the child subconscious-self. This imprinting may then slip out the door, which was opened by the sacred medicine. The principal conclusion is that this behavior has no rightful place in a healing space and must be assertively discouraged in ayahuasca sessions.

Failure to Feel Significant Effects

We have witnessed several participants who don't receive any significant effects during an ayahuasca session, despite their expressed intention and strong desire to receive it. Most of these participants have persevered in their quest by drinking an unusually long series of consecutive doses. However, even with these multiple doses, they respond with no significant reaction besides slight drowsiness and nausea. Some, though not all, reach a point of purging. This is an anomaly that intrigues us all.

In these scenarios, frustration often ensues, and participants often dismiss the medicine as 'not meant to be' for them. Often, they will decide never to try ayahuasca again. However, we have had a few more resilient participants who have experienced this situation but tried it again at a later date with very positive results.

My impression is that in these circumstances, the subconscious-self has developed robust protective mechanisms to isolate from the lower aspects of the self. Think of a crust of hardened energy as a shield to survive a very hostile upbringing or environment. The subconscious-self may have created this shield to protect the identity and avoid dissolution into the whole or to block undesirable encrypted memories. This subconscious crust prevents the subject from experiencing the typical disruption of the ego-self, from opening up, and from developing their natural intuitive abilities. In neurological terms, for some reason, the participant's Default Mode Network has created a neurochemical immunity to the active ingredients of ayahuasca. As such, the ego-self remains relatively unaltered. This immunity may be the product of conscious or unconscious actions across many years of protective behavior where thought patterns have crystallized in neural pathways and chemical alterations. This anomaly shows us how strong habitual thoughts can become, creating an impenetrable armor from such a potent substance as ayahuasca.

This armor may be a useful survival tool while dealing with stress throughout daily life. However, it comes at the expense of self-realization. To understand why it happens, we should consider that at the other end of this continuum is the lack of adequate protection, where the ego-self remains too permeable, and disturbing memories may happen to emerge on an ongoing basis. This end of the spectrum can be incredibly disruptive to daily life. In other words, the lack of reaction to the medicine could potentially be protection from triggering a latent mental condition like psychosis or schizophrenia. Only future scientific research can settle such a question.

Negligent Psychonauts and Bad Trips

We have covered the aspect of ayahuasca safety in Chapter 1 (The Safest Medicine Ever?) and in Chapter 15 (About Fatalities Associated with Ayahuasca Sessions). It is now pertinent to make a case against the irresponsible use of the sacred medicine.

Most sources of information about ayahuasca use include clear recommendations about consuming the medicine under the supervision of responsible, experienced shamans or facilitators. Some of them include warnings about the dangers of using it under the wrong conditions. Notwithstanding, there are many explorers of psychedelic substances, or psychonauts, that dismiss these warnings as plain exaggerations. They have experienced the most potent strains of cannabis, different classes of mushrooms, LSD, Peyote, Ecstasy, smoked DMT, and other three-letter compounds that promise a dose of fun and entertainment. Why could ayahuasca be dangerous? They may argue, maybe with a kernel of validity. With such a fearless attitude, many move forward finding the ingredients or analogs, and carefully plan their next expedition into their inner space. What they ignore is the little surprise Mother Ayahuasca has in store for them.

In 2016, the Journal of the American College of Medical Toxicology (ACMT) published a short technical report analyzing the data of reported ayahuasca-related medical emergencies in the United States. The ACMT is a professional, non-profit association of approximately 800 physicians with recognized expertise in medical toxicology. [4]

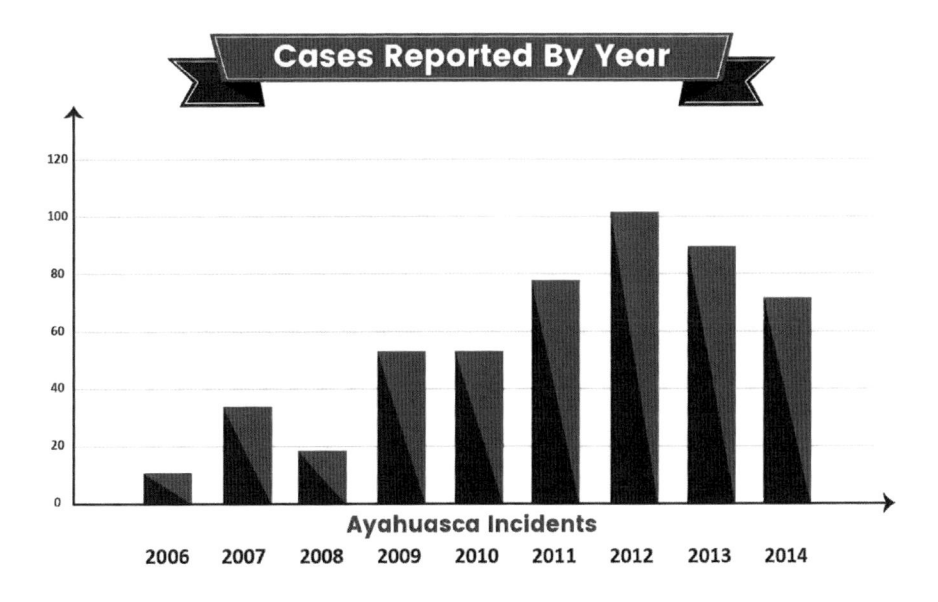

Cases Reported By Year

Ayahuasca Incidents
2006 2007 2008 2009 2010 2011 2012 2013 2014

The researchers that published this report obtained permission to access the central database of the American Association of Poison Control Centers (AAPCC), who has detailed records of emergency calls received from people or institutions in need of urgent advice to handle poison incidents. AAPCC is a nonprofit organization dedicated to actively advancing the health care role and public health mission of its members through information, advocacy, education, and research. The researchers filtered the data to segregate poison emergency calls associated with ayahuasca for a ten-year period comprising from September 2005 to September 2015. A total of 538 ayahuasca-related poison calls were identified for this time period.

Note that after the peak frequency experienced in 2012, the incidence of ayahuasca-related emergencies began to gradually decline. It would be interesting to evaluate an updated study that includes more recent data.

A factor that may partially explain the relatively high incidence of these emergency calls is in the very own nature of the ayahuasca experience. Since the fear of death is a frequent occurrence while having an ayahuasca experience, we can safely infer that inexperienced users working without proper guidance would quickly turn into panic mode and rush to seek emergency help. I would not expect anything different from anyone who feels death approaching nearby.

It's common knowledge that thousands of ayahuasca sessions are conducted every year across the United States. The vast majority of them are very likely populated by organizers and participants that are knowledgeable about the requirements and procedures. It's hard to envision experienced shamans or facilitators holding ayahuasca sessions in the USA calling a government-sponsored poison control unit seeking advice to handle an ayahuasca participant in crisis. Knowing what we know today about the sacred medicine mechanics, it's not difficult to infer that the vast majority of these cases must have been negligent at worst or very inexperienced at best.

The data suggest that dangerous experiences with ayahuasca or "bad trips" are mostly experienced by audacious young people experimenting with homemade mixtures prepared with ingredients purchased online, people mixing ayahuasca with other dangerous drugs or even longtime users of counter-indicated medications who didn't prepare properly. These must have been victims, in most cases, of their ignorance who went in panic and desperately called the nearest poison control unit. The following study findings support these views:

- **Fact:** The vast majority of cases were men (487 / 87%) with a median age of twenty-one years-old. A total of (107 / 20%) of the cases were youngsters under eighteen-years-old and remarkably, ten of those were children under ten-years-old.
- **Fact:** A total of (332 / 62%) cases reported ingesting only ayahuasca and

nothing else, but 148 reported consuming one additional substance, 45 reported consuming two additional substances, 43 consuming three or more additional substances.

- **Fact:** Assistance from the poison center was requested in the vast majority (447 / 83%) by the healthcare facilities, which were already handling the cases while the remainder was requested by the concerned victims themselves.

- **Fact:** Of the 538 exposures, 258 (48%) were treated and released from a healthcare facility. Ninety-two were admitted to a critical care unit (17%). Fifty-eight were admitted to a non-critical care unit (11%). Thirty-three were medically cleared and admitted to a psychiatric unit (6%). The remaining 97 did not have complete information on file (18%).

- **Fact:** The most severe effects noted were seizures (12 / 2%), respiratory arrest (7 / 1%), and cardiac arrest (4 / 1%). Three fatalities were reported to poison control, all adults, with two cases marked as indirect reports.

Researcher's Note: One case in the medical literature described the death of a young person with very high levels of some of the psychoactive substances found in ayahuasca, although the psychoactive substances, in this case, may have been synthetic rather than botanically derived. Many forms of DMT are synthetically derived and may have sympathomimetic activity not usually found in the botanical versions. These synthetic agents cause hyperthermia, rhabdomyolysis, seizure, and potentially death. Case reports of adverse outcomes and human deaths maybe not from botanical ayahuasca at all.

I hope this evidence equips readers with a solid argument to discourage anyone who intends to adventure with ayahuasca on its own terms. Conclusion: Ayahuasca is an extremely safe substance when skillfully administered with care and responsibility.

CHAPTER SIXTEEN

How to Advise for Psychological Wellbeing

Spiritual Guidance for Enduring the Storms

Thanks to the ability of the sacred medicine to erode the heavily resilient defense mechanisms of the ego-self, session participants are often inclined to access intimacy about their emotions and beliefs. By expressing enough empathy and compassionate probing, spiritual healers should be able to establish an adequate level of rapport with their participants. As mentioned earlier, the real guidance is provided by Mother Ayahuasca during the sessions while the spiritual healing advisor acts as her assistant in the process. Many participants, depending on their prior experience in the spiritual path, often guide themselves through their spiritual healing process, but often find themselves in a dead-end street where any further progress seems out of reach. This is when the spiritual healing advisor makes its valuable contribution.

The spiritual healing advisor must develop the skill to recollect its current understanding of the particular case and look at the person as a whole. Understand their childhood and family dynamics, the conscious issues that they are trying to heal, and the barriers that seem to be holding them back. With this mental review, the spiritual healing advisor can apply the powerful tool of the projection principle. They must find a way to articulate the well-structured leading question for the session of the participant. What aspects unknown to the participant are blocking the process? The participant should ask: "How is my ego-self trying to justify my reality based on external factors?, How is my ego-self avoiding to look at an aspect of myself to preserve its status quo?, In what manner is this barrier, a projection of an unseen angle in my psyche? Where is the blind spot I am missing? These leading generic questions that apply to a wide variety of situations and invariably generate valuable insights in the participant. This Socratic dialogue between participant and spiritual healing advisor often yields new perspectives that substantially shift the direction of the initially intended agenda of the consultation. It frequently leads to a different lead question for the session than the one originally envisioned. When a new horizon of work opens up in the heart of the participant, the energy changes, it shows in the body language, and the spiritual healing advisor feels that the participant has moved from a stagnant to a more fluid space. When this happens, the consultation session is ready to be summarized and closed.

Setting Intentions & Asking the Right Questions

Much has been said about advice and recommendations to set clear intentions before an ayahuasca session. Meditating about them or fixing them deeper in the subconscious-self by writing them down on paper is always a good idea. By doing that, the ego-self is consciously seeking alignment within its SIE, in this way inducing the soul-self to "take note" and increases the odds of having them considered in the forthcoming experience. Explicit intentions may be useful, but they don't determine the experience. There are unconscious processes that need to unfold, and even without the intentions, the participant may experience amazing life-changing breakthroughs. Once the intentions are set, they don't need to be repeatedly reminded during the session. However, they come as handy reminders during the experience if you find yourself grappling with distracting thoughts that pull you away from the focus of your work.

Intentions, by definition, are general requests or wishes that the participant would like to address during the session. "I want to understand why I have these anger episodes," or "Show me my mission in life" are typical examples of intentions from participants.

But the most powerful tool for self-realization and spiritual healing is to ask well-structured questions during the peak stage of the experience. This is a more effective way to establish a flow of messages or insights with the soul-self. Our soul-self doesn't usually engage in a dialogue, taking us by the hand, for example, in leading us to step by step about what our mission in life is.

We need to walk our inner path to identify the specific area that would yield the most guidance in our quest or path. Then, we need to articulate a question that is answered with an image or message that contains feeling or meaning. When the answer is received during the session, even if not visually or audibly transparent, you know what it means in your heart. That is the answer right there; don't expect a dissertation. The answer comes intuitively more than rationally in the vast majority of cases. We have to make it easy for our soul-self with questions that require short answers while carrying high significance in our quest.

Think of you physically approaching the wisest guru or spiritual master. He is overwhelmed by hundreds of followers like you and is your turn to receive the full attention of the teacher for fifteen seconds. Since you don't want to waste any time, you probably ask a question that you have articulated beforehand in the least number of words, and as precise as possible. It's a precious moment that you have been anxiously anticipating. Such is the emotional tone we recommend participants to seek in their hearts when asking questions during ayahuasca sessions. We need to do it with maximum emotional energy possible. This can only be achieved by being honest and truthful in your desire to know, as it will bring progress in your path to the light. Pray, beg for help, and do it from the heart.

There is one way that has worked for many and goes like this: "Show me the origin of" This refers to the origin of so many failures, contradictions, and inconsistencies in our character that bring about so much pain, trouble, and unhappiness to our lives. This implies that you have already identified the area that needs to be improved in your persona. You have done your homework, but you are still stuck in a persisting pattern of behavior, and you need help to find the key to the riddle. This question sends an explicit request to your soul-self, and it is quickly answered with a memory from childhood, a feeling from the past, or similar. Another powerful one is: "What is going on with ..." or similar phrasing. This applies to life situations that you don't understand and need clarity to be able to make important life decisions.

Another essential element is the relative transcendence and the sense of urgency of the question at hand. When your heart urgently needs clarity, it comes faster than when inquiries are made just to confirm what you already feel or already have a good idea of the answer. This reminds me of one participant that asked whether her boyfriend truly loved her. The answer that quickly followed was nothing short of hilarious. She got this answer emotionally charged with a reprimanding tone: "You know that! Why are you asking?" We may find surprises when using the sacred medicine as a psychic oracle. She was obviously trying to convince herself of not ending a relationship that was not working for her.

How to Dissolve Resistance Barriers

Here is advice for situations of participants experiencing frustration for not being able to break through a psychological blockage that refuses to give-in. A participant may have identified a particular blockage, had properly articulated the right questions, but still, during the session, there appears to be strong resistance to their efforts. The answer is a technique that I have personally tried successfully and other practitioners as well.

Two elements are crucial for it to work effectively. First, the unbreakable will to break through the barrier of resistance. As the peak of the session begins, one must feverously pray and reach out for the strongest honest desire appealing the soul-self. Stay focused in such an emotional state for a few minutes and then suddenly stop and let go. One must explicitly declare to be receptive and ready to accept whatever new information is about to be unleashed. That one has the emotional strength to process any shocking truth that may be revealed. This is about sending a strong message to the soul-self requesting to bypass the encryption protocols being firmly held by the subconscious-self. The message must be heavily wrapped in emotional energy for which an amount of desperate call for mercy is in order.

The second step is to suddenly stop, relax, do nothing, think about nothing, surrender fully, and let the experience flow. Just be passively alert to the sensations that subsequently unfold. When resistance is extreme, the participant is often carried towards irrelevant or random thoughts that manifest freely due to the permission given by the assumed attitude of total surrender. Time is very elastic in those moments, but relatively speaking, after a few minutes, there is a point where it becomes clear that the attempt is not working.

If the desire for resolution is strong enough, the participant should be able to assume control of the experience again and repeat the process one more time. It can be repeated two or three times before the medicine experience begins to show signs of fading off. At this point, it becomes evident is time to shift consciousness to other areas to maximize the time remaining in the experience. The good news is that this technique has proven to work with remarkable breakthroughs for the delightful rejoice of many participants. These are the outcomes that make the ayahuasca unique among all plant medicines.

The Tricks of the Trickster

In Carl Jung's collection of archetypes, there is one not often mentioned, that of the trickster. The description of Jung archetypes is known for containing profound conceptual abstractions and ancient historical references. The concept of trickster has some relevance in the ayahuasca experience and deserves a simple description to which we may relate.

There are popular myths that speak about this unconscious trickster that play tricks in our consciousness, such as when we thoroughly search for our misplaced car keys to realize later they were located in its usual place or searching for our eyeglasses when we are actually wearing them. In mythology and the study of folklore and religion, a trickster is a character in a story (god, goddess, spirit, human, or anthropomorphized) which exhibits a great degree of intellect or secret knowledge and uses it to play tricks or otherwise disobey standard rules and conventional behavior. Since the message must be heavily wrapped in emotional energy, making a desperate or passionate call to your soul-self or to God is highly recommended. The *heyoka* is a kind of sacred clown in the culture of the Lakota people of the Great Plains of North America who manifests by doing things backward or unconventionally—riding a horse backward, wearing clothes inside-out, or speaking in a backward language.

I bring the trickster in the historical context of Jung as an element of the subconscious-self that sometimes manifests during the peak of ayahuasca experiences and succeeds in deceiving the ego-self, who is partially disabled at the moment. Practitioners should be aware that they may perceive insights that appear to originate from their soul-self but, in reality, were deceptions crafted by this rogue element in the subconscious.

It appears that the subconscious-self, in its function to protect the belief system of our SIE it pulls from its almost infinite diversity of programmed resources this sophisticated tool to combat a formidable opponent like the ayahuasca. Most of the time, the subconscious-self subverts the interpretation process to suit the ego-self inherent needs of continuity. We know how belief systems entrench themselves, objecting, rationalizing, and even confronting outside threats that attempt to change or modify them. Survival depends on our understanding of reality, and the subconscious-self has spent our entire lifetime building a belief system that works for us. The subconscious-self, conveniently allied with certain subpersonalities and independent psychological entities, is not going to give up the fight easily. These are very intelligent, resilient, and never surrender.

Clearly, at the peak of the ayahuasca experience, the presence of the intruder has been detected, and the partially disabled ego-self is no longer capable of rationally resisting it. They will avoid at all costs the ayahuasca's forced entry into the control room where all the programming is stored and protected. The belief system that was painstakingly developed for decades must be protected from "hackers."

Within this context, I describe here a few tricks used by this team of players in the subconscious-self in their desperate attempts to derail your intention of hacking your programming. When everything else fails, they bring the last weapon in its arsenal, that is tricks and deception. Here is a partial list of those tricks:

Classical Psychological Projection- This is what we do all the time in our daily lives; it's the most common subconscious trick. This is discussed extensively in Chapter 9. Psychological projection is highly effective in the preservation of our belief systems, projecting outside of ourselves, the weaknesses which we are not prepared to accept to avoid the stress of dealing with them. In some ways, it is helpful and necessary, but we must be aware that it's detrimental to our soul's desire for self-realization as it avoids change while preserving the status quo.

During the ayahuasca experience, participants often find themselves projecting excessively, wasting valuable prime time from experience. One of the most prevalent projections is the judgment to others, from the "annoying noises of the participant next to me," to "the terrible way my sister back home treats my mother." From suddenly realizing that "this shaman is a pervert" to deeply understanding that "this session is full of insane people." Inexperienced participants fail to realize that precious time intended for profound spiritual healing is being sadly diverted into unproductive wanderings of the ego-self.

Spiritual Exaltation - Some session participants describe flamboyant visions of them visiting exotic places, sacred temples, Egyptian gardens, wearing colorful or pristine white robes, sitting in thrones, and sometimes crowned with exuberant jewelry. Higher beings generally accompany these, or solemn voices gently telling them messages to the effect that they have reached an exalted level of spirituality. I have personally experienced some of these before, for which I can recognize them well when described to me by others.

Another style of exaltation comes when the participant has visions of being taken to other planets or even spaceships, and advanced information is revealed as to the inner workings of the mind, or human civilization in general, or the evolution of life, just to name a few. These kinds of visions leave the participant very exalted about the achievement of being "chosen" or the privilege having reached "a high level of spiritual development." Ironically, these get them no closer to their real healing goal, and their psychological condition remains unchanged. When advised adequately about it, participants "wake up" from the deception and get back to the real work. Our advice to participants about these visions being tricks of the subconscious-self has proven useful in obtaining better results in the intended purpose of the sessions.

We can't deny or invalidate the visionary experiences described above, for these can be very fulfilling and boosters of self-esteem and other possible benefits. However, indulging in them during a healing retreat is considered a distraction and does not contribute to the healing efforts within the scope of this spiritual healing methodology.

I am ok; I don't need more of this! - This trick appears in a variety of shades but is essentially the same. The participant may receive it as a sudden realization, a "message from above" or from Mother Ayahuasca herself. It consists in the absolute certainty that the participant's psychological or spiritual condition is currently well above average, in excellent good standing, for which there is not much to improve. Therefore, resorting to doing ayahuasca work is unnecessary, there is no need to do it again, even if it was the first time to experience the medicine. This trick makes the participant feel relieved from their original assumption that ayahuasca would have helped them in whatever personal issues they wanted to address.

I Want to be a Shaman – When a highly experienced ayahuasca participant receives the call from Mother Ayahuasca to consider becoming an ayahuasca facilitator or any other form of spiritual guide, this is something that may authentically happen from time to time. It happens typically to persons that have the possibility of doing it within their reach. It is something viable by making life changes here and there. However, a common occurrence in the ayahuasca practice is when relatively inexperienced participants receive these calls from Mother Ayahuasca or other spiritual guides to become ayahuasca facilitators. They suddenly realize their mission in life is to help others in their spiritual path, express a notable desire to receive training to become shamans right away. Some of them actually research training programs, trips to Peru, or similar alternatives. This should be viewed with suspicion as the ego-self is undoubtedly trying to focus the attention away from the crux of the healing process. The immediate consequence of such a shift is that the pursual of inner spiritual healing becomes a second priority, making the exaltation strategy successful. Not necessarily it is always the case, but the rule of thumb should be to assume that it's a deceptive distraction. In the end, their interest in shamanism or spiritual healing fades away, and the intensity in seeking true spiritual healing rarely returns to the original levels. The relevant lesson for ASA's is that, as a general rule of thumb, while guiding participants in their integration of ayahuasca experiences, their narratives are not to be taken at face value, but instead scrutinized with investigative rigor to identify these deceptions correctly. In the case of "aspiring shamans," for example, note that their sudden desire for helping others is the psychological projection of helping themselves. This means they are genuinely invigorated in the path of self-realization.

Another essential consideration while listening to participant's stories is that despite ayahuasca's excellent reputation in its ability to "dissolve the ego," the inconvenient truth is that ayahuasca may also strengthen certain subpersonalities or entities of the ego-self. There are people with too hardened ego-self whose entities learn to bypass the medicine. One example is individuals suffering from a severe addiction to hard drugs. Their neurology has developed a sort of immunity or callousness due to the intense drug use that the sacred medicine falls short of causing a significant impact in their subconscious-selves. When this happens, the entities assume more "muscular" control over the overall ego-self, a very lamentable outcome. The entities tend to become more dangerous and mischievous than gentle and benevolent. Such is the case, for example, of shamans or facilitators that turn into sophisticated sexual predators, abusing unsuspecting vulnerable women with numerous lies, tricks, and even direct criminal behavior.

Is the Progress in Spiritual Healing Fast or Slow?

The spiritual healing may occur incredibly fast in some participants, while others may occur remarkably slow. The ASA must have the sensibility and ability to understand the unfolding process of spiritual healing to provide relevant suggestions or advice to the participants properly. The ASA should pay attention to the speed at which progress is occurring.

On multi-day ayahuasca retreats, during advisory sessions conducted after the ayahuasca sessions, you may observe some participants' energy and wakefulness level at an average or even enhanced state despite them likely not having many sleeping hours the night before or maybe none at all. It becomes more evident with their positive facial expressions and body language without saying a word. Then you can confirm your perceptions when you listen to their answers to your open question: "Describe to me something about what happened last night during the session?" or something to that effect, kicking off the advisory session. In such cases, participants describe different levels of perceived progress, from mild to significant. Others tell short or lengthy passages of their favorable experiences but fail to recognize them as such. In both instances, the advisor should validate and congratulate them on their progress and proceed with a brief interview to understand their experience. The advisory session ends with an agreement about the right attitude and intention for the next session. These advisory sessions may be as brief as five minutes since the only objective is to monitor their progress. Those who exhibit fast progress allow the advisor to finish the programmed advisory sessions faster, allowing the advisor to move into other participants, if any.

There will be other participants, however, that require closer and more dedicated attention. It often becomes evident by their facial expressions and demeanor. Almost always, they look tired, low energy, and exhibit a diversity of attitudes. Some appear confused by the intensity of the previous night experience, others frustrated or disappointed, and feel like giving up and quit the process. Also, others have rationally organized their feelings and experiences and are ready for a productive advisory session.

The advisor should probe them for details about how they feel, identify the pitfalls, fallacies, and biased judgments in their minds and refocus them towards a positive attitude towards the next ayahuasca session and their spiritual healing process. It is essential to convey a special message to those who tend to compare their healing process with the ones of other participants who they perceive are doing relatively better than them. To avoid any frustration about their process, they need to understand that the speed of the healing process is a function of many factors and is highly variable among participants. Some require more than one retreat to see the process moving from its previous stagnant state, while others experience extraordinary breakthroughs that re-launch their lives to new highs and never come back for more. Here are a few of those factors:

(1) Many subjects that seek participation in ayahuasca retreats do so because they have reached a point in their lives where they have tried several types of conventional therapies with little or no results. They tend to become over-hopeful after finding the "miracles" of ayahuasca in social media and other publications. The general health profile and medical record of these participants are often

plagued with compromised conditions or appear to have many layers of personal and family emotional dramas and anxiety. When they don't find immediate relief after only a few ayahuasca sessions, they tend to judge that ayahuasca is not working for them. An advisor should bring them to realize with simple examples that they have complicated situations, and Mother Ayahuasca is working on them at the subconscious level and is still not being physically manifested yet. Mother Ayahuasca is untangling a bunch of ensnared wires in their subconscious-self, and this takes time while some patience is appropriate.

(2) Other participants don't exhibit significant complexities in their recent or medium terms health history but may have indications of early childhood trauma. Some of them acknowledge their suspicions that something may have happened to them as little children. Others may have clear or faint memories of child abuse and may recall the circumstances and the parties involved. Participants in this category should be able to understand that the earlier the trauma has occurred, the longer it takes to repair and heal the damage created. The hardest to identify and treat are the cases of physical or sexual abuse in the infant-toddler stage of development when the child's memory capacity has not developed sufficiently to record and retain images of the traumatic events. However, they remain stored in the cellular memory. They are retrievable in the form of touch, sound, and even faint visual memories that get re-enacted when the participant is prepared during the ayahuasca sessions to handle the underlying emotional impact that comes with them. Mother ayahuasca is wise and compassionate enough to release details from the cellular memory banks only when the subject is capable of processing its impact. Remember the axiom that participants shall never end up worse than they originally were without the medicine.

(3) Some participants, after the initial short period of the relatively good healing process, find themselves stuck as if having found a brick wall in their path. Intuitively, it feels that there is something else that needs to be unveiled but remain clueless about what it may be. We may be facing a case of deeply encrypted memories. Unlocking these requires a resilient desire of the participant and great patience to keep persisting while waiting for the sparkling wine's cork to pop. The problem is that in many cases, participants don't find such desire due to the intense fear of uncovering very unpleasant, or even terrifying memories. They tend to overthink about finding very negative scenarios such as feeling permanently troubled or disturbed by the memory, going insane, or having an uncontrollable violent reaction toward a possible aggressor, who often is a family member. Fear is the most potent defense mechanism of the survival program, which unfortunately happens to be a stumbling block encrypted memory retrieval. If participants are paralyzed by fear to the extent of not being able to control it consciously, then it means they are not ready to experience such breakthroughs. If they can't be skillfully persuaded to confront the fear in their next ayahuasca session, then they should be led to a different intention containing less emotional stress. They

could address the issue on a future occasion with regained inner strength. John Welwood, [1] makes an eloquent description of the ego-self resisting ayahuasca's healing power:

" *[the ayahuasca experience]....its like the warmth of the Sun starts to wake up a dormant seed within us. The soul is that seed, which wants to grow, blossom, and bear fruit, to become all that it can be. But often, the shell around the seed is so thick that it blocks those expansive possibilities. Instead of the light penetrating us to the core, transmuting us wholly, we let it shine only the places we want, the safe places we know, because deep inside, we are afraid of lowering our defenses. We remain stuck in the same neurotic pathways as before, endlessly wondering why we don't feel better when nausea will end, and why we aren't having visions while our neighbor is head to head with a large bioluminescent snake. "I want that she is having!"*

The Joy of Feeling Healed and the Agony of Relapse

By reading through numerous internet forums and listening to several practitioners from our observational sample, there is a pattern that is relevant to ASA's. Some practitioners have described the situation where, after experiencing remarkable psychological breakthroughs with the sacred medicine, they later feel "back to square one." It often happens to people who travel to Peru for their ayahuasca retreats, experience notable progress, post the great news in social media, and enthusiastically film a YouTube testimonial. But later, weeks after returning home, they begin to witness a gradual regression to the old habits; the previous patterns were coming back, making them feel frustrated, disappointed, but worse of all, confused.

Closely examining these cases led us to realize that these practitioners never reached the bottom of the psychological issues that were bothering them. They only had scratched the surface of a much deeper situation that had remained encrypted in their subconscious. But then we faced the question: If they haven't reached the point of true permanent resolution in their issues, then what was the factor that was making them feel well, at least temporarily? Answer: the harmine molecule.

When we review the chemistry of ayahuasca, we find a magnificent family of molecules found in the vine component of the medicine. The chemical analysis of Banisteriopsis Caapi reveals the presence of harmine, harmaline, and tetrahydro harmine. The properties of these chemicals have been studied for decades by the pharmaceutical industry due to its promising health benefits. Among them is the property of acting as a chemical inhibitor of Mono Amine Oxidase (MAO) enzymes, making possible the entry of the DMT into the bloodstream bypassing the destroying gastric fluids after we ingest the ayahuasca brew. The potent experience of ayahuasca is mostly thanks to the combination of DMT and MAO inhibitors. The MAO enzymes in our bodies quickly respond to DMT and break it down, dramatically shortening the life span and reducing the potency of any DMT ingested. By combining DMT with harmine, the later interferes with the function of these enzymes, preventing them from breaking down any DMT for some time. As you can imagine, this gives the DMT within ayahuasca plenty of time to work its "magic."

But harmine is not only crucial for the effectiveness of the ayahuasca brew ingested orally. What is relevant here is another vital role of harmine once it has made an entrance in the brain territory. For being a chemical MAO inhibitor, harmine belongs to a class of drugs best known as highly efficacious anti-depressants, as well as effective therapeutic agents for panic disorder and social phobia. This is why most participants of ayahuasca sessions feel "very well" not only immediately afterward but also during the following days or weeks as well. Consequently, the symptoms of undiagnosed anxiety, issues of self-esteem, and mild depression, which many people unknowingly suffer, get immediate improvement. This is often misinterpreted by many participants as a "cure" from whatever perceived psychological condition they were concerned about.

Like any other chemical remedy that only treats the symptoms, their effects gradually fade away, and the underlying condition surface back again. In other words, there has been an enormous number of people that have erroneously believed in the excitement of the moment that ayahuasca has changed their lives. Unfortunately, when we revisit them six months later, we find that their lives remain more or less unchanged, except that they now carry the added misgivings and confusion derived from their failed attempt.

This brings us to the inevitable conclusion that there are two distinct healing mechanisms inherent to ayahuasca. As the wise and well known late "curandera," Norma Panduro [2] used to say: "Ayahuasca has two faces: a loving face and a terrifying face." Many experienced shamans from Peru not only agree but also teach this shamanic principle. Translating shamanism into spiritual healing terminology, I would say that the loving face, the one that heals without causing much havoc, corresponds to the bio-chemical, neurological stabilizer effect of the medicine. This is the effect that could be temporary for substantially variable periods, and also can be extended as long as additional ayahuasca sessions are conducted. The terrifying face, on the other hand, corresponds to the psychological kind characterized by a deep understanding and undeniable clarity about the subject's resolution of issues hidden deep in the Jungian shadow. The latter is predominantly long-lasting and almost always permanent, being ultimately the real motive behind embarking in the intensity of ayahuasca healing journeys. I call these two mechanisms chemical relief and spiritual healing, respectively.

Having learned this lesson along the way, advisors should make participants aware of this phenomenon to prepare them to understand the possible occurrence in their particular case. When participants relapse into their previous emotional states, it means that they haven't reached rock bottom on the issue at hand, and there is more work to be done. There is nothing more gratifying than persisting in the quest and reach the precious eureka moment when the subconscious-self finally surrenders the tightly gripped secret that makes spiritual healing permanent and irreversible. When that happens, after the joy and celebration, a different conscious work must begin to actually start manifesting the gained wisdom into practice and truly enjoy a happier and more fulfilling life free of the burdens that once dwelled in the shadows. When people in the community repeatedly state the caveat to the effect that ayahuasca is not a magic pill or panacea, they are being sharply accurate.

Unfortunately, thousands of ayahuasca tourists spend their savings traveling to South America to find themselves empty and confused only a few months after returning home. On the other hand, we have to acknowledge that many participants may experience profound, permanent healing with just a few sessions and feel their trips were worthwhile, similar to many participants in the retreats in other parts of the world. Generally, those success stories are associated with cases relatively mild compared to the ones referred above, which include severe trauma, early childhood abuse, PTSD, and other conditions that temporarily improve but sooner or later relapse if not treated in depth.

CHAPTER SEVENTEEN

INTEGRATION AND CLOSURE

The Ideal Ayahuasca Session for Spiritual Healing

There is a myriad of different styles of ayahuasca sessions. They are as numerous as the number of facilitators or shamans out there. The traditional shamanic sessions are not conducted in the spirit of holding space the way we described it before. On the contrary, the role of the conventional shaman is one of an active participant, the one of the healer. Since shamans are considered an intrinsic part of the healing process, while the session is unfolding, they often intervene with the participants, asking them to sit up from the laydown position for smudging, perfuming, tobacco-blowing, or chanting icaros to them on a one-to-one basis. They may also begin to physically touch the participant by rubbing the forehead, or even more intrusive, massaging the abdomen area to identify or remove negative energies. If the participant begins to cry or scream uncontrollably, they often intervene in a diversity of ways to calm them down or talk them out of the "crisis" in their honest effort to help them.

The ideal behavior for a shaman leading an ayahuasca session conducted for spiritual healing purposes in one of a passive space holder, compassionately following the participants' processes, and other supervisory functions. The unfolding of the personal process of a participant during the peak of the experience must be protected from interference because these not only disrupt important and necessary inner resolution of personal issues but also may instill undesirable programming in the subconscious-self. To that effect, note that using the label of "facilitator" instead of a "shaman" is more appropriate in the context of spiritual healing as it better illustrates its essential role. The facilitator facilitates, it is the agent of allowance, holding the space to make healing possible.

Another aspect of the ideal session for spiritual healing is the music. Sessions are traditionally adorned with beautiful ancestral icaros that are chanted by the shamans with specific intentions. These also celebrate and honor themes around animals and plants. The ancestral musical instruments of the traditional shamans are the rattle, the flute, and a bundle of leaves called chakapa [1]. With the recent explosion of new shamans and facilitators, they have introduced the use of new musical instruments. It began expanding into a wide diversity of percussion instruments, followed by strings such as *charangos* [2] and guitars. With an increased variety of facilitators, sessions became increasingly focused on the quality and entertainment value of their musical performance. Then came the introduction of beautiful non-icaro songs specially composed for ayahuasca sessions, where those with singing abilities perform for the rejoice of their ayahuasca-influenced audience. Ayahuasca sessions for spiritual healing should have a moderate element of live music as it has proven to play an essential role in the unfolding of the experience. Simple repetitive rhythms can sustain and, more importantly, transmute the psychic state of the participants, removing them from often stagnant psychological states that don't contribute to the healing process. Music that may elicit memories of popular rhythms or that contain lyrics allusive to any kind of storyline, no matter how noble, infuse an element of distraction that captures the attention of the participant away from important subconscious events that need to be revealed. Therefore, over-emphasis on music performance is not recommended for spiritual healing sessions. Extended periods of silence combined with short periods of unadorned live music are preferable over an amusing and often distracting music repertoire.

We can conclude that only a limited number of abilities are required from facilitators or shamans during spiritual healing ayahuasca sessions. It means that the most admired skill of traditional shamans, interventions, are not at all necessary. Holding space with respect and strict moral integrity must be the most critical requirement for a facilitator or shaman in spiritual healing sessions. It can be a mediocre musician as long as the intention remains pure and follow the essence of the guidelines discussed earlier in Chapter 12.

Watching for the Shaman's Moral Integrity

Historically, spiritual healing hasn't been the primary mission of Amazonian shamanism. For centuries and until now, the shamanic practice has focused on other areas such as curing physical ailments, divination, and even sorcery. The idea of spiritual healing is relatively modern as it emerged from the Western mindset over the last two decades when it recognized the fundamental impact of ayahuasca in the human psyche. When the self-improvement community embraced ayahuasca's potential for spiritual healing, ayahuasca tourism was born. For years, hordes of people have been flowing to South America seeking physical healing, resolution of traumas, blockages, and above all, an enhanced sense of existential meaning. Many of them, especially women, naively forgot that similar to the cases of priests, gurus, and ministers, you will find wolves in sheep's clothing.

Without going into details about the well know problem with sexual predators infiltrated in the shaman's world, participants should be aware, especially women, that sexual predators do not always look or feel like the creepy characters we see in the movies. On the contrary—they're often charming and charismatic. Seduction in this context is part of their larger repertoire, one of many tools along with manipulation, promises of spiritual, emotional, even physical healing, and the administration of other substances known to elicit dizziness. Unethical shamans recognize behaviors characteristic of vulnerable women, and at this point, they become prey.

These are individuals who have developed callous sexual entities in their subconscious-selves and have embraced the ayahuasca medicine work as an instrument to achieve their heinous goals. Women must walk away from shamans who claim to have special powers, thrive on authority and praise, or boast about their ancestry, lineage, or power. They often offer "special" healing treatments in private, which involve some form of physical contact such as rubbing of "special" ointments, diagnosis of abdominal "bad spirits," or just relaxing massages. Be aware that authentic shamans are generally respectful, introvertive, and unassuming.

Integration Work

The single most neglected aspect of ayahuasca healing is the integration of the experience into the deeper parts of the self. Integration is the final step of the process, which warrants real transformation in the work. Transpersonal psychologist Katherine Coder [3] offers a definition:

"Visionary plant medicine integration is the process by which a participant is transformed by the teachings, visions, and experiences…. and incorporates those changes into daily life. Integration can often necessitate attending to traumas to release them fully, understanding the manifestations of ego in one's day-to-day experience; and, practicing new ways of thinking, conceptualizing, and being that is in alignment with wisdom teachings."

This definition brilliantly captures its essence as the second sentence pinpoints the integration process with four verbs: attending, understanding, practicing, and being. For integration to be successful after ayahuasca, sessions participants should:

1. Please pay close attention to the spiritual and emotional areas that were moved in the session, take notes, or use a journal to keep track of them.

2. Be mindful of those areas in terms of the implications they will have in your conscious daily life, understanding how the past is now seen differently. This may imply to make an in-depth review of your beliefs about life in general.

3. Put those realizations and well-thought conclusions into practice by looking at future situations with new eyes and rehearsing new attitudes in your heart and mind. In summary, you need to change your eyeglasses with which you look at reality.

4. Being the new person you have become, knowing the work done was successfully, and you have embraced new ways of being. Integration is now complete.

There is no specific time required to integrate ayahuasca session experiences properly. The process lasts as long as it takes, and no value judgment should be placed on the time invested. It all depends on the magnitude of the emotional impact experienced. The majority of the participants work on effective integration instinctively and even unconsciously, as we all have an inherent urge to make sense of everything we experience in general. Our subconscious-self is an automatic meaning-making machine, and most of us can adequately integrate the experience within a reasonable time frame after the session.

Also, assuming a healthy and stable overall emotional condition of the participant, the process may take as little as one day. Others may need a few days before they finally feel grounded. Allowing ample time for naps, sleep, passive recreation, time in nature, creative expression, and physical exercise are the essential components in achieving a healthy grounding. In contrast, crowded places, loud music, spicy foods, and drinking alcoholic beverages should be avoided. Sexual activity should also be avoided with new partners as your energy channels are still open and vulnerable and may absorb unwanted vibes in the process.

One particular aspect that participants often find challenging is the interpretation of their visions during sessions. Here the advisor plays a role of utmost importance. Ideally, retreats of consecutive sessions should include individual confidential advisory interviews after each ayahuasca session. It is highly recommended to provide some meaningful context to a unique experience before engaging in the next one. One of the main reasons why numerous travelers to South America return confused or disillusioned with their ayahuasca retreat is that integration services were limited or non-existent. They often realize too late that ayahuasca healing is much more than just drinking the medicine.

We must recognize that ayahuasca visions and messages can be confusing, and we often find ourselves lost about their meaning. As we grow spiritually, we become increasingly aware of our subconscious-self, and our insights become sharper with a strong sense of conviction in our hearts. Advisors may provide their valuable guidance and hermeneutical skills, but indeed, the participants are the ones that ultimately make the final assessment of its meaning and implications in their lives. There is a guiding light within each of us that, if we calmly listen, tells us its purpose.

It is not advisable to over-share your experience with others around you and don't pressure yourself trying to make rational sense too early. Just relax and let your soul-self work at its own pace. We often seek assurance or confirmation of what we already suspect, but deep inside, we knew it all the time. Such whispers of inner certainty come from our soul-self, speaking through our subconscious-self. The real challenge is dealing with our slippery ego-self, which tends to persist during deliberations, always adding its convenient angle to avoid being "reprogrammed" in the process.

We may have experienced a profound insight or vision but may also remain ambivalent about how to make it part of our lives. Being shown that you are depressed is one thing, but recovering from depression is another. This is when an ayahuasca spiritual healing advisor may contribute the most by offering further support to help you understand what happened and fully integrate the healing.

In many cases, experts in energy clearing, psychological healing, physiological healing, and bodywork can assist in the integration process. Specialists such as energy healers, acupuncturists, psychologists, psychotherapists, somatic therapists, and those in similar professions could play an essential role in the process. [3]

When opting for a psychologist or psychotherapist, it is crucial to ensure they are experienced in handling cases associated with visionary plant medicines. The professional should be unbiased so that they don't project their fear and beliefs onto you as part of the therapeutic process. A professional should be seriously considered when these symptoms are observed in severe intensity: (1) sleep disturbance for weeks or months after an experience, (2) paranoid or delusional thoughts recurring for days or weeks after an experience, (3) thoughts of harming yourself or others, and (iv) sustained manic behavior, depression, or anxiety. Consultation with the ayahuasca advisor would provide valuable support in reaching the final decision.

To truly bring our journey to completion, we must learn how to accept difficulty with graciousness, how to grow through the mistakes we make. It is our courage that allows us to find a place of serenity and truth amid the storms and difficulties.

The Power of Journaling after Ayahuasca Sessions

During ayahuasca retreats, we encourage participants to journal their experiences the morning after the session. The first most apparent convenience of this practice is the logging of private events. They remain handy for future reference, especially when subsequent sessions are scheduled shortly after that. Sometimes if the journaling is skipped, it is harder to do it later because the memories of the subjective experiences of two ayahuasca sessions tend to merge together or, worse, important details are forgotten. Therefore, it is convenient to use journaling as a powerful tool for integration. If you can't come back weeks or months later to review your integration process, if you only rely on memory, you will be missing a substantial portion of your process. Remember that the ego-self will always attempt to block selected memories that may work against its best interests of self-preservation. Important realizations and dot-connecting that occur during sessions may be conveniently forgotten if not written down for future reference. I learned disciplined journaling during my early years as a practitioner when more than once I found myself realizing essential aspects of my inner self while also realizing that I had realized it before and had forgotten about it. When I realized that forgotten realizations need to be recognized again to continue my progress, my journal book became an inseparable companion when doing ayahuasca work. I felt like I had wasted my time and energy the first time around as I didn't integrate fundamental pieces of my hard work. Conscious ayahuasca work is too important to let precious pearls of wisdom fall through the cracks of memory fragilities.

Emotional Healing and Writing from your Heart

Both the advisor and the participant may realize that an altered emotional state continues to be relatively active after one or several sessions. Notable sadness, anxiety, or confusion are clear clues that indicate unfinished integration requiring further work. When a participant is emotionally charged or overwhelmed, the advisor should be sensitive enough to avoid imposing a conversation about the subject that contributed to the emotional state at hand. In such delicate situations, ignoring it is not an option either. This would lead the participant into rumination, the act of focusing, and indulging in the emotion, something that has shown to be unhealthy.

There is one simple and highly effective technique that is worth trying as an initial option to soothe or reduce the tension that still lingers in their souls. The advisor may ask the participant to put negative emotions into words. It doesn't have to be comprehensive; just a few words will do the trick. This is called "affect labeling." Research has shown that it helps to mitigate the effects of negative feelings and jumpstart the process of climbing back from stress.

Psychology professor Matthew Lieberman and his colleagues conducted a series of brain imaging experiments. They noticed that when research subjects were asked to label a strong emotion, they showed less activity in the amygdala and higher activity in a region of the brain associated with vigilance and discrimination. The perception shifted from objects of fear to subjects of scrutiny. In other words, the feeling of being attacked morphed into a detective asking questions.

The clarifying effect of putting feelings into words was observed by philosopher Baruch Spinoza, who, in his 17th Century classic "Ethics," noted: "*an emotion, which is a passion, ceases to be a passion, as soon as we form a clear and distinct idea thereof.*" Classical psychotherapy has also heavily relied on making patients talk about their feelings with well-documented, favorable results. It is well known that patients often express relief when the therapist gives them a "diagnose" that names or labels the condition. The fact that there is a name for the feelings we are having means that other people have experienced it as well, making an overwhelming emotion feel less insolating. While this effective therapy has been used successfully for decades, it has taken a lot longer to figure out why it works. We now have a scientific basis to encourage and promote its practice.

Advisors may also recommend a similar technique for less urgent situations, called "*expressive writing*," [4] which may work as another powerful integration tool in the privacy of the participant's home. Dr. James Pennebaker has notably explored the connection between expressive writing and wellness at the University of Texas. Expressive writing is personal and emotional writing without regard to form, style, or correctness. Spelling, punctuation, and verb agreements are irrelevant opposite to its emotional content; it merely expresses what is in your mind and heart. Feelings are more important than events, memories, objects, or people in the context of a narrative. Sometimes expressive writing behaves like a good storyline that builds up and resolves itself to the ground. Other times, it can be turbulent, unpredictable, and inconclusive, which is also perfectly acceptable. How you feel about what happened is more important than what happened.

CHAPTER EIGHTEEN

DOING YOUR PART AFTER AYAHUASCA

Bypassing Roadblocks

Ayahuasca may bring remarkable results to anyone with just one single session. But significant permanent changes almost always require multiple sessions supported by effective advising. The powerful effects of the medicine mainly drive the transformation of the person and its lifestyle. Still, we must not ignore that there is much that can be done to boost or maintain the personal benefits being harvested while running our daily lives.

Any technique that helps in improving the state of consciousness or that contribute to the psychological wellbeing can prove invaluable to the whole spiritual healing process. There is an increasing number of self-help techniques available to the resilient souls that strive forward in their quest for self-realization. From holotropic breathing to heartfelt prayer, the diversity of approaches continues to grow in this exciting era of personal growth. When you embark on such exploration, you often find the method that best resonates with your soul-self. Instead of providing a long list of recommended techniques for you to explore, below find some relevant areas intricately connected with the spiritual process. Please pay careful attention to them as you progress in your self-realization work after ayahuasca.

Psychological Traps

Rumination - In ordinary language, this word means "pondering" or reflecting," both of which can be healthy ways of carefully considering something. But here we refer to a type of thinking that is negative, repetitive, prolonged, and unhelpful. This unconstructive way of thinking, worrying, and turning something over and over don't reach to any creative solution and end up making us feel worse. People often fall into rumination while desperately seeking temporary protection from painful emotions or safe distraction from constructive but challenging behavior. The short-term benefits of rumination are only the illusion that it may help us. This illusion is a psychological trap. In the long run, rumination worsens negative moods, deflates motivation to behave constructively, and keeps the physical body in an unhealthy state of tension.

Thought Avoidance - There is an interesting paradox in psychology: the more we try not to think about something, the more we think about it. It is well known that avoiding indulging in certain kinds of thoughts has been proven to be a futile task. In experiments conducted during the 1980s psychologists designed a series of experiments that clearly illustrated this fact. Compared with control groups, subjects who were instructed not to think in a polar bear started thinking of them more frequently than the group that was told to think about them as an option. Then, when they were told not to think about them for five minutes, they observed what was later labeled as the "rebound effect," where subjects thought about white bears even more frequently than in the initial session. Thought suppression is a common psychological trap that comes disguised as a sensible way of dealing with unwanted thoughts. The same thing happens with unwanted emotions and urges. The more we try to suppress them, the stronger they become. We end up doing it because we tend to believe we can succeed in doing it, unaware that it is not an effective strategy. The best approach to deal with unwanted thoughts or emotions is to acknowledge them and put your attention in finding the necessary space and time to process them properly. Unwanted thoughts are an unequivocal sign that there is inner work to do. Work with them at your own pace and reach meaningful conclusions about them, and they will stop altogether.

Unhealthy Emotional Reactions - Emotions are the most sublime expressions of the soul-self. These are the torrents of energy that make life worth living as they define the magnificence of being human. Emotions have their innate corresponding facial expressions that are similar all over the world. Research has shown that even people who have been blind since birth smile when they are happy, frown when they are sad, and clench their teeth when they are angry, despite having never seen these expressions on other people's faces. Scientists believe these are universal expressions product of human evolution because they are necessary for survival. Most emotions come and go like waves in the ocean. When allowed to run their natural course, feelings usually last only a few seconds or minutes. Repeated or ongoing events and circumstances, such as the loss of a loved one, can prolong them. Emotions evolved to be useful, yet often cause trouble. They are often triggered quickly, and bodily reactions and impulses arise before we have time to think about them. Sometimes these quick responses are essential for survival, but this legacy from ancestral evolution needs to be tamed in modern civilized society for effective interaction while working toward common goals. When we are emotionally upset or under severe stress, people often snap and do things that they later regret. We usually know that we are behaving unwisely, but we lose control and follow our urges anyway because it relieves the intensity of our feelings. Unfortunately, the relief is temporary, and the behavior is usually inconsistent with our long-term goals. The alternative is to observe our emotions mindfully, accepting them as temporary visitors to our SIE. Acknowledge the urges to behave in particular ways without necessarily acting on them. Over time, emotions will become less dramatic and more comfortable to understand, even when they are complex. Mindfulness creates a healthy space between the emotion and the corresponding behavior providing an opportunity to choose what we do.

Self-Criticism - Many of us believe that self-criticism prevents laziness, complacency, and self-indulgence, that it helps us meet responsibilities and maintain self-discipline. This is probably learned from childhood, perhaps from parents or school teachers who did not understand the difference between constructive and unconstructive criticism. We need to be aware that if we are going to criticize ourselves, we should do it constructively. Why not say to ourselves: "Oh, I just made the same mistake again!" instead of "How could you be so careless, stupid?" Facing our mistakes is already tricky enough, insulting ourselves with harsh self-criticism makes us feel worse. It interferes with our ability to improve and from accepting aspects of ourselves that are acceptable the way they are. Many of us forget that constructive suggestions work better when improvement is required, and that kindness works better than cruelty regardless of whether the improvement is needed or not. Suppose you make a mistake at work, and the thought "I am so incompetent" pops into your mind. If you get fixed with this thought, you believe it unquestionably. It feels like the truth, like an important fact. You are inserting very toxic programming in your subconscious-self. If you are mindful, you recognize that "I am so incompetent" is just a thought. You observe the emotions that it triggers and the urges that follow. Now you are in a position to decide what to do; you may curse, throw your coffee mug, and scream out, or just take a deep breath and allow yourself time to settle down. When it comes to self-criticism, use the following rule of thumb: Never say to yourself anything that you would never say to a loved one. Just love yourself, plain and simple.

Spirituality Traps

Numerous sidetracks lead to a distorted, ego-centered version of spirituality; we can deceive ourselves into thinking we are developing spirituality when instead, we are strengthening our egocentricity through spiritual techniques. We must admit that there are significant challenges in the spiritual path, and discussing a few of them is worth mentioning.

One of the biggest challenges of self-realization is to be able to expand consciousness, to align with the soul-self in a way that allows us a clear view of the intricate complexities of our ego-self. The ego-self is the part of us that appears to be continuous and stable. This struggle to maintain a sense of solid, permanent self is the action of the ego-self. The pursual of such continuity by the ego-self often includes trying to achieve spirituality. This objective should be the last one the ego-self should be pursuing as the ultimate consequence of seeking spirituality implies the substantial de-construction or dissolution of subpersonalities and entities. Notwithstanding, the ego-self persists as it grabs anything that may provide security, status, and recognition. Besides, it hopes to exist in a transcended exalted state eventually.

It is essential to see that the main point of any spiritual path is to step out of the bureaucracy of the ego-self. This means stepping out of the ego's constant desire for a higher, more spiritual, more intuitive version of knowledge, religion, virtue, judgment, comfort, or whatever it is that the particular needs are seeking. One must step out of the continuous pursual of spiritual disciplines; otherwise, we may eventually find ourselves just possessing a vast collection of spiritual paths without advancing in anyone of them. Many of us spend decades joining many spiritual disciplines, approaches, or groups in the constant migration of a nomadic lifestyle, never finding our permanent home. This is a spiritual trap we must avoid. It is essential to relate non-judgmentally to our soul-self, to our own experience. Otherwise, the spiritual path becomes dangerous, becomes purely external entertainment, rather than an organic personal experience.

Another spiritual trap is that once we have the blessing of experiencing a powerful spiritual epiphany, the idea of evaluation suddenly appears. "Wow, fantastic, I have to catch that, I have to capture and keep it because it is an infrequent and valuable experience." Thus, we try to hold onto the experience, and the problem starts there, as soon as we try to capture the experience, a chain reaction begins. We create mental concepts about the event, and we disconnect from the beauty of the experience and its relationship to us. And the opposite of self-deception is just working with the facts of life. If one searches for any kind of bliss or joy, the mere act of attempting will make it elusive and impossible to attain. This is the whole point: a fear of separation, the hope of achieving transcendence, these are not actions of the ego-self, as if the ego-self were a real thing which performed specific actions. The ego-self IS the actions, the mental events. The ego-self IS the fear of losing the joy and bliss. We must live life fully conscious that the real experience, beyond the dream world, is the beauty and color and excitement of the actual experience of NOW in everyday life.

A third spiritual trap comes when we force ourselves into the experience of bliss. It is a kind of self-hypnosis; in that, we refuse to see the background of what we are. We focus only on the immediate experience of bliss. We ignore the entire primary ground over which we are built, and we embark on seeking and ultimately finding it. Yes, it is possible. You may have resorted to planting medicines, cannabis, or a sensory deprivation chamber, but you did it successfully. This kind of experience is based purely upon watching oneself. It is an entirely dualistic approach. We would like to experience something, and by working hard, we do achieve it. However, once we come down from our "high," once we realize that we are still here, reality checks-in and a depression feeling follow. We are still here, which where we must start in the first place. Again, the ego-self attempting to secure continuity.

I learned about these spiritual traps from the Buddhist teachings of Chögyam Trungpa. [1] They had walked such labyrinthic paths for centuries, and there is evident wisdom in their teachings associated with the ego. Buddhism is by far the doctrine most highly developed in knowledge and understanding about the ego-self. They had focused on it for millennia, and there is something to learn from them if self-realization is our "goal." But again, when I hear their message, embarking in the path of ultimate nirvana is a project not for everyone, and not viable for all humanity to follow. There is more to living life than exclusively focusing on spiritual ascension.

Throughout years of doing spiritual healing advice to hundreds of participants, I gradually developed a pragmatic approach vis-a-vis the elusive problem of the ego-self. It was essential to advise participants about the evident realities that surface during ayahuasca sessions, the undeniable elements of ego-self, subpersonalities, and entities. Developing practical advice about the ego-self tailored to ordinary people was not an easy task. After all, the ego-self is about the conscious distinction between "me and I," and this is deeply intertwined with the nature of consciousness, which we also reviewed earlier.

At some point, we must reach the balance of ego-self acceptance and live with it in peaceful, productive terms. Waging war against the destructive entities is mandatory and must be prioritized, while also reaching negotiated peace treaties with some subpersonalities. Each one should find by themselves how far to take the self-realization journey to reach an acceptable level of inner psychological wellbeing.

Along those lines, I reflected on where to find such middle ground. I started with a careful evaluation of my subpersonalities, to what extent these were harmful or beneficial to my spiritual development. I started right there with my subpersonality of ayahuasca usage. It was a valid question after many years of passionately pursuing my spiritual healing with it. It was a strong subpersonality created and fed by my desire to be happy and help others. When the subject matter of ayahuasca arises in any social conversation, in a flash, it kicks-in, takes over my personality and starts doing what it does best, passionately learning, sharing information, teaching, and assisting others. After close examination, I concluded that it should not be considered an entity, as this aspect of my personality, contrary to bringing difficulties in my life it provides a profound sense of satisfaction as well as benefits to the ones around me. This tree was giving apples; therefore, it must be an apple tree.

Another one I recognized was my subpersonality of self-observation practices. Since the 1980s, I became a devoted practitioner of self-observation when I joined an esoteric Gnostic religion whose central "dogma," very extreme by the way, was the total annihilation of the ego-self, to reduce it, as they used to say, to cosmic dust. From them, I learned advanced techniques of self-observation with the warrior mission of watching the ego-self in action at all times. After a few years with them, I left the organization, but the habit stayed with me ever since. Decades of self-observation had created another subpersonality. When I realized that this practice of an ego-self observing the ego-self was becoming too extreme, I decided to let go and reduce its intensity of action partially. However, after carefully reflecting on it, I decided that this subpersonality was right for me and "negotiated" its acceptance.

Can you see a pattern emerging here? Who is deciding to negotiate? Clearly, there is another subpersonality that wants to be enlightened and has established alliances with the other two, the one that loves ayahuasca work and the one constantly self-observing. This can become an intricate and extraordinarily complex mind game which common sense told me it must stop at some point. I either quit most of my life projects and dedicate full time to a Buddhist lifestyle or decide where to stop and develop a lifestyle that fits the personal and family circumstances currently unfolding in my life. The latter is the one I recommend to participants seeking advice about these more profound aspects of spiritual healing.

Once you have gone through a productive period of spiritual healing with ayahuasca or other psychedelics, I recommend to engage in the process of life restructuring consisting in doing a patient and thoughtful inventory of your SIE, and (i) identify the areas that you sincerely diagnose to be harmful entities, and prioritize working for their removal, (ii) identify those subpersonalities which are not helping you and work to redesign them, and (iii) identify the subpersonalities that work in your favor, the ones that evidently help your overall life process and accept them always with the caveat that any of them may turn into a harmful entity if you let it run out of control.

Harmful Legal Addictions

Expansion of consciousness is the mantra of spiritual self-realization. The primary strategy toward such an objective should be to continuously keep our mindful attention focused on identifying areas that may decrease our vibrational frequency. I find it necessary to emphasize certain activities in which harmful effects against consciousness expansion have not been sufficiently highlighted. Responsible spiritual advice must include a message of caution of the dangers hidden behind certain legal and socially acceptable practices. Let us review some of them:

Alcohol – It has been throughout history the most widely used psychoactive substance. From the earliest civilizations, Asian, Middle Eastern, or American, these have all independently discovered the properties of fermented fruits and have indulged in its use in a variety of ways. It has been the universal relief for the hardships of survival, for the stress, anxiety, and insecurities of human existence. The highly developed mammalian brain seems to be inclined to embrace mind-altering substances to escape the prison of physical reality temporarily. Monkeys are well known to enjoy beer and elephants for feasting on fermented batches of rotten fruits. The domestic production of beer, as confirmed by ancient archeology, has occurred since the Neolithic era. In modern times, the U.S. struggled with the social consequences of alcoholism. It went through a period of prohibition to later acknowledge that the remedy was harming society more than the illness. Alcohol is now universally accepted, except in specific religious populations that prohibit, offer ineffectively, its consumption. The relevancy to spiritual growth has to do with the effects of vibration resonance in the human body. Those who do not like to drink alcohol dislike the awful flavor but also its initial effect of drunkenness. Alcohol is an acquired taste. We force ourselves into the unpleasant act of ingestion induced by the promise of the subsequent reward. Masking its aggressive attack on our taste buds has become a commercial industry by itself with fruits and sugars being the forefront runners. Close your eyes and remember your reaction to your first try with an alcoholic beverage. If you do not recall, just go online, and watch a few of the hundreds of anecdotal videos showing the squirming faces of curious children discovering their natural reactions. One thing must be clear. Your soul, your master program, your subconscious, do not like alcohol in the physical vehicle. It is only your ego, disconnected from its divine source that likes to escape the unbearable uncertainty inherent in physical existence. That said, seekers of self-realization should be aware of this fact to self-observe its urges and attraction towards alcohol. For those who engage in the occasional glass of wine, they should pay close attention to this habit turning into a subpersonality and, even worse, an uncontrollable entity.

Tobacco - Millennia of human history went about without tobacco until the XVI Century when European conquistadores saw the indigenous people of the Caribbean intoxicate themselves smoking rolled dried leaves of tobacco with their "Y" shaped straw inserted into their nostrils. The ego is always avid to experiment with new ways of intoxication as long as it does not awaken you from the illusion of itself. Spaniards embraced tobacco, coffee, and chocolate from the New World but demonized peyote, psilocybin, and ayahuasca. Well, the craving for new escapes spread rapidly all over Europe in the case of tobacco and continue today every time drug cartels introduce new modalities such as crack cocaine, meth, and a multitude of poisons with three-letter acronyms. New ways of escaping is always attractive to the ego. The most crucial fact about tobacco is its impressive skill to lure its victims into addiction.

Tobacco smoking is at the bottom of the scale of drug sensorial gratification. It merely gives you nothing in exchange for the energy invested in consuming it. Besides the mild dizziness caused by the smoke intoxication of the lungs, you get no psychoactive effects whatsoever, no enhanced perceptions, no euphoria, nothing. Do not overlook the fact that the smoke itself produces the mild intoxication; any kind of smoke would do the trick, nothing to do with its active ingredient, nicotine. But there is one thing that nicotine surely does, and that is the physical addiction of craving for more. Once you are addicted, which happens only after only a few smoking sessions, you feel anxious as a withdrawal symptom. Now you are trapped in the cycle. Smoke to feel better is the solution, giving the smoker the false sense of satisfaction, that nice, relaxed sense of wellbeing so well exploited by the seductive advertising campaigns pushed by the multinational tobacco empires. When you think about it, nicotine is the dumbest drug possible as it only offers relief to the anxiety it produces in the first place. It gives smokers nothing in return, except a monetary leak in their wallets and a long list of adverse side effects, including one called death.

Cannabis - This natural substance has been used for thousands of years, as evidenced by archeological findings ranging from Egyptian tombs to permafrost burials of noblewomen in Russia. It has been revered as well as demonized, which suggests a sort of duality in its nature. Much has been written and said about its virtues and dangers and, to focus on the relevant aspects of our discussion, I here emphasize the latter. Depending on a few key factors, cannabis may contribute to the advancement of your self-realization agenda. In my case, for instance, cannabis was my first mind-altering experience when I was nineteen during my freshman year in college. It made a profound shift in my perception of reality and redirected my life path for the better. One single cannabis experience was enough to destroy my then firmly held belief in the Newtonian model of reality. The indisputable fact that my state of mind was fundamental in how reality is perceived left me with the big question: What is reality then? It took me a few days to reshuffle my deck of cards and start building a new house from scratch. My then ultra-orthodox mechanistic universe worldview turned into a lifelong journey of self-exploration that ended up defining my persona and providing me with the privilege of having a fulfilling spiritual life. After mother ayahuasca made its grand entrance in my life in 1998, my relationship with her led me to a deeper understanding of what she called the spirit of cannabis. Without getting into lengthy anecdotal storytelling of how these came about, I share here some of my realizations about it.

Before I start, one important message I received from ayahuasca was that cannabis nor tobacco or any other plant should be taken in smoke form. Burning the plant destroys essential healing properties that can be acquired via our digestive system instead. The negative aspects of the plant are enhanced when smoked while the most beneficial are destroyed. It all makes sense to me when we observe the incredible diversity of benefits derived from cannabis and tobacco consumed in ways other than smoked.

Back to spiritual aspects of cannabis, besides its highly praised health enhancement virtues, cannabis has several severe limitations when considered for self-realization purposes. Speaking about limitations, let us start by acknowledging cannabis's limited potential for assisting in personal spiritual development. Although it may provide newcomers with valuable initial insights, as in my case mentioned above, and a few other spiritually relevant ones along the way, cannabis falls short when compared with other traditional psychedelics. Spiritual seekers must take note of the fact that cannabis should be considered a sort of entry-level substance in the consciousness expansion spectrum. They should be aware that cannabis simply will not meet their highest expectations for self-realization.

On the contrary, they should expect with its continued use, start harvesting its other qualities that are not helpful, and harmful for increasing vibration resonance and psychological wellbeing. If you develop the habit of smoking cannabis regularly, it will show you to be seldom valuable. Think of you throwing an occasional bone to your pet to keep it happy and loyal to you; such is the analogy of cannabis and the user, the only difference being that the user is the pet and cannabis the master. That brings us to my next objection; cannabis is highly addictive despite the effective marketing campaign asserting the contrary. The addictive cycle of cannabis goes something like this: you start smoking having a good time and enjoying it all the way until you reach the scoop of ice cream to close the session. Then you begin increasing the frequency until you find yourself doing it daily and if your lifestyle allows it, even more than once a day. Then you gradually make an important discovery: its enjoyable effects run inversely proportional to its frequency of use. You stop for a little while. The cycle starts again when you resume the habit and get the renewed excitement of enjoying its powerful effects again, with the fresh feeling of the first time. Once again, the fun gradually diminishes, creating this endless loop that may endure for years or decades. This undeniable pattern is the classical addictive behavior. It perpetuates indefinitely due to a conspiracy of denial that involve users and a strong advocacy movement that promote the cause in the media. Frequent users opt to believe that they are not addicted because they can stay without cannabis for short periods. They take this as evidence of their freedom of choice and reject addiction as a reasonable diagnosis of their habit. Cannabis advocates paint a rosy scenario to avoid the inconvenient label that works against social acceptability but more importantly, it is the ego of the smoker, the cannabis subpersonality or perhaps the cannabis entity, that looks the other way for the same reason and to mask the underlying guilt associated with being a drug addict. It is interesting to observe that cannabis has become legal and widely used in many countries, but the subject of cannabis addiction is almost totally absent in the cultural narrative. The media is often flooded with alcohol and tobacco addiction prevention campaigns, but one for cannabis is yet to be seen.

Cannabis enjoys strong support from many sectors of society for different reasons. Still, one that constitutes a solid contender for the number one reason is its amazing quality as an emotional anesthetic. For the same reason that tobacco and alcohol have been used to relieve the existential anxiety of the ego, cannabis does it more effectively and with less secondary effects. Their obvious health hazards have already demonized these two, but cannabis is currently at its infant stage in its integration into mainstream society. Cannabis is the rising star when compared to the other two obsolete alternatives. Emotional numbness is ultimately what alcohol drinkers and tobacco smokers are seeking; and cannabis is here to offer instant numbness, without getting drunk, or endlessly inhaling an unpleasant smoke. Recreational cannabis is here to stay escorted by its gorgeous and good-looking companion of authentic medical applications.

Finally, I cannot close this section without mentioning the two most harmful qualities of cannabis opposite self-realization work: laziness and forgetfulness. Frequent users often experience fantastic episodes of creativity, come up with viable plans and projects for the future, but these never even reach the drawing board. Also, their "things to do" lists rarely get updated, and laziness becomes part of the personality affecting the smoker's potential for success and, therefore, depleting all interest in pursuing a healthy spiritual life. As if that was not enough, they find themselves arriving late or missing .important appointments, and often forget to exit the highway correctly. When absent-mindedness is not considered a problem for a productive lifestyle, then the entity of cannabis has won the war until the soul-self can awaken the ego-self.

Pornography - I left this legal addiction for last because it is the most important one of all. Pornography is the most harmful drug for its potential of embracing the entire human species under its spell, something practically impossible for any other drug. Porno does not require a physical-chemical to assault the brain; it does it by visually hijacking the most powerful survival program of all, the reproductive imperative command. The chemical drug is already in generous amounts in your brain, dopamine, serotonin, and other neurotransmitters that are typically subconsciously controlled by the soul end up being manipulated at will by the ego. For the first time in evolution, the ego has, at its disposal, a mechanism to play a visual dirty trick onto your subconscious-self and go around the, brain mechanics, which unfortunately can't distinguish between physical sex and a well-modulated stream of pixels dancing on a flat-screen.

Porno has always existed, but its harmful reach was held back by the fact that subpersonalities and entities always crave novelty. In the old days, pornographic material was available to a handful of wealthy lascivious noblemen that we're able to afford secret drawings and color sketches discreetly hidden in dark places. It later expanded its reach with the newly discovered photographic techniques, which was quickly put at its service. Then came magazines followed by celluloid films. But still, the porno entities got bored with the same repetitive graphic stimuli. It required the acquisition of new fresh material, new magazines, new DVDs, which resulted in the inconvenience of occupying an increasing volume of space as well as a notable depletion of the bank's account balance. But with the advent of high-speed internet, it became the new paradise of the porno industry. A constant flow of new stimuli tailored-made to the most bizarre preferences met the requirements of demanding porno addicts. Porno is extremely addictive as it hijacks the subconscious-self who cannot tell the difference between a real sexual encounter and the graphic illusion on a computer screen. There are several programs to overcome porno addiction, and I encourage those entangled in this sticky web of erotic energy to seek help and find the strength to heal it.

Fanatical Passions - Fanatism is a very smart subpersonality that often turns into dangerous and even lethal entities. All forms of fanaticism start when our intellect agrees with a concept and finds emotional comfort in it. This happens because this concept balances an already existing deficiency caused by prior trauma, childhood neglect, abuse, or other deeply rooted anomalies in the SIE. These are fed by the constant input of conceptual data that supports the concept and gradually grows into a subpersonality. As mentioned before, subpersonalities can be useful to our survival and even self-development. It is essential, however, to be aware of how they increase in strength with the potential of detaching from the ego-self and turning into a free-standing entity. The word "fanatism' already carries a negative connotation, and western culture has created the short version of "fan," which is no more than a euphemism to underplay its true nature. Being a "fan" is now socially acceptable while being a fanatic is a pejorative term, although we are referring to the same energy. For this reason, fanatism quickly turns into rogue entities that live comfortably under the sponsorship of the ego-self, in a way not different from an alcoholic that is in denial of the problem and enjoys drinking regularly.

By carefully examining the following checklist, you can identify subpersonalities and entities that are currently installed in your subconscious-self while interfering with your human potential:

- **Political Fanaticism** - Republicans and Democrats, Globalists and Nationalists, Capitalists and Socialists, Anarchists, Libertarians, Armed Militias, Conspiracy Theorists, Terrorists.
- **Religious Fanaticism** - Christian, Muslim, Buddhists, Zionist Funda-

mentalism, Jihadists, Amish lifestyle, Snake Worshipers, Santeria, Voodoo, Black Magick Cults, Scientologists.

- **Racial Fanaticism** - White Supremacists, Black Power, Nation of Islam, Zionism, Nazism, Anti-Semitism, Pro-Semitism, Racial Purity groups, Black Lives Matter movement.

- **Fanatical Activism** - Environmentalists, Social Justice Crusaders, Feminism, Gender Equality Groups, Humanitarian Causes.

- **Sports Fanaticism** - All kinds of Team Sport Loyalty groups, World Cup Soccer, European Leagues, FIFA Tournaments, National Football League, National Basketball Association, Major League Baseball, Boxing Championships, Ultimate Fighting Championships, NASCAR races.

- **Personal Celebrity Fanaticism** - Rock Stars, Politicians, Movie Stars, Sports Stars, Famous People, Royalty, Scientists, Folk Heroes, Book Authors, intellectual personalities, Comedians.

- **Fads Fanaticism** - Cartoon heroes, Tattoos, Vampires, Piercing, Goth, Emo, Gangs, Motorcycle Renegades, Manga, Anime, Video Games.

All these areas of human endeavors may be practiced in a balanced way relative to one's life purpose. None of these are criticized in themselves as all of them are valid manners of being and human life. However, to properly pursue the goal of our psychological wellbeing, we must create awareness of these forms of behavior, the entities that run wild in our quantum field, creating conflict and unhappiness in our lives. Disproportionate amounts of energies invested in any kind of fanaticism are eventually reflected in severe deficits in other areas of life. Make your self-assessments of fanatical tendencies and decide which ones deserve your conscious intervention.

Practice the Moral Integrity Technique

We cannot underestimate the importance of moral integrity in our quest for psychological wellbeing. The word integrity evolved from the Latin adjective *integer*, meaning *whole* or *complete*. In this context, integrity is the inner sense of "*wholeness*" deriving from qualities such as honesty and consistency of character. As such, one may judge that others "have integrity" to the extent that they act according to the values, beliefs, and principles they claim to hold. We know what is right and wrong, and we choose to do the right thing. Doing the right thing when it is the easiest or the most profitable thing is not what matters, though. When things are easy, anyone can appear to have a backbone. It is the hard times that matter.

Someone can do harmful acts to others without lying, but we can use it as a powerful tool for self-observation. Moral integrity is deeply entwined with the act of lying. A common denominator among all humans is that almost 100% of us consciously lie to others. Politicians continuously lie to entire countries for ulterior motives, and some lie on little things to one person, many times protecting self-esteem. It is a matter of degree, but as a matter of principle, we are all liars. When you are working in spiritual healing, the observation of our moral integrity is a great technique to expose our subpersonalities and entities. The ego-self quickly comes with defense and begin arguing about the relativity of morality, that a particular action could be moral for someone but not so for others and similar arguments. There are volumes written about it in philosophy and ethics, but let us not get distracted by intellectual arguments. An aligned ego-self should be delighted with the exercise, but the territory of moral integrity seems too broad to corner the rogue liar subpersonality. To avoid such a scenario, it is more effective to focus our attention on the simple act of lying. The ego-self knows precisely when it is lying, especially after the fact when the exercise of self-observation is running in your conscious attention.

When we practice self-observation with our lies, we will notice a pattern that can be traced back to a subpersonality associated with specific traumas or emotional issues. Psychology has already discovered that when the self-esteem of the ego-self is threatened, individuals tend to lie easily. Our self-esteem must be guarded at all costs; that's why we lie when asked about something we have failed to do, in order to rectify the error without being detected quickly. The image of the "perfect person" was once more preserved. We can probably trace it back to childhood; like many other issues, we may identify scrutinizing our different patterns of lies.

This technique is highly effective for those who have reached a relatively close alignment with their subconscious-selves and soul-selves. When you are not well aligned, you will quickly realize the technique is not working because your ego-self begins to justify the lies instead of scrutinizing its origins. When we find ourselves flowing smoothly through life without lying to others, it means we are closer to, if not already, enjoying the psychological wellbeing we deserve.

Contain the Quantum Leakage

One powerful exercise in your efforts to improve your psychological wellbeing is to apply your new understanding of how energy works to revise your lifestyle under a new context. Your SIE is a quantum-based energy environment that is yours and only yours. This is your kingdom, or better said, your domain of action in this existence, which is under your exclusive control. You may visualize this envelope as your home, which has a ventilation system that produces heat to protect you from the threatening frozen environment outside your envelope. The heat is produced by a magnificent spark of light residing in your soul-self, the engine of your system. Your SIE is your "home base," and the heat that it produces is your life force. This life force, the quantum flow, is also nourished by the biological transmutation of your physical machine. All the input sources that go into your home base, finely digested nutritional chemicals, breathing oxygen, the sound harmonics going to your hearing, among others, are the physical components that feed your inherent life force. To maximize our wellbeing, we need to manage its input and output flow wisely. If it is freezing outside your home base, it is not a good idea to leave your windows open, right? We need to preserve the heat that has been produced with hard work and considerable effort and, even more important, the precious time invested in the process. We need to contain the quantum leakage from our quantum home base. It is all about vibration. The higher the frequency we can sustain, the brighter the shining light of our life force. This translates into psychological wellbeing and, ultimately, happiness. What are the windows left open that are leaking quantum flow? What about the words that come out of my mouth? Our treatment to the ones surrounding us? The physical energy spent in useless activities, in addictive behaviors, ruminating unsolvable problems? The same applies to the vibrational quality of the input material. The quality of the food that hit our stomach, the quality of the sounds that hit our eardrums, the quality of the images that hit our retina, all these are critical factors in the spiritual growth formula.

Going Entity Hunting

When we think about what entities we may "own" within us, that is, in our SIE, we often have a particularly good idea of where to look for them. Entities are often self-evident as they manifest in ways that are substantially away from your normal behavior, making themselves visible to us and others around us. However, these are also hidden behind other, more socially acceptable subpersonalities. They grow and survive with longevity until we start getting suspicious.

The more obvious ones are the addictions and compulsive behaviors. Snapping out of control in the face of specific circumstances is something anyone should pay attention to, and seek professional help before it gets worse. Most common among those are the emotional attacks of rage, which often turn violent destroying property, domestic violence, child abuse, or even darker criminal behavior. All addictions and obsessive behaviors are entities that should be targeted for conscious healing work.

A smart way of finding hidden entities is to carefully observe behavior in ourselves if we ever get under the influence of alcohol. As you most likely already know, many people do dramatic personality shifts after a few drinks, turning more friendly, sensual, romantic, or even lustful. Others find themselves feeling resentful, righteous, angry, or sad. These are strong candidates of entities that should be carefully observed and scrutinized to identify their origins and plan for a healing strategy. When we target one, we must assess whether we have it under control or relatively harmless or is otherwise a rogue entity that occasionally snaps and drags us into behavior that later deserves an apology to others or regrets in our hearts.

A great place to start in doing your part in your quest for self-realization without ayahuasca is by doing a short inventory of the ones that deserve your close attention. Think about racist, pride, greed, anger, opinionated gossip, victimhood, grungy, righteous, lascivious, etc.

The Challenge of Entity Healing

We have defined the entities as subpersonalities that have become self-aware and consciously operate in our SIE for its survival. These generally end up, with their powerfully energized repetitive behavior, these frequently end-up strengthening the neural pathways they use while acting out. Once these neural pathways are well established, it becomes much easier for the entity to manifest its compulsive or addictive patterns. Think of a grass field where frequent walking creates trail paths, which tend to be used over and over afterward. For this reason, the spiritual healing of entities is harder to accomplish than the average unwanted subpersonality behavior. It often requires multiple sessions with focused advisory work to make progress in permanently removing a specific entity or at least substantially reducing its influence. This is only possible due to the properties of the sacred medicine acting during the peak of the ayahuasca experience. This is when the ego-self awakens making important reconnections at the quantum level and reprogramming itself, while dramatically increasing the potential for brain neuroplasticity. The neural pathways become more malleable, and the combined quantum and neurochemical effects allow the creation of new pathways of reprogrammed behavior that "compete" with the old ones being used by the entity. Think of a new temporary road detour that reduces the traffic of the old road. Unfortunately, addiction entities of certain drugs such as heroin, meth, and crack cocaine harden these brain circuits firmly, making top-down spiritual healing almost ineffective in obtaining acceptable results. Dr. Lieberman describes this well when he writes:

"Drugs destroy the delicate balance that the brain needs to function normally. Drugs stimulate dopamine release no matter what kind of stimulation the user is in. That confuses the brain, and it begins to connect the drug use to everything. After a while, the brain becomes convinced that drugs are the answer to all aspects of life. Feel like celebrating? Use drugs. Feeling sad? Use drugs. Hanging out with a friend? Use drugs. Feeling stressed, bored, relax, tense, angry, powerful, resentful, tired, energetic? Use drugs."[2]

Although ayahuasca appears to be ineffective in these cases, I believe it is a matter of expectations. Ayahuasca does not seem to work well in severe addiction to certain hard drugs cases if the outcome is measured with the same standard of the vast majority of the other less severe cases. If many hardcore addicts can overcome their addictions with substance-free methods such as Narcotics Anonymous, relying only on the spiritual strength and the power of will, it is entirely possible to develop ayahuasca-based programs with drastically superior success rates. The expectations, however, must be adjusted to the situation by assuming months instead of days or weeks as the target time frame to full recovery.

Waging War with your Entity

The spiritual healing of entities is by far the hardest project in the spiritual path. I can never emphasize enough its importance, as these will impede acceptable progress in self-realization. In this section we correlate the healing process of entities with waging war with them. This is an educational metaphor, not necessarily an accurate description of the nature of the process. Our culture programs us, and we grow up as children with the hero-villain paradigm, from comic books, children stories of monsters and dragons. The following description is targeted directly to that part of your subconscious-self that understands this language, and hopefully, it spreads, strengthening your will.

When the main ego-self aligns with the soul-self and decide to join forces to confront an entity, this can only be understood as an open declaration of war. The mission has the clear-cut objective of submitting the entity to obedience, restraining it from operating freely, all this as an alternative to total obliteration. War is a serious business and is a life or death endeavor. War is not a part-time job, and not a leisurely walk in the park. It requires your full attention and power of will for total victory. That said, let us describe the entity as the enemy of your war and internalize the following advice:

1. An entity is as smart as its creator, you. Therefore, do not expect to outsmart the entity you want to defeat. This is a common mistake you must avoid. A more detailed explanation follows in another section below.

2. Entities are very slippery and excellent at hiding out of sight when you consciously try to confront them. Just close your eyes and feel a sort of negative energy and acknowledge its presence while praying in your heart for inner determination and strength.

3. An entity will tell you anything to keep you from doing your cleansing work. It will perjure, fabricate, falsify, seduce, bully, and conspire, among another long list of actions.

4. It will assume any form or shape to deceive you from seeing it the way it is.

5. It will reason with you as the best lawyer money can buy and will find arguments that may you doubt about your mission against it. Be especially wary about proposals for negotiations and peace treaties.

6. It will pledge anything to get a deal with you; then, it will stab you in the

back as soon as you lower your defenses.

7. It will lie and be warned that if you buy it, you deserve anything you get.

8. It has the survival strength of those monster machines from the movies; you may reduce it to a single cell and will continue to attack.

9. It cannot be reasoned with; it only respects the power of your will.

10. It cannot understand who you really are, and it does not care. It operates with the callousness and indifference of a psychopath criminal.

11. You can use it as a compass to direct your actions. The stronger the resistance you feel, the closer you are to hurting it with a powerful blow.

12. Remember, it has no power of its own as it feeds from the behavior you allow to happen, and from your fear of failure against it.

13. When you are winning the battle, it launches strong counter-attacks slamming you with everything it has. This means you are gaining crucial ground but be wary when it appears to be mostly defeated.

14. The harder they fight, the more gratification you will feel when you finally win. The importance of your healing project is your motivation to keep you going.

15. It dominates the art of rationalization. It elegantly adds a spin for why you should not do your work with a series of plausible, rational justifications.

16. Defeating your entity is like giving birth. It appears absolutely impossible until you remember that women have pulled the stunt successfully for those who know how many millions of years.

17. Be wary about plunging into the project with an overambitious and unrealistic timetable, as you will not be able to sustain the required level of intensity for a long time, and most likely, you shall crash. Remember to prepare your mind for a marathon, not for a 100-meter dash.

Those are the instructions to warriors receive when preparing to engage in imminent combat. Let us now review some strategic guidelines to employ during the war.

Your only edge against your entity is that your main ego-self has more valuable resources at its disposal. The main ego-self has the advantage of making alliances with other subpersonalities, and above all, a stronger will connection with your soul-self. The entity is alone by itself entrenched in its own behavior niche, while the main ego-self has a full view of the battlefield and the strategic allies to call upon for help.

The overall battle strategy from the general commander standpoint is to (i) surround it with keen self-observation, (ii) cut-off its supply lines to starve it by not feeding it with its behavior of choice, and (iii) strengthen your soul connection by prayer in your own style asking for will power and assistance from God.

Another hint is about your physical surroundings. To project law and order into your subconscious-self, where the entity dwells, you must put order in your physical surroundings. Reorganize your closets, dump useless possessions, turn over your mattress, do a deep cleaning of your house or apartment, increase order and organization anywhere you can. Eliminate chaos outside, to banish it from your inner SIE.

You Can't Out Smart Your Entity

Those who have created and experienced their entities in action understand they must exist due to the inconspicuous ways they see them manifesting. The Alcoholics Anonymous movement, for example, acknowledges the alcoholic entities by calling them "the enemy" in their programs. They recognize the need to put a label and objectify the addiction in a way the patients can relate and understand. They accept and use the term freely because it is evidently real in their lives and in no way fear to be considered delusional by using it.

The "enemy" or the alcoholic entity operates at sub-perceptual levels. Observant alcoholics in recovery generally acknowledge how it manifests in mysterious ways. Consider an alcoholic in recovery, for example, who, for no apparent reason one day decides to switch his regular route driving back home from work. He happens to drive by a bar he used to frequent with his old drinking friends and suddenly gets overcome by cravings and stops there relapsing once again. In his next therapy session, they speak about how the enemy impaired his ability to appreciate the danger of taking a new route and then convinced him to drink only one more time. Translating this Alcoholics Anonymous narrative into our model of the psyche, I believe that his self-conscious entity was feeling symptoms of starvation and sensed a moment of weakness in the ego-self. It pushed back hard, influencing the main ego-self "decide" to switch routes and have him closer to a place with strong appeal. Once nearby, it found the energy to take over the command post, displacing the main ego-self aside. The entity dwells in the SIE equipped with most of the resources of the main ego-self and strives to survive using its intelligence. The ego-self created the entity at its "image and likeness" for which you cannot outsmart it. The entity just patiently waits while processing the flow of input from the host's senses, and at the right time, it jumps at a quick gap of attention, hacks its behavior, and makes him detour en route to the bar. Then it launches a full attack, and the host feels the strong temptation to get into it.

These relapses or sort of "something made me do it" behavior is a phenomenon generally acknowledged by addicts of different kinds, and we often find references to them in their testimonials. Food addicts hiding a piece of pecan pie for later after midnight, porno addicts that "accidentally" end-up in a porno site while they were searching an unrelated subject in Google, sex addicts at a party that "unintendedly" bump into another compatible sex addict, are just a few of many examples of how entities drive behavior to secure their food supply.

They feed on the quantum psychic energy produced by the brain while the addicted behavior is in progress. Neuroscientists may explain it with the alternate narrative of dopamine circuits and neurochemical reactions that "make the addict act" in such ways. Addicts also report that the more determined they get into staying "good," the easier it becomes to go "bad" due to the frequent opportunities that just fall on their lap out of nowhere, opportunities than rarely appear when they are actually on the hunt for the addictive behavior. These are the product of starving entities desperately doing hard work in the SIE before they go "off-line" or defeated by the strong will of the recovering addict. When this happens is a good sign, the recovering addict is doing great abstinence work and should take it as motivation to continue resilient in their goals. When grappling with addictive behavior, some addicts see the total success from the addiction as a goal too big too soon and instead attempt to trick the entity by negotiating, like "I will stop for thirty days, after that, we negotiate again." Although the intention is good, they fail to realize that this is the entity negotiating with them. With this approach, they better prepare well for the 31st day when the entity comes back demanding its food payment. Sometimes it may work successfully, but most of the time, the addict is not able to outsmart the entity in this or other creative strategies that addicts develop wishing for a smoother transition out of it. In the end, self-awareness, mindfulness, is the only effective method to overcome any addiction, of course, supported by a good measure of strong will.

CHAPTER NINETEEN

Epilogue

To summarize, this book:

- Rescues the soul from long-standing neglect by science relocating it to its rightful place inside our personal identity.

- Renovates the traditional definition of personal human identity with the renewed proposition of an SIE described as a trinity of merged but distinct personal selves: ego, subconscious, and soul.

- Debunks the notion of the subconscious mind, an abstraction that confuses more than assists the process of human self-realization.

- Embraces the universal morphogenetic field of the torus geometrical shape as the causative formation pattern of all living organisms, including humans, to provide a tool to develop visualization techniques for ayahuasca spiritual healing and psychedelic-assisted therapies.

- Places the limbic imprinting phenomenology in human behavior as a primary area of focus for spiritual healing techniques as well as its crucial role in our deeply hidden fundamental beliefs.

- Promulgates the importance of creating awareness of the meta-psychological projection principle, which is implicit and necessary to physical existence and to achieve optimum spiritual healing.

- Describes a series of valuable but previously unpublished observations about the healing process.

- Presents a series of recommendations targeted to ayahuasca spiritual advisors, -psychedelic-assisted therapists, and advanced ayahuasca practitioners, which can be integrated with their existing alternative healing techniques.

I have shared most of my belief system, which I constructed for the last two decades as instinctively followed my hardwired subconscious command for agenticity (remember Chapter 6). This is the subconscious imperative of infusing our perceived reality patterns with meaning and intention. I hope these ideas find a place in readers interested in opening to new ways of interpreting reality. Spiritual healing begins with brutal self-honesty. Deconstructing and unlearning are requirements for fundamental inner change. When equipped with a road map to embark on a convoluted journey, the mission becomes easier and expectations brighter. Achieving personal spiritual healing with a quantum model of the psyche is within reach of anyone with access to sacred plants and responsible assistance. I promote the instinctive pursual of our self-realization programs to increase the number of people in this Planet that may join the relatively small critical mass necessary to change it for the better. When we heal ourselves, we heal the world.

To close this fascinating discussion that had captured my curiosity for the last two decades, let us shift from the analytical focus into the verbal right-brain realm of storytelling. This is a selection of nine first-hand accounts I have received over the years directly from ayahuasca session participants. We will see that despite having a fairly congruent model of the psyche at our disposal, these stories still trigger a sense of awe, intrigue, and thoughtfulness in our ego-self. I reiterate a label I often use to describe her: Ayahuasca, the Unknowable.

BONUS SECTION

TALES FROM THE QUANTUM FIELD

A Jungian Psychologist's Dream

There is a saying in the ayahuasca community that has become popular over the years - "You don't find ayahuasca; instead, it's ayahuasca who finds you." The key message is that "when the student is ready, the master appears," or "there are no coincidences" when you learned about what ayahuasca is, or when you face the opportunity of actually having the experience. When we apply that saying to a situation, it is because either a friend or stranger mentioned ayahuasca, or you stumbled onto an ayahuasca book in a bookstore in an unusual way or another unlikely scenario. The story of Dr. Warren Tucker is mind-boggling because it brings "the ayahuasca finds you" cliché to a higher plane. I was fascinated when Dr. Tucker asked me to translate the story to Don Jose. This curandero had just initiated him during a ten-day dieta at his jungle retreat in the Peruvian Amazon. He waited until the last moment before returning to the U.S. because he was still processing the awe of how he discovered ayahuasca and the myriad of synchronicities that followed. This is the story he told us.

Dr. Tucker was a prominent Jungian psychoanalyst running a successful private practice in a major city in the American Midwest. He had a stable family life while working 60-hour weeks. For stress management, he practiced 10K running and mountain biking regularly with friends as a hobby. As a successful regular guy enjoying his local lifestyle, traveling was not one of his favorite activities, and he had never gone outside the U.S. frontiers. Since he was in college pursuing his Ph.D. in clinical psychology, he was naturally fascinated by the well-known Carl Jung dream theories and became an avid student of his dreams. As a result, Dr. Tucker accumulated an enormous collection of dream journals. Studying his own dreams proved to help become an expert in dream interpretation, and eventually, he started earning a living practicing his passion for interpreting the dreams of his patients.

Observing his own dream patterns, he noticed that during the last several months, he had dreamt with a new character never found before after many years of journaling - a shaman. He found it curious and decided to pay close attention the next time it popped up in a dream. Shortly after, he dreamt that a female shaman approached him, put a passport in his hand, and told him to hold it carefully because he was going to travel outside the U.S. in the near future. In the dream, he rejected the passport and told the female shaman, "No, thank you. Don't worry about it because I have no plans to travel soon, much less outside the U.S.". He found it strange and was unable to interpret the dream in the context of his current lifestyle. He concluded that this was a recurring dream that would bring similar ones in the future. He was right. A couple of weeks later, the same female shaman approached him again in a dream. This time she gave him the passport insisting that he must hold it because he was going to travel outside the U.S. When he was about to reject the passport again, she interrupted him and suggested that he look inside the passport before dismissing it. He proceeded to browse through the passport pages and felt a sense of shock and fascination with what he saw. Every page of the passport contained very profound and detailed stories of the different creation myths of different cultures of the world. This was especially relevant because this was a subject matter that had fascinated him for many years as it has to do with the Jungian archetypes he was so interested in understanding. This dream caught his attention, and he interpreted it as a call from his higher self to explore shamanism. "Maybe an incursion into this new area of knowledge would give me a deeper understanding of this lifelong intellectual curiosity I always have had about the origins of mankind," he thought.

The following night he went online and searched for "shamanism." It didn't take long before he read about this strange brew named ayahuasca, something about he had never heard of before. After learning about its entheogenic properties, he felt that maybe the recurring dreams were a call to drink this shamanic brew, and the passport was the sign that he should travel to Peru. It all made sense now. The professional expert in dream interpretation had just interpreted his recurring dream, and it was pointing at a trip to South America.

He asked himself, "But where in Peru and with whom I am going to do this?" He figured that if this was meant to be, he would get another sign, basically that all plans must unfold smoothly without inconveniences of any sort. What happened next was the key that turned Dr. Tucker from a bit hesitant and undecided all the way to firmly committed into action.

He searched online for ayahuasca retreat centers and clicked on donjosecampos.com, which is one website that I used to manage as a webmaster. I was one of the organizers of the dietas being conducted at Don Jose's jungle campsite, and the emails addressed to his website from potential participants were forwarded to me for the initial contact and orientation. He said, "If this is meant to be, I will send an information request to this shaman and see what happens." There I was at the other end in Miami, Florida, going on with my life when I received Dr. Tucker's email in my mobile device. I usually replied to those emails later at night, but at that specific moment, I was idle and responded immediately. In less than three minutes there it was, a full information package with all the dates, prices, and pertinent information needed to make a decision. He was so impressed by the synchronicity that he decided right there on the spot to travel to Peru. The next day he applied for a passport, and two months later, he participated in a ten-day retreat with five ayahuasca ceremonies conducted by Don Jose himself.

When I finished translating this story to Don José, he asked Dr. Tucker whether his questions about the origins of mankind were correctly answered. Dr. Tucker stared in his eyes for a second and replied: "I now not only have a much deeper understanding about our origin, which is totally spiritual but also my understanding of dream interpretation has multiplied tenfold. I can't wait to go back home to meet my patients again." We were all delighted to hear such an intriguing story and to watch a Ph.D. professional in awe of the power and potential of ayahuasca.

After returning to his professional practice, Dr. Tucker adjusted his therapy and coaching sessions and developed a retreat format that offered participants the opportunity to deepen their awareness and appreciation for sacred prayer. He was touched in a way that allowed him to evolve both personally and professionally.

Going back to the "ayahuasca finds you" saying, I can't think of a better example. No intermediaries, friends, books, or coincidences were needed for Dr. Tucker to discover the wonders of the sacred medicine. It was like he was directly recruited from the spiritual world via the medium he trusted most, his dreams.

A Muslim Tobacco Smoker Quits in One Session

Meet Abdullah Sein, a 40-year-old immigrant from Jordan who heard about ayahuasca from his friends. After doing some research, he thought it could help him quit smoking. Since he was a teenager in Jordan, he started smoking with friends, and it became part of his life. After moving to the U.S., he continued his habit of sharing different strains of tobacco with his new Middle Eastern friends in New York City. Besides chain-smoking up to two packs of cigarettes per day, he enjoyed meeting with friends over the weekend to smoke a recently purchased 30-inch tall hookah. This Middle Eastern smoking device creates a smoke that is passed through a water basin, often glass-based, before going out through one or several inhalation hoses.

Abdullah was living a life of contradiction because while he was enjoying it, he knew deep in his heart that it was wrong. This feeling was partial because of his Muslim belief that smoking was contrary to Koran's teachings but also because he was well informed with western medical knowledge about the significant health risks. He had a couple of family members that suffered smoking-related lung ailments and knew he was enlisted in a dangerous club.

For about fifteen years, Abdullah had tried quitting the habit without success. He had tried meditation, hypnosis, acupuncture, nicotine patches, among other alternatives, but his best result so far was only three months off the habit. On multiple occasions, he regretfully fell back into it, feeling defeated and hopeless. He regained some hope after learning that smoking was one of the problems that the sacred medicine can heal. His friend that initially mentioned ayahuasca to him, was delighted about Abdullah's decision to give it a try. He quickly made the arrangements with his ayahuasca community for his friend to participate in one of their ayahuasca sessions.

The big day arrived, and he had his first ayahuasca experience. Everybody at the event knew that Abdullah had a powerful healing experience because they reported afterward that during the ceremony, Abdullah was for a reasonable period of time struggling, moaning, choking, and cuffing, and after a period of silence, he started repeatedly screaming: "Ayahuasca healed me, Allah! Ayahuasca healed me!" Being unaware of all the background information mentioned above, when we had hot soup and fruit after the ceremony, I casually asked Abdullah how the experience was for him. To my delight, he immediately jumped of excitement to tell me about the details of his healing experience:

"At some point, I was lost in a dark place full of smoke and had no idea where I was. Then I heard a voice asking me whether I really wanted to quit smoking because a part of me really loved to smoke. I was so happy to hear that question because I knew then that my intention and prayers were being answered. Yes! I want to quit smoking, no matter how much I enjoy it! Please I beg you to help Mother Ayahuasca, I want to quit forever. Then I heard the voice again: 'Do you really want to do this? It's going to be hard and painful,' to which I answered with a convincing affirmative. I relaxed, and a bit later, it started like a whirlpool of energy growing from the bottom of my sexual center and getting bigger and stronger as it moved upwards. Then I felt a pressure in my belly, like something growing inside my stomach. It felt like a ball and became so big that it started to stretch the inner walls of my belly and cause pain. I knew this big healing event was unfolding but had no idea what was next. I opened wide my stiff legs while firmly grabbing the grass under my hands to prepare for what was imminent. The ball started to push up my esophagus, but it was too big for it. A strong force was pushing up while the ball began to elongate as it slowly moved up, and the pain intensified. I wanted to scream in pain, but for some reason, I couldn't. As it started to move further upwards, I realized that eventually, it would reach my mouth, and something would come out. When it approached my throat, it started blocking my airways, and I couldn't breathe. I began to panic, feeling that death was possible. My rational mind was telling me to hold on, that if it would get expelled in one minute, I was going to be okay. I consciously held my breath, hoping for the trusting inner voice that warned me about it. I felt the tissues stretching in my throat to a point where the pain was unbearable. I almost fainted but held on by mere survival instinct. I opened my mouth wide as it was starting to make its way out of my body. I was running out of breath, but I found strength feeling that the end was getting closer. Finally, when it was about twelve inches out of my mouth, I squeezed my eyes shut very firmly in pain, and I saw a crystal-clear vision of the thing coming out of my mouth. It was my hookah! My thirty-inch hookah was coming out of my throat in one piece. It reminded me of my mother giving birth to me 40 years earlier. I gasped a huge breath and immediately started to laugh. The pain was over, and, in my vision, the hookah dissolved in its own smoke and disappeared. What a relief! At that moment, I knew that my tobacco addiction was totally healed. I am so grateful for this incredible medicine. Thank you, Mother Ayahuasca, thank you."

I grabbed Abdullah, hugged him, congratulated him, and celebrated the story with others around us. It was a cheerful moment for everybody. It was a memorable moment that enlightened the space with an air of awe and satisfaction.

About six months later, Abdullah paid me a visit and brought some presents and food to share. He wanted to celebrate his sixth month without tobacco. He never smoked again. He confessed that the mere smell of other people's smoke gives him goosebumps and mild nausea. In this compelling story, a strong addiction was healed in just one session. He continues to drink ayahuasca to expand in other areas of his spiritual life.

When I think about Abdullah's healing, I can rationally refer to current scientific investigations that have shown statistically significant evidence about the healing properties of ayahuasca with certain addictions. Indeed, we may find a chemical explanation of such healing in terms of molecular mechanisms in the brain, neurotransmitters, reprogramming, but when I review what happens in the similar emotional, spiritual subjective experience of the patient I have no option but to validate a model of the psyche that transcends the Newtonian cause-effect principle. How was Abdullah healed? Was his volitive energy emerging from the quantum level of reality that caused chemical changes in Abdullah's brain, or was it the chemically active ingredient in the ayahuasca brew that caused the hookah hallucination in his brain?. Regardless, the story ends with the immense gratitude Abdullah developed for the sacred medicine. A couple of years later, he departed from his family tradition of naming newborn babies with Muslim-oriented names. His wife gave birth to a healthy and beautiful baby girl who they officially named "Aya."

An Unborn Girl Named Penelope

Lillian Lock is a 42-year-old woman with ten years of active service as a firefighter in Atlanta, Georgia. She was having mild episodes of anxiety from time to time and suspected that these were related to the inherent stress from her job. Being alert for many hours at a time, and acting in emergency mode was clearly the reasonable cause for her anxiety. She felt upset and sometimes annoyed for having these mild anxiety episodes during the most unexpected moments of her free time and holidays. She decided to make a career change before things got worse. She knew that seeking medical help would result in getting prescription medications, something she did not want. She already had obtained a bachelor's degree in nursing, which helped her qualify for the firefighter job, and going back to college to pursue a master's degree seemed like a great idea. This would allow her to apply for less demanding jobs in the medical world that offered comparable salaries. She enrolled in graduate school and started a night study program. In casual conversation with her new friends in school, she heard for the first time about ayahuasca. One thing led to another, and before she knew it, the opportunity to drink ayahuasca knocked on her door.

I met Lillian in 2016 when she participated in a group ayahuasca ceremony. When someone comes to drink ayahuasca for the first time, I invariably conduct a private and confidential interview not only to confirm the participant's health profile but also to ask a few personal questions about their intention and expectations in order to guide them properly. She spoke about her anxiety episodes and her current firefighter job. It all made sense, but I wondered what else may be causing those episodes. In one of my questions, I asked her about being married and having children, and I sensed energy that may relate to her anxiety. "Lillian, you are 42 years old now and have been married for the last seven years. Have you ever considered having a child?" I asked. She nonchalantly replied that having children was something she had never felt the call for, and her husband felt the same way. In fact, it was an important thing they had in common that got them closer and helped both decide to get married.

Motherhood is an extraordinarily strong genetic drive in women in general, and deciding not to have children for just "not having the call" was suspicious to me. My intuition was telling me that for some reason, she was not having the call, which could be a source of unconscious anxiety besides the more obvious rationale of job-related stress. It also came to my attention that after graduating from nursing school, she decided to pursue a firefighter career, like bypassing a naturally feminine career for which she was properly trained to look into a more masculine type of job. Moreover, her husband was a police officer, and they both invested most of their free time in heavy physical fitness training, including some weightlifting.

I invited her to ask Mother Ayahuasca to show the origin of her anxiety, to open her mind to accept any information, feeling, or vision during the ceremony that would give her a clue about it. I said: "Get into the ceremony with the assumption that there is something hidden that needs unveiling, explore your childhood, find sources of abuse, trauma, or anything that may strike your consciousness with the notion that you found a missing link." She later confirmed that this guidance was crucial for what she discovered during the ceremony.

She followed my advice and found something big, a deeply repressed memory that got released. She recalled that while in the tenth grade of high school, she fell in love for the first time with a twelve-grade senior. She was sixteen, and he was eighteen when they made love in secret. Then a big nightmare began. She got pregnant; the boyfriend denied accepting any responsibility, and after a couple of unbearably anxious weeks, she decided to get an abortion to avoid confessing to her parents. Her boyfriend assisted with money, some care, and the problem went away. Lillian was crying uncontrollably as she described in detail her painful memory.

I told her that she indeed had found a missing link and encouraged her to drink ayahuasca again, this time with the firm conviction of going back to re-live the event and ask Mother Ayahuasca to remove and heal this pain and anxiety from her subconscious-self. The mere awareness of the origin of the trauma is not enough to heal it. The link can be unveiled, but a deep wound that has been forgotten for a long time requires more profound healing work. She was impressed by the power of ayahuasca and agreed to come back for more.

On her second ceremony, she got it. Ayahuasca operates in strange ways. What happened next is the reason why I included Lillian's story in this collection. For four hours, Lillian cried, screamed, sobbed, moaned, and finally laughed in joy and gratefulness. When it started, Lillian prayed and begged for healing with sincere intent from her heart. After a few minutes, she fell into a sort of trance while experiencing an intense vision. The soul of a baby girl appeared before her eyes. It was amorphous, a presence that she knew was there in front of her, that came from a mysterious place. Then, the baby soul started to talk to Lillian. She said: "You know who I am, do you recognize me?" She yelled in response, "Yes! You are my daughter!"

Lillian's vision was about connecting with the soul of the baby girl that was incarnated in her womb when she was sixteen years old. A compassionate conversation flowed smoothly between the two, and the baby soul answered all of Lillian's questions and concerns. The baby soul said a few things that were absolutely necessary for Lillian's mental health. The most important one was that she made Lillian feel innocent of murder, that it was okay, and was meant to be. This is the subconscious guilt carried by all women that consciously end their pregnancies with abortion. Regardless of the attitudes and moral directives that society has developed over time regarding abortion at the rational level, the fact remains that deeply at the emotional or spiritual level, the woman doing the abortion retains subconscious guilt that years later comes back to haunt her. In one way or another, the unresolved conflict manifests in a variety of ways such as insomnia, anxiety, aggressive attitudes, and in the case of Lillian, developing the unconscious preference of not having children. Her conscious conclusion of "not having the call" was an unconscious excuse to hide the real trauma lying underneath as an encrypted memory.

Here we have a 42-year-old woman that missed her main period of fertility working as a firefighter, married to a policeman that rejected having children, and obsessed with physical fitness and looking good. This was the best way she found to run away from the innate instinct of motherhood. The natural consequence of realizing what really happened is a feeling of regret and remorse. But here comes the second part of her healing. During their conversation, the baby soul was referring to Lillian as "mother" all the time. For some period, Lillian was talking to her daughter, listening to her saying, "because mother this; mother, you should know that, etc.". Amazingly, this was sufficient to reprogram her brain with the feeling of motherhood. She started the ceremony as a woman that didn't want to have children and came out of the experience as a mother that had lost her daughter. That was a huge difference for Lillian. She changed entirely from a tough woman to a softer, more compassionate one. Her husband could not believe the woman that came back home. They are now living happier times as a couple.

The epilogue of this story is fascinating. At the end of Lillian's conversation with the baby soul, she asked what name she would have preferred if she had been born. She answered in one word without hesitation - Penelope. This sealed the healing process as Lillian experienced becoming a mother that lost a daughter named Penelope. She loved this name, and a few days later, she got curious and decided to research its origins online. What she found was awesomely meaningful. Penelope is a Greek name that originates from the Odyssey, which is one of two major ancient Greek epic poems attributed to Homer. She was the wife of Odysseus, who remained faithful to him for twenty years while she waited for his return during his long absence at Troy. It literally means "weaver," as Penelope spent all that time weaving beautiful fabrics while patiently waiting for her husband. Penelope is, therefore, associated with patience and faithfulness. For Lillian, it all made sense now. The daughter had patiently waited twenty-six years for the acceptance of her mother. This added another layer of healing and acceptance in Lillian's new life free of anxiety.

The Penelope twist was a curious part of this story. It reminds me of the concept of the collective unconscious developed by the Swiss psychiatrist Carl Jung. How did this ayahuasca vision come up with a name from Greek mythology that perfectly fits the Lillian situation? Is ayahuasca a key opener to the Jungian collective unconscious data banks? Is Lillian's soul-self, or her higher divine nature, responsible for creating the perfect vision necessary for the psychological healing of her lower self?

A Deceased Mother Helping Her Son in Depression

Andrea Segarra is a successful businesswoman that many years earlier discovered the benefits of drinking ayahuasca. She tries to drink regularly for her ongoing process of self-improvement and spiritual awakening. One day she felt that it was time to drink again and made the arrangements accordingly. She never expected that this occasion would be any different. At the last stage of her ayahuasca experience, she connected with the spirit of her aunt, who had passed away two months earlier. This was not new for Andrea, as she has had similar connections before with other deceased dear ones. Her aunt was a developed soul when she was alive as she always followed the spiritual path until she died at age 72. She spoke to Andrea about a few things on the other side but explained that the reason for her visit was a cry for help. She wanted Andrea to help her cousin, her aunt's son, by inviting him to do several ayahuasca ceremonies. Andrea knew precisely that her aunt was referring to her cousin James and not his brother Felix. It is fascinating to learn about a deceased soul that had never experienced ayahuasca while alive, to irrupt into the consciousness of a living family member, and beg for his depressed son to experience ayahuasca. Did she find out on the other side that ayahuasca, and not any other, is the powerful remedy that can help her son?

James was a 45-year-old man that grew very emotionally dependent on her mother, and after her departure, he fell in a severe depression that was ruining his life. James never married and lived with his mother until the tragic day of her death. As a youngster, he was a privileged student, eventually earned a Ph.D. degree in history, and became an associate professor at a prominent university in California. Although he was in denial about his sudden depressed condition after his mother's death, it was apparent that his work performance declined significantly. It was so evident to students and fellow professors that the university administration acted by forcing him into a sabbatical leave until he got better. Felix, his concerned brother, rescued him from the darkness of his messy bedroom and placed him under the care of a quality psychiatric facility.

Soon after the ceremony, Andrea phoned his cousin Felix to find about the latest on James' condition. Andrea suffered deeply after learning about James' struggle to achieve progress at the psychiatric clinic after four weeks of treatment. She told Felix about her experience and the request from his mother to help James. Felix understandably reacted in disbelief, and it took a great deal of Andrea's persuasion to have him agree to the request. Felix visited James at the clinic and dropped the bomb. James interpreted that this was his brother playing mind tricks on him with good intentions, in an effort to get him hopeful about an alternative treatment.

James was convinced that the unbelievable story about his mother was just a merciful lie from his brother to induce him to end his hospitalization. After some time persuading him, the incredulous James agreed but threw at Felix a menacing caveat: "Okay brother, I am going to quit this treatment and try ayahuasca, but if I find out that your mother's story was a lie, I will commit suicide right away because I cannot live with this anymore. And you will have to carry with the guilt of what you did to me for the rest of your life". Felix smiled and staring intensely into his eyes, replied: "Yes, brother, you got a deal; let's get out of here."

A few days later, Andrea called James and told him the extended version of her experience. James felt more at ease and agreed to make the arrangements to participate in a series of private ayahuasca ceremonies. When the day came, James was totally ready. He started sobbing as soon as he arrived at the ceremony location as if already feeling what was about to unfold. Then it happened.

In the first few minutes after feeling the effects of ayahuasca, the visions started. With his eyes shut, he saw a small spark of light in the center of his dark field of vision. It began to get bigger and closer to him. Then it turned into a bright, round cloud, and he gradually started feeling the unmistaken presence of his mother. "Mom?" he asked. Then he burst in an intense, repeating cry, screaming, "Mom, mom, mom!" His mother's compassionate face appeared clearly from the dissolving smoke. She told him that she was waiting for him, that asking Andrea for help was the most natural way she could help; that the most important message she has for him is that she is not dead but alive in another plane, that she is doing fine; and that he should not grieve so much for her departure; also that they will one day be together again, and that committing suicide would separate their souls forever instead of getting them closer. She also wanted him to promise her that he would move on with his life and continue his successful path as before. At the end of the ceremony, James remained silent for hours and refused to talk or interact with anyone. It took a couple of days of quiet integration for James to finally say: "I promise."

After a couple of weeks, the old James was back, and he traveled across the country to spend time with his father in New York, with whom he was moderately distant for the last few years. He reconciled past grudges he still had in his heart, and it was an extremely good reunion for both of them. He went back home and learned to enjoy living by himself during the few weeks left of the teaching semester. The doctors at the psychiatric clinic were amazed at his recovery and wondered how it happened. James decided to keep the ayahuasca story for himself and just requested the certifying paperwork of his mental health to enable him to report back to work. When James returned to the faculty staff, Andrea traveled to his hometown to celebrate the achievement with lots of gratitude and good family times.

An exciting sequel of the story is that a few months later, James felt the urge to communicate with his mother again and decided for another ayahuasca ceremony. This time was different. His intention was firm and was able to connect with his mother the second time. However, the connection was brief, leaving James disenchanted with the encounter but in acceptance at the same time. His mother told him that she would not be able to stay in contact with him the way he wanted; that more communication between them would constitute a continuation of the toxic emotional codependence that he had thankfully healed. It would cause him to fall back into sickness, and that was the last thing she wanted. It was time to grow up and assume full responsibility for his life while completely releasing the remnants of the mother attachment that still existed in his heart.

For many ayahuasca enthusiasts, this is irrefutable proof of life after death, the eternal nature of the spirit, even supporting the reincarnation beliefs. For traditional science, however, it's just still unexplained brain phenomena currently beyond the reach of scientific theories. But that one day, science will get there as it has done with other mysteries. These are exciting moments for scientific movements of the 21st century; science continues to evolve as people open to novel understandings of reality, blending physical with metaphysical in refreshing quantum cocktails.

Leaving the mysteries to future scientists, understanding the quantum field in this story can explain how such a tremendous amount of wisdom found its way to a grieving man, resulting in instant relief to his condition. It may take decades before this kind of phenomena can be explained by science, but in the meantime, the story of a divine spirit comforting her grieving son through the ayahuasca portal is strong evidence of its healing effects.

Helping Elder WW2 Veterans to Die in Peace

I met Henry Benjamin when he was referred to ayahuasca sessions by his massage therapist. He was a remarkably exciting fellow with a fascinating life. He was 50 years old when I met him. He never married or had children, and with all the time we spent together for the next couple of years, I got the impression that Henry was a highly intelligent person living a lonely inner life while often reluctant to engage in casual conversations. Consequently, Henry had few friends and a history of very brief relationships with women. His talks were short, rarely describing his emotional state, and were always limited to replying to questions or suggestive comments. When I looked in his eyes, I got the feeling he was absent, but on the contrary, he was an acute observer. I liked him a lot and spent hours talking to him as the more questions I asked, the more fascinating his answers became.

I was able to confirm everything he told me as factual after checking the Internet. He was a shy, introspective, and highly intelligent child living in a remote area of Montana. When he turned 18, he stole his father's car and credit cards and disappeared without a trace. A year later, he reappeared with the same car and almost a million dollars in his bank account. He made a lot of money buying and selling cars and trucks along with other side hustles. After making peace with his relieved parents, he purchased a few thousand acres of forest land, obtained government permits, and started exploiting the lumber business after investing in a couple of trucks and machinery. Five years later, a major corporation became interested in his successful forestry operation and bought him out for five million dollars. After that, he moved to the east coast and spent years in real estate development, becoming very wealthy throughout his thirties and forties.

As a hobby, he became a treasure hunter and found a sunk Spaniard wreck off the coast of Virginia. Prior to his successful expedition, he had obtained a letter from the Spanish government confirming that they did not object to his search and relinquished any discoveries. After he publicly announced his discovery, a higher Spanish authority reversed their position and declared the discovery as national heritage. He went to Federal Court and lost his case. Disgruntled and extremely upset, Henry destroyed the buoys he had placed at the site of the high sea, and all the technical documentation indicated its exact location. He decided to forget this chapter of his life while absorbing the substantial financial loss associated with the expensive treasure hunt. He told the Spanish government: "Go and find it yourselves!". Such controversy made the news in Virginia while his only reward ended up being a memento he kept for himself - a gorgeous bundle of gold coins blended in a coral formation.

When Henry arrived for the ayahuasca ceremony, he was in good physical health, and there were no emotional or spiritual issues that were bothering him at the time. Henry liked his experience but did not share much about what happened. Over the next few months, Henry acted very similarly in several ceremonies. He would lay down on the grass, facing up with his pillow, stayed there for five hours without using the restroom, no vomiting, while displaying the happiest childlike smile, with occasional bursts of laughter. Sometimes he asked for additional cups of ayahuasca only to continue a bit longer and more in-depth. To my amazement, he consistently did that every time. Just imagine a skinny guy joining a group of experienced bodybuilders in a gym and then doing record-breaking weightlifting in front of them. That's a fair analogy of Henry and ayahuasca. I spent a few hours interviewing him every time I could, especially inquiring about his subjective experience during his ayahuasca journeys. A few times, he confessed to visiting other dimensional spaces that were just too strange to describe. All he could say is that he felt a divine joy, an eternal presence, a cosmic bliss as he interacted with souls of other parts of the world.

After a year doing ceremonies regularly, Henry enrolled in one of the Amazon trips I used to organize for Don Jose Campos. As the webmaster of Don Jose's website, I was responsible for replying to the inquiring emails from potential participants interested in traveling to Peru from all over the world. After lots of email coordination, I would spend a day or two welcoming every incoming participant at the Lima airport and then have dinner with them in order to introduce each other and provide final instructions for our journey to the Peruvian Amazon. Don Jose was awaiting us.

I enjoyed watching how Henry, who came from the comforts of a wealthy urban lifestyle, quickly adapted and enjoyed the bare basics of jungle life like a native. The impressive part of Henry's story comes after the fourth ceremony of the five scheduled. At the end of the retreat, Henry visited me in my jungle shack because he wanted to share two things that impressed him to a great extent. I was very attentive as he began to talk. After the ceremony, he went to his shack and laid down to relax with his eyes closed. He sensed a light inside his cabin and opened his eyes to see a ball of light about two feet in diameter, floating about three feet from the floor and about five feet from his face. Too close and fascinating to ignore, the ball was just passively standing there glowing softly but not showing any details inside of it. He reacted calmly, staring at it and expecting something to happen. But a few minutes passed by with no change at all. He was collapsing from being so tired after the ceremony but could not turn over to sleep with a ball of light floating in his room. Moreover, he felt it would be a lack of respect to ignore it. He briefly closed his eyes for a couple of minutes, and the ball disappeared. He wanted to know the meaning of it, but I was speechless in my ignorance.

The second thing that impressed him was his visions he experienced at the last ceremony. For the first time, Henry revealed details about his journeys. He was clearly moved when he revisited my cabin to share his experience. First, he confessed that in many of his ceremonies in the U.S., he had compelling visions of astral travel to different parts of the world. In these travels, he would meet World War 2 veterans in their late eighties and nighties that were going through their last moments before dying. He admitted that this happened on several occasions, and while not exactly knowing what it meant, his mission was to help them detach from the physical body because they were too scared to surrender to death. Apparently, their unresolved war traumas made it extremely agonizing to let go and die in peace.

Henry felt pulled towards them, feeling the urge to provide his loving assistance to end their struggle. After dying, the souls of the veterans invariably acknowledged that Henry's help allowed them to feel incredible joy. This happened to him four or five times in the past. He never told me or anyone else because he was not sure whether he was helping someone, or it just was a "hallucination" provoked by the DMT in the ayahuasca brew. For months he was quietly longing for confirmation on whether his mission of compassion with war veterans was true or only existed in his mind. His question was answered.

During his vision that night, he found himself astral traveling again, but contrary to previous occasions, he knew exactly where he was going and who he was approaching. It was a 95-year-old war veteran named Andrew Gallagher who served as a young army private in the Japanese front and was dying in Honolulu, Hawaii, at that exact moment he was in the Peruvian Amazon. For the first time, I saw Henry expressing emotions; he was anxious to find out whether this was true.

Henry received something incredibly special in his last ceremony. The next day was scheduled for integration and relaxation, and the following day, the group embarked on a three-hour ride in motorized river canoes streaming the Ucayali river back to Pucallpa. A little tourist bus was waiting at the port to take us to our guesthouse. When we arrived at the guesthouse, Henry jumped off the bus, desperately running to his room. He picked up his mobile phone, plugged it in the wall, and waited for the Wi-Fi signal to connect. He spent less than thirty minutes searching the Internet when he approached me with excitement and said: "Look at this!" I could not believe my eyes. There it was, in the obituary section of a Hawaiian newspaper's website: "Oldest war veteran in town, Andrew Gallagher, dies at 95."

It was an incredible experience for both of us. When we told the story to Don Jose, a highly experienced curandero, he was not impressed: "You have seen nothing, kids." He was right. We were beginners just scratching the surface of the potential of ayahuasca for the spiritual awakening of the human species.

Being a financially resourceful person, Henry invited a female friend to accompany him on a cruise ship vacation the following year. Not surprisingly, the destination was Hawaii. He visited all the beautiful spots of the Hawaiian Islands, but he had something special on his mind. He took a day off to rent a car and visit the cemetery where he knew the veteran was buried. Henry found Andrew Gallagher's grave, placed a huge flower arrangement on it, and prayed a few minutes for his soul. He could not have devised a better closure to his experience. Henry Benjamin is now a profoundly spiritual person.

The Daughter of Audrey Hepburn That Never Was

Jane Haulotte was a 20-year-old girl, the daughter of Phillip Claude, a dear friend of mine. For many years, my friend was a Canadian entrepreneur living in Montreal. He traveled the world doing international consulting work for several industries. We met a few years earlier when he came to experience ayahuasca, something that proved to be particularly suitable for him. We discovered lots of things in common and became good friends. One thing we had in common was our passion for the entertainment industry. In my case, this passion was circumstantial, as described in the Pedro Capo story shown later in this book section, but in his case, it was more fundamental. Since he was a teenager, he had this dream of one day producing a major feature film designed to awaken the people to become more politically engaged and change the world. He was doing something about it by writing a script during his free time while taking specialized training courses about the film production industry.

At one point, he approached me to speak about his daughter Jane. He wanted to explore the possibility of introducing her to ayahuasca, as he felt she was having difficulties finding her sense of direction in life. Being a common situation for young adults her age, I agreed to talk to her to confirm that this was something she really wanted to do. Ayahuasca is not for everyone, and it's a very personal decision. A friend, and especially any father, should never persuade, induce, or much less pressure anyone to try ayahuasca; it should never go beyond a graceful invitation or a friendly suggestion.

When I met Jane a couple of months later, I agreed with Phillip Claude. Jane carried a contradiction within her that was making her unhappy. She was atypical for her age in several areas. Jane wanted to be an actress, and after graduating from high school, she enrolled in an acting oriented college. She was struggling with college as she felt left behind due to the highly competitive school atmosphere. This was understandable because Jane was extremely introverted and insecure. She was aware of these characteristics but also knew that it wasn't a deal-breaker for pursuing this career. After all, great actors had succeeded with her personality type. However, for some reason, she was failing to come out of her shell.

In addition, Jane was extremely sensitive emotionally and didn't communicate much, even with her immediate family circle. Both her mom and brother confirmed this besides Phillip Claude. She resorted to the Internet to hide away from the world and quickly became addicted, a condition confirmed by online diagnostic tests I suggested her to take. At her age, she admitted to never having any kind of sex or ever having a boyfriend. Luckily, she was aware of needing help but was unsuccessful after trying a couple of therapists and counselors. Convinced that conventional therapy was not going to help, she was eager to try ayahuasca and hopeful of getting good results.

Jane had a series of ceremonies without much revelation or understanding. She could feel going through very intense processes, but despite many efforts, she failed to remember them. However, she remained strongly committed to drinking ayahuasca as frequently as possible because she felt the unexplainable certainty that something big was waiting for her.

Five ceremonies later, there she was in the middle of the ceremony crying intensively, going through the big breakthrough she was waiting for. The following morning, I went to interview her, and luckily, she was prepared to talk.

In her visions, she saw herself as a talented and successful actress; they were idealized images of herself in the way she longed them. Then she saw the other Jane - insecure, introverted, and not as beautiful as her true self. This was a recreation of her confused life, trapped between what she was and what she wanted to be. This contradiction had kept her frozen for several years now. "I want this to end! I can't take it anymore! Help!" she screamed. But nobody in the ceremony noticed anything. It was all an inner emotional release. It is interesting that her shyness had control over her even during the ceremony. Most people in those circumstances would cry out loud, something that occurs often. As she fervently wanted this to end, she was shown the source of the two different "Janes" living in her.

First, she was shown the introvert Jane. This Jane was the product of numerous childhood traumas she had forgotten but was still inhibiting her self-expression because of fear. She saw that she was sexually molested by the second husband of her grandmother. Between ages two and five, her grandmother was doing daycare for her, as Jane's mother had a day job. When her grandmother occasionally went out for groceries, her husband, not the biological grandfather, took advantage of her. She immediately understood her instinctive repulsion toward the male figure in general. She was even confused about her gender identity, as sometimes she asked herself whether she was lesbian, but quickly changed her mind when realizing that she liked to fantasize about handsome men. It all made sense now. That's why she never had a boyfriend; she was unconsciously projecting her dislike for men, and potential prospects would sense this energy and lost interest. She also saw that she was projecting this repulsion towards Phillip Claude, her father. It was quite easy to do because her father was very demanding during her teenage years, which helped solidify the emotional shell she was creating around herself.

Then came the visions of the other Jane. These ones came totally unexpected. She saw the talented actress Jane again, knowing that it was an aspect of herself. But then the actress began to regress in age back to a child, then an infant, and finally inside the womb of her mother. The strange thing was that this mother of the actress Jane was not her biological mother, the wife of Phillip Claude. To her amazement, the mother was none other than Audrey Hepburn, the famous Hollywood actress of the 1950s and 60s. Being an aspiring actress, she recognized her immediately because she had watched some of her classic movies. When she asked, "Where am I?" she found herself in the womb of Audrey Hepburn and began to feel a terrible pain all over her body. She felt the anguish and sorrow of Audrey and the fear in her own life. She felt like she had died inside the womb but suddenly was alive again inside the womb of her biological mother.

It was like waking up from a horrible nightmare. She opened her eyes and stood up, heading for the bathroom. On the way to the bathroom, she got the classical ayahuasca nausea and stopped to throw up. She vomited violently, loudly, and extensively. While this was happening, she saw she was releasing her past life. She was the daughter of Audrey Hepburn in her previous life, and this is where the passion for acting comes from. Jane started laughing uncontrollably for quite some time. She just could not believe her incredible breakthrough.

The two Janes have split apart like the surgery of Siamese twins. A sturdy brick wall was built between the two, and she can now perceive who is who. She can decide which way to go. She felt transformed into the woman she wanted to be, as she broke free from contradiction and confusion. Gratitude poured out of her eyes while the effects of the sacred medicine gradually receded.

During the next few days, she continued ruminating about her connection with the famous actress. The notion of being the daughter of Audrey Hepburn in her previous life fascinated her, and she even felt a sort of ego trip or pride. Then she felt curious about the details of her former life, especially since her mother was a celebrity. Jane went online to research her biography, and it didn't take long. A single click at Wikipedia said it all. It turns out that Audrey had a total of four miscarriages, two before her only son, and two more thereafter. Jane stared at her computer screen for a long time while she connected all the dots. "Of course!" The painful experience inside Audrey's womb and the sudden transfer to the womb of her current mother all made sense. Her soul was conceived in one of Audrey Hepburn's pregnancies, and then a miscarriage occurred, allowing her to continue towards her next step in her spiritual evolution. She already knew such was the case since the night of the ceremony, but having this convincing real-life confirmation sealed the covenant of truth in her heart. It's a privilege a few happen to receive.

My question is: Given that Phillip Claude was an aspiring film producer, did Jane's soul selected him as a father because she would have better chances to manifest the actress in her, something that she tried but failed with Audrey? Did she know that Phillip Claude would eventually produce a movie, and she may end up acting in it?

Although Jane was able to make a clear distinction between her "double personality," she continued to grapple over the choice of blindly following the instinct from a previous incarnation or to accept that it was only the remnants of a time gone past and she should just pursue a new lifestyle in her current life. Not an easy question to answer.

A Baby Soul Complains to His Future Dad.

Jimmy Mendez was a 32-year-old Mexican American electronic technician living a stable and comfortable married life with no children. He came to drink ayahuasca to "find his purpose in life." This is not an unusual intention for many first-time participants, especially those in the 30-35 age bracket. In fact, I have compiled statistical evidence that shows the 30-40-year-old demographic as the most significant number of participants seeking initiation in ayahuasca. This is the time when people have already figured out the basics of survival and the mechanics of society but start feeling that something is missing. Ayahuasca has already established an excellent reputation in helping people in that situation.

Jimmy was in such a life stage when he attended a group ceremony on a beautiful summer night. The ceremony unfolded smoothly, and the next morning, we were sharing our experiences in an integration circle. This is when participants speak about their experience the night before, ask questions, and share opinions. It's a very healthy exercise highly recommended after every group ceremony.

Jimmy shared his experience and made a few listeners crack up in laughter, and those who didn't, were left with frowning glances. Jimmy told us that he was experiencing some childhood memories when he felt interrupting energy. When he was trying to clear up his confusing state of mind, he felt the presence of a baby boy. Jimmy felt warm and comfortable and wished to talk to him. Before Jimmy thought about what to say, the baby boy said: "Daddy! Here I am." "What the heck!" Jimmy replied while jerking up a couple of centimeters above the ground. Besides being a bit funny, the conversation that happened next shakes up the notions of space-time and cause-effect for most people.

Jimmy Junior, let's say, was communicating with his future father. He explained that he has been "there" waiting for a long time, and he was getting desperate. He had been "assigned" to Jimmy and his wife and described a few things he needed to accomplish in his next lifetime. Jimmy was so confused about the whole situation that he was speechless. He decided to reply with the truth in an apologetic tone: "But Boy, you have to understand that my wife and I have decided to work hard and save enough money to purchase a house before we look into having children." Jimmy Junior replied with a strong sense of urgency: "No, no, no, dad, YOU don't understand that I am running out of time to achieve the things I need to do as your son. I need you to get mom pregnant right NOW!" Jimmy reacted in laughter, and Junior faded away from his consciousness.

He shared the story with the integration circle and asked for advice, as he felt that this was a fun trip of the DMT component of ayahuasca or something of that sort. The comments from participants were varied, and in the end, Jimmy went home, not knowing what to make of it all. His wife was the next to hear the story as soon as he arrived home.

How can this be? The notion that a soul is "assigned" and having to wait is new information to many people, including me. Jimmy Junior did not have the option of finding another set of parents or asking the "reincarnation process" to find them for him. According to this experience, there are specific rules, and Jimmy Junior apparently was just an impatient soul burning with the desire to incarnate again.

About three years later, Jimmy returned to drink ayahuasca again, this time accompanied by his wife. She was carrying a one-year-old baby, and as soon as I approached her, she said: "Hi, Julio! I brought him because I wanted you to meet him in person. This is Jimmy Junior. I wanted to thank you personally because you were an instrument that got us inspired to change our plans and bring Junior to life." I almost broke into tears—what a beautiful story. I can imagine at some point in the future when Jimmy Junior hears his own story from his father. When we think about it, Jimmy went to ayahuasca with the intention of finding his life purpose. And he found it. The answer is now apparent.

Ayahuasca Composes A Song and Becomes A Hit

By the year 2020, Pedro Capo was a thriving Puerto Rican pop artist. In 2001, he was just an aspiring young pop singer and composer who I introduced to ayahuasca. He is the grandson of Bobby Capo, a Latin American music legend, and in those days, I knew that Pedro had the magic blend of talent and enormous inheritance entangled in his DNA. I got convinced that he would eventually gain widespread recognition and success. He had lost his father, another musician but not as famous as his dad, just three years before I met Pedro. He was seventeen, and his hunger to follow in his ancestor's footsteps was an awakening. With his father gone and an alcoholic mother, the inevitable happened. He started misusing controlled substances and needed help. I had met him not long before he ran into trouble. It was also only three years after I had my first ayahuasca experience. I knew that ayahuasca could help this youngster, and as it had helped me.

I introduced him to the sacred medicine with excellent results. He saw the emotional issues that were haunting his heart and literally fixed his twisted ways. After several years of working his way up the financially difficult path to become a successful pop artist, he attended one of the ceremonies led by Don Jose Campos. It was conducted in a beautiful temple in upstate New York, and Pedro was happy as he had been waiting a long time for this moment. The ceremony went very well for him, with numerous insights and understandings genuinely relevant to his family relationships and professional career. This brew was extraordinarily strong, and after five hours, Don Jose had performed the ceremonial closing. He stayed the rest of the night, still processing the experience, and in the early morning, Mother Ayahuasca was still working within him. He could not believe that after nine hours, he still was feeling dizzy and unable to drive back home safely. He decided to go out for a walk to exercise and feel more grounded. Then something unexpected happened.

Pedro was an experienced song composer and could easily recognize the feeling of being "in the zone" or getting in touch with his composer's muse. It's a feeling that he was able to voluntarily evoke when pondering ideas for a song. But this time was different. While walking through a beautiful wooded trail, he started to get the feeling of inspiration coming on. He wondered why this was happening as he was not thinking about songwriting. He was just exhausted and wanted to feel ready for the drive back home. As he later said jokingly: "Clearly, Mother Ayahuasca had other plans in mind."

The feeling of inspiration became gradually more reliable, but he was confused about the theme or subject matter. He headed to his car and grabbed his composer notebook, knowing that something was going to come up. He sat in his driver's seat, sighed a couple of times, closed his eyes, and after a moment of nothingness, the dam broke. It was like an Internet download and not a line by line communication; in computer terms, it was a compressed zip file that contained the entire content in one piece. Pedro described a bust of light in his field of vision that included a song for him, a celebration of his work with ayahuasca, a song for the world to hear. He started to slowly discern the verses of the song, not by-word channeling, but as if he was writing it himself. Pedro said: "It's too hard to describe how it happened exactly. The point is that I have never composed a song that quickly without scratching out words or verses, all in one final version.

In less than ten minutes, there it was."

When he drove back home, he ran for his guitar to find the melody for his new song. He was excited about his latest creation, knowing that it came from the spirit of ayahuasca herself. The melody flowed effortlessly as well. All in one day, this was the fastest creation in his expanding repertoire. He kept composing dozens of other songs not only for other artists but for his own album that was soon to start production under the Sony Latin label. This was his favorite song, evidently confirmed by the fact that the song title in Spanish, "Vivo," ended up deeply inked in his skin with a styled calligraphy tattoo in his left arm.

When Pedro's album production started, the record label executives reviewed dozens of recorded demos Pedro had created. He fell in ecstasy when "Vivo" was one of the songs they selected for the album. About a year later, in 2014, his "Aquila" album was released in Puerto Rico, which included a collection of songs with a common thread depicting how to stay positive and find happiness while dealing with heartbreak. It was definitely an ayahuasca inspired album. It was a total success in terms of record sales, and several songs made it to the top ten of the popularity charts, including "Vivo." It's interesting to note that the lyrics of "Vivo" are generally interpreted by the general public as a man singing to a woman, but when we listen carefully, there are verses that sound very awkward. This is because it describes the passionate cry of Pedro singing to Mother Ayahuasca. The song's lyrics have the dual meaning of parallel interpretation.

Pedro's popularity skyrocketed with this album to the extent that the Sony Latin executives decided to promote a major concert at the largest venue in San Juan, Puerto Rico. This happened in 2016 before a full house of 12,000 fans, including my wife Rosalia and my seating in the front row. The concert began with "Vivo," and the rest was history. After the show that night, Pedro shared some intimate quality time with fellow musicians, his family, and a few close friends at a nearby restaurant. It was a moment of celebration, accomplishment, and overall happiness. He grabbed the microphone for a few words and said: "I am so happy tonight because the concert went really well. It was that way because we were aligned with the divine. I started the concert with "Vivo" because the first verse of the song says: Somos Dios (We are God), we started the concert declaring that we, all 12,000, were God. What a grand opening".

We still fail to fully comprehend other instances where ayahuasca opens channels. Perhaps a higher reality wanted to convey a message to the world through Pedro, an up and coming artist. It was not a typical positive message but a lesson about ayahuasca. Along with music, the spirit of ayahuasca is manifesting in different ways worldwide, and I hope it continues. Pedro's career continued to soar, including a music video with over two billion views on YouTube and several Latin Grammy Awards.

My Banking Career in Imminent Danger

This is the story of my first ayahuasca experience. It was a Friday afternoon in June of 1998. I was a real estate banker in charge of the bank's construction financing department when ayahuasca found me. After a series of synchronicities too long to describe here, I was finally about to experience Mother Ayahuasca for the first time. For years, I thought that I would be traveling to Peru one day to experience this brew prepared by the Amazon shamans. All I knew about it was what I had read in one of the first ayahuasca articles published in 1988 in the Science section of the Sunday edition of The New York Times. I'll never forget the phrase that caught my attention: ". When shamans drink the brew, they can see the past, present, and future." It sharply struck my imagination due to my firm scientific "beliefs" that I had cultivated over the years. The notion of a chemically induced vision of the future was only too hard for me to comprehend. I had previously experienced all the hallucinogens available during the eighties and was willing to settle with having visions of the past or the present. But the future was too much to take. I was very skeptical based on my understanding of quantum physics, after having read several paperback publications for laymen. Such an intellectually daring proposition was the original spark that triggered my interest in ayahuasca.

I had previously decided to participate in a group ceremony led by Peruvian curandero Don Jose Campos, who was visiting Puerto Rico in those days. I believe he was one of the first Peruvian shamans traveling to the U.S. offering ayahuasca sessions. I took the Friday afternoon off at my bank job and headed to the grand event. I arrived at a beautiful farm in the Puerto Rico countryside and met the organizer of the event. I was still wearing my business attire, which pulled frowny looks from many of the participants, a bunch of relaxed freestyled casually dressed youngsters. Any forty-two-year-old banker would feel out of place but not in my case.

Don Jose conducted a beautiful ceremony which did not have a substantial effect on me except in the last part when I felt the urge to throw up. At that moment, I had a visual and auditory "vision" at the same time. Difficult to describe, but in the simplest terms, it was a warning message related to my bank job. I was shown and told that I must be cautious with the situation I was facing in my work environment. It's a long story, but the main message was that my boss was a secret practitioner of evil Santeria witchcraft, and this would bring serious problems if I didn't handle it with intelligence and wisdom.

He was a very reputable community member, public speaker, and smart bank executive; in short, a role model for my professional banking career. After the ceremony, I was driving back home and reviewing my experience. I could not accept this message as authentic at all. This was too weird; it didn't match in any possible angle making sense in my thoughts. It was the only message I got from the experience. "This is ayahuasca?" I said to myself. I was disillusioned because I expected a lot more, and all I got was a warning sign related to my career. My conclusion was that this was a trick my mind played on me, not different from the hallucinations I remembered when I experienced LSD during my college years in the seventies. Then, while driving alone, I switched into disappointment mode and began to argue with Mother Ayahuasca: "Do you want me to trust you? You want me to believe that my boss is into black magic? Well, I need proof, ok? Do you hear me? I need proof! I am not going to change my attitude towards my boss just because I had this crazy hallucination, period." I was extremely frustrated because my bright expectations faded into nothingness, and it was also a waste of time and money.

Next Monday morning, I was back on my desk, just another day in the office. Two weeks later, my boss asked me to drop by his office because he met a potential bank client the night before and wanted me to use the connection to solicit business for the bank. It was about 7:00 PM when I sat in front of his elegant wooden desk at his enormous office. When he pulled out his wallet to grab the business card from the bank prospect the night before, a strange object inadvertently fell from his wallet on top of his desk. It was a Santeria amulet, which I quickly recognized because I grew up in Puerto Rico and heard many stories earlier in life. Santeria witchcraft is the evil side of the Santeria religion, which you may research for more information. I might have dismissed the whole coincidence of an amulet falling from my boss's wallet as unimportant if it wasn't for my boss's quick reaction of putting it out of sight. I looked away as if I hadn't noticed anything and acted naturally casual. I grabbed the business card, said good night, and rushed out to my office.

When I was walking through the long hallway leading to the floor elevators, I was pensive about what just happened. Then, suddenly, and out of nowhere, I heard a voice inside my head: "Did you want proof?" I was shaken up by surprise and intrigued about this "thought." I felt the presence of ayahuasca in my body as if I was feeling the symptoms in the ceremony. Exactly sixteen days after the ceremony, I felt the same voice from my ayahuasca vision without being under the influence of any substance. I felt a sense of surprise, disconcertedness, and finally fear that the danger warning received in the ceremony might be real.

I went back to my office and marveled at the power of ayahuasca. This was more than a substance. This was a connection with another dimension. It defied all my scientific concepts, and my paradigm of reality was collapsing right there inside of me. How was this possible? Anyway, I looked at it; I was blown away. I could even imagine someone in another dimension laughing at me as they witnessed a hardcore skeptic turning into a faithful devotee in a blink of an eye.

The next day, I called the organizer of the ceremony to ask about Don Jose. Suddenly I was interested in whether more ceremonies had been scheduled and Don Jose's contact information in Peru. I also passionately researched ayahuasca endlessly on the Internet. That was my initiation, my Chapter One.

I had no other choice but to conclude that ayahuasca opens specific channels in my brain, mind, soul, and spirit. It goes beyond a chemical reaction; this substance was making modifications in my brain circuitry in ways far from my comprehension. I was starting to understand concepts that I had previously learned in metaphysical books but had remained at the intellectual level. Terms such as "universal mind," "collective unconscious," and "higher self" began to acquire new meanings in my inner dictionary. My life just got split into two distinct parts: before ayahuasca and after ayahuasca. I was just beginning to live out the second part.

Acronyms and Definitions

AINDE — Ayahuasca-Induced Near Death Experience

ASA — Ayahuasca Spiritual Advisor

Beliefs: Personal understandings and ways of thinking that are assumed to be true.

DMN — Default Mode Network

Dieta: Shamanic healing process from the Peruvian Amazon region which involve an individual undergoing isolation for a period of time, from days to months, during which it is fed a ritually prepared and symbolically significant diet of foods such as plantain, cassava, and certain river fish. Sugar, salt, spices, pork, acidic fruits, fermented foods, alcohol, and stimulants are avoided, as well as excessive exposure to sun, rain, fire, and unpleasant smells. Social interactions that involve ill individuals, sexual activity, and speaking of outside concerns, are likewise eschewed. By doing so humans are more open to guidance and power from the natural world.

Ego-self: the part of the psyche which is experienced as the "self" or "I" and is in contact with the external world outside our bodies. It is the part which remembers, evaluates, plans, and is otherwise responsive to, and acts in the surrounding physical and social world.

Entity: a subpersonality that has become self-aware, gaining relative independence from the ego-self and operating under the survival program run by the subconscious-self as if being the ego-self itself. It cares about its own survival and not about the organism from which it feeds. A quantum parasite that learned how to hack the system.

Free Will: The ability of the ego-self to decide and act in accordance with its beliefs, and not in accordance with its instincts.

Limbic Imprinting: the automatic function of the nervous system to absorb and memorize all our sensations in a non-cognitive manner. This takes place during the whole formative period; from the moment of conception, through birth, and the first few years of childhood.

Mind: the intrinsic natural ability of a quantum structure to think thoughts, feel emotions, interpret perceptions, judge decisions, recall memories, and desire objectives

Quantum Field: (i) A continuum of energy potential encompassing the entire Universe where every wave and every particle in existence is simply a partial excitation of such continuum. (ii) a discrete quantity of energy proportional in magnitude to the frequency of the vibration it represents.

Quantum Psychology: the study of the human soul -- an actual spiritual entity with a quantum presence in the quantum field-- and its relationships with the other parts of the human psyche, collective unconscious, the subconscious-self and the ego-self.

Quantum Structures: These are hypothetical structures that exist in the quantum field with a high degree of order and organization. They represent the elements of our spiritual nature, invisible and undetectable. They contain the software that runs the physical hardware of the human brain. These structures are partially congruent with Sheldrake's hypothesis of morphic resonance.

Soul-self: the traditional concept of soul integrated as an intrinsic part of the human psyche, the highest component of the human SIE.

Subconscious-Self: the part of the psyche that acts in concert with, but independently of the ego-self, which runs analogous to a powerful computer in charge of the survival program while responding to the default settings in the system of beliefs. The middle component of the SIE.

SIE   Self-Identity Envelope

VIRS   Visionary Intense Release Syndrome

Volitive Energy: Refers to the efferent flow of energy that is transmitted by an organized quantum structure from its habitat in the quantum field into the neural networks of the brain. Volitive: That exercises volition; the power of choosing or determining (will); an act of making a choice or decision.

Bibliography & Notes

Preface

1. Tafur, J., (2017) The Fellowship of the River: A Medical Doctor's Exploration into Traditional Amazonian Plant Medicine. Espiritu Books, Phoenix, AZ.

2. Tupper, K., & Labate, B. (2015). Ayahuasca, Psychedelic Studies and Health Sciences: The Politics of Knowledge and Inquiry into an Amazonian Plant Brew. Current Drug Abuse Reviews, 7(2), 71–80. https://doi.org/10.2174/1874473708666150107155042

Chapter 1

1. Tafur, J., (2017) The Fellowship of the River: A Medical Doctor's Exploration into Traditional Amazonian Plant Medicine. Espiritu Books, Phoenix, AZ.

2. Learn more at www.esalen.org

3. Learn more at www.takiwasi.com

4. Labate, B. C., & Cavnar, C. (Eds.). (2014). The Therapeutic Use of Ayahuasca. Springer-Verlag. https://doi.org/10.1007/978-3-642-40426-9
This book focuses on the potential of Ayahuasca in the treatment and management of various diseases and ailments, presents a series of perspectives on the therapeutic potential and clinical use, and stimulates discussion on the methodological, ethical, and political aspects of research on psychedelics.

5. The Global Ayahuasca Project is a multidisciplinary research project based at the University of Melbourne that is being undertaken in partnership with an international team of researchers from Australia, Brazil, Spain, the Czech Republic, and Switzerland. The project aims to increase understanding of the drinking of ayahuasca in different contexts around the globe and will explore motivations and contexts of drinking, reported effects on health and well-being, and any potential risks. It holds a vast collection of ayahuasca research papers and articles spanning biomedical, anthropological and psychological fields. [www.globalayahuascaproject.org/]

6. Light, D. W., Lexchin, J., & Darrow, J. J. (2013). Institutional Corruption of

Pharmaceuticals and the Myth of Safe and Effective Drugs. The Journal of Law, Medicine & Ethics, 41(3), 590–600. https://doi.org/10.1111/jlme.12068

7. Touzani, K., & Sclafani, A. (2009). Learned Flavor Aversions and Preferences. In L. R. Squire (Ed.), Encyclopedia of Neuroscience (pp. 395–399). Academic Press. https://doi.org/10.1016/B978-008045046-9.00478-2

8. Protecting Traditional Knowledge: Ayahuasca Patent Dispute. (n.d.). Center for International Environmental Law. Retrieved August 26, 2020, from https://www.ciel.org/project-update/protecting-traditional-knowledge-ayahuasca/

Chapter 2

1. Cohen D, Crabtree B. "Qualitative Research Guidelines Project." July 2006. http://www.qualres.org/

Chapter 3

1. Diccionário Quechua. (n.d.). Retrieved August 26, 2020, from www.runasimi.org/cgi-bin/dict.cgi?LANG=es

2. Internet Encyclopedia of Philosophy | An encyclopedia of philosophy articles written by professional philosophers. (n.d.). Retrieved August 26, 2020, from https://iep.utm.edu/

3. Hofstadter, D. R. (1979). In Gödel, Escher, Bach: An Eternal Golden Braid (p. 710). Basic Books.

4. Soon, C. S., Brass, M., Heinze, H.-J., & Haynes, J.-D. (2008). Unconscious determinants of free decisions in the human brain. Nature Neuroscience, 11(5), 543–545. https://doi.org/10.1038/nn.2112

5. Vivekananda, S. (not dated). Chapter 3. In Raja Yoga (p. 28).

6. Schwartz, J. M., Stapp, H. P., & Beauregard, M. (2005). Quantum physics in neuroscience and psychology: A neurophysical model of mind–brain interaction. Philosophical Transactions of the Royal Society B: Biological Sciences, 360(1458), 1309–1327. https://doi.org/10.1098/rstb.2004.1598

7. Clarke, A. C. (1994). Space Drive: A Fantasy That Could Become Reality. A Source of Clean, Inexpensive, and Abundant Energy. pg. 38. Sir Arthur C. Clark (1917-2008), British science fiction writer, science writer and futurist, inventor, undersea explorer, and television series host. During WW2 he served in the Royal Air Force as a radar specialist. After the war he attained degrees in mathematics and physics from King's College in London before working as assistant editor at Physics Abstracts. Clarke then served as president of the British Interplanetary Society, wrote the 2001: A Space Odyssey, and co-authored the screenplay for the movie.

8. Bearden, T.E., (2008) Energy from the Vacuum: Concepts & Principles, Cheniere Press, ISBN 10: 0972514600 ISBN 13: 9780972514606. Tom Bearden

Ph.D., nuclear engineer, retired Lieutenant Colonel (U.S. Army), CEO of CTEC, Inc., Director of the Association of Distinguished American Scientists, and Fellow Emeritus of the Alpha Foundation's Institute for Advanced Study. Bearden is a theoretical conceptualist active in the study of scalar electromagnetics, advanced electrodynamics, unified field theory, KGB energetics weapons and phenomena, free energy systems, electromagnetic healing via the unified field action of extended Sachs-Evans electrodynamics, and human development. Particularly known for his work establishing a theory of over-unity electrical power systems, scalar electromagnetic weapons, energetics weapons, and the use of time-as-energy in both power systems and the mind-body interaction.

9. Millis, M. G., & Davis, E. W. (Eds.). (2009). Frontiers of Propulsion Science. American Institute of Aeronautics and Astronautics. https://doi.org/10.2514/4.479953
The Institute for Advanced Studies at Austin was founded in 1985 by Harold Puthoff, PhD, and later incorporated under EarthTech International, Inc., in 1991 as an innovative research facility with a high powered creative staff dedicated to exploring the forefront reaches of science and engineering. Their corporate website describe their mission: "Our research interests include theories of spacetime, gravity and cosmology; studies of the quantum vacuum; modifications of standard theories of electrodynamics; interstellar flight science; and the Search for Extraterrestrial Intelligence, specifically as these topics may apply to developing innovative space propulsion and sources of energy. We strive to translate these ideas into laboratory experiments." https://earthtech.org/

10. Burns, J. E. (2002). Quantum Fluctuations and the Action of the Mind. Noetic Journal, 3(4), 312–317.

11. Hiscock, H. G., Worster, S., Kattnig, D. R., Steers, C., Jin, Y., Manolopoulos, D. E., Mouritsen, H., & Hore, P. J. (2016). The quantum needle of the avian magnetic compass. Proceedings of the National Academy of Sciences, 113(17), 4634–4639. https://doi.org/10.1073/pnas.1600341113

12. European Science Foundation publication: A Foresight Activity on Research in Quantum Biology. http://archives.esf.org/fileadmin/Public_documents/Publications/FarQBio_01.pdf

13. LiveScience is a popular science news website that breaks down the most interesting stories on the Internet, while also digging up discoveries from dinosaurs and archaeology to wacky physics and astronomy to health and human behavior. https://www.livescience.com/65501-fetal-heartbeat-at-6-weeks-explained.html

14. Eccles, J. C. (2012). How the Self controls its brain. Springer Science & Business Media. p.38

Chapter 4

1. Sheldrake, R. (2012). The Science Delusion: Freeing the Spirit of Enquiry. Coronet..

2. Hampden-Turner, C., (1981) Maps of the Mind: Charts and Concepts of the

Mind and its Labyrinths, Collier Books, New York, N.Y.

3. Sheldrake, R., (1995) The New Science of Life: The Hypothesis of Morphic Resonance, Park Street Press, Rochester, Vermont.

4. Jung, C. G. (1981). In The Archetypes and the Collective Unconscious (p. 44). Princeton University Press.

5. Mills, J. (2019). The myth of the collective unconscious: MILLS. Journal of the History of the Behavioral Sciences, 55(1), 40–53. https://doi.org/10.1002/jhbs.21945

6. Chardin, T.D. de, & Huxley, J. (1975). The Human Phenomenon, New York: Harper & Row, (B. Wall, Trans.).

7. Probability Cloud: A distribution through a region of space of the probability of detecting a given particle, such as an electron in orbit around the nucleus of an atom, determined by the wave function of the particle.

8. Stafford-Clark, D., PhD., "What Freud Really Said: An Introduction to His Life & Thought" Little Brown Book Group, London. (1965).

Chapter 5

1. Overbye, D. (2003, March 11). Universe as Doughnut: New Data, New Debate. The New York Times. www.nytimes.com/2003/03/11/science/universe-as-doughnut-new-data-new-debate.html

2. Reul, H., Talukder, N., & Mu¨ller, E. W. (1981). Fluid mechanics of the natural mitral valve. Journal of Biomechanics, 14(5), 361–372. https://doi.org/10.1016/0021-9290(81)90046-4

3. Gorvett, Z. (n.d.). The mystery of the lost Roman herb. BBC FUTURE. Retrieved August 27, 2020, from www.bbc.com/future/article/20170907-the-mystery-of-the-lost-roman-herb

4. Bible Gateway. Passage: Genesis 1:3 - New International Version. "God said, "Let there be light," and there was light". www.biblegateway.com/

5. Definition of MIND. (n.d.). Retrieved August 27, 2020, from www.merriam-webster.com/dictionary/mind

6. Floyd, K. (1973). Of time and the mind. Fields Within Fields, 10, 17.

7. Bible Gateway. Passage: Matthew 7:3-5 - New International Version. "Why do you look at the speck of sawdust in your brother's eye and pay no attention to the plank in your own eye? www.biblegateway.com/

8. Stafford-Clark, D., & Inc, S. R. (n.d.). What Freud Really Said: An Introduction to His Life and Thought.

9. Byrne, R. (2006) The Secret, Astria Books, New York, N.Y.

10. Definition of PSYCHE. (n.d.). Retrieved August 27, 2020, from https://www.merriam-webster.com/dictionary/psyche

11. Claudio Naranjo, MD (1932 – 2019) was a Chilean-born psychiatrist who is considered a pioneer in integrating psychotherapy and the spiritual traditions. He was a principal developer of Enneagram of Personality theories and a founder of the Seekers After Truth Institute. In the 1960s, Naranjo introduced ibogaine and harmaline into psychotherapy as a "fantasy enhancing drug." He was also an advocate of the global human potential movement and the spiritual renaissance of the late 20th century. He was the author of over a dozen books.

12. Sheldrake, R. (1987). Part I: Mind, memory, and archetype morphic resonance and the collective unconscious. Psychological Perspectives, 18(1), 9–25. https://doi.org/10.1080/00332928708408747

13. Sheldrake, R. (1981). Morphic Resonance: The Nature of Formative Causation.

14. Sheldrake, R. (2018). Science and Spiritual Practices: Transformative Experiences and Their Effects on Our Bodies, Brains, and Health.

15. Wallis, K. F. (2014). Revisiting Francis Galton's Forecasting Competition. Statistical Science, 29(3), 420–424. JSTOR.

16. Surowiecki, J. (2005). In The Wisdom of Crowds (p. Introduction).

17. David R. Hawkins, M.D., Ph.D., (1927-2012) was a world-famous author, spiritual teacher and consciousness researcher. His work represents the leading edge of consciousness research and the verification of spiritual realities. With a scientific and clinical background, he verbalized and explained the consciousness phenomenon in a manner that is clear and comprehensible. A nationally renowned physician, researcher and lecturer, Dr. Hawkins is a world renowned author of numerous books translated in over than 20 languages.

18. Hawkins, David, MD, PhD, (2014) Power vs Force: The Hidden Determinants of Human Behavior" Hay House, Carisbad, CA.

Chapter 6

1. Shermer, M. (2011). In The Believing Brain: From Ghosts and Gods to Politics and Conspiracies—How We Construct Beliefs and Reinforce Them as Truths (p. 5). Macmillan.

2. Shermer, M. (n.d.). Patternicity: Finding Meaningful Patterns in Meaningless Noise. Scientific American. https://doi.org/10.1038/scientificamerican1208-48

3. In addition to Bible passages on 1Kings 8:63, 1Chr 29:21, and 2Chr 7:5, according to historian Josephus a Passover-feast at Jerusalem in Nero's time, the priests counted 256,000 sacrifices confirming the capacity of such large numbers.

4. Dharma: Sanskrit word derived from the etymological root meaning "to hold", and in this context the word has a broader meaning: any behavior or understanding that serves "to hold one back" or protect one from experiencing suffering and

its causes.

5. Bstan-'dzin-rgya-mtsho, & Cutler, H. C. (1998). The art of happiness: A handbook for living. Riverhead Books.

6. Lipton, B. H. (2016). The biology of belief: Unleashing the power of consciousness, matter & miracles.

Chapter 7

1. Jogalekar, A. (n.d.). Is psychology a "real" science? Does it really matter? Scientific American Blog Network. Retrieved August 27, 2020, from https://blogs.scientificamerican.com/the-curious-wavefunction/is-psychology-a-e2809creale2809d-science-does-it-really-matter/

2. DE NANTES BARRERA, O. S., WAITHE, M. E., VINTRÓ, M. C., & ZORITA, C. A. (2007). New Philosophy of Human Nature: Neither Known to nor Attained by the Great Ancient Philosophers, Which Will Improve Human Life and Health. University of Illinois Press; JSTOR. www.jstor.org/stable/10.5406/j.ctt1xcqnn

3. Lieberman, D. Z., & Long, M. E. (2018). In The Molecule of More: How a Single Chemical in Your Brain Drives Love, Sex, and Creativity—And Will Determine the Fate of the Human Race (p. 62). BenBella Books, Incorporated.

4. Principle of Parsimony: Also known as the Occam's Razor principle, common to all science, it postulates that, when making logical deductions, we should choose the simplest scientific explanation that fits the evidence. It is especially embraced by biologists studying evolution where, for example, the best hypothesis is the one that requires the fewest evolutionary changes. It was developed by the 14th-century logician William of Ockam.

5. Parallax: the effect whereby the position or direction of an object appears to differ when viewed from different positions, e.g. through the viewfinder and the lens of a camera.

6. David Bohm (1917–1992) was an American scientist who has been described as one of the most significant theoretical physicists of the 20th century who contributed unorthodox ideas to quantum theory, neuropsychology and the philosophy of mind. Bohm advanced the view that quantum physics meant that the old Cartesian model of reality – that there are two kinds of substance, the mental and the physical, that somehow interact – was too limited.

7. Biase, F. D. (2009). Quantum-Holographic Informational Consciousness. An Interdisciplinary Journal of Neuroscience and Quantum Physics, Volume 7(No 4), 657–664. https://doi.org/10.14704/nq.2009.7.4.259

8. Simanonok, K. (n.d.). An endogenous light nexus theory of consciousness. In R. L. Amoroso (Ed.), Complementarity of Mind and Body: Realizing the Dream of Descartes, Einstein and Eccles.

9. Bradley, R. T. (2007). The Psychophysiology Of Intuition: A Quantum-Ho-

lographic Theory Of Nonlocal Communication. World Futures, 63(2), 61–97. https://doi.org/10.1080/02604020601123148

10. Rowan, J. (1990). In Subpersonalities: The People Inside Us (p. 7). Routledge.

11. Ibid.

12. Ferrucci, P. (1982). In What We May be: Techniques for Psychological and Spiritual Growth Through Psychosynthesis (pp. 47–48), citing Roberto Assagioli, course given at the Accademia Tiberina, 1967.

13. Dissociative Identity Disorder - Previously known as multiple personality disorder, is a mental disorder characterized by the maintenance of at least two distinct and relatively enduring personality states. This is accompanied by memory gaps beyond what would be explained by ordinary forgetfulness. The name was changed in 1994 to reflect a better understanding of the condition—namely, that it is characterized by a fragmentation or splintering of identity, rather than by a proliferation or growth of separate personalities.

14. Critique: A Journal of Conspiracies & Metaphysics. – A printed quarterly journal published by Bob Banner during the 1980's out of Santa Rosa, California. It's self-described purpose was "to question, explore, and expose consensus reality to assist in the transformation from consumer idiots to critically thinking, aware and developing individuals. And to prepare the way for the new paradigms and the new species."

15. Genesis 1:26 - Then God said, "Let us make man in our image, after our likeness. And let them have dominion over the ……"

Chapter 8

1. The default mode network (DMN) is a system of connected brain areas that show increased activity when a person is not focused on the outside world. It is especially active when one engages in introspective activities such as daydreaming, contemplating the past or the future, or thinking about the perspective of someone else. It is also active when a person is awake, but in a resting state, not engaged in any demanding, externally oriented mental task—hence the word "default."

2. The Gift of Neuroplasticity. (2013, December 31). David Perlmutter M.D. https://www.drperlmutter.com/gift-neuroplasticity/

3. Kleim, J. A., & Jones, T. A. (2008). Principles of experience-dependent neural plasticity: Implications for rehabilitation after brain damage. Journal of Speech, Language, and Hearing Research: JSLHR, 51(1), S225-239. https://doi.org/10.1044/1092-4388(2008/018)

4. Pollan, M. (2018). In How to Change Your Mind: What the New Science of Psychedelics Teaches Us About Consciousness, Dying, Addiction, Depression, and Transcendence (pp. 301–302). Penguin.

5. Brown, A. S. (2011). The environment and susceptibility to schizophrenia. Progress in Neurobiology, 93(1), 23–58. https://doi.org/10.1016/j.pneurobio.2010.09.003

6. Chamberlain, D. B. (1999). Babies are not what we thought: Call for a new paradigm. Journal of Prenatal & Perinatal Psychology & Health, 14(1–2), 127–144.

7. Elena Tonetti-Vladimirova. (n.d.). Birthintobeing. Retrieved August 27, 2020, from www.birthintobeing.com/elenasarticlesmain

8. Lipton, B. H. (2016). The biology of belief: Unleashing the power of consciousness, matter & miracles.

9. Kier, E. L., Kim, J. H., Fulbright, R. K., & Bronen, R. A. (1997). Embryology of the human fetal hippocampus: MR imaging, anatomy, and histology. AJNR. American Journal of Neuroradiology, 18(3), 525–532.

10. Chamberlain, D. (1998) The Mind of Your Newborn Baby, 3rd edition. Berkeley, CA: North Atlantic Books.

11. Simborg, D. (n.d.). Lamarckian Evolution is Making a Comeback. Retrieved August 27, 2020, from /2018/01/08/lamarckian-evolution-is-making-a-comeback/

12. Rosenblatt, F., Farrow, J. T., & Rhine, S. (1966). The transfer of learned behavior from trained to untrained rats by mean of brain extracts. I. Proceedings of the National Academy of Sciences of the United States of America, 55(3), 548–555.

13. Heijmans, B. T., Tobi, E. W., Stein, A. D., Putter, H., Blauw, G. J., Susser, E. S., Slagboom, P. E., & Lumey, L. H. (2008). Persistent epigenetic differences associated with prenatal exposure to famine in humans. Proceedings of the National Academy of Sciences, 105(44), 17046–17049. https://doi.org/10.1073/pnas.0806560105

14. Rodriguez, T. (2015, March 1). Descendants of Holocaust Survivors Have Altered Stress Hormones. Scientific American. https://doi.org/10.1038/scientificamericanmind0315-10a

Other Suggested Reading:

15. CurryJul. 18, rew, 2019, & Pm, 2:05. (2019, July 18). Parents' emotional trauma may change their children's biology. Studies in mice show how. Science | AAAS. https://www.sciencemag.org/news/2019/07/parents-emotional-trauma-may-change-their-children-s-biology-studies-mice-show-how

16. Damian, R. I., Spengler, M., Sutu, A., & Roberts, B. W. (2019). Sixteen going on sixty-six: A longitudinal study of personality stability and change across 50 years. Journal of Personality and Social Psychology, 117(3), 674–695. https://doi.org/10.1037/pspp0000210

17. Horsthemke, B. (2018). A critical view on transgenerational epigenetic inheritance in humans. Nature Communications, 9(1), 2973. https://doi.org/10.1038/

s41467-018-05445-5

18. Lieberman, S. (1979). A transgenerational theory. Journal of Family Therapy, 1(3), 347–360. https://doi.org/10.1046/j..1979.00506.x

Chapter 9

1. Lanza, R., & Berman, B. (2009). Biocentrism: How Life and Consciousness are the Keys to Understanding the True Nature of the Universe.

2. Lochtefeld, J. G. (n.d.). The Illustrated Encyclopedia of Hinduism, Vol. 2: N-Z.

3. Kiddushin 70a. (n.d.). Retrieved August 27, 2020, from https://www.sefaria.org/Kiddushin.70a.11

4. Jung, C. G. (2014). General Aspects of Group Psychology. In The Structure and Dynamics of the Psyche. Routledge. https://doi.org/10.4324/9781315725857

Chapter 10

1. Ayahuasca Manifesto. (n.d.). Retrieved August 27, 2020, from https://cutt.ly/ayahuascamanifesto

2. Dean, J. G., Liu, T., Huff, S., Sheler, B., Barker, S. A., Strassman, R. J., Wang, M. M., & Borjigin, J. (2019). Biosynthesis and Extracellular Concentrations of N,N-dimethyltryptamine (DMT) in Mammalian Brain. Scientific Reports, 9(1), 9333. https://doi.org/10.1038/s41598-019-45812-w

3. Lolley, R. N., Craft, C. M., & Lee, R. H. (1992). Photoreceptors of the retina and pinealocytes of the pineal gland share common components of signal transduction. Neurochemical Research, 17(1), 81–89. https://doi.org/10.1007/BF00966868

4. Osteopathic medicine: 125 years of history. (2017, November 15). The DO. http://thedo.osteopathic.org/2017/11/osteopathic-medicine-125-years-history/

5. Khetrapal, A. (2018, August 23). Psychosomatic Disorders. News-Medical.Net. https://www.news-medical.net/health/Psychosomatic-Disorders.aspx

6. Zipfel, S., Herzog, W., Kruse, J., & Henningsen, P. (2016). Psychosomatic Medicine in Germany: More Timely than Ever. Psychotherapy and Psychosomatics, 85(5), 262–269. https://doi.org/10.1159/000447701

Chapter 11

1. London Real—YouTube. (n.d.). Retrieved August 27, 2020, from https://www.youtube.com/user/LondonRealTV

2. Epstein, M. (1995). In Thoughts Without a Thinker: Psychotherapy from a Buddhist Perspective (p. 119). MJF Books.

3. Park, S. Q., Kahnt, T., Dogan, A., Strang, S., Fehr, E., & Tobler, P. N. (2017). A neural link between generosity and happiness. Nature Communications, 8(1),

15964. https://doi.org/10.1038/ncomms15964

4. Quoidbach, J., Dunn, E. W., Petrides, K. V., & Mikolajczak, M. (2010). Money giveth, money taketh away: The dual effect of wealth on happiness. Psychological Science, 21(6), 759–763. https://doi.org/10.1177/0956797610371963

5. A quote by William J. Bennett. (n.d.). Retrieved August 27, 2020, from www.goodreads.com/quotes/214763-happiness-is-like-a-cat-if-you-try-to-coax

6. Frankl, V. E. (1946). Man's search for meaning (Mini book ed.). Beacon Press.

7. Romanelli, D. (2014). Happy Is the New Healthy. http://search.ebscohost.com/login.aspx?direct=true&scope=site&db=nlebk&db=nlabk&AN=954393

Chapter 12

1. Tolle, E., (2005) "A New Earth: Awakening to Your Life's Purpose" Penguin Books, New York, N.Y.

Chapter 13

1. Rogers, C. R. (1951). Client-centered therapy; its current practice, implications, and theory (pp. xii, 560). Houghton Mifflin.

Chapter 14

1. Helene, Z. (n.d.). Sex + Setting: Friends Don't Let Friends Sleep With Shamans - Mind & Body - Utne Reader. Utne. Retrieved August 27, 2020, from www.utne.com/mind-and-body/sex-setting-friends-dont-let-friends-sleep-with-shamans-zb0z1608zsau

2. Stefani, L., Galanti, G., Padulo, J., Bragazzi, N. L., & Maffulli, N. (2016). Sexual Activity before Sports Competition: A Systematic Review. Frontiers in Physiology, 7. https://doi.org/10.3389/fphys.2016.00246

3. Giordano Bruno (1548 – 1600) was an Italian Dominican friar, philosopher, mathematician, poet, cosmological theorist, and Hermetic occultist. He proposed that the stars were distant suns surrounded by their own planets, and he raised the possibility that these might foster life of their own. He also insisted that the universe is infinite and could have no "center". Bruno's pantheism was not taken lightly by the Inquisition, as was his teaching of the transmigration of the soul or reincarnation. The Inquisition found him guilty, and he was burned at the stake in 1600. Bruno's case is still considered a landmark in the history of free thought and the emerging sciences

4. Libido—Search Results—PubMed. (n.d.). Retrieved August 27, 2020, from https://pubmed.ncbi.nlm.nih.gov/?term=libido

5. Hackney, A. C., Lane, A. R., Register-Mihalik, J., & O'leary, C. B. (2017). Endurance Exercise Training and Male Sexual Libido. Medicine and Science in Sports and Exercise, 49(7), 1383–1388. https://doi.org/10.1249/MSS.0000000000001235

6. Jiang, M., Xin, J., Zou, Q., & Shen, J.-W. (2003). A research on the relationship between ejaculation and serum testosterone level in men. Journal of Zhejiang University. Science, 4(2), 236–240. https://doi.org/10.1631/jzus.2003.0236

7. Levitas, E., Lunenfeld, E., Weiss, N., Friger, M., Har-Vardi, I., Koifman, A., & Potashnik, G. (2005). Relationship between the duration of sexual abstinence and semen quality: Analysis of 9,489 semen samples. Fertility and Sterility, 83(6), 1680–1686. https://doi.org/10.1016/j.fertnstert.2004.12.045

"The 5,983 normozoospermic samples showed a significant decrease in the percentage of sperm motility and normal morphology to mean values of 33.1% and 7.0%, respectively, on days 11–14 of sexual abstinence."

8. Ph.D, B. C. L. (2011). Consumption of Ayahuasca by Children and Pregnant Women: Medical Controversies and Religious Perspectives. Journal of Psychoactive Drugs, 43(1), 27–35. https://doi.org/10.1080/02791072.2011.566498

9. Ibid

10. Women and Ayahuasca | Singing to the Plants. (n.d.). Retrieved August 27, 2020, from https://www.singingtotheplants.com/2008/02/women-and-ayahuasca/

11. Harris, R. (2017). In Listening to Ayahuasca: New Hope for Depression, Addiction, PTSD, and Anxiety (p. 142). New World Library.

12. Brierley, D. I., & Davidson, C. (2012). Developments in harmine pharmacology—Implications for ayahuasca use and drug-dependence treatment. Progress in Neuro-Psychopharmacology & Biological Psychiatry, 39(2), 263–272. https://doi.org/10.1016/j.pnpbp.2012.06.001

13. Cohort: a group of individuals having a statistical factor (such as age or class membership) in common in a demographic study

Chapter 15

1. Rooks, B. (2014, June 12). Ayahuasca and the Godhead: An Interview with Wahid Azal of the Fatimiya Sufi Order. Reality Sandwich. https://realitysandwich.com/219826/ayahuasca-and-the-godhead-an-interview-with-wahid-azal-of-the-the-fatimiya-sufi-order/

2. Haoma: (a) a sacred plant of the ancient Persians; (b) a drink made from this plant

3. Aporias: (a) figure of speech in which the speaker expresses to be in doubt about a question; (b) An insoluble contradiction or paradox in a text's meanings.

4. Heise, C. W., & Brooks, D. E. (2017). Ayahuasca Exposure: Descriptive Analysis of Calls to US Poison Control Centers from 2005 to 2015. Journal of Medical Toxicology: Official Journal of the American College of Medical Toxicology, 13(3), 245–248. https://doi.org/10.1007/s13181-016-0593-1

Chapter 16

1. John Welwood (1943-2019) was a psychotherapist, teacher, and author. He was a significant figure in the leading-edge fields of transpersonal psychology and integrating East/West psychology and spirituality.

2. Norma Aguila Panduro Navarro (1944 - 2007) was one of the very few female ayahuasca shamans in the world. She conducted healing ceremonies at Estrella Ayahuasca, her Centro de Investigaciones de la Ayahuasca y Otras Plantas Medicinales between Iquitos and Nauta.

Chapter 17

1. Chakapa: A bundle of dry leaves tied together with a handle for a comfortable grip. Traditionally, these are built using "chakapa" leaves (Latifolia Olyra). Due to its high fiber content, these leaves can endure long seasons of use without disintegrating, as it would be the case of other species if submitted to the same treatment.

2. Charango: This is a small Andean guitar-shaped stringed instrument of the lute family, which probably originated in the Quechua and Aymara populations in the territory of the Altiplano in post-Colonial times after European stringed instruments were introduced by the Spanish during colonialization.

3. Elizabeth, K. (2017). After the Ceremony Ends: A Companion Guide to Help You Integrate Visionary Plant Medicine Experiences. katherinecoder.com

4. Pennebaker, J. W. (2004). Writing to heal: A guided journal for recovering from trauma & emotional upheaval. New Harbinger Publications

Chapter 18

1. Trungpa, C. (1973). Cutting Through Spiritual Materialism. Watkins.

2. Lieberman and Long, (2018) The Molecule of More, BenBella Books.

Credits

Cover Art: Alfredo Zagaceta [Peru]
www.zagacetaarts.com

Cover Design: Jules Henry Rivers

Layout Design: Abdullah Al Maruf [Bangladesh]
marufabdullah8@gmail.com

Text Editor: Ashleigh Willis [Scotland]
ajwillis91@outlook.com

Neuroscience Consultant: Ashleigh Willis, PhD Candidate
www.youtube.com/watch?v=Jh426VE3nUI

Publisher: Quantum Books [Puerto Rico]
ayaquantum@protonmail.com

Illustrations

[Cartoons] Santiago Oliveros (a/k/a Sako Asko) [Colombia]
www.facebook.com/sakoasko

[Infographics] Khawaja Aakash Ali [Pakistan]
www.behance.net/khawajaali

[Torus Images] Cristian Aquino [Argentina]
aquinocristiancg@gmail.com

[Other Images] www.freeimages.com

Image References & Credits

Chapter 5

Gable, Andrew. (2012). "Becoming Aware of the Mind", Multiple thoughts depicted over a thinking man [Drawing]. https://anartistsjourneytolife.wordpress.com/2013/06/06/i-am-different-when-i-speak-to-clients-an-artists-journey-to-life-day-383/Chapter 8

Chapter 8

Santiago, O. (2017). Scientist working with child brain [Drawing]. https://www.facebook.com/sakoasko/photos/a.448667458581062/1394649997316132/?type=3&theater

Santiago, O. (2019). Man in the ocean holding a water drop [Drawing]. https://www.facebook.com/sakoasko/photos/a.448247295289745/2342833692497753/?type=3&theater

Chapter 9

Santiago, O. (2020). Man with heart shaped eyes projecting himself into a woman. [Drawing].https://www.facebook.com/sakoasko/photo/a.448667458581062/3085841888196926/?type=3&theater

Santiago, O. (2020). Man arguing with woman while holding a mirrorover her face [Drawing]. https://www.facebook.com/sakoasko/photos/a.448247295289745/2762866773827774/?type3&theater

Santiago, O. (2015). Sequence of man wearing a contact lens [Drawing]. https://www.facebook.com/sakoasko/photos/a.448247295289745/752537404860731/?type=3&theater

Santiago, O. (2017). Human eye projecting images [Drawing]. https://www.facebook.com/sakoasko/photos/a.1339409862840146/1339410296173436/?type=3&theater

Chapter 10

Santiago, O. (2017). Young man removing sunglasses [Drawing]. https://www.facebook.com/sakoasko/photos/a.1339409862840146/1339410296173436/?type=3&theater

Escher, M. C. (1948). Drawing Hands [Lithograph]. https://mcescher.com/gallery/back-in-holland/